Fodor's 4th Edition

Belize &
Guatemala

The Guide
for All Budgets

Completely
Updated

Where to Stay, Eat,
and Explore

On and Off
the Beaten Path

When to Go,
What to Pack

Maps, Travel Tips,
and Web Sites

Fodor's Travel Publications • New York, Toronto, London, Sydney, Auckland
www.fodors.com

Fodor's Belize & Guatemala

EDITOR: Mark Sullivan

Editorial Contributors: Gregory Benchwick, Lan Sluder
Editorial Production: Tom Holton
Maps: David Lindroth, *cartographer*; Rebecca Baer, Robert Blake, *map editors*
Design: Fabrizio La Rocca, *creative director*; Guido Caroti, *art director*; Jolie Novak, *senior picture editor*; Melanie Marin, *photo editor*
Cover Design: Pentagram
Production/Manufacturing: Robert B. Shields
Cover Photo (Coffee Canoe, Guatemala): Bo Zaunders/Corbis Stock Market

Copyright

Fourth Edition

ISBN 1–4000–1056–X

ISSN 1522–6123

Important Tip

Although all prices, opening times, and other details in this book are based on information supplied to us at press time, changes occur all the time in the travel world, and Fodor's cannot accept responsibility for facts that become outdated or for inadvertent errors or omissions. So **always confirm information when it matters,** especially if you're making a detour to visit a specific place.

Special Sales

Fodor's Travel Publications are available at special discounts for bulk purchases for sales promotions or premiums. Special editions, including personalized covers, excerpts of existing guides, and corporate imprints, can be created in large quantities for special needs. For more information, contact your local bookseller or write to Special Markets, Fodor's Travel Publications, 280 Park Avenue, New York, NY 10017. Inquiries from Canada should be directed to your local Canadian bookseller or sent to Random House of Canada, Ltd., Marketing Department, 2775 Matheson Boulevard East, Mississauga, Ontario L4W 4P7. Inquiries from the United Kingdom should be sent to Fodor's Travel Publications, 20 Vauxhall Bridge Road, London SW1V 2SA, England.

PRINTED IN THE UNITED STATES OF AMERICA

10 9 8 7 6 5 4 3 2 1

CONTENTS

Maps

ON THE ROAD WITH FODOR'S

A TRIP TAKES YOU OUT OF YOURSELF. Concerns of life at home completely disappear, driven away by more immediate thoughts—about, say, what marvels will beguile the next day, or where you'll have dinner. That's where Fodor's comes in. We make sure that you know all your options, so that you don't miss something that's around the next bend just because you didn't know it was there. Mindful that the best memories of your trip might have nothing to do with what you came to Belize and Guatemala to see, we guide you to sights large and small all over the region. You might set out to climb the pyramids at Tikal, but back at home you find yourself unable to forget diving near Ambergris Caye and gazing into a smoldering volcano near Antigua. With Fodor's at your side, serendipitous discoveries are never far away.

About Our Writers

Our success in showing you every corner of Belize and Guatemala is a credit to our extraordinary writers. Although there's no substitute for travel advice from a good friend who knows your style, our contributors are the next best thing—the kind of people you would poll for travel advice if you knew them.

Freelance writer **Gregory Benchwick** first fell in love with Latin America when he travelled via chicken bus from Costa Rica to Belize in 1995. Returning to Latin America in 1999, this time to Chile, Gregory first glimpsed the rugged, enchanting, and often inhospitable landscape of El Norte Chico and El Norte Grande, which he wrote about for *Fodor's Chile*. A former editor of the *Bolivian Times*, Gregory has written extensively about travel in Latin America.

Belize First magazine editor and publisher **Lan Sluder** has been banging around that country for more than a decade. In addition to writing the *Belize First Guide to Mainland Belize* and *Adapter Kit: Belize*, he has written about the country for *Caribbean Travel & Life*, the *Bangkok Post*,

and Canada's *Globe & Mail*, among other publications.

Editor **Mark Sullivan** has spent much time in Central America, scaling the heights of Volcán Pacayá in Guatemala and discovering the depths of the coral reef surrounding the Bay Islands in Honduras. He has also traveled farther south, editing *Fodor's Chile* and *Fodor's South America* along the way. His next project, after a quick dip in the waters of Aruba, is the first edition of *Fodor's Central America*.

You can rest assured that you're in good hands—and that no property mentioned in the book has paid to be included. Each has been selected strictly on its merits, as the best of its type in its price range.

How to Use This Book

Up front is Smart Travel Tips A to Z, arranged alphabetically by topic and loaded with tips, Web sites, and contact information. Destination: Belize and Guatemala helps get you in the mood for your trip. The country chapters that follow are divided geographically; within each area, towns are covered in logical geographical order, and attractive stretches of road between them are indicated by the designation En Route. To help you decide what you'll have time to visit, all chapters begin with our writers' favorite itineraries. (Mix itineraries from several chapters, and you can put together a really exceptional trip.) The A to Z section that ends every chapter lists additional resources. At the end of the book you'll find Background and Essentials, including an essay about bus travel in Guatemala, followed by a wildlife glossary and a Spanish vocabulary. The Books section suggests enriching reading.

Icons and Symbols

★   Our special recommendations
✕   Restaurant
🏠   Lodging establishment
✕🏠   Lodging establishment whose restaurant warrants a special trip
⚠   Campgrounds

☺   Good for kids (rubber duck)

☞   Sends you to another section of the guide for more information

✉   Address

☎   Telephone number

✆   Opening and closing times

🎟   Admission prices (those we give apply to adults; substantially reduced fees are almost always available for children, students, and senior citizens)

Numbers in white and black circles ③ ❸ that appear on the maps, in the margins, and within the tours correspond to one another.

For hotels, you can assume that all rooms have private baths, phones, TVs, and air-conditioning unless otherwise noted and that all hotels operate on the European Plan (with no meals) if we don't specify another meal plan. We always list a property's facilities but not whether you'll be charged extra to use them, so when pricing accommodations, do ask what's included. For restaurants, it's always a good idea to book ahead; we mention reservations only when they're essential or are not accepted. All restaurants we list are open daily for lunch and dinner unless stated otherwise; dress is mentioned only when men are required to wear a jacket or a jacket and tie. Look for an overview of local dining-out habits in Smart Travel Tips A to Z and in the Pleasures and Pastimes section that follows each chapter introduction.

Don't Forget to Write

Your experiences—positive and negative—matter to us. If we have missed or misstated something, we want to hear about it. We follow up on all suggestions. Contact the Belize and Guatemala editor at editors@fodors.com or c/o Fodor's at 1745 Broadway, New York, New York 10019. And have a fabulous trip!

Karen Cure

Karen Cure
Editorial Director

Belize and Guatemala

Chetumal
Corozal
Orange
Walk
Blue Creek Village
Altun Ha
Ladyville
Río Hondo
Belize City
Tikal
Río Belize
Gales
Point

BIOSPHERE
RESERVE

San Ignacio
Belmopan

MEXICO

Flores
BELIZE

Santa Elena

Sayaxché
Dolores
Dangriga

Ceibal
Placencia

San Antonio
*Golfo de
Honduras*

San Luis

ALTA VERAPAZ
Punta Gorda

Modesto
Mendez
Livingston

Soloma
GUATEMALA
*RÍO DULCE
NAT'L PARK*
Puerto
Barrios

Cobán
San Pedro
Carchá
*Lago
Izabal*
Río Dulce

Huehuetenango
Los Amates

San Marcos
Motagua
Copán

Chichicastenango
El Progreso
HONDURAS

Totonicapán
El Florida

Quetzaltenango
*Lago
Atitlán*
Chimaltenango

Antigua
Guatemala
City

INTERAMERICAN HWY.

Santa Ana

Santa Marta
Puerto
San José
EL SALVADOR

San
Salvador
San
Miguel

*PACIFIC
OCEAN*

N

0		100 miles

0		150 km

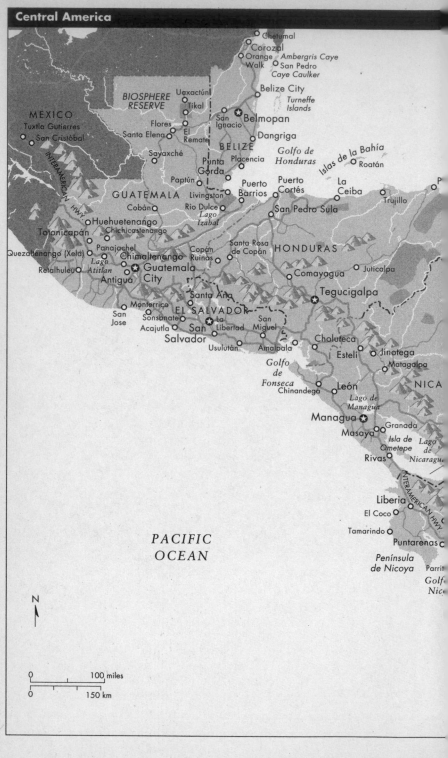

Central America

Chetumal

Corozal
Orange
Walk · San Pedro
Ambergris Caye
Caye Caulker

Belize City

Turneffe
Islands

MEXICO
Tuxtla Gutierres
San Cristóbal

BIOSPHERE
RESERVE
Uaxactún
Tikal

San
Ignacio
Belmopan

Flores
El
Remate
Santa Elena
BELIZE
Dangriga

Sayaxché

Punta
Gorda
Placencia
Golfo de
Honduras
Islas de la Bahía
Roatán
P

Paptún

GUATEMALA
Livingston
Puerto
Barrios
Puerto
Cortés
La
Ceiba
Trujillo

Cobán
Rio Dulce
Lago
Izabal
San Pedro Sula

Huehuetenango
Chichicastenango
Copán
Ruinas
Santa Rosa
de Copán
HONDURAS

Totonicapán
Panajachel

Juticalpa

Quezaltenango (Xela)
Retalhuleu
Lago
Atitlán
Chimaltenango
**Guatemala
City**
Comayagua

Antigua
Santa Ana
Tegucigalpa

Monterrico
EL SALVADOR

San
Jose
Sonsonate
Acajutla
La
Libertad
San
Miguel

San
Salvador
Usulután
Amapala
Choluteca
Estelí
Jinotega

Golfo
de
Fonseca
Chinandega
León
Matagalpa

NICA

Lago de
Managua

Managua
Granada
Masaya
Isla de
Ometepe
Lago
de
Nicaragua

Rivas

**PACIFIC
OCEAN**

Liberia
El Coco

Tamarindo
Puntarenas

Península
de Nicoya
Parrit
Golf
Nic

INTERAMERICAN HWY

INTERAMERICAN HWY

N

| 0 | 100 miles |
| 0 | 150 km |

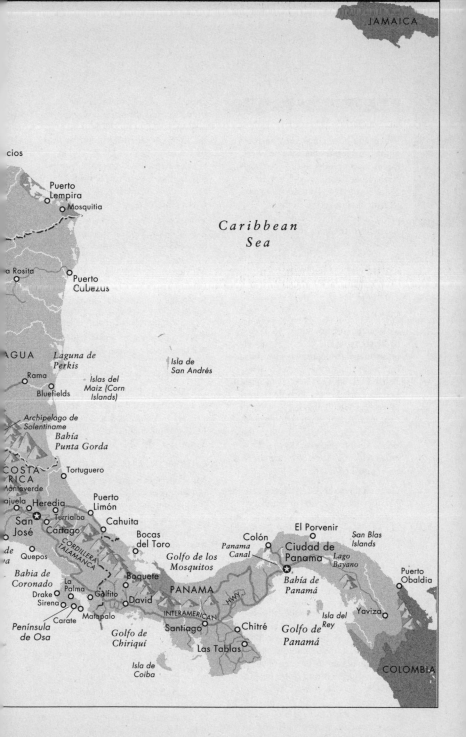

cios

Puerto
Lempira
Mosquitia

Caribbean
Sea

a Rosita

Puerto
Cubezus

JAMAICA

AGUA

Laguna de
Perkis

Isla de
San Andrés

Rama

Bluefields

Islas del
Maiz (Corn
Islands)

Archipelago de
Solentiname

Bahía
Punta Gorda

COSTA
RICA

Tortuguero

Monteverde

ajuela   Heredia

Puerto
Limón

San
José

Turrialba

Cartago

Cahuita

Bocas
del Toro

Colón

El Porvenir

San Blas
Islands

de
a

Quepos

CORDILLERA
TALAMANCA

Panama
Canal

Ciudad de
Panama

Golfo de los
Mosquitos

Lago
Bayano

Puerto
Obaldia

Bahía de
Coronado

La
Palma

Baquete

PANAMA

Bahía de
Panamá

Drake
Sirena

Golfito

David

HWY.

INTERAMERICAN

Isla del
Rey

Yaviza

Carate

Matapalo

Santiago

Chitré

Golfo de
Panamá

Península
de Osa

Golfo de
Chiriquí

Las Tablas

COLOMBIA

Isla de
Coiba

ESSENTIAL INFORMATION

AIR TRAVEL

BOOKING

When you book, **look for nonstop flights** and **remember that "direct" flights stop at least once.** Try to avoid connecting flights, which require a change of plane. Two airlines may operate a connecting flight jointly, so ask if your airline operates every segment of the trip; you may find that the carrier you prefer flies you only part of the way. To find more booking tips and to check prices and make on-line flight reservations, log on to www.fodors.com.

CARRIERS

American, Continental, and Taca fly to Belize from the United States. The major departure gateways are Houston, with daily nonstop service to Belize City on Taca and Continental; Dallas–Fort Worth, with daily nonstop service to Belize City on American; and Miami, with daily nonstop service on American. Taca also flies to Belize City from several other U.S. cities with a change of planes in San Salvador, El Salvador.

Guatemala is served by American via Miami or Dallas, Continental via Houston, Iberia via Miami, Mexicana via Mexico City, Taca via Miami or Dallas, and United via Los Angeles. From New York the only nonstop flights are on Taca. From London, Iberia flies direct to Guatemala City via Madrid.

Whereas Guatemala uses regular 727 airplanes for domestic travel between the capital and Flores, Puerto Barrios, Río Dulce, and Huehuetenango, domestic planes in Belize are single- or twin-engine island hoppers. The main carriers are Tropic Air and Maya Island Air, both of which fly to San Pedro, on Ambergris Caye, and Caye Caulker, as well as Corozal, Dangriga, Placencia, Punta Gorda,

and Flores, Guatemala. Domestic flights to and from the municipal airport are between BZ$96 and BZ$380 round-trip, except for those flights arranged on Javier Flying Service, which will take you pretty much anywhere for around BZ$340 per hour. It also has regular flights to Chan Chich Lodge.

➤ INTERNATIONAL CARRIERS: **Aeroméxico** (☎ 800/237–6639). **American** (☎ 800/433–7300). **Continental** (☎ 800/525–0280). **Iberia** (☎ 800/772–4642). **Mexicana** (☎ 800/531–7921). **Taca** (☎ 800/535–8780).

➤ BELIZEAN CARRIERS: **Javier Flying Service** (☎ 223/5360, FAX 223/1731). **Maya Island Air** (☎ 226/3838; 800/521–1247 in the U.S., FAX 226/2192, WEB www.mayaairways.com). **Tropic Air** (☎ 226/2012; 800/422–3435 in the United States, FAX 226/2338, WEB www.tropicair.com).

➤ GUATEMALAN CARRIERS: **Aeroquetzal** (☎ 334–7689). **Aerovias** (☎ 332–5686). **Inter Airline** (☎ 361–2144). **Tikal Jets** (☎ 334–5568).

CHECK-IN AND BOARDING

Most carriers require you to check in two hours before your scheduled departure time for domestic flights and 2½ to 3 hours before international flights. Always **ask your carrier about its check-in policy.**

For international flights, except for short hops between Belize and Guatemala, you should be at the airport at least two hours before your scheduled departure time; for domestic flights, about half an hour. Assuming that not everyone with a ticket will show up, airlines routinely overbook planes. When everyone does, airlines ask for volunteers to give up their seats. In return, these volunteers usually get a certificate for a free flight and are rebooked on the next flight out. If there are not enough volunteers, the airline must choose who will be denied boarding. The first to get bumped are passengers who checked in late and those flying on discounted tickets, so **get to the gate and check in as early as possible,** especially during peak periods.

Always **bring a government-issued photo ID to the airport.** You will be asked to show it before you are allowed to check in. The international airports in Belize City and Guatemala City have security precautions that are similar to those in the United States; the domestic airstrips have more limited security systems in place.

CUTTING COSTS

The least expensive airfares to Belize and Guatemala must usually be purchased in advance and are nonrefundable. Airfares to Belize are often twice or more the cost of a ticket to Mexican destinations such as Cancún or Cozumel. If you have the time, **consider flying into Mexico and taking a bus to Belize.** From the Yucatán a first-class or deluxe bus costs BZ$30 or less and takes between five and six hours to Chetumal, Mexico, a border town where you can transfer to a Belize bus. (If you fly into Cozumel, you'll first have to take a ferry to Playa del Carmen.)

You'll save up to 45% on flights within Belize by flying to and from the municipal airport near downtown Belize City, rather than to or from the international airport north of the city in Ladyville. For example, a one-way flight from municipal to San Pedro is BZ$48, but almost twice that from Ladyville.

On international flights it's smart to **contact a number of airlines, and when you are quoted a good price, book it on the spot**—the same fare may not be available the next day. Always **check different routings** and look into using different airports. Travel agents, especially low-fare specialists (☞ Discounts and Deals, *below*), are helpful.

Consolidators are another good source. They buy tickets for scheduled international flights at reduced rates from the airlines, then sell them at prices that beat the best fare available

directly from the airlines. Sometimes you can even get your money back if you need to return the ticket. Carefully read the fine print detailing penalties for changes and cancellations, purchase the ticket with a credit card, and **confirm your consolidator reservation with the airline.**

When you **fly as a courier,** you trade your checked-luggage space for a ticket deeply subsidized by a courier service. There are restrictions on when you can book and how long you can stay. Some courier companies list with membership organizations, such as the Air Courier Association and the International Association of Air Travel Couriers; these require you to become a member before you can book a flight.

➤ CONSOLIDATORS: **Cheap Tickets** (☎ 800/377–1000 or 888/922–8849, WEB www.cheaptickets.com). **Discount Airline Ticket Service** (☎ 800/576–1600). **Diversified Travel Management** (☎ 800/458–8281). **Fly Cheap** (☎ 888/702–4242, WEB www.flycheapol. com. **Latin Discounters** (☎ 877/426–8676, WEB www.latindiscounters.com). **Pino Welcome Travel** (☎ 800/247–6578, WEB www.pinotravel.com). **Traveland** (☎ 800/321–6336, WEB www.traveland.com). **Unitravel** (☎ 800/325–2222, WEB www. unitravel.com). **Up & Away Travel** (☎ 212/889–2345). **World Travel Network** (☎ 800/409–6753).

➤ COURIER RESOURCES: **Air Courier Association** (☎ 800/282–1202, WEB www.aircourier.org). **International Association of Air Travel Couriers** (☎ 352/475–1584, WEB www. courier.org). **Now Voyager Travel** (☎ 212/431–1616).

ENJOYING THE FLIGHT

State your seat preference when purchasing your ticket, and then repeat it when you confirm and when you check in. For more legroom, you can request one of the few emergency-aisle seats at check-in, if you are capable of lifting at least 50 pounds—a Federal Aviation Administration requirement of passengers in these seats. Seats behind a bulkhead also offer more legroom, but they don't have underseat storage. Don't sit in the row in front of the emergency aisle or in front of a bulkhead, where seats may not recline.

If you have dietary concerns, **ask for special meals when booking.** These can be vegetarian, low-cholesterol, or kosher, for example. It's a good idea to pack some healthy snacks and a small (plastic) bottle of water in your carry-on bag. On long flights, try to maintain a normal routine, to help fight jet lag. At night, **get some sleep.** By day, **eat light meals, drink water** (not alcohol), and **move around the cabin** to stretch your legs. For additional jet-lag tips consult *Fodor's FYI: Travel Fit & Healthy* (available at bookstores everywhere).

FLYING TIMES

To Belize City it's roughly two hours from Miami and 2½ hours from Dallas and Houston.

To Guatemala City from Dallas or Houston the flying time is two hours; from Miami, 2½ hours; from Los Angeles, 7 hours; from New York or Chicago, 5½ hours; from Toronto via Miami or Mexico City, about seven hours.

HOW TO COMPLAIN

If your baggage goes astray or your flight goes awry, complain right away. Most carriers require that you **file a claim immediately.** The Aviation Consumer Protection Division of the Department of Transportation publishes *Fly-Rights,* which discusses airlines and consumer issues and is available on-line. At PassengerRights.com, a Web site, you can compose a letter of complaint and distribute it electronically.

➤ AIRLINE COMPLAINTS: **Aviation Consumer Protection Division** (✉ U.S. Department of Transportation, Room 4107, C-75, Washington, DC 20590, ☎ 202/366–2220, 〈WEB〉 www. dot.gov/airconsumer). **Federal Aviation Administration Consumer Hotline** (☎ 800/322–7873).

RECONFIRMING

Check the status of your flight before you leave for the airport. You can do this on your carrier's Web site, by linking to a flight-status checker (many Web booking services offer these), or by calling your carrier or travel agent. Always confirm international flights at least 72 hours ahead of the scheduled departure time.

AIRPORTS

International flights to Belize arrive at the Philip Goldson International Airport in Ladyville, 15 km (9 mi) north of Belize City. It's probably the only airport in the world with a mahogany roof. Domestic airports (which consist of landing strips with one-room check-in buildings nearby) are in Belize City, Corozal, Dangriga, Placencia, Punta Gorda, and San Pedro.

The international airports in Guatemala are Aeropuerto Internacional La Aurora, in Guatemala City, and the smaller Aeropuerto Internacional Santa Elena, in El Petén.

➤ BELIZE AIRPORTS: **Belize Municipal Airstrip** (✉ Belize City, ☎ no phone). **Philip Goldson International Airport** (✉ Ladyville, ☎ 225/2014).

➤ GUATEMALA AIRPORTS: **Aeropuerto Internacional La Aurora** (✉ Guatemala City, ☎ 332–6084 or 332–6085). **Aeropuerto Internacional Santa Elena** (✉ El Petén, ☎ 950–1289).

DUTY-FREE SHOPPING

The international airports in Belize and Guatemala have several duty-free shops selling liquor, cigars, perfume, and other items.

BIKE TRAVEL

In Belize, the lightly traveled rural byways are good for biking, although the rough roads mean you should be prepared for lots of flats. Mountain Pine Ridge, with hardly any traffic on the miles of old logging roads, is an ideal spot for mountain biking. Bicycle racing has become an important sport in Belize, and you often see teams training.

Mountain biking is growing in popularity in Guatemala, particularly in highland towns like Antigua and Huehuetenango. Here the rolling hills, beautiful scenery, and decent (but not too crowded) roadways make for excellent two-wheel excursions. Road biking is less advisable, primarily because Guatemala's narrow highways can barely accommodate the growing number of cars and trucks on the road.

BIKES IN FLIGHT

Most airlines accommodate bikes as luggage, provided they are dismantled and boxed; check with individual airlines about packing requirements. Airlines sell bike boxes, which are often free at bike shops, for about $15 (bike bags start at $100). International travelers often can substitute a bike for a piece of checked luggage at no charge; otherwise, the cost is about $100. Domestic and Canadian airlines charge $40–$80 each way.

BIKE RENTALS

In Belize you can rent mountain bikes in Cayo and road bikes in the resort areas of Ambergris Caye and Placencia. In Guatemala bike-rental shops are in all the good biking towns: Antigua, Panajachel, and Huehuetenango. Plenty of ecolodges and hotels throughout the country also rent bikes or lend them to guests free of charge: mind you, these are not always in the best of shape.

BOAT AND FERRY TRAVEL

Since Belize has about 325 km (200 mi) of coastline and some 400 islands dotting the Caribbean, water taxis and small ferries are a primary form of transportation. There is scheduled ferry service three or more times a day from Belize City to Ambergris Caye, Caye Caulker, and Caye Chapel, as well as between those cayes. One-way fare from Belize City to Ambergris Caye is BZ$25, and the trip takes 1¼ hours. To Caye Caulker the fare is BZ$15, and the trip takes 45 minutes. A ferry runs at least five days a week between Corozal Town and San Pedro. The fair is BZ$35 one-way, and the trip takes 1½ hours. To reach the more remote cayes, you're basically left to your own devices, unless you're staying at a hotel where such transfers are arranged for you. The resorts on the atolls run their own flights or boats, but these are not available to the general public.

If you are headed to Honduras, ferries run once a week from Placencia and Dangriga, in Belize, to Puerto Cortes, in Honduras, for BZ$100

each way. *Lanchas* (private motor boats) shuttle passengers between Livingston, Guatemala, and Omoa, Honduras, every Tuesday and Friday. The boats leave Livingston at 7:30 and depart Omoa for the return trip at noon. The trip takes 2–3 hours and costs Q240.

For boat travel between Belize and Guatemala, water taxi service is available daily at 9 AM from Punta Gorda, in Belize, to Puerto Barrios and Livingston, in Guatemala, for BZ$20–BZ$25 each way). They return late in the afternoon. A boat leaves Puerto Barrios for Punta Gorda on Tuesday and Friday at 7 AM and takes 2½ hours. Lanchas depart around 8–9 and 1–2; the trip takes 50 minutes.

Note that life jackets are typically not provided on boats and that the seas can be rough. Postpone your trip if the weather looks bad, and don't be shy about waiting for another boat if the one offered looks unseaworthy or overcrowded.

BUSINESS HOURS

BANKS AND OFFICES

Belize has three local banks, Alliance Bank, Atlantic Bank, and Belize Bank, and two international banks, Barclays and Bank of Nova Scotia. Hours vary, but the branches are typically open Monday–Thursday 8–1 and Friday 8–1 and 3–6. The Belize Bank branch at Philip Goldson International Airport is open 8:30–4 daily.

In Guatemala most banks are open 9–4 but sometimes stay open until 7 PM. Major banks, such as Bancafe, Banco Industrial, and Banco Occidente, will exchange traveler's checks.

MUSEUMS AND SIGHTS

It's a good idea to plan your visit to Belize's museums and archaeological sites for early in the day, as many of them, including popular attractions like Cahal Pech and Xunantunich, close at 4 or 4:30. Many have abbreviated hours on weekends, closing as early as noon.

In Guatemala many museums are closed on Monday. Most are open normal business hours, but some close for a few hours in the afternoon. Tikal is open daily 8–6.

SHOPS

Belize is a very laid-back place that requires a certain amount of flexibility when browsing around stores. Shops operate according to the whim of the owner but are generally open 8–noon and 2–8. Larger stores and supermarkets in Belize City do not close at lunch. Some shops and businesses are open a half day on Wednesday and Saturday. On Friday many shops close early for the weekend. On Sunday Belize takes it easy—few shops are open.

In Guatemala shops are generally open 10–7, with many closing for a 1–3 lunch break.

BUS TRAVEL

Belize has frequent and inexpensive bus service on the Northern and Western highways, as well as reasonable service in the south along the Hummingbird, Manatee, and Southern highways. Elsewhere, service is spotty. There is no municipal bus service in Belize City, although most of Belize's private bus companies have their main terminals in Belize City. In Belize, because of many mergers, the dominant bus line is Novelo's, which also owns Southern Transport. Together, these companies dominate bus service on main routes around the country. Other companies have a handful of buses on limited routes.

In Guatemala brightly colored buses are the transportation of choice for locals and visitors alike. They can get you just about anywhere cheaply and quickly, making them great for short trips. They aren't as convenient for longer journeys, as you'll probably have to change buses once or twice along the way. The down side is that buses can be extremely crowded. Always **be prepared for a tight squeeze**—this means three to a two-person seat.

Large bags are typically stowed on top—this may make you nervous, but thefts are not common. Except for occasional pickpocketings, incidents involving foreign travelers on public buses are rare. Drivers and their assistants, called *cobradors* or *ayudantes,* are often a bit gruff but really know their stuff. They can tell you if you're on the right bus and remind you when and where to get off. To be sure you aren't forgotten, **try to sit near the driver.**

From Guatemala City Autobuses de Oriente has service to the Atlantic Lowlands, Las Verapaces, and El Petén. Transgalgos travels to the Western Highlands. Between Guatemala City and Antigua, Transportes Turísticos Atitrans and Turansa are both reputable companies. Línea Dorada offers direct bus service between Guatemala City and Santa Elena and Flores.

➤ BELIZE COMPANIES: **Novelo's** (✉ W. Collet Canal, Belize City, ☎ 227/2025). **Southern Transport** (✉ 3 Havana St., Dangriga, ☎ 522/2160).

➤ GUATEMALA COMPANIES: **Autobuses de Oriente** (✉ Guatemala City, ☎ 238–3894). **Línea Dorada** (✉ Calle Principal, Santa Elena; ✉ Calle de la Playa, Flores, ☎ 232–9658). **Transgalgos** (✉ Guatemala City, ☎ 253–4868).

CLASSES

Expect to ride on old U.S. school buses or retired North American Greyhound buses. On some routes of Belize there are a few express buses with air-conditioning and other comforts. These cost a few dollars more.

In Guatemala inexpensive public buses, also of the converted school bus variety, crisscross the entire country, but they can be slow and extremely crowded. Popular destinations, such as Santa Elena and Río Dulce, are serviced by Pullman buses, which are as well equipped as American bus lines and are considerably more comfortable. Your hotel or Inguat office can make bus travel recommendations and arrangements for you.

FARES AND SCHEDULES

Belizean buses are cheap, running about BZ$2–BZ$22 for trips between towns. In Belize most buses on main routes run according to more-or-less reliable schedules; on lesser-traveled routes the schedules may not mean much.

In Guatemala fares on public buses are a bargain at Q2–Q24. Public buses follow loose schedules, sometimes delaying departures until buses fill up. Be aware that on some routes the last bus of the day isn't always a sure thing. Always ask before waiting around.

PAYING

The main terminals in Belize City and some larger towns have ticket windows where you pay in advance and secure a reserved seat. If you board at other points, you pay the driver's assistant and take any available seat.

In Guatemala you pay the bus driver as you board. On intercity buses a fare collector will pass through the bus periodically to take your fare. These fare collectors have an amazing ability to keep track of all riders who have not paid on a jam-packed bus.

Advance-purchase bus tickets and reservations are usually unnecessary for routes within Belize and Guatemala. Arrive at bus terminals about a half hour before your departure.

SHUTTLE TRAVEL

Belize has minivans that shuttle riders between Belize City and San Ignacio. Discovery Expeditions charges BZ$70 per person for journeys between these cities and provides service to other parts of the country as well. Línea Dorada runs vans between Belize City and Flores, Guatemala, for BZ$50, and between Belize City and Chetumal for BZ$70 (plus border crossing fees.)

Shuttles in Guatemala are private minivans that hold up to eight passengers. They are faster and more comfortable than public buses and maintain a fairly reliable schedule. Advance reservations are usually required. Shuttles can be arranged at the airport, at travel agencies, and at most hotels. Popular routes, like those between Guatemala City, Antigua, Chichicastenango, Panajachel, and Quetzaltenango, run 3–5 times daily; other routes may have less frequent departures. Prices run $7–$35. Atitrans and Servicios Turísticos Atitlán are two reputable companies that operate shuttles throughout the country.

➤ BELIZE COMPANIES: **Discovery Expeditions** (☎ 223/0748). **Línea Dorada** (☎ 926/3649).

➤ GUATEMALA COMPANIES: **Atitrans** (☎ 832–1381 or 363–0178). Servicios Turísticos Atitlan (☎ 832–1493 or 762–2075).

CAMERAS AND PHOTOGRAPHY

With their incredibly varied landscapes, Belize and Guatemala are a photographer's dream. Frothy waves in a turquoise sea and palm-lined crescents of beach are relatively easy to capture on film if you **don't let the brightness of the sun on sand and water fool your light meter.** You must compensate or else work early or late in the day when the light isn't as brilliant and contrast isn't such a problem. Do **invest in a telephoto lens** if you intend to photograph wildlife: even standard zoom lenses won't capture a satisfying amount of detail. Remember to **bring high-speed film** to compensate for low light in the jungle. The thick tree canopy blocks out more light than you realize.

It's best to **always ask permission before taking pictures of indigenous people,** particularly in market areas and rural villages. Although many are more than happy to comply, others may find it disrespectful, invasive, or even threatening. In Guatemala's smaller towns children may offer to pose for a picture in exchange for a small tip. Or if you snap a candid shot of a child, you may be asked for a few quetzales. This is off-putting to some, but others realize it's a small price for a priceless memento. A nice alternative is to bring an instant camera; the photos are a great gift for youngsters who very likely have never seen a picture of themselves.

Casual photographers should **consider using inexpensive disposable cameras** to reduce the risks inherent in traveling with expensive equipment. One-use cameras with underwater functions make your snorkeling and diving adventures more memorable.

The *Kodak Guide to Shooting Great Travel Pictures* (available at bookstores everywhere) is loaded with tips.

➤ PHOTO HELP: **Kodak Information Center** (☎ 800/242–2424, WEB www.kodak.com).

EQUIPMENT PRECAUTIONS

In Belize sand and high humidity are enemies of your camera equipment. To be on the safe side, **pack your gear in plastic bags** to protect it from the elements. Always **keep film, video-tapes, and computer disks out of the sun. Don't pack film and equipment in checked luggage,** where it is much more susceptible to damage. X-ray machines used for viewing checked luggage are becoming much more powerful and therefore are much more likely to ruin your film. Remember to **ask for hand inspection of film,** which becomes clouded after repeated exposure to airport X-ray machines. Carry an extra supply of batteries, and **be prepared to turn on your camera, camcorder, or laptop** to prove to airport security personnel that the device is real.

FILM AND DEVELOPING

In Belize there are photofinishing services in most major towns, and in Belize City you'll have no trouble locating one-hour photo labs. Guatemala has reliable and affordable photo-development shops, especially in big cities and tourist destinations. Many offer one-hour developing at no extra cost.

CAR RENTAL

Belize City and Aeropuerto Internacional La Aurora, in Ladyville, are where you'll find most major car-rental agencies, as well as several local operators. Prices vary from company to company, but all are high by U.S. standards (BZ$120–BZ$260 per day). For instance, the cost of renting a four-wheel-drive Suzuki from Budget, including unlimited mileage, is about BZ$150 per day; the weekly rate, about BZ$900, is cheaper. Off-season rates are lower. Most major hotels offer all-terrain vehicles for about BZ$400 per day, including a person to guide you. Some hotels include transportation as part of your room rate. A few resorts have rental cars for about BZ$150–BZ$200 per day.

For serious safaris **rent a four-wheel-drive vehicle,** particularly a Land Rover or an Isuzu Trooper. But because unpaved roads, mudslides in rainy season, and a general off-the-beaten-path landscape are status quo here, it will be comforting to have a four-wheel-drive vehicle no matter where you are going. Note that most Belize agencies do not permit you to take their vehicles over the border into Guatemala or Mexico.

Renting cars has never really caught on in Guatemala, which, given the state of many of the roads, is understandable. However, a car can be an asset to your trip. You don't have to worry about unreliable bus schedules, you have a lot more control over your itinerary and the pace of your trip, and you can head off to explore on a whim. If you do rent a car, **consider a *doble-tracción* (four-wheel-drive) vehicle,** which can manage poorly maintained or unpaved roads. Always **look for guarded lots or hotels with private parking** to prevent theft or damage.

➤ MAJOR AGENCIES: **Alamo** (☎ 800/522–9696; 099/0999–4000 in the U.K.; WEB www.alamo.com). **Avis** (☎ 800/331–1084; 800/879–2847 in Canada; 02/9353–9000 in Australia; 09/526–2847 in New Zealand; 0870/606–0100 in the U.K.; WEB www.avis.com). **Budget** (☎ 800/527–0700; 0870/156–5656 in the U.K.; WEB www.budget.com). **Dollar** (☎ 800/800–6000; 0124/622–0111 in the U.K., where it's affiliated with Sixt; 02/9223–1444 in Australia; WEB www.dollar.com). **Hertz** (☎ 800/654–3001;800/263–0600 in Canada; 020/8897–2072 in the U.K.; 02/9669–2444 inAustralia; 09/256–8690 in New Zealand; WEB www.hertz.com). **National Car Rental** (☎ 800/227–7368; 020/8680–4800 in the U.K.; WEB www.nationalcar.com).

CUTTING COSTS

For a good deal, **book through a travel agent who will shop around.**

INSURANCE

When driving a rented car you are generally responsible for any damage to or loss of the vehicle. You may also be liable for any property damage or personal injury that you may cause while driving. Before you rent, **see what coverage you already have** under the terms of your personal auto-insurance policy and credit cards.

REQUIREMENTS AND RESTRICTIONS

In Belize and Guatemala rental-car companies routinely accept without question driver's licenses from the United States, Canada, and most other countries. Most car-rental agencies require a major credit card for a deposit, and some require you be over 25.

SURCHARGES

Before you pick up a car in one city and leave it in another, **ask about drop-off charges or one-way service fees,** which can be substantial. Note, too, that some rental agencies charge extra if you return the car before the time specified in your contract. To avoid a hefty refueling fee, **fill the tank just before you turn in the car,** but be aware that gas stations near the rental outlet may overcharge. It's almost never a deal to buy the tank of gas in the car when you rent it; the understanding is that you'll return it empty, but some fuel usually remains.

CAR TRAVEL

EMERGENCY SERVICES

When renting a car, ask the rental agency what it does if your car breaks down in a remote area. Most in Belize send a driver with a replacement vehicle or a mechanic to fix the car. For help in Guatemala, your best bet is to call the National Police or Tourist Police. In either country **consider renting a cellular phone** in case you need assistance along the way.

➤ CONTACTS: **Guatemalan National Police** (☎ 110). **Guatemalan Tourist Police** (☎ 832–0532 ext. 35 or 832–0533 ext. 35).

GASOLINE

Modern, U.S.-style gas stations—Texaco, Esso, and Shell brands, some of them with convenience stores and 24-hour service—are found in Belize City and in most major towns. In more remote areas, especially in the southern part of the country, **gas up whenever you see a service station.** Premium unleaded gas costs close to BZ$6 a gallon. Attendants who pump gas for you do not expect a tip.

You will find that prices at Guatemala's service stations are as high as in Belize. At most gas stations an attendant will pump the gas and make change. Plan to **use cash,** as credit cards are rarely accepted.

ROAD CONDITIONS

Three of the four main roads in Belize—the Western Highway, Northern Highway, and Hummingbird Highway—are completely paved. These two-lane roads are generally in good condition. The Southern Highway, running from Dangriga to Punta Gorda, is paved for about two-thirds of the way, and work on the rest continues. Aside from these major thoroughfares, expect to find the surfaces of the dirt, gravel, and limestone roads anywhere from fairly smooth to incredibly rough. Always **call ahead during the rainy season,** as a few unpaved roads may be impassable.

Immense improvements have been made to Guatemala's ravaged roads. A highway from Río Dulce to Tikal has dramatically reduced travel time along this popular route. It still has no guard rails, however, so it isn't for the squeamish. Roads in remote areas are frequently poorly paved, rife with potholes, and treacherous in the rainy season. Always **pick a four-wheel-drive vehicle for travel off the beaten path.** You'll generally find signs pointing to large towns, but routes to smaller towns may not be clearly marked. Look for intersections where people seem to be waiting for a bus—that's a good sign that there's an important turnoff nearby.

ROAD MAPS

The best road map to Belize is the *Belize Traveller's Map* (ITMB, Vancouver), which was last updated in 2001. It's a good idea to buy this map before your trip, as it is not always readily available in Belize. *Emory King's Driver's Guide to Beautiful Belize,* updated annually and available in Belize, is a mile-by-mile guide to most roads in Belize. Guatemala's tourism agency and all major car-rental companies have maps of Guatemala.

RULES OF THE ROAD

Drivers in Belize and Guatemala stick to the right. Seat belts are required, although the law is seldom enforced. There are few speed-limit signs, and police generally ignore speeders. However, as you approach small towns, **watch out for "sleeping policemen,"** a local name for raised speed bumps on the road. Belize has about a dozen traffic lights in the entire country, and only Belize City has anything approaching a traffic jam. Belizean drivers aren't always as skilled as they think they are, and drunk drivers can be a problem.

Guatemala's highways are an adventure, especially when they run along the edges of cliffs soaring high above a valley. Trucks and buses drive unbelievably fast along these routes; if you don't feel comfortable keeping up the pace, pull over periodically to let them pass. The narrow roads mean you can be stuck motionless on the road for an hour while a construction crew stands around a hole in the ground. **Always allow extra travel time** for such unpredictable events, making sure to **bring along snacks and drinks.** Otherwise, if you observe the rules you follow at home, you'll likely do just fine. Just don't expect everyone else to follow them.

CHILDREN IN BELIZE AND GUATEMALA

The people of Central America love children, and having yours along may prove to be your special ticket to meeting the locals. Children are welcomed in most hotels and restaurants, especially on weekends, when families go out for lunch in droves. If you are renting a car, don't forget to **arrange for a car seat** when you reserve. For general advice about traveling with children, consult *Fodor's FYI: Travel with Your Baby* (available in bookstores everywhere).

FLYING

If your children are two or older, **ask about children's airfares.** As a general rule, infants under two not occupying a seat fly at greatly reduced fares or even for free. When booking, **confirm carry-on allowances** if you're traveling with infants. In general, for babies charged 10% of the adult fare you are allowed one carry-on bag and a collapsible stroller; if the flight is full,

the stroller may have to be checked or you may be limited to less.

Experts agree that it's a good idea to use safety seats aloft for children weighing less than 40 pounds. Airlines set their own policies: U.S. carriers usually require that the child be ticketed, even if he or she is young enough to ride free, since the seats must be strapped into regular seats. Do **check your airline's policy about using safety seats during takeoff and landing.** Safety seats are not allowed everywhere in the plane, so get your seat assignments as early as possible.

When reserving, **request children's meals or a freestanding bassinet** (not available at all airlines) if you need them. But note that bulkhead seats, where you must sit to use the bassinet, may lack an overhead bin or storage space on the floor.

LODGING

Considering a kid-friendly hotel? Kids traveling in Belize will see monkeys and parrots at Banana Bank Ranch, outside Belmopan, and Lamanai Outpost Lodge, in Lamanai. Villas at Banyan Bay, on Ambergris Caye, has family-friendly two-bedroom condos, a big pool, and a nice beach. In Guatemala the Posada de Don Rodrigo, overlooking Lago Atitlán in Panajachel, has a pool with a huge waterslide.

Many hotels in Belize and Guatemala allow young children to stay in their parents' room at no extra charge, but many charge children older than age 11 or 12 as extra adults; be sure to **find out the cutoff age for children's discounts.**

SIGHTS AND ATTRACTIONS

Kids love Belize, especially those who enjoy the beach and water activities. Among the top attractions are the Belize Zoo, Belize's six butterfly farms, and the many Maya sites where kids can clamber up and down ancient temples. Children may enjoy taking a guided nature tour to see howler monkeys, crocodiles, snakes, and tarantulas in the wild. In Guatemala consider taking the kids to the Reserva Natural Atitlán, in Panajachel, which has winding tree-lined paths, suspension footbridges, waterfalls, a spider monkey lookout, a butterfly terrarium, and a beach. Climbing Volcán Pacayá, an active volcano near Antigua, is a thrilling and accessible hike for those over 10, and the ruins of Tikal will make history come alive for kids all ages. Places that are especially appealing to children are indicated by a rubber-duckie icon (🦆) in the margin.

SUPPLIES AND EQUIPMENT

Baby formula and diapers are available in Belize and Guatemala, but prices are up to twice those in the United States. Pasteurized milk is sold in some groceries, and canned or boxed milk is widely available.

COMPUTERS ON THE ROAD

If you're traveling in Belize with a laptop, be aware that the power supply may be uneven, and most hotels do not have built-in current stabilizers. At remote lodges power is often from generators. **Ask about electrical surges** before plugging in your computer.

Electricity is a little more reliable in Guatemala, especially in the larger cities. In either country **keep your disks out of the sun** and **avoid excessive heat for both your computer and disks.**

CONSUMER PROTECTION

Whether you're shopping for gifts or purchasing travel services, **pay with a major credit card** whenever possible, so you can cancel payment or get reimbursed if there's a problem (and you can provide documentation). If you're doing business with a particular company for the first time, **contact your local Better Business Bureau and the attorney general's offices** in your state and (for U.S. businesses) the company's home state as well. Have any complaints been filed? Finally, if you're buying a package or tour, always **consider travel insurance** that includes default coverage (☞ Insurance, *below*).

➤ BBBs: **Council of Better Business Bureaus** (✉ 4200 Wilson Blvd., Suite 800, Arlington, VA 22203, ☎ 703/276–0100, FAX 703/525–8277, WEB www.bbb.org).

CRUISE TRAVEL

Cruising is an increasingly popular way to see Belize. The government says that each year about 250,000 passengers visit Belize by boat. There are many choices, so **look into several companies before you decide a ship is right for you.** Many choose a small ship, one holding fewer than 200 passengers, because it can visit small cayes and atolls such as Turneffe Atoll, Goff Caye, Tobacco Caye, and West Snake Caye, along with resort areas such as Ambergris Caye and Placencia. If you prefer, you can opt for a large cruise ship, which carry thousands of passengers and provide all the amenities of a resort. These big boats dock in Belize City. Because of shallow water near shore, passengers are brought ashore in small boats called tenders. Once aboard, you can snorkel around the islands, explore Maya ruins, or wander around the historic parts of Belize City.

To learn how to plan, choose, and book a cruise-ship voyage, consult *Fodor's FYI: Plan & Enjoy Your Cruise* (available in bookstores everywhere).

➤ CRUISE LINES: **American Canadian Caribbean Line** (☎ 800/556–7450, WEB www.accl-smallships.com). **Carnival Cruise Lines** (☎ 888/227–6482, WEB www.carnival.com). **Celebrity Cruises** (☎ 800/722–5941, WEB www.celebritycruises.com). **Windstar Cruises** (☎ 800/258–7245, WEB www.windstarcruises.com).

CUSTOMS AND DUTIES

When shopping abroad, **keep receipts** for all purchases. Upon reentering the country, **be ready to show customs officials what you've bought.** If you feel a duty is incorrect, appeal the assessment. If you object to the way your clearance was handled, note the inspector's badge number. In either case, first ask to see a supervisor. If the problem isn't resolved, write to the appropriate authorities, beginning with the port director at your point of entry.

IN BELIZE

Duty-free allowances for visitors entering Belize include 1 liter of liquor and one carton of cigarettes.

All electronic and electrical appliances, cameras, jewelry, or other items of value must be declared at the point of entry. You should have no trouble bringing a laptop computer into Belize. Firearms of any type and spearguns are prohibited.

To take home fresh seafood of any kind from Belize, you must first obtain a permit from the Fisheries Department. There is a 20-pound limit. The export of Maya artifacts is strictly prohibited.

IN GUATEMALA

Visitors may enter Guatemala duty-free with a camera, up to six rolls of film, any clothes and articles needed while traveling, 500 grams of tobacco, 3 liters of alcoholic beverages, 2 bottles of perfume, and 2 kg of candy. Unless you bring in a lot of merchandise, customs officers probably won't even check your luggage, although a laptop may attract some attention.

It's illegal to export most Maya artifacts. If you plan on buying such goods, do so only at reputable stores, and keep the receipt. You may not take fruits or vegetables out of Guatemala.

IN AUSTRALIA

Australian residents who are 18 or older may bring home A$400 worth of souvenirs and gifts (including jewelry), 250 cigarettes or 250 grams of tobacco, and 1,125 ml of alcohol (including wine, beer, and spirits). Residents under 18 may bring back A$200 worth of goods. Prohibited items include meat products. Seeds, plants, and fruits need to be declared upon arrival.

➤ INFORMATION: **Australian Customs Service** (Regional Director, ✉ Box 8, Sydney, NSW 2001, ☎ 02/9213–2000, FAX 02/9213–4000, WEB www.customs.gov.au).

IN CANADA

Canadian residents who have been out of Canada for at least seven days may bring in C$750 worth of goods duty-free. If you've been away fewer than seven days but more than 48 hours, the duty-free allowance drops to C$200; if your trip lasts 24 to 48 hours, the allowance is C$50. You may not pool allowances with family members. Goods claimed under the C$750 exemption may follow you by mail; those claimed under the lesser exemptions must accompany you. Alcohol and tobacco products may be included in the seven-day and 48-hour exemptions but not in the 24-hour exemption. If you meet the age requirements of the province or territory through which you reenter Canada, you may bring in, duty-free, 1.5 liters of wine or 1.14 liters (40 imperial ounces) of liquor or 24 12-ounce cans or bottles of beer or ale. If you are 19 or older you may bring in, duty-free, 200 cigarettes and 50 cigars. Check ahead of time with the Canada Customs and Revenue Agency or the Department of Agriculture for policies regarding meat products, seeds, plants, and fruits.

You may send an unlimited number of gifts (only one gift per recipient, however) worth up to C$60 each duty-free to Canada. Label the package UNSOLICITED GIFT—VALUE UNDER $60. Alcohol and tobacco are excluded.

➤ INFORMATION: **Canada Customs and Revenue Agency** (✉ 2265 St. Laurent Blvd. S, Ottawa, Ontario K1G 4K3, ☎ 204/983–3500; 506/636–5064; 800/461–9999 in Canada, WEB www.ccra-adrc.gc.ca).

IN NEW ZEALAND

All homeward-bound residents may bring back NZ$700 worth of souvenirs and gifts; passengers may not pool their allowances, and children can claim only the concession on goods intended for their own use. For those 17 or older, the duty-free allowance also includes 4.5 liters of wine or beer; one 1,125-ml bottle of spirits; and either 200 cigarettes, 250 grams of tobacco, 50 cigars, or a combination of the three up to 250 grams. Meat products, seeds, plants, and fruits must be declared upon arrival to the Agricultural Services Department.

➤ INFORMATION: **New Zealand Customs** (✉ Head Office, The Customhouse, 17–21 Whitmore St., Box 2218, Wellington, ☎ 09/300–5399, WEB www.customs.govt.nz).

IN THE U.K.

From countries outside the European Union, including Belize and Guatemala, you may bring home, duty-free, 200 cigarettes or 50 cigars; 1 liter of spirits or 2 liters of fortified or sparkling wine or liqueurs; 2 liters of still table wine; 60 ml of perfume; 250 ml of toilet water; plus £145 worth of other goods, including gifts and souvenirs. Prohibited items include meat products, seeds, plants, and fruits.

➤ INFORMATION: **HM Customs and Excise** (✉ St. Christopher House, Southwark, London SE1 OTE, ☎ 020/7928–3344, WEB www. hmce.gov.uk).

IN THE U.S.

U.S. residents who have been out of the country for at least 48 hours and who have not used the $600 allowance or any part of it in the past 30 days may bring home $600 worth of foreign goods duty-free. This allowance, higher than the standard $400 exemption, applies to the 24 countries in the Caribbean Basin Initiative—including Belize and Guatemala. If you visit a CBI country and a non-CBI country, you may still bring in $600 worth of goods duty-free, but no more than $400 may be from the non-CBI country.

U.S. residents 21 and older may bring back 1 liter of alcohol duty-free. In addition, regardless of your age, you are allowed 200 cigarettes and 100 non-Cuban cigars. Antiques, which the U.S. Customs Service defines as objects more than 100 years old, enter duty-free, as do original works of art done entirely by hand, including paintings, drawings, and sculptures. You may also send packages home duty-free, with a limit of one parcel per addressee per day (except alcohol or tobacco products or perfume worth more than $5). You can mail up to $200 worth of goods for personal use; label the package PERSONAL USE and attach a list of its contents and their retail value. If the package contains your used personal belongings, mark it PERSONAL GOODS RETURNED to avoid paying duties. You may send up to $100 worth of goods as a gift; mark the package UNSOLICITED GIFT. Mailed items do not affect your duty-free allowance on your return.

➤ INFORMATION: **U.S. Customs Service** (for inquiries, ✉ 1300 Pennsylvania Ave. NW, Washington, DC 20229, WEB www.customs.gov, ☎ 202/354–1000; for complaints, ✉ Customer Satisfaction Unit, 1300 Pennsylvania Ave. NW, Room 5.5A, Washington, DC 20229; for registration of equipment, ✉ Office of Passenger Programs, 1300 Pennsylvania Ave. NW, Room 5.4D, Washington, DC 20229,☎ 202/927–0530).

DINING

You can eat very well in Belize. The country has no unique cuisine, but a gastronomic gumbo of Mexican, Caribbean, Maya, Garífuna, English, and other cuisines provides a tasty variety of dining choices. Belize also has restaurants serving French, Thai, Indian, Chinese, and even Sri Lankan food. On the coast and cayes, seafood—especially lobster, conch, and locally caught fish such as snapper and grouper—is fresh, inexpensive, and delicious. Try creole specialties such as cow-foot soup (yes, made with real cow's feet), "boil up" (a stew of fish, potatoes, plantains, cassava and other vegetables, and eggs), and the ubiquitous "stew chicken" with rice and beans. Many creole dishes are seasoned with red or black *recado*, a paste made from annatto seeds and other spices. In border areas, enjoy mestizo favorites such as *escabeche* (onion soup), *salbutes* (fried corn tortillas with chicken and a topping of tomatoes, onions, and peppers), or *garnaches* (fried tortillas with refried beans, cabbage, and cheese). In Dangriga, Punta Gorda, and other Garífuna areas, try dishes such as *sere lasus* (fish soup with plantain balls) or cassava dumplings. In most areas of Belize you can chow down on American classics like fried chicken, pork chops, and T-bone steaks.

In general, Guatemala does not have a distinguished national cuisine; most top restaurants serve European or American fare. The classic Guatemalan dish is tasty but unremarkable: it has eggs, cheese, refried black beans, meat (either sliced beef or the sausage called *chorizo*), and Guatemala's thick corn tortillas. There are a few standouts, though, including *róbalo*, a common and delicious fish called snook elsewhere; ceviche, chilled marinated seafood flavored with lime or tomato broth; and a few dishes not seen on North American menus, such as *tepisquintle*, (the world's largest rodent) and *sopa de tortuga* (turtle soup). Street vendors typically sell fried chicken and french fries, or *churrosquitos* (sliced beef or chorizo served with pickled cabbage and tortillas). *Huevos motuleños* (layers of fried eggs served on a crispy tortilla with cheese, beans, hot sauce, and sometimes ham) make an amazing breakfast. Vegetarians in both Belize and Guatemala may be "beaned out" after a week or so, although *ensalada aguacate* (avocado salad), *pan de banana* (banana bread), and flan (a crème caramel dessert) never get dull.

Only the most expensive restaurants in Belize and Guatemala accept credit cards and traveler's checks. The restaurants that we list (all of which are indicated by a ✕ symbol) are the cream of the crop in each price category. Properties indicated by a ✕▥ are lodging establishments whose restaurant warrants a special trip.

MEALTIMES

In Belize breakfast is usually served from around 7 to 9, lunch from 11 to 2, and dinner from 6 to 9. Few restaurants are open late. Remember that small restaurants in Belize may open or close at the whim of the owner. Off-season, restaurants may close early if it looks as if there are no more guests coming, and some restaurants close completely for a month or two, usually in September and October.

In Guatemala lunch is the biggest meal, or at least the longest, running from noon to 2 or 3. Breakfast starts at 7, and dinner is not long after sundown. Restaurants in major tourist areas may stay open later, but most places are all but deserted by 9.

Unless otherwise noted, the restaurants listed in this guide are open daily for both lunch and dinner.

RESERVATIONS AND DRESS

Reservations are always a good idea; we mention them only when they're essential or not accepted. Book as far ahead as you can, and reconfirm as soon as you arrive. (Large parties should always call ahead to check the reservations policy.) We mention dress only when men are required to wear a jacket or a jacket and tie.

WINE, BEER, AND SPIRITS

Although many restaurants in Belize serve terrific tropical mixed drinks, few offer wine. The beer you'll see in Belize most often is Belikin. The lager is also available in a premium version that is sold mostly in more expensive bars and restaurants. The richer Belikin Stout and the milder Lighthouse are also available. Both Belikin and Lighthouse are from Bowen & Bowen brewery, the same brewery that makes the local version of Guinness Stout. American and other imported beers are available in some grocery stores, but prices are high. Due to restrictive import laws, the fine beers of neighboring Mexico and Guatemala are rarely available in Belize. Several Belize companies manufacture liquors, primarily rum but also gin and vodka. Traveller's One Barrel Rum is a particularly good choice, spicing up drinks with a hint of vanilla flavor. Imported wines are available in supermarkets and better restaurants, but at about twice the price of the same wines in the United States. The drinking age in Belize is 18, although IDs are rarely checked.

Guatemala has no real wine market to speak of, but restaurants catering to tourists often have excellent imported bottles. The national beer, called Cabro, is decent, while Gallo is as good as any brand in the United States. Imported liquor and local spirits distilled from sugarcane can be found most everywhere. The official drinking age in Guatemala is 20.

DISABILITIES AND ACCESSIBILITY

Wheelchair accessibility in Central America is extremely limited. Few laws require accessibility for those with disabilities. However, there is a growing awareness of the needs of people with disabilities, and the friendly, helpful attitude of the people goes some way toward making up for the lack of provisions. Exploring Central America's attractions usually involves walking down steep trails, muddy paths, or cobblestone streets. In Belize boats and small planes with no accommodations for those with mobility problems are used to get to the cayes and other remote areas. Airplanes often lack jetways, meaning passengers must walk down steps to get off the plane. Because the docks cannot accommodate larger vessels, cruise-ship passengers are brought to shore in small boats that are difficult to get into without assistance. Buses are not equipped to carry wheelchairs, so wheelchair users should hire a van to get around.

➤ LOCAL RESOURCES: In Belize, **Central American Information Center** (✉ Box 50211, San Diego, CA 92105, ☎ 619/262–6489). In Guatemala, **Inguat** (✉ 7 Av. 1–17, Zona 4, ☎ 331–1339 or 331–1333).

LODGING

When discussing accessibility with an operator or reservations agent, **ask hard questions.** Are there any stairs, inside *or* out? Are there grab bars next to the toilet *and* in the shower/tub? How wide is the doorway to the room? To the bathroom? For the most extensive facilities meeting the latest legal specifications, **opt for newer accommodations.** If you reserve through a toll-free number, consider also calling the hotel's local number to confirm the information from the central reservations office. Get confirmation in writing when you can.

SIGHTS AND ATTRACTIONS

Few sights in Guatemala were designed with travelers in wheelchairs in mind, and fewer still have been renovated to meet that need. Newer destinations may have the necessary facilities and accommodations, but don't count on it—it's best to call ahead or get a recommendation from someone who has visited the property.

➤ COMPLAINTS: **Aviation Consumer Protection Division** (☞ Air Travel, *above*) for airline-related problems. **Departmental Office of Civil Rights**

(for general inquiries, ✉ U.S. Department of Transportation, S-30, 400 7th St. SW, Room 10215, Washington, DC 20590, ☎ 202/366–4648, FAX 202/366–9371, WEB www.dot.gov/ost/docr/index.htm). **Disability Rights Section** (✉ U.S. Department of Justice, Civil Rights Division, Box 66738, Washington, DC 20035-6738, ☎ 202/514–0301 or800/514–0301, for ADA inquiries; WEB www.usdoj.gov/crt/ada/adahom1.htm).

TRAVEL AGENCIES

In the United States, the Americans with Disabilities Act requires that travel firms serve the needs of all travelers. Some agencies specialize in working with people with disabilities.

➤ TRAVELERS WITH MOBILITY PROBLEMS: **Access Adventures** (✉ 206 Chestnut Ridge Rd., Scottsville, NY 14624, ☎ 716/889–9096, dltravel@prodigy.net), run by a former physical-rehabilitation counselor. **Flying Wheels Travel** (✉ 143 W. Bridge St., Box 382, Owatonna, MN 55060, ☎ 507/451–5005 or 800/535–6790, FAX 507/451–1685, WEB www.flyingwheelstravel.com).

DISCOUNTS AND DEALS

Be a smart shopper and **compare all your options** before making decisions. A plane ticket bought with a promotional coupon from travel clubs, coupon books, and direct-mail offers or purchased on the Internet may not be cheaper than the least expensive fare from a discount ticket agency. And always keep in mind that what you get is just as important as what you save.

DISCOUNT RESERVATIONS

Many of the hotels in Belize and Guatemala—including some budget ones—have Web sites. Discounts, typically 10%–20%, are often available for reservations made on-line.

To save money, **look into discount reservations services** with Web sites and toll-free numbers, which use their buying power to get a better price on hotels, airline tickets, even car rentals. When booking a room, always **call the hotel's local toll-free number** (if one is available) rather than the central reservations number—you'll often get a better price. Always ask about special packages or corporate rates.

When shopping for the best deal on hotels and car rentals, **look for guaranteed exchange rates,** which protect you against a falling dollar. With your rate locked in, you won't pay more, even if the price goes up in the local currency.

➤ AIRLINE TICKETS: ☎ 800/AIR–4LESS.

PACKAGE DEALS

Don't confuse packages and guided tours. When you buy a package, you travel on your own, just as though you had planned the trip yourself. Fly/drive packages, which combine airfare and car rental, are often a good deal.

DIVING

Belize offers some of the best scuba diving in the world. There are scores of dive sites accessible from the beach. The cayes and atolls offer world-class diving experiences. The water throughout the Caribbean is crystal clear, often to 200 ft (61 m), and the quantity and variety of marine life are astounding.

Resorts often offer guests introductory scuba instruction in a pool, followed by a shallow dive; some hotels have on-site dive shops. All shops offer instruction and certification according to the standards set by either the National Association of Underwater Instructors (NAUI) or the Professional Association of Diving Instructors (PADI). They also have a variety of day and night dives to wrecks, reefs, and underwater walls.

DIVERS ALERT

Don't fly within 24 hours after scuba diving.

➤ ORGANIZATIONS: **NAUI Worldwide** (✉ Box 89789, 1232 Tech Blvd., Tampa, FL 33619, ☎ 800/553–6284 or 813/628–6284, WEB www.naui.org). **PADI** (✉ 30151 Tomas St., Rancho Santa Margarita, CA 92688, ☎ 800/729–7234 or 949/858–7234, WEB www.padi.com; ✉ 3771 Jacombs Rd., Bldg. C, #535, Richmond, British Columbia, Canada V6V 2L9, ☎ 604/273–0277 or 800/565–8130;

✉ Unit 7, St. Philip's Central, Albert Rd., St. Philip's, Bristol, United Kingdom BS2 0PD, ☎ 0117/300–7234; ✉ Unit 3, 4 Skyline Pl., French's Forest, New South Wales, Australia 2086, ☎ 2/9451–2300).

ECOTOURISM

Central America is the original eco-tourism destination; as a result, you'll see the term used liberally everywhere. For lodging it can be used to describe a deluxe private cabaña on a tidy beach or a hut in the middle of nowhere with pit toilets. It may also point to environmental conservation efforts by parks or tour companies that are conscious of natural resources and their role in not depleting them. Or it may mean just the opposite. Wildlife parks, butterfly farms, cloud forests, and Maya ruins are some of the incredible eco-destinations in this area. And mountain biking, bird-watching, jungle hiking, scuba diving, cave tubing, fishing, and white-water rafting are just some of the eco-activities.

ELECTRICITY

Don't bring a converter or adapter as the electrical current in Belize and Guatemala is 110 volts, the same as in the United States. Outlets in both countries take U.S.-style plugs. In a few remote areas lodges and hotels may generate their own electricity. After the generators are turned off at night, light comes only from kerosene lanterns or your flashlight.

ENGLISH-LANGUAGE MEDIA

BOOKS

Because of import taxes, books are more expensive in Belize than in North America or Europe. Almost every major tourist destination in Guatemala has one or two stores with used paperbacks in English. Some are willing to trade or lend books. Guatemala City and Antigua are the only places in the country where you will find a significant selection of new books.

NEWSPAPERS AND MAGAZINES

Belize has no daily newspapers, but it has a number of brash weeklies. As in most countries, crime and politics make the front pages, often in sensational headlines. The *Re-*

porter, published in Belize City, is the best independent newspaper. For visitors the chatty *San Pedro Sun,* one of two weeklies on Ambergris Caye, is a good source of information, as is the monthly *Placencia Breeze* in Placencia.

The U.S. travel magazine *Belize First* also has an online edition (www.belizefirst.com). Both the print and electronic editions are good sources for cultural, dining, lodging, and service information.

The monthly Guatemalan journal *Revue* (⊠ 4 Calle Oriente 23, Antigua, Guatemala, ☎ 832–4619) has a few articles on local trends. *Lugares y Destinos* is a free bilingual guide produced by the Guatemalan Tourist Commission. *Destination Guatemala* and *Central America Guide* are detailed visitor guides available in most upscale hotels.

The international chain hotels usually have fairly current editions of a few major U.S. and European publications, typically *USA Today,* the *Economist,* and *Newsweek.*

RADIO AND TELEVISION

Belize's most informative television news is on Channel 5, which also offers its daily news summaries on the Web (www.channel5belize.com). Many hotels have cable or satellite TV, with 50 or more channels from the United States and Mexico. Love-FM Radio (95.1) is the nation's leading radio station, playing standards and soft rock.

Cable TV is a popular amenity in Guatemalan hotels. You can expect HBO, Showtime, ESPN, TNT, the Discovery Channel, MTV (a Spanish variety), and one or two feeds from regional stations in the United States (usually from Denver, curiously). Radio stations generally play a mix of American pop, rock, and Latin favorites.

ETIQUETTE AND BEHAVIOR

Belizeans and *Chapins* (a nickname for Guatemalans) are incredibly kind and friendly. You will let them know the same is true about you if you **always greet someone with a "good morning," or "buenos días,"** before asking for directions, inquiring about a table in a restaurant, and when entering a store or museum. It will set a positive tone for the conversation, and you'll be received much more warmly.

Don't be tempted to take pictures inside churches. (You'll probably spot clueless tourists snapping away during services, ignorant to the angry looks from worshipers.) Do not take pictures of indigenous people without first asking their permission; is customary to thank them by offering a small amount of money.

With the exception of luxury buses and shuttles, the seats on Guatemalan buses are expected to fit three abreast. Always **make room for others on buses.** It's perfectly fine to step into the aisle to let someone take a middle or window seat. In Guatemala it is acceptable to make a quick hiss or whistle to get someone's attention— you may find that you even take up the habit yourself, particularly with waiters. You also may hear men catcall women in this way, which unfortunately is not considered terribly rude either.

BUSINESS ETIQUETTE

Business dress in Belize is casual. Men rarely wear suits and ties, and even the prime minister appears at functions in a white shirt open at the neck. The business environment is more formal in Guatemala, where suits for men are more the norm. Women can wear blouses and skirts.

GAY AND LESBIAN TRAVEL

Although many tour operators book trips for gays to Belize and Guatemala, it cannot be said that the countries welcome gays with open arms. In fact, Belize has a law that went on the books in 1992 banning gay travelers from entering the country. There have been some signs of progress, however. A few years later the country invited a cruise ship full of gay men that had been turned away from the Cayman Islands to visit Belize instead.

As most are very religious, Belizeans have a very conservative view toward gay people. There are no openly gay or lesbian clubs or bars. Likewise, Guatemala frowns on gay life. There is a handful of gay clubs in Guatemala City, like Pandora's Box, which has been around forever.

➤ GAY- AND LESBIAN-FRIENDLY TRAVEL AGENCIES: **Different Roads Travel** (⊠ 8383 Wilshire Blvd., Suite 902, Beverly Hills, CA 90211, ☎ 323/651–5557 or 800/429–8747, FAX 323/651–3678, lgernert@tzell.com). **Kennedy Travel** (⊠ 314 Jericho Turnpike, Floral Park, NY 11001, ☎ 516/352–4888 or 800/237–7433, FAX 516/354–8849, WEB www.kennedytravel.com). **Now, Voyager** (⊠ 4406 18th St., San Francisco, CA 94114, ☎ 415/626–1169 or 800/255–6951, FAX 415/626–8626, WEB www.nowvoyager.com). **Skylink Travel and Tour** (⊠ 1006 Mendocino Ave., Santa Rosa, CA 95401, ☎ 707/546–9888 or 800/225–5759, FAX 707/546–9891, WEB www.skylinktravel.com), serving lesbian travelers.

HEALTH

Belize has a high standard of health and hygiene. You can drink the water in Belize City, on Ambergris Caye, and in most other areas you are likely to visit. In remote villages, however, water may come from shallow wells or cisterns and may not be safe to drink. In Guatemala it's best to **drink only bottled water,** called *agua purificada* in Spanish. It is available even at the smallest *tiendas* (stores) and is much cheaper than in North America.

HIV/AIDS is an increasing concern in Central America, especially in Belize, where the incidence is the highest in the region.

FOOD AND DRINK

The major health risk in Belize and Guatemala is traveler's diarrhea, caused by eating contaminated fruit or vegetables or drinking contaminated water. So **watch what you eat.** Skip uncooked foods and unpasteurized milk and milk products. In Guatemala avoid iced beverages. Ask for your drinks *sin hielo,* meaning "without ice." In Belize most resort areas have ice that is perfectly safe. Mild cases of traveler's diarrhea may respond to Pepto-Bismol or Imodium (known generically as loperamide). Both can be purchased over the counter in both countries, but you

should bring along your own stash in case you are not near a pharmacy. Drink plenty of purified water or tea—chamomile is a good folk remedy. In severe cases rehydrate yourself with a salt-sugar solution: ½ teaspoon salt (*sal*) and 4 tablespoons sugar (*azúcar*) per quart of water.

MEDICAL PLANS

No one plans to get sick while traveling, but it happens, so **consider signing up with a medical-assistance company.** Members get doctor referrals, emergency evacuation or repatriation, hot lines for medical consultation, cash for emergencies, and other assistance.

➤ MEDICAL-ASSISTANCE COMPANIES: **International SOS Assistance** (WEB www.internationalsos.com; ⊠ 8 Neshaminy Interplex, Suite 207, Trevose, PA 19053, ☎ 215/245–4707 or 800/523–6586, FAX 215/244–9617; ⊠ 12 Chemin Riantbosson, 1217 Meyrin 1, Geneva, Switzerland, ☎ 4122/785–6464, FAX 4122/785–6424; ⊠ 331 N. Bridge Rd., 17-00, Odeon Towers, Singapore 188720, ☎ 65/338–7800, FAX 65/338–7611).

OVER-THE-COUNTER REMEDIES

Most medicines requiring a doctor's prescription in your home country also require one in Belize, although drugstores often sell prescription antibiotics and painkillers without asking to see a prescription. In Belize private physicians often own an associated pharmacy, so they sell you the medicine they prescribe. In Guatemala, *farmacias* (drugstores) sell a wide range of medications over the counter, including some drugs that would require a prescription in the United States. Ask for what you want with the generic name. Some pharmacies are open 24 hours and deliver directly to hotels. Most hotel proprietors will direct you to such services.

PESTS AND OTHER HAZARDS

Along the Caribbean coasts of Belize and Guatemala, sand flies (also known as sand fleas or no-see-ums) are common on many beaches and in swampy areas. They can infect their victims with leishmaniasis, a disease that in its cutaneous form may cause the skin to develop sores that can sometimes leave scars. In very rare cases the visceral form of leishmaniasis can be fatal if untreated. Always **use a strong insect repellent** containing a high concentration of DEET. Some say that slathering on Avon's Skin So Soft or a citronella product called Naturapel can also deter sand flies.

The botfly, or beef worm, is one of the most unpleasant of Central American pests. Botfly eggs, deposited under your skin by a mosquito, can grow into larvae. To rid yourself of your unwanted pals, see your doctor. Virtually all honeybees in Belize and Guatemala have mixed with African bees. The sting of these creatures is no worse than that of regular bees, but they are much more aggressive. If attacked by these bees, try to get inside a building or vehicle or under water.

If you're a light sleeper, you might want to **pack ear plugs.** Monkeys howling throughout the night and birds chirping at the crack of dawn are only charming on the first night of your nature excursion.

SHOTS AND MEDICATIONS

According to the U.S. Centers for Disease Control and Prevention, there is a limited risk of malaria, hepatitis A and B, dengue fever, typhoid fever, and rabies in Central America. In most urban or easily accessible areas you need not worry. However, if you plan to spend a lot of time in the jungles, rain forests, or other remote regions, or if you want to stay for more than six weeks, **check with the CDC's International Travelers Hotline.**

In areas where malaria and dengue are prevalent, **sleep under mosquito nets.** Pack your own—it's the only way to be sure there are no tears. Always **wear clothing that covers your arms and legs,** apply strong repellent, and spray for flying insects in living and sleeping areas. You might **consider taking antimalarial pills**; Chloroquine is sold as Aralen™ in Central America, and mefloquine is marketed as Lariam. There is no vaccine for dengue.

Rabies is always a concern when you get bitten by a stray dog or a wild animal; scrub the wound under clean running water with soap or iodine—

or, failing those, some local rum—and get antirabies shots immediately.

Children traveling to Central America should have current inoculations against measles, mumps, rubella, hepatitis, and polio.

➤ HEALTH WARNINGS: U.S. Centers for Disease Control and Prevention (✉ 1600 Clifton Rd. NE, M/S E-03, Atlanta, GA 30333, ☎ 888/232–3228 general information, 877/394–8747 travelers' health line, FAX 888/232–3299, WEB www.cdc.gov).

INSURANCE

The most useful travel-insurance plan is a comprehensive policy that includes coverage for trip cancellation and interruption, default, trip delay, and medical expenses (with a waiver for pre-existing conditions).

Without insurance you will lose all or most of your money if you cancel your trip, regardless of the reason. Default insurance covers you if your tour operator, airline, or cruise line goes out of business. Trip-delay covers expenses that arise because of bad weather or mechanical delays. Study the fine print when comparing policies.

If you're traveling internationally, a key component of travel insurance is coverage for medical bills incurred if you get sick on the road. Such expenses are not generally covered by Medicare or private policies. U.K. residents can buy a travel-insurance policy valid for most vacations taken during the year in which it's purchased (but check pre-existing-condition coverage). British and Australian citizens need extra medical coverage when traveling overseas. Always **buy travel policies directly from the insurance company**; if you buy them from a cruise line, airline, or tour operator that goes out of business you probably will not be covered for the agency or operator's default, a major risk. Before making any purchase, **review your existing health and home-owner's policies** to find what they cover away from home.

➤ TRAVEL INSURERS: In the U.S.: **Access America** (✉ 6600 W. Broad St., Richmond, VA 23230, ☎ 800/284–8300, FAX 804/673–1491 or 800/346–9265,

WEB www.etravelprotection.com).
Travel Guard International (⊠ 1145Clark St., Stevens Point, WI 54481, ☎ 800/826–1300; 715/345–0505 international callers, FAX 800/955–8785, WEB www.travelguard.com).

➤ INSURANCE INFORMATION: In the U.K.: **Association of British Insurers** (⊠ 51 Gresham St., London EC2V 7HQ, ☎ 020/7600–3333, FAX 020/7696–8999, WEB www.abi.org.uk). In Canada: **RBC Travel Insurance** (⊠ 6880 Financial Dr., Mississauga, Ontario L5N 7Y5, ☎ 905/791–8700 or 800/668–4342, FAX 905/813–4704, WEB www.rbcinsurance.com). In Australia: **Insurance Council of Australia** (⊠ Level 3, 56 Pitt St., Sydney, NSW 2000, ☎ 02/9253–5100, FAX 02/9253–5111, WEB www.ica.com.au). In New Zealand: **Insurance Council of New Zealand** (⊠ Level 7, 111–115 Customhouse Quay, Box 474, Wellington, ☎ 04/472–5230, FAX 04/473–3011, WEB www.icnz.org.nz).

LANGUAGE

English is Belize's official language. Spanish also is widely spoken, especially in northern and western Belize. Several Maya dialects and the Garífuna language are also spoken. Creole, which uses versions of English words and a West African–influenced grammar and syntax, is spoken by many Belizeans, especially around Belize City.

In Guatemala Spanish is spoken by the majority of the population. Wherever tourist traffic is heavy, you'll also find English speakers. You'll have considerably less luck in places off the beaten path. In addition, many Guatemalans will answer "yes" even if they don't understand your question, so as not to appear unkind or unhelpful. To minimize such confusion, try posing questions as "Where is so-and-so?" rather than "Is so-and-so this way?"

LANGUAGES FOR TRAVELERS

It's a great idea to learn a few phrases of Spanish if you are traveling to Guatemala or other countries in Latin America. A phrase book and language-tape set can help get you started.

➤ PHRASE BOOKS AND LANGUAGE-TAPE SETS: *Fodor's Spanish for Travelers* (☎ 800/733–3000 in the United States; 800/668–4247 in Canada; US$7 for phrasebook, US$16.95 for audio set).

LODGING

In Belize you'll likely stay in one of four types of lodging: a traditional hotel, a jungle lodge, a beach hotel, or a lodge on a remote caye. Traditional hotels, usually found in Belize City and in larger towns, run the gamut from basic budget places to international-style hotels such as the Radisson Fort George in Belize City. Jungle lodges are concentrated in the Cayo and Orange Walk districts, but they can be found most anywhere. Jungle lodges need not be spartan; most have electricity (though the generator may shut down at night), a number have pools, and a few even have air-conditioning. The typical jungle lodge has a thatch roof and may remind you of a traditional Maya house. Beach hotels also come in various levels of luxury, from basic seaside cabins on Caye Caulker to deluxe resorts such as the Inn at Robert's Grove, on the Placencia Peninsula, or Hamanasi, near Hopkins. On Ambergris Caye many resorts are "condotels"—small condominium complexes whose individually owned units are managed like a hotel. Lodging choices on remote cayes appeal to the diving and fishing crowd. Amenities vary greatly, from cabins with outdoor baths to simple cottages with chemical toilets to comfortable villas with air-conditioning. Regardless of the kind of lodging, you'll almost invariably stay at a small place of 2–25 rooms where the owners manage the property. Thus, Belize accommodations usually reflect the personalities of their owners, for better or worse.

Although hotels in Belize have published rates, in the off-season you may be able to negotiate a better rate, especially if you are staying more than one or two nights. Walk-in rates are usually lower than prebooked rates, and rooms booked direct on the Internet may be lower than those booked through agents. After the global economic slowdown that hit in 2001, hotel occupancy fell significantly in Belize, and many hotels began offering discounts and specials to lure more travelers.

Unlike 10 years ago, Guatemala now has lodging options that go well beyond the needs of the backpacker, in the forms of reliable international hotels, classy colonial charmers, and rustic retreats with local flair. International chain hotels like Radisson, Marriott, and Camino Real have rooms and facilities equal to those at home. The only thing lacking in this type of lodging is a sense of place, of something uniquely Guatemalan. Fortunately, you don't have to sacrifice hot water or room service for a touch of culture—Antigua has colonial class and modern amenities at the Hotel Santo Domingo, Posada del Ángel, Mesón Panza Verde, and others. Add to the list Casa Palopó, near Panajachel; the Mayan Inn, in Chichicastenango, and the Mansión San Carlos, in Guatemala City. For something a little cheaper and out of the way, the Posada Santiago and the Casa del Mundo, both overlooking Lago Atitlán, offer comfort and culture in utter isolation. Hammocks with remarkable views beat television sets every time.

The lodgings we list are the cream of the crop in each price category. We always list the facilities that are available—but we don't specify whether they cost extra: when pricing accommodations, always ask what's included and what costs extra.

Assume that hotels operate on the **European Plan** (EP, with no meals) unless we specify that they use either the **Continental Plan** (CP, with a Continental breakfast), **Breakfast Plan** (BP, with a full breakfast) or the **Modified American Plan** (MAP, with breakfast and dinner) or are **all-inclusive** (including all meals and most activities).

➤ TOLL-FREE NUMBERS: **Best Western** (☎ 800/528–1234, WEB www.bestwestern.com). **Choice** (☎ 800/221–2222, WEB www.choicehotels.com). **Holiday Inn** (☎ 800/465–4329, WEB www.basshotels.com).

APARTMENT AND VILLA RENTALS

If you want a home base that's roomy enough for a family and comes with cooking facilities, **consider a furnished rental.** These can save you money, especially if you're traveling with a group. Home-exchange directories sometimes list rentals as well as exchanges. In Belize, you can most easily find vacation rentals on Ambergris Caye. The Ambergris Caye Web site (www.ambergriscaye.com) has a good selection of rental houses and condos.

➤ INTERNATIONAL AGENTS: **Vacation Home Rentals Worldwide** (✉ 235 Kensington Ave., Norwood, NJ 07648, ☎ 201/767–9393 or 800/633–3284, FAX 201/767–5510, WEB www.vhrww.com). **Villas International** (✉ 4340 Redwood Hwy., Suite D309, San Rafael, CA 94903, ☎ 415/499–9490 or 800/221–2260, FAX 415/499–9491, WEB www.villasintl.com).

CAMPING

If you don't mind a few mosquito bites, you can camp in Belize. It's generally prohibited in the national parks and preserves but is allowed at Cockscomb Preserve, at Half Moon Caye National Monument, and in the Mountain Pine Ridge Reserve at Augustine Village. A number of hotels and lodges in the Cayo, including Clarissa Falls, Trek Stop, and Ian Anderson's Caves Branch Adventure Camp, permit camping. Two lodges, Chaa Creek and Mountain Equestrian Trails, have safari camps, which are permanent campsites on platforms. There are only a few RV campgrounds with hookups in Belize—two are in Corozal District, in northern Belize, the Lagoon Campground and Caribbean Village—but some hotels in rural areas allow those with RVs or trailers to park (no or limited hookups) on their property.

Camping is very popular among the backpacker crowd in Guatemala, and there are campgrounds on the outskirts of Antigua, Quetzaltenango, Santiago Atitlán, and San Pedro Atitlán. Very large cities and very small towns are less likely to have such sites. Travel agencies that arrange outdoor adventures, from climbing volcanoes to mountain biking and white-water rafting, are usually the most informed about camping options in the area, either independently or as part of a trek. In

some cases they can rent equipment
as well.

HOSTELS

No matter what your age, you can
**save on lodging costs by staying at
hostels.** In some 4,500 locations in
more than 70 countries around the
world, Hostelling International (HI),
the umbrella group for a number of
national youth-hostel associations,
offers single-sex dorm-style beds and,
at many hostels, rooms for couples
and family accommodations.

Membership in any HI national
hostel association, open to travelers
of all ages, allows you to stay in HI-
affiliated hostels at member rates;
one-year membership is about $25
for adults (C$35 for a two-year
minimum membership in Canada,
£12.50 in the U.K., A$52 in Aus-
tralia, and NZ$40 in New Zealand);
hostels run about $10–$25 per night.
Members have priority if the hostel is
full; they're also eligible for discounts
around the world, even on rail and
bus travel in some countries.

➤ ORGANIZATIONS: **Hostelling Interna-
tional—American Youth Hostels**
(✉ 733 15th St. NW, Suite 840,
Washington, DC 20005, ☎ 202/783–
6161, FAX 202/783–6171, WEB www.
hiayh.org). **Hostelling International—
Canada** (✉ 400–205 Catherine St.,
Ottawa, Ontario K2P 1C3, ☎ 613/
237–7884; 800/663–5777 in Canada,
FAX 613/237–7868, WEB www.hihostels.
ca). **Youth Hostel Association of
England and Wales** (✉ Trevelyan
House, 8 St. Stephen's Hill, St. Albans,
Hertfordshire AL1 2DY, U.K., ☎
0870/8708808, FAX 01727/844126,
WEB www.yha.org.uk). **Youth Hostel
Association Australia** (✉ 10 Mallett
St., Camperdown, NSW 2050, ☎ 02/
9565–1699, FAX 02/9565–1325,
WEB www.yha.com.au). **Youth Hostels
Association of New Zealand** (✉
Level 3, 193 Cashel St., Box 436,
Christchurch, ☎ 03/379–9970, FAX
03/365–4476, WEB www.yha.org.nz).

MAIL AND SHIPPING

When sending mail to Central America, be sure to include the town and
the district, the country name, and the
words *Central America* in the address. Belizean mail service is excellent, except to and from remote
villages. The stamps, mostly of
wildlife, are so beautiful that some
people save them as souvenirs. An
airmail letter to the United States
takes about a week. From Guatemala
letters to the United States take one to
two weeks, slightly longer to get to
Canada and the United Kingdom.

OVERNIGHT SERVICES

If you have to send something fast,
use DHL, which is expensive but does
the job right. It has offices in Belize
City and Guatemala City.

➤ MAJOR SERVICES: **DHL** (✉ 38 New
Rd., Belize City, ☎ 223/4350; ✉ 12
Calle 5–12, Zona 10, Guatemala
City, ☎ 332–3023).

POSTAL RATES

In Belize an airmail letter to the
United States is BZ60¢, a postcard
BZ30¢. If your mail is headed to
Europe, the cost is BZ75¢ for a letter,
BZ40¢ for a postcard.

A letter or postcard from Guatemala
to anywhere in the Americas costs
Q3; to Europe, Asia, and the Pacific
it's Q6.

RECEIVING MAIL

In Belize City you can receive mail
addressed to you at the main post
office, where it will be kept for at
least a month. Bring a passport or
other ID to pick it up. The post office
is open Monday–Thursday 8–5 and
Friday 8–4:30. American Express
handles mail for cardholders free of
charge. In Guatemala travelers can
receive mail addressed to "poste
restante" at the main post office in
Guatemala City. Those who have
charge cards or traveler's checks can
use the American Express office in the
capital.

MONEY MATTERS

There are two ways of looking at the
prices in Belize: the country is either
one of the cheapest in the Caribbean
or it's one of the most expensive in
Central America. A good hotel room
for two will cost you upwards of
BZ$200; a budget one, as little as
BZ$20. A meal in one of the more
upscale restaurants will cost BZ$50–
BZ$75 for one, but you can eat lobster
and salad in a seafood shack for as
little as BZ$20–BZ$30 or the classic

creole dish of stew chicken and rice and beans for BZ$8. Prices are highest in Belize City and Ambergris Caye.

Guatemala can be remarkably inexpensive, especially when you are traveling in the villages of the highlands. Prices for rooms at first-class hotels and meals at the best restaurants, however, approach those in developed countries. Trips into remote parts of the jungle and specialty travel like river rafting and deep-sea fishing are also relatively expensive.

Prices throughout this guide are given for adults. Substantially reduced fees are almost always available for children, students, and senior citizens. For information on taxes, *see* Taxes, *below.*

ATMS

Most Belizean banks have automatic teller machines, but except at Barclays Bank in Belize City and Dangriga, the machines don't accept foreign cards. Because of this, **don't expect to use ATMs to get most of your cash.** When traveling in northern Belize, you can cross into Mexico and make a withdrawal from one of the many ATM machines in Chetumal, but you will get your dough in pesos that will have to be exchanged for U.S. or Belize dollars.

In Guatemala ATMs that accept foreign cards are easy to find. Banks bearing a CREDOMATIC symbol accept most ATM cards. Before your trip, **make sure your secret code has no more than four digits.** Most ATMs in Guatemala do not accept cards with five or more digits. You can easily change yours at your local bank.

Although ATM transaction fees may be higher abroad than at home, ATM rates are excellent because they are based on wholesale rates offered only by major banks. You won't do as well at exchange booths in airports or rail and bus stations, in hotels, in restaurants, or in stores.

CREDIT CARDS

In Belize and Guatemala MasterCard and Visa are widely accepted, American Express a little less so, and Discover hardly at all. It's a good idea to **bring more than one credit card,** as

some establishments accept only one or two types. Hotels and shops in Belize sometimes levy a surcharge for credit card use, usually 5% but ranging from 2% to 10%. A few in Guatemala also add a surcharge. If you use a credit card, ask if there is a surcharge.

Throughout this guide, the following abbreviations are used: AE, American Express; D, Discover; DC, Diners Club; MC, MasterCard; and V, Visa.

CURRENCY

Belize dollars are the currency used in the Caribbean nation. There are 5-, 10-, 25-, and 50-cent coins, as well as a coin valued at BZ$1. Bills are in 1, 2, 5, 10, 20, 50, and 100 denominations. For many years the Belizean dollar (BZ$) has been pegged to the U.S. dollar at a rate of BZ$2 per US$1, although private moneychangers may give slightly different rates.

Most prices for tourists are quoted in U.S. dollars, but smaller restaurants and hotels tend to use Belize dollars. Because misunderstandings can occur, **always ask which currency is being used.**

The quetzal, named after Guatemala's national bird, is divided into 100 centavos. There are 1-, 5-, 10-, and 25-centavo coins, and a 1 quetzal coin. Bills come in denominations of ½, 1, 5, 10, 20, 50, and 100 quetzales. In April 2002 the quetzal was worth about 13¢, or 7.9 quetzales to the U.S. dollar. In this guide prices are quoted in U.S. dollar amounts.

CURRENCY EXCHANGE

Because U.S. dollars are gladly accepted everywhere, there's little need to exchange yours for Belize dollars. If you're not from the United States, it's best to convert your cash to U.S. currency before arriving in Belize. Other currencies, including Canadian dollars, are not widely accepted in Belize, and you'll have a hard time finding a place that will exchange your money. When paying in U.S. dollars, you may get change in Belize or in U.S. currency, or in both.

Moneychangers at the Mexico and Guatemala borders operate on a free-market system and pay a rate depending on the demand for U.S. dollars, sometimes as high as BZ$2.20 to US$1. Banks generally exchange at BZ$1.98 to US$1 or less. In late 2001, facing a national shortage of U.S. dollars, the Belize government cracked down on private money-changers, which, although technically illegal, had for years operated openly, and tried to require that all U.S. dollar exchanges go through official banks.

When leaving Belize, you can exchange Belizean currency back to U.S. dollars (up to BZ$200). The Belize dollar is difficult, if not impossible, to exchange outside Belize. In this guide all prices are quoted in Belize dollars. The best place to exchange Belize dollars for Mexican pesos is in Corozal, where the exchange rate is quite good. At the Guatemala border near Benque Viejo del Carmen, you can exchange Belizean or U.S. dollars for quetzales—moneychangers will approach you on the Belize side.

In Guatemala, U.S. currency is almost never turned away in shops and restaurants. You can exchange cash on the street in the area around the central post office for slightly more than the official rate, but you run the risk of being shortchanged.

➤ EXCHANGE SERVICES: **International Currency Express** (☎ 888/278–6628 orders, WEB www.foreignmoney.com). **Thomas Cook Currency Services** (☎ 800/287–7362 orders and retail locations, WEB www.us.thomascook. com).

TRAVELER'S CHECKS

Do you need traveler's checks? It depends on where you're headed. If you're going to rural areas and small towns, go with cash; traveler's checks are best used in cities. Lost or stolen checks can usually be replaced within 24 hours. To ensure a speedy refund, buy your own traveler's checks—don't let someone else pay for them: irregularities like this can cause delays. The person who bought the checks should make the call to request a refund.

OUTDOORS AND SPORTS

Nearly everything worth doing in Belize involves the outdoors. Diving

and snorkeling are why visitors come to the cayes and coast of Belize. Fishing for tarpon, bonefish, and sailfish is another good reason to visit. Birding, wildlife spotting and photography, and hiking are world-class attractions of Belize's mainland rain forests and lagoons. Canoeing and sea kayaking are growing by leaps and bounds in Belize. There is no surfing in Belize—the offshore barrier reef limits the waves—but windsurfing is excellent off many cayes, thanks to the prevailing 15–20 mph winds.

With miles of limestone caves, Belize has some of the best caving in the region. Bicycle racing has many fans, as does mountain biking. Until recently you couldn't play golf in Belize, but in late 1999 a championship 18-hole course opened in a spectacular setting on Caye Chapel. There also is a small 9-hole course on the Old Northern Highway near Altun Ha. In 2002 a 9-hole dunes course on synthetic turf was set to open at Jaguar Reef Lodge, near Hopkins. Tennis is not big in Belize, but you can play on hotel courts on Ambergris Caye, on Caye Chapel, and in Placencia. The British colonial legacy didn't succeed in leaving many cricket fans, but the game is played here and there in Belize.

Hiking is surely Guatemala's greatest outdoor attraction. For climbing up the steaming black shoulder of an active volcano or exploring Maya ruins and dense rain forests, a pair of sturdy shoes and a sense of adventure are essential in Guatemala. More specialized ecotourism is expanding, with a few operators offering bird-watching, white-water rafting, caving, and mountain-biking trips. The Pacific coast has what many consider to be the best billfishing in the world, and world records have been set here.

PACKING

Baggage carts are scarce at Central American airports, and international luggage limits are increasingly tight. Whatever you do, **pack light**—casual, comfortable, hand-washable clothing. T-shirts and shorts are acceptable near the beach, while more conservative attire is appropriate in smaller towns.

Long-sleeve shirts and long pants will protect your skin from the relentless sun and ferocious mosquitoes. Always **bring along a hat** to block the sun from your face and neck. If you're heading into the Cayo, the mountains, or the highlands, especially during the winter months, bring a light sweater or jacket, as nights and early mornings can be chilly. Sturdy sneakers or hiking shoes or boots with rubber soles are essential. A pair of sandals (preferably ones that can be worn in the water) are indispensable, too.

Be sure to bring along insect repellent, sunscreen, sunglasses. An umbrella is handy in the rainy season. Other items you'll be glad you brought along include a box of tissues, a plastic water bottle, and a flashlight (for occasional power outages, streets without proper lighting, or caves). A mosquito net is a good idea if you're staying at places with no screens in the windows (or no windows at all). Snorkelers should consider bringing their own equipment if there's room in the suitcase. Last, but not least, **bring your favorite brand of condoms and tampons.** You won't find either easily or in familiar brands.

In your carry-on luggage, **pack an extra pair of eyeglasses or contact lenses and enough of any medication** you take to last the entire trip. You may also ask your doctor to write a spare prescription using the drug's generic name, since brand names may vary from country to country. In luggage to be checked, **never pack prescription drugs or valuables.** And don't forget to carry with you the addresses of offices that handle refunds of lost traveler's checks. Check *Fodor's How to Pack* (available in bookstores everywhere) for more tips.

To avoid customs and security delays, carry medications in their original packaging. Don't pack any sharp objects in your carry-on luggage, including knives of any size or material, scissors, manicure tools, and corkscrews, or anything else that might arouse suspicion.

CHECKING LUGGAGE

You are allowed one carry-on bag and one personal article, such as a purse or a laptop computer. Make sure that everything you carry aboard will fit under your seat or in the overhead bin. Get to the gate early, so you can board as soon as possible, before the overhead bins fill up.

If you are flying internationally, note that baggage allowances may be determined not by piece but by weight—generally 88 pounds (40 kilograms) in first class, 66 pounds (30 kilograms) in business class, and 44 pounds (20 kilograms) in economy.

Airline liability for baggage is limited to $2,500 per person on flights within the United States. On international flights it amounts to $9.07 per pound or $20 per kilogram for checked baggage (roughly $640 per 70-pound bag) and $400 per passenger for unchecked baggage. You can buy additional coverage at check-in for about $10 per $1,000 of coverage, but it excludes a rather extensive list of items, shown on your airline ticket.

Before departure, **itemize your bags' contents** and their worth, and label the bags with your name, address, and phone number. (If you use your home address, cover it so potential thieves can't see it readily.) Inside each bag, **pack a copy of your itinerary.** At check-in, **make sure that each bag is correctly tagged** with the destination airport's three-letter code. If your bags arrive damaged or fail to arrive at all, file a written report with the airline before leaving the airport.

PASSPORTS AND VISAS

When traveling internationally, **carry your passport** even if you don't need one (it's always the best form of I.D.) and **make two photocopies of the data page** (one for someone at home and another for you, carried separately from your passport). If you lose your passport, promptly call the nearest embassy or consulate and the local police.

U.S. passport applications for children under age 14 require consent from both parents or legal guardians; both parents must appear together to sign the application. If only one parent appears, he or she must submit a written statement from the other parent authorizing passport issuance for the child. A parent with sole authority must present evidence of it when applying; acceptable documentation includes the child's certified birth certificate listing only the applying parent, a court order specifically permitting this parent's travel with the child, or a death certificate for the non-applying parent. Application forms and instructions are available on the Web site of the U.S. State Department's Bureau of Consular Affairs (www.travel.state.gov).

ENTERING BELIZE AND GUATEMALA

To enter Belize, only a valid passport is necessary for citizens of Australia, Canada, Great Britain, New Zealand, and the United States—no visa is required. If, upon arrival, the customs official asks how long you expect to stay, give the longest period you might stay—you may legally stay in each country for up to 30 days—otherwise the official may endorse your passport with a shorter period. In Belize you can renew your entry permits for up to six months for a fee of BZ$25 per month. If you're young and entering Belize by land from Mexico or Guatemala, you may be asked to prove you have enough money to cover your stay. You are supposed to have US$50 a day, although this requirement is rarely enforced. If you enter Guatemala by land, you may need a multiple-entry visa, available at the Guatemalan consulate in your home country.

PASSPORT OFFICES

The best time to apply for a passport or to renew is in fall and winter. Before any trip, check your passport's expiration date, and, if necessary, renew it as soon as possible.

Consider renewing by mail or check out express renewal services near you or on the Internet that might reduce the time and hassle. Officially, Belize and some airlines flying there require that your passport be valid for six months past your arrival date, though this rule may not be enforced.

➤ AUSTRALIAN CITIZENS: **Australian State Passport Office** (☎ 131–232, WEB www.dfat.gov.au/passports).

➤ CANADIAN CITIZENS: **Passport Office** (☎ 819/994–3500; 800/567–6868 in Canada, WEB www.dfait-maeci.gc.ca/passport).

➤ NEW ZEALAND CITIZENS: **New Zealand Passport Office** (☎ 04/494–0700 or 04/474–8100 application procedures, WEB www.passports.govt.nz).

➤ U.K. CITIZENS: **London Passport Office** (☎ 0870/521–0410, WEB www.ukpa.gov.uk) for application procedures and emergency passports.

➤ U.S. CITIZENS: **National Passport Information Center** (☎ 900/225–5674; calls are 35¢ per minute for automatedservice, $1.05 per minute for operator service; WEB www.travel.state.gov).

REST ROOMS

You won't find many public rest rooms in Belize, but hotels and restaurants usually have clean, modern rest rooms with American-style—indeed American-made—toilets. Hot-water showers in Belize often are the on-demand type, powered by butane gas.

Rest rooms in Guatemala use Western-style toilets, although bathroom tissue generally should not be flushed but discarded in a basket beside the toilet.

SAFETY

While traveling in Central America, use common sense. Wherever you go, **don't wear expensive clothing, don't wear flashy jewelry or watches,** and **don't handle money in public.** It's a good idea to **keep your money in a pocket rather than a wallet,** which is easier to steal. On buses and in crowded areas, hold purses or handbags close to the body; thieves use knives to slice the bottom of a bag and catch the contents as they fall out. **Keep cameras in a secure camera bag,** preferably one with a chain or wire embedded in the strap. Always **remain alert for pickpockets,,** especially in the larger cities.

There is considerable crime in Belize City, but it rarely involves visitors. When it does, Belize has a particularly rapid justice system for such crimes, meaning that the offender often gets a trial within hours and, if convicted, can be sent to prison ("the Hattieville Ramada") the same day. Tourist police patrol Fort George and other areas where visitors convene. Police are particularly in evidence when cruise ships are in port. If you **avoid walking alone at night** (except in well-lighted parts of the Fort George area), you should have no problems. If you're returning to your hotel after dark, use a taxi. If you have to ring the bell to enter the hotel, ask the driver to wait until you are safely inside. Outside Belize City, and possibly the rougher parts of Dangriga and Orange Walk Town, you'll find Belize to be safe and friendly.

Pickpockets are probably the most common threat in Guatemala. They typically work in pairs or in threes; one will distract or disrupt you in some way, while another slips a hand into your pocket or backpack during the commotion. This typically happens in a crowded market or street corner, especially if your hands are full with your luggage or purchases. They are so skilled, you often won't realize you've been robbed until later. If you know you'll be passing through a crowded area (entering or leaving the bus terminal, for example), **carry only the money you'll need** and stow the rest in your money belt. If you have a home base, just bring along a day pack—you'll be significantly less vulnerable without a lot of stuff.

In 2001 there were sporadic incidents in Belize near border areas with Guatemala. In two or three cases masked men believed to be from Guatemala held up tourist vehicles near San Ignacio in western Belize. Several Guatemala–Belize border incidents also have taken place in recent years, including in late 2001 the killing of three machete-wielding Guatemalan farmers by Belize Defence Forces soldiers near San Ignacio. In 2000 a water taxi returning from Puerto Barrios, Guatemala, to Punta Gorda, Belize, was hijacked by Guatemalan nationals who shot and killed six people. Given the hundreds of thousands of visitors to Belize, however, these incidents are isolated, and the vast majority of travelers never experience any crime in Belize.

LOCAL SCAMS

Most Central Americans are extremely honest and trustworthy. It's not uncommon for a vendor to chase you down if you accidentally leave without your change. That said, most organized scams arise with tours and packages, in which you're sold a ticket that turns out to be bogus. **Arrange all travel through a legitimate agency,** and always get a receipt. If a problem does arise, the tourist boards may be able to help mediate the conflict.

WOMEN IN BELIZE AND GUATEMALA

If you carry a purse, choose one with a zipper and a thick strap that you can drape across your body; adjust the length so that the purse sits in front of you at or above hip level. Store only enough money in the purse to cover casual spending. Distribute the rest of your cash and any valuables (including credit cards and your passport) between a deep front pocket, an inside jacket or vest pocket, and a hidden money pouch. Do not reach for that money pouch in public.

Many women travel alone or in small groups in Belize without any problems. Machismo is not as much an issue in the former British Honduras as it is in neighboring countries. Unfortunately, Guatemala has been the site of some disturbing assaults on women. These have occurred on buses, usually late at night in remote areas. Always **avoid traveling alone at night.** There's very little crime outside the major cities, but it does happen. In 2001 two Dutch women were raped while hiking along the shore of Lago Atitlán. Hiring a guide through the local tourist office or through a respectable tour agency can help to avoid situations such as this.

The most common complaint by women is catcalling, which is typically more of an annoyance than a threat. Most women, locals and foreigners alike, try to brush it off.

SENIOR-CITIZEN TRAVEL

Discounts for seniors in Belize and Guatemala are pretty rare, unless you travel with a North American tour company or educational program that offers them.

To qualify for age-related discounts, **mention your senior-citizen status up front** when booking hotel reservations (not when checking out) and before you're seated in restaurants (not when paying the bill). Be sure to have identification on hand. When renting a car, ask about promotional car-rental discounts, which can be cheaper than senior-citizen rates.

➤ EDUCATIONAL PROGRAMS: **Elderhostel** (✉ 11 Ave. de Lafayette, Boston, MA 02111-1746, ☎ 877/426–8056, FAX 877/426–2166, WEB www.elderhostel. org). **Interhostel** (✉ University of New Hampshire, 6 Garrison Ave., Durham, NH 03824, ☎ 603/862–1147 or 800/733–9753, FAX 603/862–1113, WEB www.learn.unh.edu).

SHOPPING

Belize does not have the rich artistic tradition of neighboring Guatemala, Honduras, and Mexico. Gift shops offer the usual collection of off-color T-shirts and bad-taste gewgaws. There are handicrafts, furniture, music (punta rock), foods and drinks, and other items that make good souvenirs from Belize. Rum, Belikin beer, Marie Sharp's hot sauces and jams, coffee from Gallon Jug, colorful Belize postage stamps, and high-quality chairs and other furniture made from tropical hardwoods are all reasonably priced.

For souvenir seekers, Guatemala's handicrafts, called *artesanía* or *típica,* always draw the most attention, particularly the handwoven tapestries, carved wooden masks, hand-blown glass, and traditional clothing such as women's colorful *huipiles.* Such goods are beautiful and inexpensive, and they're sold throughout the country. Miniature wooden or ceramic frames make great little keepsakes, as do small hand-painted wooden jewelry boxes or masks. More exclusive items include jade carvings and jewelry, antiques, and particularly complex weavings, especially those made of silk instead of cotton, and are best purchased in Guatemala City, Antigua, and, to a lesser extent, Quetzaltenango.

WATCH OUT

The sale of some items contributes to the destruction of the natural environment, so **avoid items made from coral** and turtle or tortoise shells. Always **avoid purchasing items pilfered from archeological sites,** particularly stone carvings. They may be confiscated when you leave the country, and perhaps worse, your souvenir shopping aids in the destruction of irreplaceable historical and cultural relics. The export of Maya artifacts is strictly prohibited.

SIGHTSEEING GUIDES

In Belize all tourist guides are required to take a series of training courses and must be licensed by the government. If in doubt about the credibility of a guide, ask to see a license.

A guide's license in Guatemala means little. Here, nothing beats a personal recommendation. Ask other travelers first, and your hotel second. Otherwise, stick to the established agencies to avoid getting cheated. Tikal is an exception: official guides wear a "Carnet de Guía de Turismo" (Tourist Guide ID) and can be hired at the visitor center. Many hotels also arrange guided tours to the ruins and surrounding sights.

STUDENTS IN BELIZE AND GUATEMALA

Central America is a fantastic place for students and those on a budget. You can live well on Q100 a day in Guatemala. Belize is more expensive; expect to shell out BZ$70–BZ$90 a day. There are few hostels as such, but Guatemala and Belize are packed with cheap lodging possibilities. Any option near the bus station is usually affordable. One of the cheapest ways to spend the night, of course, is camping, and as long as you have your own tent or hammock, it's easy to set up camp in many areas (always ask for permission, of course). To get good tips and advice on traveling within a budget, look for informational bulletin boards and talk to other backpackers.

➤ IDs AND SERVICES: **Council Travel** (CIEE; ✉ 205 E. 42nd St., 15th floor, New York, NY 10017, ☎ 212/822–

2700 or 888/268–6245, FAX 212/822–2699, WEB www.counciltravel.com). Travel Cuts (⊠ 187 College St., Toronto, Ontario M5T 1P7, Canada, ☎ 416/979–2406; 800/667–2887 in Canada, FAX 416/979–0956, WEB www.travelcuts.com).

TAXES

The Belizean government levies a hotel tax of 7% and an airport-departure tax of BZ$10, which must be paid in either U.S. or Belize dollars when you leave the country. An on-land border fee is BZ$20 and is charged at the Guatemalan and Mexican borders, even for day trips. In this case you can **ask that your border-crossing fee be applied toward your airport-departure tax** as credit. For most consumer goods and services, including restaurant meals, tours, rental cars, and diving, there is an 8% sales tax.

Most Guatemalan hotels and some tourist restaurants charge an additional 10% tourist tax. The airport-departure tax is US$20.

VALUE-ADDED TAX

The unpopular Belize value-added tax has been repealed. Guatemalan stores, restaurants, and hotels charge a 10% VAT.

TELEPHONES

AREA AND COUNTRY CODES

The country code for Belize is 501; for Guatemala, 502. The country code is 1 for the United States, 61 for Australia, 64 for New Zealand, and 44 for the United Kingdom.

CELLULAR PHONES

You can rent a cell phone in Belize starting at BZ$10 a day. Check at the BTL office at the international airport, across the parking lot near the rental car offices. It is also possible use your own cell phone in Belize, but you will have to have it reprogrammed. This costs about BZ$100 and can be done at the BTL office at the international airport. In Guatemala you can rent a phone, not to mention a car, from Avis.

DIRECTORY AND OPERATOR ASSISTANCE

To obtain directory information for Belize from the United States, dial 412/555–1515. For Guatemalan operator assistance (in Spanish) dial 121; for information (in Spanish) dial 124.

INTERNATIONAL CALLS

When calling a Belize number from abroad, dial international long distance code of 011, the country code of 501, the area code, and the number, in that order. When calling from another city in Belize, dial 0, then the area code and the number.

For numbers in Guatemala, you don't need to dial an area code when calling from abroad or from within the country.

LONG-DISTANCE SERVICES

AT&T, MCI, and Sprint access codes make calling long distance relatively convenient, but you may find the local access number blocked in many hotel rooms. First ask the hotel operator to connect you. If the hotel operator balks, ask for an international operator, or dial the international operator yourself. One way to improve your odds of getting connected to your long-distance carrier is to travel with more than one company's calling card (a hotel may block Sprint, for example, but not MCI). If all else fails, call from a pay phone.

➤ BELIZE ACCESS CODES: **AT&T** (☎ 811 from pay phones; 555 from hotels). MCI (☎ 815 from pay phones; 557 from hotels). **Sprint** (☎ 812 from pay phones; 556 from hotels).

➤ GUATEMALA ACCESS CODES: **AT&T** (☎ 190). MCI (☎ 189). **Sprint** (☎ 195).

PHONE CARDS

In Belize you can buy phone cards from any BTL office or at many shops for amounts ranging from BZ$5 to BZ$50. Guatemala's public pay phones use prepaid calling cards, which you can purchase at small markets, pharmacies, and Telgua offices. Ask for a *tarjeta telefónica*. They come in denominations of Q20, Q30, and Q100; calls within Guatemala cost 15–50 centavos per minute.

PUBLIC PHONES

Belize has a good nationwide phone system. There are pay phones on the street in the larger towns. Nearly all pay phones in Belize now require a prepaid phone card. Local calls cost 25¢; calls to other districts cost BZ$1.

In Guatemala it's easier to make local calls from your hotel. Telgua is the national phone company, and every decent-size town has a Telgua office, most of which are open daily 7 AM–midnight. You usually have to wait to submit your number to the cashier and then wait again to be called to use a phone. Do not use the black, red, or blue wall-mounted phones with signs that read FREE COLLECT CALL. They charge a whopping $10 per minute and have a five-minute minimum.

TIME

Belize and Guatemala time is the same as U.S. central standard time. Daylight saving time is not observed.

TIPPING

Belize restaurants rarely add a service charge, so in better restaurants you should tip 10%–15% of the total bill. At inexpensive restaurants leave small change or tip 10%. Many hotels and resorts add a service charge of 10% to bills, so at these places additional tips are not necessary. In general, Belizeans tend not to expect tips. It's not customary to tip taxi drivers.

In Guatemala restaurant bills do not typically include gratuities in *la cuenta,* or the bill; 10% is customary. Bellhops and maids expect tips only in the expensive hotels. Guards who show you around ruins and locals who help you find hotels or give you little tours should also be tipped.

TOURS AND PACKAGES

Because everything is prearranged on a prepackaged tour or independent vacation, you spend less time planning—and often get it all at a good price.

BOOKING WITH AN AGENT

Travel agents are excellent resources. But it's a good idea to collect brochures from several agencies, as some agents' suggestions may be influenced by relationships with tour and package firms that reward them for volume sales. If you have a spe-

cial interest, **find an agent with expertise in that area**; the American Society of Travel Agents (ASTA; ☞ Travel Agencies, *below*) has a database of specialists worldwide.

Make sure your travel agent knows the accommodations and other services of the place being recommended. Ask about the hotel's location, room size, beds, and whether it has a pool, room service, or programs for children, if you care about these. Has your agent been there in person or sent others whom you can contact?

Do some homework on your own, too: local tourism boards can provide information about lesser-known and small-niche operators, some of which may sell only direct.

BUYER BEWARE

Each year consumers are stranded or lose their money when tour operators—even large ones with excellent reputations—go out of business. So **check out the operator.** Ask several travel agents about its reputation, and try to **book with a company that has a consumer-protection program.** (Look for information in the company's brochure.) In the United States, members of the National Tour Association and the United States Tour Operators Association are required to set aside funds to cover your payments and travel arrangements in the event that the company defaults. It's also a good idea to choose a company that participates in the American Society of Travel Agents' Tour Operator Program (TOP); ASTA will act as mediator in any disputes between you and your tour operator.

Remember that the more your package or tour includes the better you can predict the ultimate cost of your vacation. Make sure you know exactly what is covered, and **beware of hidden costs.** Are taxes, tips, and transfers included? Entertainment and excursions? These can add up.

➤ TOUR-OPERATOR RECOMMENDATIONS: **American Society of Travel Agents** (☞ Travel Agencies, *below*). **National Tour Association** (NTA; ⊠ 546 E. Main St., Lexington, KY 40508, ☎ 859/226–4444 or 800/ 682–8886, WEB www.ntaonline.com).

United States Tour Operators Association (USTOA; ⊠ 275 Madison Ave., Suite 2014, New York, NY 10016, ☎ 212/599–6599 or 800/468–7862, FAX 212/599–6744, WEB www.ustoa.com).

PACKAGES

Like group tours, independent vacation packages are available from major tour operators and airlines. The companies listed below offer vacation packages in a broad price range.

➤ AIR/HOTEL: **Tropical Travel** (☎ 800/365–6232).

➤ FROM THE U.K.: **Journey Latin America** (☎ 0208/747–8315, FAX 0208/742–1312). **South American Experience** (☎ 0207/976–5511, FAX 0207/976–6908).

THEME TRIPS

➤ ADVENTURE: **Adventure Center** (⊠ 1311 63rd St., #200, Emeryville, CA 94608, ☎ 510/654–1879 or 800/227–8747, FAX 510/654–4200, WEB www.adventurecenter.com). **American Wilderness Experience** (⊠ Box 1486, Boulder, CO 80306, ☎ 800/444–0099, FAX 303/444–3999, WEB www.gorptravel.com). **Himalayan Travel** (⊠ 110 Prospect St., Stamford, CT 06901, ☎ 203/359–3711 or 800/225–2380, FAX 203/359–3669, WEB www.gorp.com/himtravel/htm). **International Expeditions** (⊠ One Environs Park, Helena, AL 35080, ☎ 205/428–1714 or 800/633–4734, FAX 205/428–1714, WEB www.internationalexpeditions.com). **International Zoological Expeditions** (⊠ 210 Washington St., Sherborn, MA 01770, ☎ 503/655–1461 or 800/543–5343, FAX 503/655–4445), WEB www.ize2belize.com. **Mountain Travel-Sobek** (⊠ 6420 Fairmount Ave., El Cerrito, CA 94530, ☎ 510/527–8100 or 888/687–6235, FAX 510/525–7710, info@mtsobek.com, WEB www.mtsobek.com). **Slickrock Adventures** (⊠ Box 1400, Moab, UT 84532, ☎ 800/390–5715, FAX 435/259–6996, WEB www.slickrock.com). **Wilderness Travel** (⊠ 1102 Ninth St., Berkeley, CA 94710, ☎ 510/558–2488 or 800/368–2794, WEB www.wildernesstravel.com).

➤ ART AND ARCHAEOLOGY: **Archaeological Conservancy** (⊠ 5301 Central Ave. NE, #1218, Albuquerque, NM 87108, ☎ 505/266–1540, FAX 505/266–0311, WEB www.gorp.com/archcons). **Far Horizons Archaeological & Cultural Trips** (⊠ Box 91900, Albuquerque, NM 87199, ☎ 505/343–9400 or 800/552–4575, FAX 505/343–8076, WEB www.farhorizon.com). **Meetings and Incentives in Latin America (MILA)** (⊠ 100 S. Greenleaf Ave., Gurnee, IL 60031, ☎ 847/249–2111 or 800/367–7378, FAX 847/249–2772, WEB www.milatours.com or www.mayapath.com). **Sanborn's Viva Tours** (⊠ 2015 S. 10th St., Box 519, McAllen, TX 78505, ☎ 956/682–9872 or 800/395–8482, FAX 210/682–0016, WEB www.sanborns.com).

➤ BIRD-WATCHING: **Victor Emanuel Nature Tours** (⊠ Box 33008, Austin, TX 78764, ☎ 512/328–5221 or 800/328–8368, FAX 512/328–2919, WEB www.ventbird.com).

➤ FISHING: **Artmarina** (1390 S. Dixie Hwy, Suite 2221, Miami, FL 33146, ☎ 305/663–3553, FAX 305/666–6445, fish@artmarina.com, WEB www.artmarina.com). **Fishing International** (⊠ Box 2132, Santa Rosa, CA 95405, ☎ 707/542–4242 or 800/950–4242, FAX 707/546–3474, fishint@wco.com, WEB www.fishinginternational.com). **Rod & Reel Adventures** (⊠ 566 Thomson La., Copperopolis, CA 95228, ☎ 209/785–0444 or 800/356–6982, FAX 209/785–0447, WEB www.rodreeladventures.com).

➤ SCUBA DIVING AND SNORKELING: **Go Diving** (⊠ 5610 Rowland Rd. #100, Minnetonka, MN 55343, ☎ 612/931–9101 or 800/328–5285, FAX 612/931–0209). **Rothschild Dive Safaris** (⊠ 900 West End Ave., #1B, New York, NY 10025, ☎ 212/662–4858 or 800/359–0747, FAX 212/749–6172). **Scuba Diving & Snorkeling Worldwide** (⊠ Box 471899, San Francisco, CA 94147, ☎ 415/922–5807, FAX 415/922–5662). **Tropical Adventures** (⊠ 111 2nd Ave. N, Seattle, WA 98109, ☎ 206/441–3483 or 800/247–3483, FAX 206/441–5431).

➤ HIKING/TREKKING/WALKING: **Backroads** (⊠ 801 Cedar St., Berkeley, CA 94710, ☎ 510/527–1555 or 800/462–2848, FAX 510/527–1444). **Country Walkers** (⊠ Box 180, Waterbury, VT 05676-0180, ☎ 802/244–1387 or 800/464–9255, FAX 802/244–

5661). **Quetzalventures** (✉ 4 Calle Poniente 38, Antigua, Guatemala, ☎ 406–8709 or 406–8710, WEB www.quetzalventures.com).

➤ YACHT CHARTERS: **Ocean Voyages** (✉ 1709 Bridgeway, Sausalito, CA 94965, ☎ 415/332–4681, FAX 415/ 332–7460). **TMM (Belize) Ltd.** (✉ Coconut Dr., San Pedro, Belize, ☎ 226/3016, FAX 226/3072, WEB www. sailtmm.com/Belize/beaut2.htm).

TRAVEL AGENCIES

A good travel agent puts your needs first. Look for an agency that has been in business at least five years, emphasizes customer service, and has someone on staff who specializes in your destination. In addition, **make sure the agency belongs to a professional trade organization.** The American Society of Travel Agents (ASTA)—the largest and most influential in the field with more than 26,000 members in some 170 countries—maintains and enforces a strict code of ethics and will step in to help mediate any agent-client disputes involving ASTA members if necessary. ASTA (whose motto is "Without a travel agent, you're on your own") also maintains a Web site that includes a directory of agents. (If a travel agency is also acting as your tour operator, *see* Buyer Beware *in* Tours & Packages, *above.*)

➤ LOCAL AGENT REFERRALS: **American Society of Travel Agents** (✉ 1101 King St., Suite 200, Alexandria, VA 22314, ☎ 800/965–2782 24-hr hot line, FAX 703/739–7642, WEB www. astanet.com). **Association of British Travel Agents** (✉ 68–71 Newman St., London W1T 3AH, ☎ 020/7637–2444, FAX 020/7637–0713, WEB www. abtanet.com). **Association of Canadian Travel Agents** (✉ 130 Albert St., Suite 1705, Ottawa, Ontario K1P 5G4, ☎ 613/237–3657, FAX 613/237–7052, WEB www.acta.net). **Australian Federation of Travel Agents** (✉ Level 3, 309 Pitt St., Sydney, NSW 2000, ☎ 02/9264–3299, FAX 02/9264–1085, WEB www.afta.com.au). **Travel Agents' Association of New Zealand** (✉ Level 5, Tourism and Travel House, 79 Boulcott St., Box 1888, Wellington 10033, ☎ 04/499–0104, FAX 04/499–0827, WEB www.taanz.org.nz).

VISITOR INFORMATION

➤ TOURIST INFORMATION: **Belize Tourist Board** (✉ New Central Bank Bldg., Level 2, Gabourel La., Belize City, Belize, ☎ 223/1913; 800/624–0686 in the U.S., FAX 223/1943, WEB www.travelbelize.org). **Inguat** (✉ 7a Av. 1-17, Zona 4,Guatemala City, Guatemala, ☎ 331–1333, FAX 331–4416, WEB www.guatemala. travel.com.gt).

➤ IN THE UNITED KINGDOM: **Belize High Commission** (✉ 10 Harcourt House, 19A Cavendish Sq., London W1M 9AD, ☎ 0207/499–9725). **Guatemalan Embassy** (✉ 13 Fawcett St., London SW10 9HN, ☎ 0207/ 351–3042).

➤ IN THE UNITED STATES: **Belizean Embassy** (✉ 2535 Massachusetts Ave., NW, Washington, DC 20008, ☎ 202/332–9636, FAX 202/332–6888). **Guatemalan Embassy** (✉ 2220 R St., NW, Washington, DC 20008, ☎ 800/464–8281, FAX 561/ 241–7687).

➤ U.S. GOVERNMENT ADVISORIES: **U.S. Department of State** (✉ Overseas Citizens Services Office, Room 4811, 2201 C St. NW, Washington, DC 20520, ☎ 202/647–5225 interactive hot line, WEB www.travel.state.gov); enclose a self-addressed, stamped, business-size envelope.

WEB SITES

Belize is wired—most hotels now have Internet access, and many will permit guests to send or receive e-mail for a small fee. Internet cafés can be found in San Pedro, Caye Caulker, Belize City, San Ignacio, Placencia, Corozal Town, Punta Gorda, and other areas. Rates are usually around BZ$15 an hour. By law BTL is the only Internet service provider in Belize. Service is usually good, but rates are much higher than in the United States. Contact BTL to arrange Internet access for longer stays.

Business-friendly hotels in Guatemala have Internet access in their rooms and in computer rooms where they charge guests by the hour for access. Cybercafés are everywhere and are the best places for checking e-mail.

Do check out the World Wide Web when planning your trip. You'll find everything from weather forecasts to virtual tours of famous cities. Be sure to **visit Fodors.com** (www.fodors.com), a complete travel-planning site. You can research prices and book plane tickets, hotel rooms, rental cars, vacation packages, and more. In addition, you can post your pressing questions in the Travel Talk section. Other planning tools include a currency converter and weather reports, and there are loads of links to travel resources.

For information on Belize, visit: www.travelbelize.org or www.belizefirst.com (at this site, Lan Sluder, a contributor to this guide and the author of four books on Belize, offers to answer any reasonable question about Belize by e-mail, usually within 48 hours, a free service). For destination-specific information check out www.ambergriscaye.com; www.belizex.com for the Cayo district; www.placencia.com for Placencia; www.hopkinsbelize.comfor the Hopkins area; and www.corozal.com for northern Belize.

For general information on Guatemala, go to www.guatemala.travel.com.gt or www.travel-guatemala.org.gt. For information on Lago Atitlán destinations, also see www.atitlan.com, or for Río Dulce go to www.mayaparadise.com.

WHEN TO GO

The Central American climate has two basic seasons. The rainy season, which in Spanish-speaking areas is *invierno* (winter), lasts from around June through November; the dry season, which is called *verano* (summer), runs from December through May. However, by "dry season" Belizeans usually mean the months in late spring, before seasonal rains begin in June, when temperatures inland may reach 38°C (100°F).

If you want to escape crowds and high prices and don't mind getting a little wet, visit in the rainy season. Though some restaurants may close and hotels may offer limited facilities, reservations are easy to get, even at top establishments, and you'll have the Maya ruins and beaches to yourself. Note that Guatemala's busiest time of the year is around Holy Week, from Palm Sunday to Easter Sunday, and that hotels in Antigua, Panajachel, and Chichicastenango fill up months ahead of time. The busiest time in Belize is the Christmas/New Year's period, followed by Easter and Thanksgiving, but mid-November through April is the high season in Belize.

CLIMATE

Belize's Caribbean coasts get sweltering, humid weather with soaring temperatures, while Guatemala's mountains in the Western Highlands can have downright chilly evenings. Central America's rainy season is marked by sporadic downpours that occur without warning; rainfall is generally heavier in the afternoon than in the morning, so you may want to do the majority of your sightseeing and shopping in the morning, leaving the afternoon flexible. In Belize only in the far south can the rainy season really be called rainy; the Toledo district gets 160 inches or more of rain annually. However, northern Belize gets about the same amount of rain annually as Atlanta, Georgia, and on the cayes rain usually comes in brief squalls, after which the sun comes out. The wet season on the cays is often accompanied by lashing northerly winds known in Creole as Joe North. In a bad year Joe North can turn into Hurricane Hattie. Hurricane season in the western Caribbean is June through November, but historically storms usually hit September through early November.

Central America's tropical temperatures generally hover between 21°C and 29°C (70°F and 85°F). It's the high humidity that'll make you sweat. Remember to drink plenty of bottled water to avoid dehydration.

The following are average daily maximum and minimum temperatures for cities in Belize and Guatemala.

➤ FORECASTS: **Weather Channel Connection** (☎ 900/932–8437), 95¢ per minute from a Touch-Tone phone.

BELMOPAN, BELIZE

Jan.	81F	27C	May	87F	31C	Sept.	87F	31C
	67	19		75	24		74	23
Feb.	82F	28C	June	87F	31C	Oct.	86F	30C
	69	21		75	24		72	22
Mar.	84F	29C	July	87F	31C	Nov.	83F	28C
	71	22		75	24		68	20
Apr.	86F	30C	Aug.	88F	31C	Dec.	81F	27C
	74	23		75	24		73	23

GUATEMALA CITY, GUATEMALA

Jan.	73F	23C	May	84F	29C	Sept.	79F	26C
	52	11		60	16		60	16
Feb.	77F	25C	June	81F	27C	Oct.	76F	24C
	54	12		61	16		60	16
Mar.	81F	27C	July	78F	26C	Nov.	74F	24C
	57	14		60	16		57	14
Apr.	82F	28C	Aug.	79F	26C	Dec.	72F	22C
	58	14		60	16		55	13

FESTIVALS AND SEASONAL EVENTS

➤ MAR.: **Baron Bliss Day,** celebrated on March 19, is when locals give three cheers for Baron Henry Edward Ernest Victor Bliss, a wealthy English sportsman who offered Belize an immense estate in return for a holiday devoted to sailing and fishing.

➤ APR.: The celebrations on **Good Friday** show off Guatemala at its most festive. Processions of costumed disciples weave their way through flower-carpeted streets, leaving behind a trail of incense.

➤ MAY: In Belize, Crooked Tree celebrates the local cash crop with the annual **Cashew Festival.** Held the first weekend of the month, the festival includes sale of jams, jellies, juices, preserves, and other delicacies produced here. On May 24 the country celebrates Commonwealth Day, which commemorates the birthday of Queen Elizabeth II, with a bicycle race form Belize City to San Ignacio.

Every year on the second Sunday in May the Guatemalan city of Cobán fills up with runners and spectators for the 21-km (13-mi) **International Cobán Half Marathon,** which is run over and around the area's beautiful green hillsides. About 2,800 runners from around the world participate annually.

➤ JUNE: The **Día de San Pedro,** a three-day festival honoring St. Peter, is celebrated in San Pedro, Belize. The early morning boat parade is worth a trip here.

➤ JULY: Celebrated in Cobán, **Rabin Ajau** is a traditional festival that runs July 21–26. The week culminates with the crowning of the "daughter of the king."

➤ AUG.: The Belizean village of San Pedro Columbia observers the **Día de San Luis Rey** on August 5 with religious ceremonies and dancing. The **San Pedro Costa Maya Festival,** held in mid-August, is a four-day multicultural bash that takes over Ambergris Caye; those entertaining come from Belize and other Central American and Caribbean countries. September 21 is **National Independence Day,** which honors Belize's independence from Great Britain in 1981. The Guatemalan village of San Felipe de Jesús, just north of Antigua, celebrates the **Día de San Felipe** on August 30.

➤ SEPT.: The **Battle of St. George's Caye** celebrates the David-and-Goliath defeat of the Spanish navy by a motley crew of British settlers, buccaneers, and liberated slaves. This week of merrymaking in Belize begins September 10. Guatemalans nationwide celebrate their **Independence Day** on September 15 with traditional music, dances, and costumes. In southern Belize, the village of San Antonio holds a colorful Maya celebration that culminates in the **Feast of St. Luis** on September 25.

➤ OCT.: Todos Santos Cuchumatán is the most frequently visited village in Guatemala, especially during **Festival de Todos Santos.** The longest festival in Guatemala, it begins each year on October 21. The high point of the celebration is a horse race with the competitors riding bareback. The **Festival de San Simón** is held in the village of Zunil each year on October 28, the date that the statue of this cigar-smoking deity, also known as Maximón, takes up residence in a new household.

➤ NOV.: On **All Saints' Day,** celebrated November 1, huge kites fly from the cemetery of Santiago Sacatepéquez, near Guatemala City. **Garífuna Settlement Day** marks the arrival of Black Carib settlers, known as Garífunas, from the West Indies in 1823. Processions and traditional dancing are held throughout Belize, especially in Dangriga.

➤ DEC.: In Guatemala, Cobán's **International Orchid Festival** is held annually in early December in the main square. The charming Guatemalan village of Chichicastenango marks the **Día de Santo Tomás** on December 13. During the festivities men wear elegant silver costumes and carry staffs topped by a magnificent sun medallion.

1 DESTINATION: BELIZE AND GUATEMALA

A Study in Contrasts

Pleasures and Pastimes

What's Where

New and Noteworthy

Fodor's Choice

A STUDY IN CONTRASTS

ALTHOUGH THEY SIT SIDE BY SIDE, Belize and Guatemala could hardly be more different. Belize has always had more in common with the islands of the Caribbean Sea than with the rest of Central America. Its astounding stands of coral have made it a world-class diving destination, second only to Australia's Great Barrier Reef. Travelers who come here usually have only three things in mind: sun, sand, and surf.

Guatemala also has a short coastline on the Caribbean, as well as a much longer one on the Pacific, but most of its population lives in the towns and villages of the highlands. The lively outdoor markets, where locals sell everything from piles of freshly picked fruit to yards of colorfully dyed fabrics, show just how little these communities have changed over the centuries. Guatemala has long been a popular destination for backpackers seeking out the mysteries of the Maya temples.

There are other differences as well. Belize has relatively few inhabitants, while Guatemala is one of the most densely populated regions in Central America. Belizeans share a generally high standard of living, while their counterparts in Guatemala struggle with a wide gap between rich and poor. Most people in Guatemala speak Spanish, while their neighbors to the east speak English.

One thing both countries share, however, is a steady increase in tourism. The number of visitors to the region rose 69% between 1994 and 1999. Even in 2001, when the threat of terrorism and a sour economy made many people stay close to home, travel to Central America, including Belize and Guatemala, continued unabated.

At the top of the seven-country isthmus that connects North and South America, Guatemala is, in the words of poet Pablo Neruda, the "sweet waist" of Central America. It's true that the weather can sometimes be unbearable; the sun beats down over lowland fields of sugarcane that seem to expand, then to melt away, in the dreamlike heat. But in the highlands the invigorating mountain air provides a respite from the taxing tropical climate.

The people who live here are mostly descendents of the Maya, but they comprise at least 22 ethnicities, differentiated by sometimes subtle distinctions in language, dress, and customs. They take great pride in the hundreds of Maya ruins that dot the landscape.

A mere sliver on the Caribbean just south of Mexico's Yucatán Peninsula, Belize extends beyond the boundaries of land, incorporating cayes, atolls, and reefs into its surreal landscape. This is a place where it isn't hard to get away from it all. On a clear night make sure to look up at the sky for a view of so many stars it will leave your knees weak. Among the many ethnic groups who make their home here are an Afro-Caribbean folk called the Garífunas, who proceed at their own relaxed pace.

Central America offers unequaled opportunities for the adventurous visitor, but enjoying the continent's natural wonders doesn't necessarily mean you have to sacrifice your creature comforts. In Guatemala you can spend an afternoon hiking up the imposing Volcán Pacayá, peering into pools of boiling lava from its narrow rim, and then spend that evening pampering yourself with a mug of rich coffee in one of nearby Antigua's luxurious hotels. In Belize you can spend the morning at a sandbar where you can snorkel with manta rays, taking time to feed these gentle creatures, and still be back at your hotel in time for a gourmet lunch featuring shrimp in watermelon sauce or crab claws with garlic butter. You could even skip the "adventure" altogether and enjoy a cozy holiday just relaxing on coral sands at a resort on the shore or reclining before a crackling fireplace at an inn in the highlands.

Until rather recently, a rather tiny pool of budget-minded travelers were the only ones to choose Central America as their vacation destination. The biggest reason the region hadn't been an obvious choice among most travelers, despite its exceptional natural beauty and rich cultural heritage, is a volatile political legacy that continued to plague most of the region. In the late 1970s guerrilla groups calling for the rights of indigenous peoples took up arms against Guatemala's right-wing leaders. The government responded with the "scorched-earth" campaigns of the early 1980s, in which more than 100,000 Guatemalans were tortured and killed as the military razed hundreds of villages. Belize was spared that kind of political unrest, but it, too, was affected when Guatemalan and other refugees fleeing the violent spasms that gripped their homelands flooded into the country.

But in the 1990s a gentler wind finally blew across the region. The transformation from guerrilla warfare to political dialogue, which gave Central America a desperately needed break from the violence, has since brought about democratic elections, plans for land redistribution, and some acknowledgment of human rights abuses in those volatile countries— reconstruction *de cabo a rabo* (from head to toe).

For the most part Belize and Guatemala have reaped the benefits of the growing tourism industry, drawing in much-needed capital to bolster national coffers. The costs of tourism are less obvious, however. Among other effects, indigenous communities are undermined by increasingly tourist-oriented economies—cultivating a plot of land may no longer support a family, but selling knickknacks in the streets just might. There is no easy solution to this dilemma, and balancing the advantages of tourism against its drawbacks is, and will remain, a constant struggle for these nations. The long-term effects are as much dependent on the attitudes and behavior of visitors as they are on prudent national policies.

There are still problems, of course. The highway system is still underdeveloped, due in no small part to the mountains running through each country. Because of the topography, travel is slow on the best-paved roads. Electricity is still lacking in the most isolated corners of these countries. Political problems persist, especially in Guatemala, where there is a growing call for those responsible for the killings of the 1980s to finally be brought to justice.

What does the future hold for Belize and Guatemala? In a region characterized by the extremes of the political pendulum, the future is difficult to predict. What does seem clear is that tourism will continue to play an increasingly important part. Walk lightly, with a sense of humility, and try not to disturb the cultures and landscapes that brought you to Central America in the first place.

PLEASURES AND PASTIMES

Archaeological Treasures

The ancient Maya empire once occupied much of present-day Guatemala and extended east into Belize, north into Mexico, and south into Honduras and El Salvador. The empire crumbled in the middle of the 16th century, but it still left one of the richest cultural and archaeological legacies in the world. Only a fraction of the thousands of Maya ruins have been excavated from the jungle that over the centuries has swallowed the splendid temples and sprawling cities. Of the many sites in the northernmost reaches of El Petén, Tikal is the most majestic; a visit to the top of one of the temples is an unforgettable experience. Evidence of the Maya is everywhere in the area, from the harder-to-reach pillars in the jungle at Aguateca to the crumbling pottery found in the caves at Actun Tunichil Muknal.

Bird-Watching

Belize and Guatemala will make a birdwatcher out of anyone. Those who make it their business to memorize their field guide will have to share their binoculars with one and all when the toucans at Tikal fly from tree to tree. If you're a skilled birder in search of the hard-to-find motmot, you can make a beeline for Belize's Cayo or head off the beaten path to Guatemala's Lago Izabal. Guatemala's Biotopo del Quetzal is the place to see the bird whose plumage is as green as emeralds. Come between April and June, when your chances of seeing the bashful beauty are greatest.

Nature's Bounty

Central America has a nearly unfathomable array of flora and fauna. The rain forests are home to howler monkeys, which have a roar that will doubtless wake you up in the morning. Forge farther into the jungle and you'll encounter ocelots, pumas, or even the elusive jaguar. To preserve its natural wonders, Belize has created a well-run system of national parks, nature reserves, and wildlife sanctuaries. Guatemala has set up protected areas known as *biotopos* that, despite chronic underfunding, aim to preserve the country's natural resources as well as its archaeological heritage. Many of the protected areas in both countries are in remote locations that are difficult to reach; some are accessible only by all-terrain vehicles or only by boat. As long as you're prepared for the long journey ahead, getting there will indeed be half the fun.

Fishing

Some of the world's most exciting fishing lies off the coast of Belize. Fly-fishing is excellent on the shallow flats between the reef and the coast, giving anglers a rare opportunities to achieve the "triple crown"—tarpon, bonefish, and permit—in one day. Farther out to sea, sailfish, wahoo, and marlin abound. Several resorts and fishing camps, such as Turneffe Flats, El Pescador, and the Setee River Lodge, cater to anglers, but most hotels can help you organize excellent fishing expeditions.

Underwater Adventures

It's no secret that Belize's Barrier Reef, a coral necklace stretching the length of the country, offers some of the world's best diving. The reef is not only the longest in the western hemisphere, but also the most spectacular: graceful sea fans and great chunks of staghorn coral make a visit here an exhilarating experience. Although the diving is excellent almost anywhere along the reef, the very best is around the many coral atolls farther out to sea. Extremely popular are Turneffe Island and Lighthouse Reef, the latter the site of the famous Blue Hole. First dived by Jacques Cousteau in 1970, this breathtaking vertical chute has become something of a pilgrimage site for divers from all over the world. But you'll be amazed at what you can see without a tank. Snorkelers will see moray eels at Hol Chan Marine Reserve and nurse sharks at Shark-Ray Alley.

WHAT'S WHERE

Belize

Wedged between Guatemala and the Yucatán Peninsula, Belize is a sliver of land on the Caribbean Sea. Along its coastline coast are 175 cayes, some no larger than a tennis court. In the Maya Mountains—the central highlands that form the watershed for Belize's thousands of streams and rivers—there is dense rain forest; in the north, savannas and fields of sugarcane. Because it has the lowest population density of any Central American nation—El Salvador, though a smaller country, has 10 times the population—most of this green interior is still the province of scarlet macaws, tapirs, kinkajous, pumas, and howler monkeys. Even reduced to vapid statistics—300 species of birds, 250 varieties of orchids, dozens of butterfly species—the sheer variety of Belize's wildlife is breathtaking. The same goes for its nearly 600 Maya ruins, which range from the metropolitan splendor of Caracol to the humble burial mounds sprinkled throughout the countryside.

Guatemala

Belize may have the beaches, but Guatemala has just about everything else—misty cloud forests, tremendous mountain ranges, smoldering volcanoes, and rain forests of massive mahogany trees draped with mosses, bromeliads, and rare orchids. In the highlands around Lago Atitlán are sleepy villages that come to life each week with vibrant markets. Here you'll find Antigua, the colonial capital filled with quaint cobblestone streets, crumbling monasteries, and the country's finest restaurants and hotels. Take a white-water rafting trip to the Pacific coast, or go boating in the Atlantic Lowlands. Water sports are popular on the Atlantic coast, which spices things up with its distinctive Caribbean flavor. Everywhere are traces of the Maya, especially in El Petén, where the stately pyramids of Tikal rise from the steamy jungle.

NEW AND NOTEWORTHY

It's increasingly difficult to find low-priced lodging in Belize. Even the most remote resorts are increasing their rates as they add amenities like swimming pools. Although you can still find a clean, pleasant place to stay for a reasonable rate, you can also spend hundreds of dollars a night at luxurious resorts such as Cayo Espanto and Caye Chapel Golf Course & Marina.

All-inclusives—where you pay a flat price for lodging, meals, and activities—are an increasingly popular option in Belize. Jungle lodges like Chan Chich and dive resorts like Lighthouse Reef have long offered such plans. Then Mopan River Resort opened in Benque Viejo and upped the ante, including everything from transfers to tours to tips in the rate. Kanantik Reef & Jungle Resort, near Hopkins, is the latest to jump on the bandwagon.

Developers of time-share properties, perhaps running out of space in Cancún, are moving south to Belize. Several more "interval ownership resorts" are planned for Ambergris Caye, including one that would be the largest resort in Belize. But don't reach for your wallet just yet. Government regulation of time-shares is virtually nonexistent, leading to some sad situations. One time-share on North Ambergris Caye, sold sight unseen on the Internet, is well over a year behind schedule, with its fractional owners so far left high and dry.

In Guatemala new lodgings are opening in Antigua, in Chichicastenango, and in the increasingly charming city of Flores. Tour companies are opening more wilderness areas to travelers every year. Jungle treks, white-water rafting trips, cave explorations, volcano climbs, and deep-sea fishing can all be combined with trips to charming villages or ancient ruins.

FODOR'S CHOICE

Archaeological Sites

Belize

Actun Tunichil Muknal, Belize. Some of country's most interesting Maya sites are underground, as is this cavern on Roaring Creek near Belmopan. The "Cave of the Stone Sepulcher" holds remarkable artifacts and well-preserved skeletons of human sacrifices.

Caracol, Belize. The most spectacular Maya site in Belize, Caracol has the remains of five plazas and 32 large structures covering nearly a square mile. As many as 200,000 people are believed to have lived here.

Lamanai, Belize. Nearly 60 Maya structures are spread over this 950-acre reserve, including a massive temple that is the largest Preclassic building in the country.

Guatemala

Quiriguá, Guatemala. This important erstwhile trading center is renowned for its massive stelae, the largest in the Maya world.

Tikal, Guatemala. Guatemala's most famous ruin is the embodiment of the extraordinary accomplishments of the Maya. The vast array of awesome temples and the intricate acropolis once formed a part of a teeming metropolis.

Dining

Belize

Capricorn, Ambergris Caye. You'll have to take a water taxi to this romantic ocean-side eatery, but the excellent seafood makes it worth the trip. $$$

Smoky Mermaid, Belize City. This oasis of flowering plants is set in the garden courtyard of the Great House, an old colonial inn in Belize City. This is Belize at its most sophisticated. $$$

Rendezvous, Ambergris Caye. Even if it weren't Belize's first and only Thai–French restaurant, this Ambergris Caye favorite would still be known for its inventive sweet-and-hot dishes. $$–$$$

Elvi's Kitchen, Ambergris Caye. Massive mahogany doors lead you into this seaside favorite. The banner states that this IS DI PLACE FOR SEAFOOD, and we cannot but agree. $$

Guatemala

Jake's, Guatemala City. The best wine list in Central America is the draw at this Guatemala City restaurant. Twenty-five daily specials augment the excellent international menu featuring such creative dishes as smoked chicken tortellini. $$$

Welten, Antigua. The handmade pasta, topped with inspired sauces and organic vegetables, couldn't be more satisfying. Enjoy your meal on the plant-filled patio, where orchids cascade from above. $$$

El Bistro, Panajachel. Hummingbirds dart among flowering vines at this romantic eatery on the shores of Lago Atitlán. Enjoy homemade Italian pastas in the lovely garden. *$$*

Las Puertas, Flores. Six sets of swinging doors give Las Puertas its name. Fresh ingredients for the sandwiches and just-picked fruit for the smoothies give this popular spot its lasting appeal. *$*

Lodging

Belize

Hamanasi, Hopkins Village. Most dive resorts pay little attention to the accommodations. This one has stylish suites, a beautiful pool, and, as mascots, cats that came from Moscow. The diving isn't bad, either. *$$$–$$$$.*

Inn at Robert's Grove, Seine Bight Area. The terrific food—mostly tropical takes on Continental dishes—and the attention to every detail mean this lodging on the coast near Placencia won't be a secret for long. *$$$–$$$$*

Chan Chich Lodge, Gallon Jug. Built atop the plaza of a Maya temple, this lodge is one of the most scenic in Central America. It's so close to nature that your neighbors are howler monkeys and toucans and so safe that your cabin door doesn't have a lock. *$$$*

The Lodge at Chaa Creek, The Cayo. A mixture of the seclusion of the jungle and the conviviality of candlelighted dinners make Chaa Creek the queen of the jungle resorts. Add to this impeccable service, delicious food, and a decadent spa. *$$$*

Guatemala

Ni'tun Ecolodge, San Andrés. Hidden in the forest on the shores of Lago Petén Itzá is this cluster of thatch-roof cabins. Culinary considerations are brought to the forefront, so you won't miss out on wonderful meals. *$$$$*

Posada del Angel, Antigua. This truly angelic inn, set around a sparkling blue pool, may be the most charming lodging in Central America. The rooms are spacious and luxurious, with lovely corner fireplaces to keep out the chill. *$$$$*

Hotel La Posada, Cobán. You won't be able to resist the lovely café on the porch of this simple colonial inn off Cobán's main square. Nap in one of the hammocks swinging in the breeze or retreat to your tastefully decorated room with exposed hardwood beams and fireplace. *$$*

Posada de Santiago, Santiago Atitlán. Sandwiched between two volcanoes on the shores of a lagoon, this hotel brings you every modern convenience while preserving a traditional Indian-village environment. *$$*

Special Moments

Belize

Diving at night, Hol Chan Marine Reserve. If you're a strong swimmer, this is a special treat. Nocturnal animals, including long-legged spider crabs, casually go about their business in water that sparkles from bioluminescence.

Sunrise over the New River Lagoon, Lamanai. This secluded jungle paradise wrapping around a romantic lagoon is the perfect place to greet the dawn. Nearby Maya ruins beckon to be explored.

Guatemala

Sunrise atop a temple, Tikal. Imagine that you're Maya royalty—or an intrepid archaeologist—as the emerging rays wake the jungle into its noisy daily activity.

Looking for dolphins, Río Dulce. You will probably only get to see these magical mammals from a canoe, but the paddling will be well worth it as you float quietly between banks of jungle foliage, with egrets and iguanas perched overhead.

Soaking in the clear water pools, Semuc Champey. Here the beautiful white water of the Río Cahabón momentarily comes to a pause at a land bridge: the universe's intention, it seems, is serene soaking for the weary traveler.

2 BELIZE

Most visitors to this tiny country head out to the cayes and atolls that dot the Caribbean Sea, lying on the brilliant white beaches or discovering the colorful coral that begins just a few feet from shore. But Belize has much more to offer—hundreds of Maya ruins, ranging from ancient cities to humble individual dwellings, make this a magical place. Nowhere else can dedicated divers and archaeology addicts find as much to invigorate their spirits.

By Lan Sluder
and Simon
Worrall

Updated by
Lan Sluder

SLIVER OF LAND wedged between Guatemala and the Caribbean Sea, Belize is only 109 km (68 mi) wide at its broadest point. But don't let its diminutive size fool you. Within its borders Belize probably has the greatest variety of flora and fauna of any country of its size in the world.

In the Maya Mountains, the central highlands that form the watershed for thousands of streams and rivers, there is dense rain forest; in the north there are savannas and vast fields of sugarcane. Because Belize has the lowest population density of any country in Central America— El Salvador, the only smaller country, has 10 times as many people— and because Belizeans are by temperament and tradition town dwellers, most of the interior remains uninhabited.

Less than an hour's flight from the mainland is the Barrier Reef, a great wall of coral stretching the entire length of the coast. Dotting the reef like punctuation marks are more than 200 cayes, and farther out to sea are three coral atolls—all superb for diving and snorkeling. Some of the cayes are no more than Robinson Crusoe islets of white coral sand and mangroves, inhabited by frigate birds, pelicans, and the occasional fisherman, who will spend a few days diving for conch and lobster, sleeping under a sheet of canvas strung between two trees. Others, like Ambergris Caye, are becoming increasingly popular, and with the crowds comes an ample supply of bars, restaurants, and inns.

The name Belize is a conundrum. According to *Encyclopaedia Britannica,* it derives from *belix,* an ancient Maya word meaning "muddy water." Anyone who has seen the Belize River swollen by heavy rains will vouch for the aptness of this description. Others trace the origin of the name to the French word *balise* (beacon), though no one ventures to explain why a French word would have caught on in a region once dominated by the English. (For years Belize was known as British Honduras.) Another theory is that Belize comes from the Maya word *belikin,* but as this is the name of the national beer, this may be a drinker's tale. Some say Belize is a corruption of Wallace, the name of a Scottish buccaneer who founded a colony in 1620; still others say the pirate wasn't Wallace but Willis, that he wasn't Scottish but English, and that he founded a colony not in 1620, but in 1638. We'll never know if Wallace and Willis were one and the same, or how a *w* could become a *b* and an *a* slip to an *e*. But what's in a name, anyway? Grab a Belikin and come up with a few theories of your own.

There was indeed a pirate named Wallace, a onetime lieutenant of Sir Walter Raleigh who later served as governor of Tortuga. Perhaps it was liquor or lucre that turned Governor Wallace into pirate Wallace. Sometime between 1638 and 1662 he and 80 fellow renegades washed up near St. George's Caye, and proceeded to live for years off the booty from cloak-and-dagger raids on passing ships. The two stout men on Belize's flag are not pirates, however, but a pair of woodcutters standing beneath a logwood tree. Under them is a Latin inscription: *sub umbra floreat*—"In the shade of this tree we flourish." What's most remarkable about the men is that one is black, the other white—a celebration of Belize's historic and emblematic racial mixture.

Belize's whites are descendants of the English buccaneers and subsequent settlers of what was first known as the Honduran Bay Settlement. They worked under grueling conditions in the jungles and forests to export logwood to England, where it was prized as a valuable textile dye. As the craftsmen of Europe learned the value of mahogany, the loggers were joined by many more.

Many of today's blacks descended from slaves who were brought from Jamaica to work in the logging industry. By the early 18th century the number of people of African descent in Belize outnumbered those of British origin, and they probably enjoyed greater human rights than do many of those in Central America today. Instead of fighting each other, white and blacks eventually united to defeat a common enemy.

That enemy appeared in 1798, in the form of a fleet of 31 ships. After more than a century of trying to uproot this upstart colony from its backyard, the Spanish had finally come to exterminate it. Residents had a total of one sloop, some fishing boats, and seven rafts, but their knowledge of the sea helped them to defeat the invaders in two hours. That was the last time the Spanish attempted forcibly to dislodge the settlement, though bitter wrangles over British Honduras's right to exist continued for nearly a century.

In the 19th century Belize's early settlers were joined by mestizos (people of mixed Indian and European heritage) and Garífunas (Caribbean people). Later came Mennonites fleeing persecution in Europe. All these peoples, like Belize's most recent refugees—people from Hong Kong unwilling to live under communist rule—found in this tiny country a tolerant and amiable home. In a country where almost everyone is a foreigner, no one is.

In many ways a landlocked island, Belize has more in common with Trinidad or St. Kitts than with Guatemala or El Salvador. English, the official language here, aligns the nation with the British Caribbean ("tea" here refers to just about any meal, for example, as it does in the West Indies and cockney London). Only in a few aspects is Belize like its Central American neighbors: Spanish is widely spoken in the north and west, while Maya dialects are heard mainly in the south. Moreover, the population is 62% Roman Catholic and only 12% Anglican.

The British, who at the request of the Belizean government had maintained a small military presence since independence in 1981, finally pulled out in 1994, but relations between the two countries remain close. Belize's defense force is still trained by the Brits; and Harrier jump jets, which used to inspire gasps from arriving tourists by flying backward over the airport, are still on call in case Guatemala should try to reassert its claim to what it once called its 13th province. At the same time, initiatives like Mundo Maya—an effort by Central American states to coordinate tourism to Maya sites—are paving the way for greater regional cooperation.

If you're intent on finding a sprawling beach resort or a golfer's paradise, look elsewhere. If, on the other hand, you want to take a night dive through a tunnel of living coral, explore a jungle resounding with the call of howler monkeys, or clamber on ancient Maya ruins, the "adventure coast"—as Belize is rightly called—will not disappoint. Experiencing the rich diversity of colorful birds and animals that make their homes here, and perhaps showing them to your children, is another of this friendly, easygoing country's richest gifts. Clever Belize will probably remain a nature lover's haven for decades to come.

Pleasures and Pastimes

Beaches

Much of the mainland coast is fringed with mangrove swamps and therefore has few beaches. The few that do exist are not spectacular. This changes dramatically on the islands off the coast, particularly Ambergris Caye. The beaches are not expansive—generally a small strip of sand at the water's edge—but their white coral sand, palm trees, and mint-

green water assure you that you're in the Caribbean. The best beach
on the mainland is in Placencia, in the south. The Hopkins/Sittee Point
area also has a good beach.

Caving

Belize is riddled with hundreds of caves, many of them unexplored in
modern times. The most easily visited are those in Cayo, in Western
Belize. Near San Ignacio are the caves at Barton Creek. Near Belmopan is Footprint Cave, where you can spend hours floating through
underground rivers in an inner tube. Also in the area is Actun Tunichil
Muknal, with its wealth of Maya artifacts, and many others. The remote Chiquibul system along the Guatemala border contains Cebeda,
thought to be the country's largest cave. You don't need a guide to visit
open caverns such as Rio Frio, but others require an experienced guide.

Dining

Belizean cuisine is not one of the world's greatest, but it might be the
best Central America has to offer. Tasty treats—like the johnnycake,
a sconelike cornmeal roll fried to a golden crisp and served at breakfast—rice and beans, fried chicken, and tasty creole "stew chicken"
are the staples. Added to these are such acquired tastes as iguana, known
as "bush chicken" or "bamboo chicken," and gibnut, a small rodent
christened the "royal rat" after Queen Elizabeth dined on it during a
state visit, and oddities of the British culinary heritage, like bread-and-
butter pudding and cow-foot soup. But with the world's second-largest
coral reef running the length of the coast, Belize whips up seafood as
tasty as any in the Caribbean. Belizean chefs have learned how to pre-
pare fish for a lighter northern palate (everything is *not* deep fried),
and at their best dishes like grilled red snapper in a papaya-pineapple
sauce, shrimp coated with coconut, or blackened shark steak squirted
with fresh lime can be sublime. Throughout the country meals are washed
down with delicious fresh-squeezed juices, such as lime, watermelon,
and mango. However, you may decide that the national drink of Belize is orange Fanta or Belikin beer.

The best restaurants are mostly in hotels and resorts and bear comparison with good, though not first-class, eateries in North America
or Europe. Ambergris Caye has established itself as Belize's epicenter
of fine dining with the opening of several excellent restaurants, such
as Capricorn, Rendezvous, and Mata Chica. An increasing number of
restaurants are carrying substantial wine lists, although the import taxes
are high, so you may pay more than you'd like. Be careful not to judge
a restaurant by the way it looks; some of the best cooking comes from
the humblest-looking cabanas. when in doubt, follow your nose.

Belize is a casual place and demands little in the way of a dress code.
A few expensive restaurants and clubs in Belize City prefer but do not
require a jacket and tie for men; otherwise, you'll probably get served
if you're wearing shoes and a shirt. On the cayes, you won't even need
shoes at most restaurants. Reservations are advisable, as cooks buy ingredients for the evening's meal based on the number of guests expected.

CATEGORY	COST*
$$$$	over BZ$34 (over US$17)
$$$	BZ$20–BZ$34 (US$10–US$17)
$$	BZ$10–BZ$20 (US$5–US$10)
$	under BZ$10 (under US$5)

*per person for a main course at dinner

Fishing

Some of the most exciting sportfishing in the world lies off Belize's coast and cayes. Fly-fishing is excellent on the shallow flats between the mainland and the reef, giving anglers a rare opportunity to achieve the "grand slam" of tarpon, bonefish, and permit in one day. Farther out to sea, sailfish, wahoo, and marlin abound. Several specialty resorts and fishing camps, such as Turneffe Flats, El Pescador, and the Lillpat Sittee River Lodge, cater to the angler, but most hotels can help you organize excellent fishing trips. Belize's attention to ecology means that catch-and-release fishing is usually the rule.

Lodging

Chain hotels are the exception rather than the rule in Belize. Here you'll find smaller establishments shaped by the personalities of their owners, most of whom are American or British. Because of the salt and humidity, operating a hotel in the tropics is an art in itself, the closest thing to keeping house on the deck of a ship. Without constant maintenance, things start to rust, the thatch (a frequently used natural building material from either the bay palm or cohune palm) leaks, and the charms of paradise quickly fade.

Rooms tend to be more expensive in Belize than elsewhere in Central America. The priciest places are in Belize City and Ambergris Caye, but they also offer more for your money because there is more competition. Hardest to find are good accommodations at moderate prices. Lodgings tend to leap from spartan to luxurious, with the middle ground occupied by either grand hotels that have fallen on hard times or small ones that are overcharging. Budget travelers, however, have a wide selection.

CATEGORY	COST*
$$$$	over BZ$400 (over US$200)
$$$	BZ$250–$400 (US$175–US$200)
$$	BZ$100–$250 (US$50–US$175)
$	under BZ$100 (under US$50)

*All prices are for a standard double room, including 7% hotel tax.

Scuba Diving and Snorkeling

The Barrier Reef, a coral necklace of 320 km (198 mi) stretching from the Yucatán Peninsula to the tip of Guatemala, is the longest in the western hemisphere. If you include the three coral atolls farther out to sea—Lighthouse Reef, Glover's Reef, and the Turneffe Islands—Belize has more than 560 km (347 mi) of reef just waiting to be explored. That's more than Bonaire, Cozumel, and all the Caymans put together.

The cast of aquatic characters here is endless. One moment you can come upon an enormous spotted eagle ray, its needlelike tail streaming out behind; the next you may find the feisty little damselfish, a bolt of blue no bigger than your little finger. There are bloated blowfish hovering in their holes like nightclub bouncers; lean and mean barracuda patrolling the depths; and queen angelfish that shimmy through the water with the puckered lips and haughty self-assurance of a supermodel. In all, several hundred species frequent the reef, including cardinal fish, squirrel fish, butterfly fish, parrot fish, and 40 kinds of grouper.

Wildlife

Within this tiny country you'll find animals like scarlet macaws, tapirs, jaguars, kinkajous, mountain lions, and howler monkeys, making Belize one of the best places on earth to get close to the color and variety of tropical wildlife. Most hotels can book you a wildlife tour, and many jungle lodges, especially in Cayo, have their own guides to lead you into the wild.

Exploring Belize

Although it's not the capital, Belize City still serves as the country's transportation hub. From here you can reach the Maya ruins of the north; the mountainous Cayo district in the west; the villages along the coast to the south, and the cayes and atolls in the Caribbean. The majority of travelers, having heard the (somewhat exaggerated) rumors about Belize City, choose to move on quickly. You may want set up a base near San Ignacio or Belmopan to explore the western part of the country, in Placencia to explore the country's southern coast, in Corozal Town to check out the north, or even on Ambergris Caye or Caye Caulker, from which you can make day trips to the mainland.

Great Itineraries

IF YOU HAVE 2–4 DAYS

If your international flight arrives early enough, say by 4:30 PM, head directly to one of the cayes. Otherwise, spend your first night in **Belize City** and take a morning flight or ferry to **Ambergris Caye.** Spend a few days poking around San Pedro, the island's main town, and exploring the nearby Barrier Reef. If you fancy a laid-back tropical paradise with fewer tourists and less development, travel to the southern town of **Placencia,** where you can also dive and snorkel.

IF YOU HAVE 5–6 DAYS

It's said that Belize is the only country where you can scuba dive before breakfast and hike in the rain forest after lunch, but to do this you have to plan carefully. Spend your first night in **Belize City,** then head to **Ambergris Caye** for a few days of fun in the sun. If you would like to extend your underwater adventures, move on to one of the remote coral atolls such as **Turneffe Atoll** or **Lighthouse Reef Atoll.** For the jungle experience, head to the **San Ignacio,** in the Cayo district, and take excursions from one of the lodges in the area. From here you can canoe down the Macal River, hike through the rain forest, or explore the Maya ruins at **Xunantunich.**

IF YOU HAVE 7–10 DAYS

If you have more than a week, it's worth spending a bit more time around **Belize City.** For Maya ruins put **Altun Ha** or **Lamanai** on your list. If it's nature you want, visit the **Crooked Tree Wildlife Sanctuary** and **Community Baboon Sanctuary.** Fly to **Ambergris Caye** for two or three days of diving and sunbathing; then fly back to Belize City and head for the resorts around **San Ignacio** to see the rain forests that makes Belize a naturalist's paradise. Finally, head south to **Placencia** or **Hopkins** for a luscious last few days of snorkeling and relaxing under palm trees. Or if you've had enough beach time, explore Belize's least visited spots, **Punta Gorda,** in the far south, or **Corozal,** in the north.

When to Tour Belize

Belize is a year-round destination, but some seasons are better than others. The dry season, from February or March to May, can be the least attractive time for inland trips, with dusty roads and wilting vegetation, but this is a fine time to visit the coast. The rainy season is June through September, extending in some areas through October. The wet weather varies dramatically depending on where you are—in the deep south as much as 160 inches of rain falls each year, but in the rest of the country there's much less. Moreover, the rain is not continuous; sudden thunderstorms are followed by sun. On the cayes the wet season can be accompanied by lashing winds, known here as "Joe North."

Hurricane season in the western Caribbean is June through November. Hurricanes have been relatively rare in Belize—usually one every decade—but two big storms slammed the country in as many years.

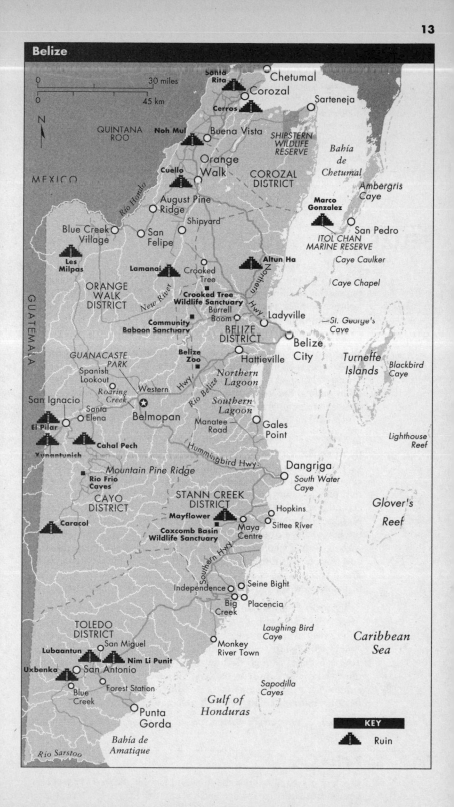

Belize

0 _____ 30 miles
0 _____ 45 km

N

Santa Rita
Chetumal
Corozal
Cerros
Sarteneja

QUINTANA ROO

Noh Mul
Buena Vista

SHIPSTERN WILDLIFE RESERVE

Bahía de Chetumal

Cuello
Orange Walk

COROZAL DISTRICT

Ambergris Caye

MEXICO

August Pine Ridge

Shipyard

Marco Gonzalez
San Pedro

ITOL CHAN MARINE RESERVE

Blue Creek Village
San Felipe

Caye Caulker

Les Milpas

Lamanai
Crooked Tree

Altun Ha

Caye Chapel

GUATEMALA

ORANGE WALK DISTRICT

New River

Crooked Tree Wildlife Sanctuary
Burrell Boom

Ladyville

St. George's Caye

Community Baboon Sanctuary

BELIZE DISTRICT

Belize City

Turneffe Islands

Blackbird Caye

GUANACASTE PARK

Belize Zoo

Hattieville

Northern Lagoon

Spanish Lookout

Roaring Creek

Western Hwy

Rio Belize

Southern Lagoon

San Ignacio
El Pilar
Santa Elena

Belmopan

Manatee Road

Gales Point

Lighthouse Reef

Xunantunich
Cahal Pech

Hummingbird Hwy

Mountain Pine Ridge

Rio Frio Caves

Dangriga
South Water Caye

Glover's Reef

CAYO DISTRICT

STANN CREEK DISTRICT

Hopkins
Sittee River

Caracol

Mayflower

Maya Centre

Coxcomb Basin Wildlife Sanctuary

Southern Hwy

Independence
Big Creek

Seine Bight
Placencia

Laughing Bird Caye

Caribbean Sea

TOLEDO DISTRICT

Lubaantun
San Miguel

Nim Li Punit

Monkey River Town

Uxbenka
San Antonio

Blue Creek
Forest Station

Sapodilla Cayes

Punta Gorda

Gulf of Honduras

KEY

Ruin

Bahía de Amatique

Rio Sarstoo

In September 2000 Hurricane Keith struck Ambergris and Caulker, killing three and doing more than BZ$400 million in damage. In October 2001 Hurricane Iris came ashore near Placencia, killing more than 20 (including 17 Americans staying in a dive boat) and leaving some 13,000 people in the southern part of the country temporarily homeless. Thanks to relief and rebuilding efforts, as well as Mother Nature's healing green thumb, today you will notice few if any effects of the storms.

Scuba enthusiasts can dive all year, but the water is at its clearest from April to June. Between November and February cold fronts from North America can push southward, producing blustery winds known as "northers" that bring rain and rough weather and tend to churn up the sea, reducing visibility. Water temperatures rarely stray from 27°C (80°F), so many people dive without a wet suit.

BELIZE CITY

From the air you realize how small Belize City is—with a population of about 60,000, it is really more of a town than a city. Few of the ramshackle buildings you'll find here are taller than the palm trees. After a couple of miles, streets simply give way to a largely uninhabited country where animals still outnumber people.

Perhaps because of its strange history, Belize was one of the most neglected colonies of the Pax Britannia. The British, who were generally generous in such matters, left little of either great beauty or interest in the capital of their former colony—no parks or gardens, no university, no museums. Indeed, one of the clichés about Belize City is that the most exciting thing that happens here is the opening of the rusty swing bridge on Haulover Creek.

In 1961 the city was almost annihilated by Hurricane Hattie, and authorities decided to move Belize's capital to Belmopan, robbing Belize City of its reason for being. Thus began a long, dark night that caused even more damage than Hurricane Hattie. So bad was Belize City's rap that press accounts of street crime made the place sound like south-central Los Angeles. It never was quite that bad, but in the mid-1990s both the government and private sector began a concerted effort to stop the hemorrhage of travelers, and thus money, away from the city. In 1995 a Tourism Police Unit was created to help cut down on crime, and officers on foot patrol are now a familiar sight. To make getting around the city easier, roads were resurfaced and traffic lights were installed. A new waterfront walkway was built along Eve Street.

At the turn of the millennium other changes were underway. More and more colonial buildings were restored, making the Fort George area an increasingly pleasant place to stay. Late 2001 saw the unveiling of a new cruise-ship terminal and a shopping area called Fort Point Tourist Village. Though shallow water in the harbor means passengers must be brought ashore in tenders, the city expects about a quarter of a million cruise-ship passengers annually. There's still a lot of work to be done, but Belize City *is* slowly re-creating itself.

Numbers in the margin correspond to points of interest on the Belize City map.

Exploring Belize City

If you're prepared to take the time and trouble, Belize City will repay your curiosity. Belizeans are natural city dwellers, and there is an infectious sociability on streets like Albert and Queen, the main shopping strips. The finest British colonial houses—graceful white buildings

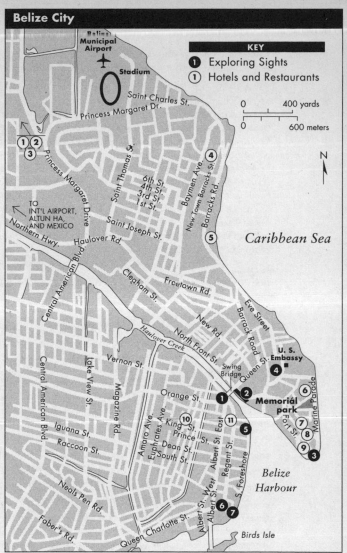

with wraparound verandas, painted shutters, and fussy Victorian woodwork—are on the North Shore, near the Radisson Fort George, the most pleasant part of the city in which to stroll.

A Good Walk

A good place to start a tour of Belize City is at the **Swing Bridge** ①, which crosses the Haulover River. If you happen to be here at 5:30 AM or 5:30 PM, you can watch it in action. Close to the Swing Bridge on North Front Street is the **Marine Terminal** ②, where you catch water taxis to the cayes. Here you'll find the Coastal Zone Museum, which has displays on the Barrier Reef, and the Marine Museum, which has displays about the country's maritime history. Walk southeast along the water on Front Street to reach the **Fort George Lighthouse** ③. You'll find a view of the bustling city harbor just over the promontory. Walk north on Marine Parade and behold the Radisson Fort George Hotel, guarded by white-helmeted attendants. Next door is the Chateau Caribbean, a beautiful colonial mansion that was once Belize's only private hospital. It adjoins Memorial Park, a tranquil respite with welcome sea breezes. Farther inland are most of the embassies, housed in well-preserved mansions; the impressive American Embassy is on Gabourel Lane just south of Queen Street. While on Gabourel Lane, stop in at the new **Museum of Belize** ④, a small space in the Central Bank Building with an eclectic collection of Belizeana.

Some beautiful buildings lie south of the Swing Bridge on Regent Street. The courthouse here is a cement reconstruction of the original wooden structure, which burned down in 1926. Along the colorfully named Southern Foreshore is a cultural center called the **Bliss Institute** ⑤. Overlooking the harbor that the baron loved so much, the center hosts a number of arts events. At the end of Regent Street you'll find **St. John's Cathedral** ⑥, built by slaves with bricks that served as ballast in the hulls of ships arriving from Europe. One block southwest lies Yarborough Cemetery, where the inscriptions on the headstones once hinted at tales of deceit, murder, and derring-do, though you'd be hardpressed to find any legible inscriptions after the passing of a century. Nearby is the **Government House** ⑦, the former residence of the governor-general of Belize.

TIMING

Belize City is fairly compact, so this walk should take only a few hours.

Sights to See

⑤ **Bliss Institute.** Overlooking the harbor from the south bank of Haulover Creek, this building houses the National Arts Council and hosts cultural events throughout the year. There are a drama series (April), Children's Festival of the Arts (May), dance festival (June and July), and a variety of musical and cultural performances during the month-long celebration of independence in September. A few Maya artifacts from Caracol are on display in the entryway. ✉ *2 Southern Foreshore, between Church and Bishop Sts.,* ☎ *227/2110.* ⊙ *Weekdays 8:30–noon and 1–5.*

❸ **Fort George Lighthouse.** Towering over the entrance to Belize Harbor, this lighthouse stands guard on the tip of Fort George Point. It was designed and funded by the country's greatest benefactor, Baron Bliss. A memorial to him is nearby. ✉ *Fort St.*

❼ **Government House.** The finest colonial structure in the city is said to have been designed by the illustrious British architect Sir Christopher Wren. Built in 1812, it was once the residence of the governor general, the queen's representative in Belize. After he and the rest of government moved to Belmopan in the wake of Hurricane Hattie, the house became a venue for social functions and a guest house for visiting VIPs. (Queen Elizabeth stayed here in 1985, Prince Philip in 1988.) It is now open to the public, and you can peruse its archival records, silver, glassware, and furniture or mingle with the tropical birds that frequent the gardens. ✉ *Regent St. at Southern Foreshore,* ☎ *227/3050.* ▣ *BZ$5.* ⊙ *Weekdays 8:30–4:30.*

❷ **Marine Terminal.** Housed in a former firehouse dating from the 1920s, this white clapboard building is where you can catch a boat to the cayes. While you wait, you can browse around the two museums on the premises. On the main level is the **Coastal Zone Museum,** which tells all about the reef and the creatures that make it their home. On the second floor is the **Marine Museum,** where you can wander among models of boats that have sailed these waters and displays of tools used by shipwrights. One ticket gets you into both museums, or you can get in free if you have booked passage on one of the ferries. ✉ *10 N. Front St., at Queen St.,* ☎ *223/1969.* ▣ *BZ$4.* ⊙ *Mon.–Sat. 8–4:30.*

④ Museum of Belize. Debuting in 2002, this small but interesting museum has displays on Belize history and culture ranging from ancient Maya artifacts to a cell from the old jail built in 1853. ⊠ *Gabourel La.,* ☎ *223/4524.* ☞ *BZ$10.* ☾ *Tues.–Fri. 10–6, Sat. 10–3*

⑥ St. John's Cathedral. At the south end of Albert Street, this lovely structure is the oldest Anglican church in Central America and the only one outside England where kings were crowned. From 1815 to 1845 four kings of the Mosquito Coast (a British protectorate along the coast of Honduras and Nicaragua) were crowned here. ⊠ *Albert St.,* ☎ *227/2137.*

① Swing Bridge. As you may have guessed, the bridge spanning Haulover Creek actually swings. Each day at 5:30 AM and 5:30 PM, four men hand-winch the bridge a quarter-revolution so a bevy of waiting boats can continue their journeys upstream (when it was the only bridge in town, this snarled traffic for blocks). The bridge, made in England, opened in 1923; it was renovated and upgraded in 1999. It's the only one of its kind left. Before the Swing Bridge arrived, cattle were "hauled over" the creek in a barge. ⊠ *Haulover Creek where Queen and Albert Sts. meet.*

Dining and Lodging

$–$$ ✕ Sea Rock. This unprepossessing restaurant has the best Indian food in Belize—period. The spicy tandoori fare is cooked in a clay oven and served in a comfortable dining room enlivened by a few trinkets from India. It's a good first stop for vegetarians, as it serves many meatless dishes. ⊠ *190 New Town Barrack Rd., near Princess Hotel,* ☎ *223/4105. AE, MC, V. Closed Sun.*

$ ✕ Dit's Saloon. Nobody does beans and rice better than Dit's, a Belize City institution. More café-cum-saloon than restaurant, it's a real local place. (Like many other older Belizean restaurants, it has a sink right in the dining room.) Cheery striped tablecloths lend the place a homey feel. The sticky and sweet baked goods are delicious, especially the three-milks cake and the coconut tarts. Stop by for breakfast—the platters of eggs, beans, and toast, washed down with ample mugs of tea, are an excellent value. The fresh-squeezed juices are delicious. ⊠ *50 King St.,* ☎ *227/3330. No credit cards.*

$ ✕ Macy's Café. You've seen the wildlife? Now you can eat it. Wrap your mouth around armadillo, brocket deer, gibnut, and, by request, stewed iguana, known locally as bamboo chicken. Macy, the Jamaican-born proprietor, says it's tough to prepare—it has to be scalded, then washed in lime juice and vinegar—but delicious to eat. Macy proudly displays a letter from the bishop of Belize congratulating the staff on its catering feats and a photo of Harrison Ford, who commandeered the table by the door during the making of *The Mosquito Coast.* ⊠ *18 Bishop St.,* ☎ *227/3419. No credit cards.*

$$$ ✕🏠 The Great House. The grand colonial facade of this house, one of
★ the largest wooden structures in Belize, is one of the most pleasing sights in the Fort George area. Owner Steve Maestre has turned his house into a fine little inn that holds one of the city's best restaurants. The large rooms have polished pine floors and beds piled with decorative pillows and colorful quilts. The wraparound verandas are pleasant places to sit and read as you catch the breeze from the sea. On the ground floor a tiny gallery of shops leads to the Smoky Mermaid, where you can dine under the stars. In a large courtyard shaded by breadfruit and sapodilla trees, the amiable servers bring Caribbean-influenced seafood dishes, inventive pasta, and savory barbecues. The best table? It's the one on the little deck on the roof of the bar. ⊠ *13 Cork St.,* ☎ *223/3400,* FAX *223/3444,* WEB *www.greathousebelize.com. 12 rooms. Restau-*

rant, fans, in-room fax, in-room safes, refrigerator, cable TV, shops, laundry service, travel services. AE, DC, MC, V.

$$$ ✕🍽 **Princess Hotel & Casino.** Big-time gambling arrived in Belize when the country's first Las Vegas–style casino opened at this sprawling hotel in 2000. The hotel, by far the largest in Belize, is still being expanded to house the new facilities. More than 60 new rooms are being built, while some of the older ones are awaiting much needed renovation. It's not quite the MGM Grand, but it's as serious. As you enter the casino, more than 400 slot, video poker, and other machines fill the central part of the room. Black jack, roulette, craps, and poker tables are toward the back. Even if you don't gamble, the hotel's all-you-can-eat buffet at lunch and dinner, of surprising quality for the price, is a bargain at just BZ$15. For the same price you can get sloshed at the all-you-can-drink happy hour from 5 to 7 on Friday. Belize's only movie theater and bowling alley are also here. ✉ *Kings Park,* ☎ 223/2670, FAX 223/2660, WEB *www.princessbelize.com. 179 rooms, 5 suites. Restaurant, room service, cable TV, pool, gym, hair salon, dive shop, marina, fishing, bowling, casino, theater, bar, laundry service, business services, meeting rooms, car rental, travel services; no-smoking rooms. AE, MC, V.*

$$$ ✕🍽 **Radisson Fort George.** Porters in pith helmets keep British colo-
★ nialism in the air at Belize City's finest hotel. Lush red and ocher fabrics, faux-leopard carpets, and reproduction rattan and hardwood antiques re-create the British raj of the 1880s. Rooms in the main building have private verandas overlooking the pool and gardens; those in the six-story tower have panoramic views of the sea through tinted glass; while those in the executive wing across the road overlook the river and one of the hotel's two pools. Service is always sprightly, and hotel staffers are relentlessly efficient and friendly. A marina can handle vessels of up to 250 ft, and one of Belize's top dive operations, Hugh Parkey's Dive Belize, is on the hotel's dock. The Bayman's Tavern is one of the city's premier watering holes, and although the hotel's dining room is not quite as well regarded, it serves up a tasty snapper fillet and grilled chops. ✉ *2 Marine Parade,* ☎ 227/7400; 800/333–3333 in the U.S., FAX 227/3820, WEB *www.radissonbelize.com. 102 rooms. Restaurant, room service, in-room data ports, some in-room safes, minibars, cable TV, 2 pools, gym, dive shop, marina, fishing, bar, shops, laundry service, business services, meeting rooms, car rental, travel services; no-smoking rooms. AE, MC, V.*

$$ 🍽 **Belize Biltmore Plaza.** Once sinking into lodging oblivion, this hotel is staging a comeback. Manager Teresa Parkey, who formerly ran Fort Street Guesthouse, has made much needed improvements to the pool and grounds and also upgraded many of the rooms. The "deluxe premier" rooms, with new carpets and mattresses, are worth the extra cost. Also turning around is the Victorian Room, which serves entrées like stew chicken and New York strip. It's a now a popular lunch spot for local businesspeople. Themed evenings, such as Thursday jazz night and Friday happy hour (5–7) draw sizable crowds. ✉ *Mile 3½, Northern Hwy.,* ☎ 223/2302, FAX 223/2301, WEB *www.belizebiltmore.com. 80 rooms. Restaurant, room service, cable TV, pool, 2 bars, shops, laundry service, business services, meeting rooms, travel services. AE, MC, V.*

$$ ✕🍽 **Chateau Caribbean.** The bright colors of the Caribbean enliven the rooms in this handsome colonial-style hotel. The suites have balconies overlooking the harbor. As this is Belize, don't expect everything to work perfectly—the louvered windows in your room may not close, defeating the air-conditioning. Fortunately, all rooms have phones, so you can call the front desk. Chateau Caribbean is best known for its second-floor restaurant. With white tablecloths, gleaming cutlery, and great ocean views, it's a charming place to eat. It's also less expensive

than most other hotel dining rooms. The menu is an unusual combination of Chinese and Caribbean dishes, so you could have grilled snapper with rice and beans while your dining companion enjoys sweet and sour pork. ⊠ *6 Marine Parade,* ☎ *223/0800,* FAX *223/0900,* WEB *www.chateaucaribbean.com. 20 rooms. Restaurant, room service, cable TV, bar, laundry service, meeting rooms. AE, MC, V.*

$$ ⊡ **Colton House.** This beautiful 1920s West Indian–style house, in a
★ prime location in Fort George, is Belize City's best small inn. Proprietors Alan and Ondina Colton take loving care of this charmer. Alan, who came here with the British armed forces, has an enormous collection of ecology books he's happy to share. He also is an enthusiastic amateur beer brewer and owner of the "Swamp Water Brewery of Belize," consisting of 5-gallon buckets in a washroom. Ondina, originally from Caye Caulker, handled the interior decoration. The wraparound veranda is furnished with hammocks and white rattan furniture; the interior has antiques and cool, polished wood floors. Reservations are essential. ⊠ *9 Cork St.,* ☎ *224/4666,* FAX *223/0451,* WEB *www.coltonhouse.com. 5 rooms, 1 suite. Some rooms with fans, library, travel services; no room phones, no TV in some rooms, no kids under 10, no smoking. No credit cards.*

$–$$ ⊡ **Embassy Hotel.** If you want a place to stay en route to somewhere else, this hotel is just steps from the international airport. It has little charm, and some of the rooms look down at heel, but it's safe, clean, and convenient. There are a restaurant and a sunny roof deck where you can relax in a hammock or challenge a friend to a game of table tennis. Staying longer? Consider one of the one-bedroom apartments. The hotel will also store your luggage or dive gear for a small fee. ⊠ *Philip S. W. Goldson International Airport,* ☎ *225/3333,* FAX *225/2267,* WEB *www.embassyhotelbelize.com. 40 rooms, 7 suites, 8 apartments. Restaurant, bar, travel services. MC, V.*

$$ ⊡ **Villa Boscardi.** If you're edgy about Belize City, this B&B in Belize's northern suburbs might be your cup of herbal tea. Franco and Francoise Boscardi (he's Italian, she's Belgian) opened their home in a quiet residential area to guests. Four rooms are bright, sunny, and stylishly decorated, with a hint of Europe here, a taste of Belize there. A new detached bungalow in the back has a refrigerator and coffeemaker. Breakfast is included, as is an evening shuttle to downtown restaurants. ⊠ *6043 Manatee Dr. (turn toward sea off Northern Hwy. at Golding Ave., then left on 2nd lane to 5th house on right),* ☎ FAX *223/1691,* WEB *www.villaboscardi.com. 4 rooms, 1 cottage. Fans, some refrigerators, cable TV, free airport shuttle, car rental. AE, MC, V.*

Outdoor Activities and Sports

Operated for years by Hugh Parkey, **Belize Dive Connection** (⊠ 2 Marine Parade, Belize City, ☎ 223/4526, FAX 27/8808) runs trips to suit your every whim from the Radisson Fort George dock. Dive trips to Hol Chan Marine Reserve near Ambergris Caye run around BZ$180 per person.

Shopping

For Belizean souvenirs try the **National Handicraft Center** (⊠ Fort St., ☎ 223/3636). Popular items include hand-carved figurines, pottery, and woven baskets. Belize's beautiful stamps are available from the **Philatelic Society** (⊠ Queen St., behind post office). Many feature lovely images of the country's wildlife. The **Book Centre** (⊠ 4 Church St., ☎ 227/7457) sells magazines and the classics.

If you want to stock up on picnic supplies, head to **Brodies** (⊠ Mile 2½, Northern Hwy., ☎ 223/5587). **Save-U** (⊠ Belikin Area Plaza, ☎ 223/1291) is a good place to browse for local bargains.

Side Trips from Belize City

Belize Zoo

☾ You turn a sharp corner on the jungle trail, and suddenly you're face to face with a black jaguar, the largest cat in the western hemisphere. The big cat growls a deep rumbling threat. You jump back, thankful that a strong but inconspicuous fence separates you and the jaguar.

The Belize Zoo is one of the smallest, but arguably one of the best, zoos in the world. It comprises just 29 acres, but it packs a lot of nature into a small space. Housing only animals native to Belize, the zoo has habitats as natural as its budget allows. As you stroll the trails on a self-guided tour, you visit several Belizean ecosystems—rain forest, lagoons, and riverine forest—and spot more than 125 species. Besides the rare black jaguar, you'll also see the country's four other wild cats: the puma, margay, ocelot, and jaguarondi. Probably the most famous resident of the zoo is named April. She's a Baird's tapir, the national animal of Belize. This relative of the horse and rhino is known to locals as the mountain cow.

The zoo exists because of the dedication and drive of one gutsy woman, Sharon Matola. An American who came to Belize as part of a film crew, Matola stayed on to care for some of the semitame animals used in the production. She opened the zoo in 1983 and in 1991 it moved to its present location. She is also an active environmentalist.

Besides touring the zoo, you also can hike or canoe through the adjacent 84-acre Tropical Education Center. The center is involved in a green-iguana breeding project. Dormitory accommodations, with outdoor toilets, are available at the center. Overnighters can take a nocturnal zoo tour. ⊠ *48 km (30 mi) west of Belize City,* ☎ *220/8004,* ⊠ *www. belizezoo.org* ⊠ *BZ$15.* ⊗ *Daily 9–4:30.*

Community Baboon Sanctuary

One of the country's most interesting wildlife conservation projects, the Community Baboon Sanctuary is actually a haven for black howler monkeys. The reserve, encompassing a 32-km (20-mi) stretch of the Belize River, was established in 1985 by a group of local farmers. The howler monkey—an agile bundle of black fur with a deafening roar—was then being zealously hunted throughout Central America and was facing extinction. Today there are nearly 1,000 black howler monkeys in the sanctuary, as well as numerous other species of birds and mammals. Thanks to ongoing conservation efforts, you can also see howler monkeys in a number of other areas, including at Lamanai in northern Belize, along the Macal and Belize rivers in western Belize, and near Monkey River in southern Belize. Exploring the Community Baboon Sanctuary is made easy by about 5 km (3 mi) of trails that start near a small museum. The visitor center has a few rooms for rent, but you need to reserve well in advance. ⊠ *50 km (31 mi) west of Belize City,* ☎ *227/7369.* ⊠ *BZ$10.* ⊗ *Dawn–dusk.*

Crooked Tree Wildlife Sanctuary

A paradise for animal lovers, this wildlife sanctuary encompasses a chain of inland waterways covering more than 3,000 acres. Traveling through by canoe, you're likely to see iguanas, crocodiles, coatis, and turtles. The sanctuary's most prestigious visitor, however, is the jabiru stork. With a wingspan up to 9 ft, it is the largest flying bird in the Americas. For birders the best time to come is in the dry season, roughly from February to early June, because lowered water levels mean birds tend to group together to find water and food, making them easy to spot. Snowy egrets, snail kites, ospreys, and black-collared hawks, as well as two types of duck—Muscovy and black-bellied whistling—and all five species of kingfisher native to Belize can be spotted.

At its center of the reserve is Crooked Tree, one of the oldest inland villages in Belize, with a population of about 800 people, mostly of Creole origin; the community has a church, a school, and one of the surest signs of a former British territory: a cricket pitch. There are a number of excellent guides in the village, including Sam Tillet. ⊠ *Turn west off Northern Hwy. at Mile 30.8, then drive 3 km (2 mi),* ☎ *223– 4987 for Belize Audubon Society.* ☜ *BZ$8.*

DINING AND LODGING

$$ ⚑ **Bird's Eye View Lodge.** Although this two-story concrete hotel covered with climbing vines and flowers looks a little out of place at the edge of the lagoon, inside you'll find someone with a smile to make you feel welcome. Choose from spic-and-span private rooms or a bed in a dorm-style room. The hotel's appealing little dining room serves no-frills but filling creole fare. ⊠ *Crooked Tree,* ☎ *225/7027, birdseye@btl.net. 10 rooms, 1 dorm-style room. Restaurant, fans, lake, canoeing, horseback riding, laundry service; no air-conditioning in some rooms, no room phones, no room TVs. AE, MC, V.*

$ ⚑ **Paradise Inn.** This is the kind of place where you'll want to stay for a week, then regret having to leave when you do. It's operated by Rudy Crawford, who started the Crooked Tree Wildlife Sanctuary with help from several of his nine children. Simply furnished, well-maintained thatch cabanas sit right on the lagoon, with sweeping views. You can have all your meals here for under BZ$30 a day. As a bonus, Rudy brews some mean cohune palm wine. ⊠ *At north end of Crooked Tree,* ☎ *025–7044. 6 cabanas. Restaurant, fans, lake, canoeing, horseback riding, laundry service; no air-conditioning, no room phones, no room TVs. MC, V.*

Belize City A to Z

To research prices, get advice from other travelers, and book travel arrangements, visit www.fodors.com.

AIR TRAVEL TO AND FROM BELIZE CITY
Philip S. W. Goldson International Airport is near Ladyville, 14 km (9 mi) north of the city. In addition to international flights, a domestic terminal has flights to Ambergris Caye and Caye Caulker and the coastal towns of Dangriga, Placencia, and Punta Gorda. Taxis to town cost BZ$35. The Belize City Municipal Airport, on the seafront about 2 km (1 mi) north of the city center, also has flights to these destinations. Fares from the municipal airport are about 10%–45% cheaper than similar flights departing from the international airport.

BUS TRAVEL TO AND FROM BELIZE CITY
Belize City is the hub of the country's fairly extensive bus network, so there's regular service to most regions and to the Guatemalan and Mexican borders. Novelo's is the dominant carrier in the country, especially on the Western and Northern Highways.
➤ BUS INFORMATION: **Novelo's** (⊠ W. Collet Canal, Belize City, ☎ 227/ 2025, novelo@btl.net).

BUS TRAVEL WITHIN BELIZE CITY
There is no bus service within Belize City. If you are headed for another part of the city, your best option is taking a taxi. Don't walk around the city at night except in the Fort George area.

CAR RENTAL

Most international rental-car agencies have locations at Philip S. W. Goldson International Airport as well as in downtown Belize City. Branches at the airport are usually are closed on Sunday. Avis has a branch at Belize City Municipal Airport as well.

Budget, with the best service in town, has a fleet of low-mileage vehicles. Some locally owned companies, such as Crystal Auto Rental, are less expensive than many of the international chains and offer service that is just as good.

➤ LOCAL AGENCIES: **Avis** (✉ Municipal Airport, Belize City, ☎ 223/ 4619; ✉ Philip S. W. Goldson International Airport, Ladyville, ☎ 225/2385). **Budget** (✉ 771 Bella Vista, Belize City, ☎ 223/2435; ✉ Philip S. W. Goldson International Airport, Ladyville, ☎ 223/2435). **Crystal Auto Rental** (✉ Mile 1½, Northern Hwy., Belize City, ☎ 223/ 1600; ✉ Philip S. W. Goldson International Airport Ladyville, ☎ 223/ 1600). **Hertz** (✉ 11A Cork St., Belize City, ☎ 223/5395; ✉ Philip S. W. Goldson International Airport, Ladyville, ☎ 223/5395). **Thrifty** (✉ Central American Blvd. and Fabers Rd., Belize City, ☎ 227/1271).

CAR TRAVEL

There are only two highways to Belize City—the Northern Highway, which leads from the Mexican border, 165 km (102 mi) away, and the Western Highway, which runs 131 km (81 mi) from Guatemala. Both are paved and in good condition. Recently installed signs point you to nearby destinations such as the Belize Zoo.

Finding your way around the city itself, however, is much more difficult. The downtown area's narrow one-way streets, usually without signs identifying where you are, often end abruptly because of construction work or an inconveniently located river. Save your nerves and explore the city by taxi or, in safer sections such as the Fort George area, on foot.

EMERGENCIES

Karl Heusner Memorial, a public hospital, and Belize Medical Associates, a private facility, both have 24-hour emergency rooms. Brodie's Pharmacy, at Market Square, is open Monday, Tuesday, Thursday, and Saturday 8:30–7, Wednesday 8:30 AM–12:30 PM, Friday 8:30 AM–9 PM and Sunday 9 AM–12:30 PM. Community Drug, with several locations in Belize City, is open daily including holidays 8–8.

Dr. Osbert Usher, a dentist, sees patients on short notice.

➤ DOCTORS AND DENTISTS: **Osbert Usher** (✉ 16 Magazine Rd., ☎ 227/ 3415).

➤ HOSPITALS: **Belize Medical Associates** (✉ 5791 St. Thomas St., ☎ 223/0303). **Karl Heusner Memorial** (✉ Princess Margaret Dr., ☎ 223/ 1548).

➤ PHARMACIES: **Brodie's Pharmacy** (✉ Regent St. at Market Sq.). **Community Drug** (✉ Farmers' Market and 18 Albert St.).

MAIL AND SHIPPING

The main post office is inside the historic Paslow Building, just north of the Swing Bridge. It is open weekdays 8–noon and 1–4:30. Mail service from Belize City to the United States and other countries is generally fast and reliable (airmail to the United States usually takes about five days). For faster service use DHL and FedEx, both of which have offices in Belize City.

➤ OVERNIGHT SERVICES: **DHL** (✉ 38 New Rd., ☎ 223/4350). **Federal Express** (✉ 32 Albert St., ☎ 227/3507).

➤ Post Offices: **Main Post Office** (✉ N. Front St. at Queen St., ☎ 223/2201)

MONEY MATTERS

U.S. dollars are accepted everywhere in Belize, but if you need to exchange another currency, you can do so at one of the five banks operating in Belize City—Alliance Bank, Atlantic Bank, Bank of Nova Scotia, Barclays, and Belize Bank. Most banks have their main offices on Albert Street in downtown Belize City, with smaller branches scattered around the city. Should you exchange U.S. dollars at a bank, expect to be charged a 1%–2% fee.

The good news is most banks in Belize City have ATMs. The bad news is many of these ATMs do not accept cards issued outside Belize. Exceptions are Barclays Bank branches in Belize City, Dangriga, and Belmopan. These machines may be out of order, so do not depend on ATMs for your cash. Most banks offer cash advances on cards issued by Visa and MasterCard for a fee ranging from BZ$5 to BZ$30.

➤ Banks: **Alliance Bank** (✉ Princess Margaret Dr., ☎ 223/5698). **Atlantic Bank** (✉ Freetown Rd., ☎ 223/4123). **Bank of Nova Scotia** (✉ Albert St., ☎ 227/7027). **Barclays Bank** (✉ 21 Albert St., ☎ 227/7211). **Belize Bank** (✉ 60 Market Sq., ☎ 227/7132).

SAFETY

Belize City earned a reputation for street crime in the early '90s, but the government has made great strides in cleaning up the problem. Still, in February 2002 hundreds of businesses in Belize City, including most of the old and largest stores in the country, closed down for a full day to protest rising crime in Belize City and countrywide. Remember to take the same precautions you would take in any city—don't wear expensive jewelry or watches, avoid handling money in public, and leave valuables in a safe. On buses and in crowded areas hold purses and backpacks close to the body. Check with the staff at your hotel before venturing into any unfamiliar areas, particularly at night.

TAXIS

Cabs cost BZ$5 for one person between any two points in the city, plus BZ$1 for each additional person. Outside the city you're charged by the distance you travel. There are no meters, so be sure to agree on a price before you leave. Pick up a taxi at Market Square or by the Swing Bridge. Cinderella Taxi and Caribbean Taxi are reputable local companies.

➤ Taxi Companies: **Cinderella Taxi** (☎ 224/5240). **Caribbean Taxi** (☎ 227/2888).

TOUR OPERATORS

Discovery Expeditions is a well-known tour operator with offices at the Philip S. W. Goldson International Airport and at several hotels in Belize City. In addition to sightseeing tours, it provides airport transfers and transportation to other parts of the country. Maya Travel's Katie Valk, a New Yorker with attitude (softened by some 15 years' residency in Belize), can organize a trip to just about anywhere in the country. She also has good connections at most hotels and can get you a room even when everything seems to be booked. S&L Travel is another long-established tour operator.

➤ Tour companies: **Discovery Expeditions** (✉ 5916 Manatee Dr., ☎ 223/0748). **Maya Travel Services** (✉ Belize City Municipal Airport, ☎ 223/1623, mayatravel@btl.net). **S&L Travel** (✉ 91 N. Front St., ☎ 227/7593).

VISITOR INFORMATION

The Belize Tourist Board, in the New Central Bank Building, is open weekdays 8–noon and 1–5.

➤ CONTACTS: **Belize Tourist Board** (✉ New Central Bank Building, Level 2, Gabourel La., Box 325, Belize City, ☎ 223/1913 or 800/624–0686, FAX 223/1943, WEB www.travelbelize.org).

THE CAYES AND ATOLLS

Imagine heading back to shore after a day's snorkeling, the white prow of your boat pointing up into the billowing clouds, the base of the sky darkening to a deep lilac, the spray from you like warm rain. To the left San Pedro's pastel buildings huddle among the palm trees like a detail from a Paul Klee canvas. To the right the surf breaks in a white seam along the reef. Over the surface of the water flying fish scamper away.

This and many other delicious experiences lie off the coast of Belize, where more than 400 cayes (pronounced "keys," as in the Florida Keys) dot the Caribbean Sea like punctuation marks in a long, liquid sentence. Most cayes lie inside the Barrier Reef, which allowed them to develop undisturbed by the tides and winds that would otherwise have swept them away. The vast majority are uninhabited except by pelicans, brown- and red-footed boobies, and some lewd-sounding creatures called wish-willies (actually a kind of iguana). The names of the islands are evocative and often humorous: there are Wee Wee Caye, Laughing Bird Caye, and—why ask why?—Bread and Butter Caye. Some names suggest the kind of company you should expect: Mosquito Caye, Sandfly Caye, and even Crawl Caye, which is supposedly infested with boa constrictors. Many, like Cockney Range or Baker's Rendezvous, simply express the whimsy or nostalgia of the early British settlers. The battle fought for control of the high seas spilled over into nomenclature. With the rout of the Spanish at the Battle of St. George's Caye, in 1798, English names took precedence: Turneffe, for Terre Nef; Lighthouse Reef, for Quattro Cayos; Glover's Reef, for Longorif.

Farther out to sea, between 48 km and 96 km (between 30 mi and 60 mi) off the coast, are the atolls, which from the air look impossibly beautiful. At their center the water is mint green: the white sandy bottom reflects the light upward and is flecked with patches of mangrove and rust-color sediment. Around the fringe of the atoll the surf breaks in a white circle before the color changes abruptly to ultramarine as the water plunges to 3,000 ft.

The origin of Belize's atolls is still something of a mystery, but evidence suggests that unlike the Pacific atolls, which formed by accretion around the rims of submerged volcanoes, these grew from the bottom up, as vast pagodas of coral accumulated over millions of years on top of limestone fault blocks. The Maya were probably the first humans to discover the atolls, using them as stopovers on their trading routes. Piles of seashells and rocks, known as "shell maidens," thought to have been placed as markers, have been found on the Turneffe Islands.

Scuba Diving

Dive destinations are often divided into two broad categories—the reef and the atolls. Most reef diving is done on the northern section, particularly off Ambergris Caye. Here the reef is just a few hundred yards from shore, making access to your dive site extremely easy: the journey by boat usually takes as little as 10 minutes. Coast and coral are farther apart as you head south, which mean a greater dependence on weather. On Ambergris Caye you might be stuck in your hotel during

The Cayes, Atolls, and Barrier Reef

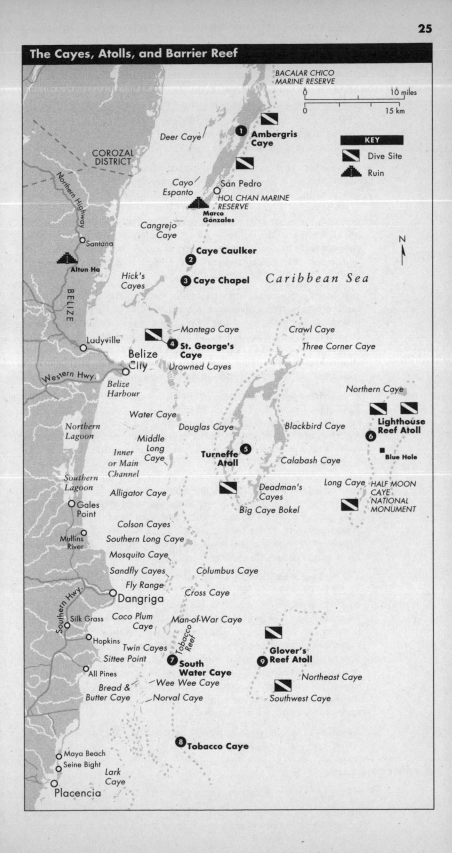

BACALAR CHICO
MARINE RESERVE

0   10 miles

0   15 km

Deer Caye

1 Ambergris Caye

COROZAL
DISTRICT

KEY

Dive Site

Ruin

Cayo
Espanto

San Pedro

HOL CHAN MARINE
RESERVE

Marco
Gonzales

Cangrejo
Caye

Santana

Caye Caulker

Caribbean Sea

Altun Ha

Hick's
Cayes

3 Caye Chapel

2

N

Montego Caye

Crawl Caye

Three Corner Caye

Ludyville

4 St. George's Caye

Belize City

Drowned Cayes

Northern Caye

Western Hwy.

Belize
Harbour

Water Caye

Douglas Caye

Blackbird Caye

Lighthouse Reef Atoll

6

*Northern
Lagoon*

Middle
Long
Caye

Inner
or Main
Channel

Turneffe Atoll

5

Calabash Caye

Blue Hole

*Southern
Lagoon*

Gales
Point

Alligator Caye

Deadman's
Cayes

Long Caye

HALF MOON
CAYE
NATIONAL
MONUMENT

Big Caye Bokel

Colson Cayes

Mullins
River

Southern Long Caye

Mosquito Caye

Sandfly Cayes

Columbus Caye

Fly Range

Cross Caye

Dangriga

Silk Grass

Coco Plum
Caye

Man-of-War Caye

Hopkins

Twin Cayes

Tobacco Reef

Glover's Reef Atoll

9

Sittee Point

7 South Water Caye

All Pines

Wee Wee Caye

Northeast Caye

Bread &
Butter Caye

Norval Caye

Southwest Caye

Maya Beach

8 Tobacco Caye

Seine Bight

Lark
Caye

Placencia

BELIZE

Northern Highway

a morning storm, but you still have a good chance of getting out in the afternoon. Most of the cayes' dive shops are attached to hotels, and the quality of dive masters, equipment, and facilities varies considerably.

Many resorts offer diving courses. A one-day basic familiarization course costs between BZ$250 and BZ$350. A four-day PADI certification course costs BZ$700–BZ$800. A popular variant is a referral course, in which you do the academic and pool training at home, then do the required dives here; the cost for two days is about BZ$500.

If you want to experience something truly dramatic, head to the atolls, which make for some of the world's greatest diving. The only problem with the atolls is that they're awfully far from the accommodations. If you're staying on Ambergris Caye, Glover's Reef is out of the question for a day trip by boat. Even when the weather is perfect—which it often isn't in winter—a trip to Lighthouse Reef takes between two and three hours. Turneffe is more accessible, but even that is a long and comparatively costly day trip, and you're unlikely to reach the atoll's southern tip, which has the best diving.

If you're determined to dive the atolls, you can stay at one of the island resorts or spend time on a live-aboard dive boat. The resorts are marvelous hangouts for those who want a real castaway experience. If, on the other hand, you like a bit of nightlife, you might go stir-crazy. You might also find yourself significantly poorer at the end of your trip. A live-aboard can be great fun if the weather is good. The cost—BZ$2,400–BZ$3,400—is about the same as staying in a resort.

The **Belize Aggressor III** (✉ Box 1470, Morgan City, LA 70381, ☎ 985/385–2628 in the U.S., FAX 985/384–0817 in the U.S., WEB www. aggressor.com) runs a shipshape operation with a khaki-clad crew of four. It uses a 120-ft luxury cruiser powered by twin 500-horsepower engines and equipped with the latest communication systems. The schedule—five single-tank dives a day, including one night dive—will leave you begging for mercy. Staterooms are, well, almost stately. The spacious double-berth cabins are brightened with sky-blue fabrics, light-wood trim, and multiple windows instead of small port-holes. All have private baths, TVs and VCRs, and individual climate controls. Weeklong tours depart from the dock at the Radisson Fort George in Belize City. The boat makes scheduled stops at all three atolls, but most dives are on the southeast corner of Lighthouse Reef.

The **Nekton Pilot** (✉ 520 S.E. 32nd St., Fort Lauderdale, FL 33316, ☎ 954/463–9324 or 800/899–6753, FAX 954/463–8938; WEB www. nektoncruises.com) operates in Belize during the winter months. The 80-ft craft has a twin hull that makes it appear to be walking across the water on four big feet. The design, based on the same technology that allows oil platforms to operate in the rough waters of the North Sea, is supposed to provide more stability and reduce the chance of seasickness, even in rough water. Up to 32 divers all stay in outside cabins. For on-board relaxation there are a sundeck and a hot tub. Most itineraries include visits to all three of Belize's atolls, with the opportunity for four or five dives a day.

Numbers in the margin correspond to points of interest on the Cayes, Atolls, and Barrier Reef map.

Ambergris Caye

❶ *56 km (35 mi) northeast of Belize City.*

At 40 km (25 mi) long and 7 km (4½ mi) wide, Ambergris is the queen of the cayes. On early maps it was often referred to as Costa de Ambar, or the Amber Coast, a name supposedly derived from the blackish substance secreted by the sperm whale that often washes up on beaches. No proof exists, however, that ambergris was ever found here, although there's also an Ambergris Caye in the Bahamas.

A few years ago, when you flew into the caye's main town, San Pedro, the tips of the plane's wings almost touched the laundry hanging in people's backyards. Once landed, you could walk from one end of town to the other in 10 minutes. Today you need a bike just to get from one end of the airstrip to the other. Every year there are more cars, more souvenir shops, and more tourists. Ambergris will never be like Cancún, but it is the most developed—some would say overdeveloped—of the cayes. In 1999, the town paved one of the island's sandy streets for the first time.

The heart of the town is still the same: a couple of rows of brightly painted wooden houses with the ocean on one side and the lagoon on the other. Old men still lean over their balconies in the evenings to watch the world go by, and many people stroll down the roads barefoot. The stores and restaurants still have names like Lily's, Alice's, or Martha's. With a population around 4,400, San Pedro remains a small, friendly, and prosperous village. It has one of the highest literacy rates in the country and an admirable level of awareness about the fragility of the reef. The large number of substantial private houses being built on the edges of town is proof of how much tourism has enriched San Pedro.

Tourism on the island was slowed down temporarily in 2000, when Hurricane Keith slammed the island with 140 mph winds. The storm killed three people on the caye and caused millions of dollars in damage. Visiting the island today, however, you won't even realize a hurricane swept through. The hotels and other businesses quickly reopened, and even the palm trees have recovered. Because the winds came in from the west, beaches actually accreted sand. Hurricane Iris, which followed in 2001, did severe damage to parts of southern Belize, but had absolutely no effect on Ambergris Caye.

One of the biggest decisions you'll make about Ambergris Caye is where to stay. You have three basic options: in or near the town of San Pedro, in the South Beach or South End area beyond town, or on the North Beach or North End of the island beyond the channel. If you prefer easy access to restaurants, bars, and other activities, you'll likely be happier in San Pedro. Accommodations in town are generally simple and not too expensive (BZ$30–BZ$200). Rooms on the main streets can be noisy, not so much from cars as from late-night revelers. There are also numerous small bistros in town where, as often as not, you'll be eating with your feet in the sand. The fish arrives at your table fresh from the ocean. If you want silence and sand, you have to go out of town for resort-style accommodations. For privacy and the feeling of being away from it all, consider the South End, which is a golf cart ride away, or the even more remote North End, which is reachable only by water taxi.

Whether you arrive in San Pedro by air or by ferry from Belize City, you'll be met by a small crowd of cab drivers, friendly but a little pushy, offering cheap deals on lodging. Keep in mind that hotels pay a commission to these drivers, and the commission is reflected in the hotel rate. For the best rates call the hotel directly when you arrive. During the off-season (May–October), hotels offer walk-in rates that are often a third less than the advertised rates.

Although development on Ambergris continues relentlessly, the far north of the island remains pristine, or close to it. At the top of the caye, butting

28

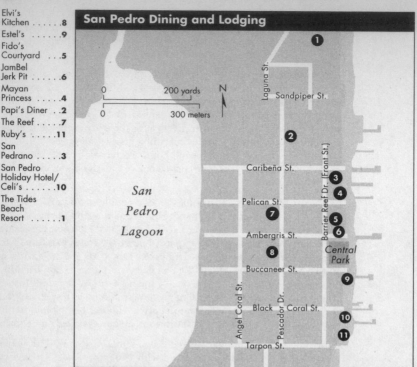

up against Mexico, **Bacalar Chico National Park** encompasses 105 square km (41 square mi) of land, reef, and sea. Here you can still find white-tail deer, ocelots, saltwater crocodiles, and, according to some reports, pumas and jaguars. Diving, snorkeling, and fishing are excellent, especially off Rocky Point. You'll need a boat and a guide to take you here. ⊠ *North end of Ambergris Caye.* ☞ *BZ$5.*

The highlight of the reef is the **Hol Chan Marine Reserve** (Maya for "little channel"), 6 km (4 mi) from San Pedro at the southern tip of Ambergris. It's a 20-minute boat ride from the island. Basically, Hol Chan is a break in the reef about 100 ft wide and 20 ft–35 ft deep, through which tremendous volumes of water pass with the tides. The 13-square-km (5-square-mi) park has a miniature Blue Hole, a 12-ft-deep cave whose entrance often attracts the fairy basslet, an iridescent purple-and-yellow fish frequently seen here. The reserve is also home to a large population moray eels.

Varying in depth from 50 ft to 100 ft, Hol Chan's canyons lie between buttresses of coral running perpendicular to the reef, separated by white, sandy channels. Some sides are very steep; others comprise gently rolling undulations. You'll occasionally find tunnel-like passageways from one canyon to the next. Not knowing what's in the next "valley" as you come over the hill can be pretty exciting. Because fishing is off-limits here, divers can see teeming marine life, including spotted eagle rays. You'll identify large numbers of squirrel fish, butterfly fish, parrot fish, and queen angelfish as well as Nassau groupers, barracuda, and large shoals of yellowtail snappers.

Shark-Ray Alley, a sandbar where you can snorkel with nurse sharks and rays (who gather here to be fed) and even larger numbers of day-trippers, was added to the reserve in 1999. Sliding into the water is a feat of personal bravery, as sight of the sharks and rays brushing past you is daunting yet spectacular. A night dive here is a special treat: the water lights up because of bioluminescence, and many nocturnal animals emerge, such as octopus and spider crab. You need above-average swimming skills, especially at night, as the current is very strong. ⊠ *Southern tip of Ambergris Caye.* ☎ *BZ$10.*

Dining and Lodging

SAN PEDRO

$$$ ✕ **Elvi's Kitchen.** Elvi Staines started out selling burgers from the win-
★ dow of her house in 1974. Soon she added a few tables on the sand under a flamboyant tree. A quarter century later the tree is still here (cut back to fit inside the roof), but everything else is changed. Enter through massive mahogany doors and you'll be tended to by a staff of a couple of dozen in snappy black-and-white outfits. The burgers at lunch are still good—if you're hungry, order the macho burger with double meat—but the place now specializes in upmarket dishes such as shrimp in watermelon sauce or crab claws with garlic butter. For dessert the coconut pie is a must. ⊠ *Pescador Dr.,* ☎ *226/2176. AE, MC, V. Closed Sun.*

$$–$$$ ✕ **Fido's Courtyard.** Sooner or later you're sure to end up at Fido's, sipping something cold and contemplating the ocean views. This casual restaurant and bar is one of the most popular places in San Pedro, serving up everything from fish-and-chips to slices of pizza. It's open every day for lunch and dinner, and some nights, depending on the season, there's live music. ⊠ *Barrier Reef Dr., just north of Catholic church,* ☎ *226/3176.*

$$ ✕ **Estel's Dine by the Sea.** Estella's father-in-law was a World War II flier with a squadron called Di Nah Might (his flight jacket is displayed on the wall). Not surprisingly, this is one of the best places in town to get a hearty American-style breakfast complete with bacon, fried potatoes, and freshly squeezed juice. Later in the day you can order burgers, Mexican meals, and excellent seafood dishes. The little white-and-aqua building is right on the beach, as you might guess from the sandy floor and porthole-shape windows. There's a terrace outside where you can sit under a thatch umbrella and watch pelicans. ⊠ *Barrier Reef Dr.,* ☎ *226/2019. No credit cards.*

$$ ✕ **JamBel Jerk Pit.** The spicy jerk-style dishes here are the way to go at this eatery that combines the cuisines of Jamaica and Belize (hence the name). This casual spot is in the middle of town next door to Big Daddy's. You can relax in the main dining room, where reggae is always playing, or upstairs on the roof, which is often so windy you'll have to hang on to your napkin. The ocean views make it worth the trouble. ⊠ *Barrier Reef Dr., next to Central Park and Big Daddy's,* ☎ *226/3303. AE, MC, V.*

$–$$ ✕ **Papi's Diner.** Atmosphere is in short supply at Papi's, as are views of the sea. Hardly more than a screened porch with a few wooden tables, Papi's is an unpretentious place tucked away at the north end of town. The seafood and other dishes are expertly prepared and served at some of the most reasonable prices in town. The grilled fish, served with all the usually side dishes, goes for BZ$16. ⊠ *Pescador Dr. at north end of town behind Seven Seas Resort,* ☎ *226/2047. No credit cards.*

$–$$ ✕ **The Reef.** There's no sea view here, and not much else beside heaping portions of fresh fish, chicken, and beans and rice. The lunch menu has Mexican dishes at rock-bottom prices. Avoid the specials at dinner, which are overpriced. ⊠ *Pescador Dr., just north of Elvi's,* ☎ *226/ 3212. No credit cards.*

$$ ⊞ **San Pedro Holiday Hotel.** This quartet of colonial-style houses, with cheery pink-and-white trim, is right in the heart of town. Owned by Celi McCorkle, one of the first Belizeans to open a hotel here, the hotel is always spic-and-span. All rooms have polished wood floors, and many have views of the hotel's small in-town beach. Celi's, one of the Caye's better restaurants, serves salads, sandwiches, and other light fare. ⊠ *Barrier Reef Dr.,* ☎ 226/2014, FAX 226/2295, WEB *www. sanpedroholiday.com. 16 rooms, 1 suite. Restaurant, fans, beach, dive shop, bar, shops, laundry service, travel services. AE, MC, V.*

$$$ ⊞ **Mayan Princess.** This pink hotel, sitting pretty right in the middle of town, has rattan furniture covered with pastel-color fabrics. Sliding doors open onto verandas where you can eat the meals you've prepared in your well-equipped kitchenette. In the low season—and sometimes even the high season, as well—managers Sheila and Rusty Nale drop room prices dramatically. When making reservations, it doesn't hurt to ask for a deal. ⊠ *Barrier Reef Dr.,* ☎ 226/2778, FAX 226/2784, WEB *www.mayanprincesshotel.com. 23 apartments. Fans, kitchenettes, cable TV, beach, travel services. AE, MC, V.*

$$ ⊞ **Tides Beach Resort.** One of the island's most experienced dive masters, Patojo Paz, opened this hotel with his wife, Sabrina, in 1999. The three-story wood-frame structure harks back to a time before everybody built with reinforced concrete. If diving is your reason for being, you couldn't do better than staying here. When you're ready to get wet, your boat is only a few feet away. When you return, there's a beach bar in which you can quench your thirst and swap stories. Standard rooms are attractive, if a bit on the small side. For a few bucks more you can upgrade to a bigger room with a king-size bed. The best are the four seafront rooms on the second and third floors, which have balconies overlooking the beach. The hotel is north of town, but you can walk along the beach to San Pedro's bars and restaurants. ⊠ *Boca del Rio Dr., north of town,* ☎ 226/2283, FAX 226/3797, WEB *www.ambergriscaye. com/tides. 12 rooms. Fans, refrigerators in some rooms, beach, dive shop, dock, bar, laundry service; no air-conditioning in some rooms, no room phones, no TVs in some rooms. AE, MC, V.*

$ ⊞ **Ruby's.** If you're a tightwad, you'll like this clean hotel on the beach. No wonder budget-minded travelers flock here—air-conditioned rooms with private baths and balconies facing the ocean go for under BZ$100. Try the breakfast burritos at the hotel's little restaurant, which opens early, at 6 for the fishing and diving crowd. ⊠ *South end of Barrier Reef Dr., at Tarpon St.,* ☎ 226/2063, FAX 226/2434, WEB *www.ambergriscaye.com/rubys. 17 rooms, 11 with bath. Restaurant, beach, fishing; no air-conditioning in some rooms, no room phones, no room TVs. AE, MC, V.*

$ ⊞ **San Pedrano.** Painted mint green, blue, and white, this is the cheeriest budget hotel in San Pedro. Each of the spotless rooms has crisp linens. The owners, members of the Gonzalez family, are friendly folks. ⊠ *Barrier Reef Dr.,* ☎ 226/2054, FAX 226/2093. 6 *rooms. Fans; no air-conditioning in some rooms, no room phones, no room TVs. AE, MC, V.*

NORTH OF SAN PEDRO

$$$$ ✕ **Capricorn.** Almost from the day it opened in 1996, this small seaside bistro has been widely considered the best restaurant on the island. Clarence and Annabel Burdes (he's French-Canadian, she's British) serve up delights like rosemary focaccia, medallion of beef with grilled lobster, and crepes with seafood. For dessert there are equally dreamy tropical treats such as key lime pie or coconut ice cream. You'll have to arrange a water taxi to get here, but once you've settled on the veranda, just steps from the sea, you'll be glad you made the trip. If you don't want to leave, there are three little cabanas. ⊠ *5 km (3 mi) north of San Pedro,* ☎ *226–2809. Reservations essential. AE, MC, V.*

$$$$ ✗ **Mambo Cuisine.** "Food and love are the most important things in the world," says the warm, exuberant Italian co-owner, Nadia Torcelli. The variety and delectability of the meals served at this restaurant in the Mata Chica resort reflect this dictum, particularly the seafood and pasta dishes. A new menu debuted in 2001 that emphasizes seafood specials such as chilled stone crabs. The dining room, in a soaring *palapa* (thatch-covered structure), has charming decorative touches, like the seashells used as salt and pepper shakers. ⊠ *8 km (5 mi) north of San Pedro,* ☎ *220/5010. AE, MC, V.*

$$$$ ✗ **Rendezvous Restaurant & Bar.** Next door to Journey's End is Belize's first and only restaurant serving Thai-French fusion. The *som tum* (shredded papaya) and *cho cho* (a local squash) in a tangy sauce with peanuts, coriander, and dried shrimp make a great starter. Follow that with chicken in a spicy red curry sauce, smoothing it out with chocolate truffle cake with Belizean *wongla* (sesame) seed candy. The owners, who have lived and worked in Thailand and Singapore, also make and bottle their own wines using imported grape concentrate. A honeymoon suite above the restaurant can be rented if you can't bear the water-taxi ride back to your hotel. ⊠ *8 km (5 mi) north of San Pedro,* ☎ ℻ *226/3426. AE, MC, V.*

$$–$$$ ✗ **Sweet Basil.** In a quiet residential area on North Ambergris, Sweet Basil is the place to get everything you need for an epicurean picnic. You'll have to take your bike or golf cart up Pescador Drive and across the "cut," a cross-caye channel where a hand-pulled ferry will take you and your vehicle across for BZ$5. Look for the pink-and-blue house a quarter of a mile on, where you can relax on the upstairs veranda eating some of Belize's scarcer commodities, like lox, prosciutto, and imported cheese. Salade *niçoise* or tapenade is served here 10–5 daily except Monday. ⊠ *Tres Cocos area, North Ambergris,* ☎ *226/3870. No credit cards. Closed Monday.*

$$$$ ▥ **Captain Morgan's Retreat.** Featured prominently on *Temptation Island,* this resort hasn't been shy about touting it (or in boosting rates to take advantage of the exposure). But instead of scantily clad beauties, here you'll find a long, quiet stretch of sand beside thatch-roof cabanas. Each has windows that let in lots of light and a porch with unobstructed ocean views. Good-size tile showers are welcome in the otherwise narrow baths. Newer condos have a sitting room and kitchen. The pool surrounded by a hardwood deck offers an alternative to a dip in the ocean, which is not at its best here. Despite the attractive setting, the staff here seems to change frequently, making for less than tempting service. The rates aren't much of a bargain, either. ⊠ *6 km (4 mi) north of San Pedro,* ☎ *226/2567; 888/653–9090 in the U.S.,* ℻ *307/587–8914,* ⅦⅧ *www.belizevacation.com. 14 cabanas, 12 condos. Restaurant, fans, pool, beach, dive shop, dock, bicycles, volleyball, bar, laundry services, travel services; no TVs in some rooms. AE, DC, MC, V.*

$$$$ ▥ **Mata Chica.** A dozen or so casitas in shades of mango, banana, and
★ blueberry accentuated by the brilliance of the white sand make this resort look like something out of a Gauguin painting. Fabrics inside echo these brilliant colors, as do the murals by a French artist in each bedroom and the Mexican tiles in the uniquely styled baths. Delectable meals are served at Mambo Cuisine, which excels at seafood. Nadia Torcelli and her husband, Philippe, worked in the fashion business for a decade before coming here. They brought with them a guest list that has included such stars as Mick Jagger, but you'll feel special even if your 15 minutes haven't arrived. If you crave the water, Philippe can

take you on day or overnight cruises on his catamaran. The beach here is postcard pretty, so you might not mind that there is no pool. A new beachside minispa with a hot tub opened in 2001. ⊠ *8 km (5 mi) north of San Pedro,* ☎ *220–5010,* WEB *www.matachica.com. 12 casitas, 2 cabanas. Restaurant, fans, beach, snorkeling, boating, fishing, bar, laundry service, travel services; no room TVs. AE, MC, V.*

$$$$ ⚂ **Portofino.** After a long series of delays, this new resort on the site of
★   the former Green Parrot finally opened in late 2001. With an eye on the success of nearby Mata Chica, it targets the tony side of the market. Here you'll find lushly landscaped grounds, an international-style restaurant called Coralino, and an "ocean pool" (a bit of dockside shore that has been scooped out to accommodate swimmers). Rooms are in thatch-roof buildings facing the ocean. Eight cabanas have bamboo four-poster beds draped with linen mosquito nets (although mosquitoes are rarely a problem). Two "tree house" suites are perched on wooden stilts above the sand. A deluxe honeymoon suite has a private whirlpool. ⊠ *10 km (6 mi) north of San Pedro,* ☎ *221/2096,* FAX *226/4272,* WEB *www. portofinobelize.com. 8 rooms, cabanas. Restaurant, room service, fans, minibars, beach, snorkeling, boating, fishing, bar, laundry service, travel services; no in-room phones, no in-room TVs. AE, MC, V.*

$$$–$$$$ ✕⚂ **El Pescador.** Every place on Ambergris Caye claims to offer fishing trips, but if you want some of the best guides, boats, and gear in Belize, this is the place for you. Occasionally described as a "fishing camp," the main lodge here is actually a handsome colonial house with comfortable, if not luxurious, rooms with mahogany floors. Adjoining the lodge are deluxe two- and three-bedroom villas (with prices to match). Other recent additions include a pool. You can enjoy a fine meal, served family style in the dining room, or a drink on the veranda. Most guests are here as part of a fishing package whose price starts at BZ$1,696 per person for three nights. ⊠ *5 km (3 mi) north of San Pedro,* ☎ *226/ 2398,* FAX *226/2977,* WEB *www.elpescador.com. 13 rooms, 4 villas. Restaurant, fans, kitchens, pool, beach, dock, boating, fishing, bar, fly shop, laundry service, travel services; no TV in some rooms. MC, V.*

$$$–$$$$ ⚂ **Journey's End.** The caye's largest resort, Journey's End caters to families who like to keep busy. There are activities day and night, from windsurfing and kayaking to snorkeling and diving. The reef is a little closer to shore here, so there's no need for snorkelers to pay for a boat trip. Come back for dinner, followed by live music. Journey's End is one of the few resorts in Belize that offers an all-inclusive option, letting you pay in advance for all meals and drinks. The landscaped grounds with coconut palms and cedar trees are well maintained, though some of the seafront cottages could use some sprucing up. The rooms facing the lagoon comfortably sleep groups of 10. And if you're lucky, you might see a crocodile from your patio. ⊠ *8 km (5 mi) north of San Pedro,* ☎ *226/2173; 800/460–5665 in the U.S.,* FAX *713/780– 1726,* WEB *www.journeysendresort.com. 70 rooms. Restaurant, fans, refrigerators in some rooms, 2 tennis courts, pool, beach, dive shop, snorkeling, windsurfing, boating, fishing, bar, laundry service, travel services; no TVs in some rooms. AE, MC, V.*

$$$–$$$$ ⚂ **Playa Blanca.** Run by Gary "Gaz" Cooper, a British expatriate who is a well-known dive operator in San Pedro, Playa Blanca feels like a private home. The pièce de résistance is the penthouse, a 2,200-square-ft suite with three bedrooms and two baths and great views of the water—it's ideal for a large family or group of friends. Packages include dives in the area. ⊠ *8 km (5 mi) north of San Pedro,* ☎ *226/ 5206,* WEB *www.playablancabelize.com. 3 suites. Fans, kitchens, refrigerators, pool, beach, dive shop, snorkeling, windsurfing, boating, fishing, bar. MC, V.*

SOUTH OF SAN PEDRO

$$ ✕ **Jade Garden.** Classic Cantonese dishes have a Caribbean twist at Jade Garden, as in the fish chow mein and the conch kebabs. You'll find American-style 12-ounce T-bone steaks and Belizean-style pork chops on the menu, too. This attractive restaurant fills the top two floors of a white colonial-style building just outside town. It's outfitted with handsome rattan furniture and pastel tablecloths, making this one of the caye's more comfortable restaurants. ✉ ¼ mi south of airstrip, Coconut Dr., ☎ 226/2126. AE, MC, V.

$$$$ 🏨 **Cayo Espanto.** After you arrive at this tiny private island west of Ambergris Caye, you may find that you don't want to leave. And why should you? Your luxurious villa comes complete with amenities like a splash pool, Egyptian cotton linens, and even a personal butler (the staff-to-guest ratio here is two to one). The walls on several of the villas literally fold back to let in the Caribbean sun. Meals, prepared by chefs who took home awards from Caribbean Culinary Federation competitions, are delivered to your own waterside table. You can expect entrées from local rock crab to grilled breast of duck. For all this personal care you'll pay a small fortune, so why not enjoy it? ✉ 5 km (3 mi) west of Ambergris Caye, Box 90, San Pedro, ☎ 888/666–4282 in U.S., ☎ FAX 221/3001, WEB www.aprivateisland.com. 5 villas. Restaurant, fans, room service, cable TV, 4 pools, beach, dock, snorkeling, boating, fishing, laundry service, travel services. AE, MC, V. AP.

$$$$ 🏨 **Victoria House.** With its bougainvillea-filled gardens, this beautiful
★   property 3 km (2 mi) south of San Pedro has the style and seclusion of a diplomatic residence. In the white colonial-style house with airy verandas and tile walkways are three ample suites with mahogany furnishings. They share a wraparound veranda that looks over the treetops to the turquoise sea. Stone-and-thatch casitas with private porches overlooking the sea are arranged around a lawn shaded by palm trees. A luxury suite on the beach has a king-size bed with silver headboard. Victoria House has made a lot of improvements over the past two years, the biggest of which is a gorgeous pool. The hotel's restaurant has also improved—dreary buffets have been replaced by dishes like shrimp beignets and conch fritters. Sea kayaks, catamarans, and a full array of diving tours are available. ✉ Coconut Dr., 3 km (2 mi) south of San Pedro, ☎ 226/2067; 800/247–5159 in the U.S., FAX 404/373–3885, WEB www.victoria-house.com. 13 rooms, 10 casitas, 3 suites, 2 villas. Restaurant, fans, kitchens, pool, beach, dive shop, dock, snorkeling, windsurfing, boating, fishing, bar, laundry service, travel services; no TVs in some rooms. AE, MC, V.

$$$$ 🏨 **Villas at Banyan Bay.** If you like little luxuries like a whirlpool bath in your room, this complex about 3 km (2 mi) south of town will suit you splendidly. The red-tile-roof buildings hold stylishly furnished two-bedroom condos that have verandas overlooking the sea. You won't feel cramped here—these are some of the largest and most luxe apartments on the island. The cathedral ceilings in the main living area sport a stunning array of tropical hardwoods. The pool is one of the largest on the island, and Mar de Tumbo is at the top of a short list of the island's best beaches. Rico's Bar & Grill, which opened in 2001, has friendly service and a beautiful setting on the water. ✉ Coconut Dr., 3 km (2 mi) south of San Pedro, ☎ 26/3739, FAX 226/2766, WEB www.banyanbay.com. 42 apartments. Restaurant, fans, in-room hot tubs, kitchens, cable TV, pool, beach, dive shop, dock, bar, laundry service, travel services. AE, MC, V.

$$$–$$$$ 🏨 **Ramon's Village Resort.** One of the first resorts to open on the cayes, Ramon's keeps on growing. In 2001 it unveiled a new collection of cottages across the street called Steve and Becky's Cute Little Hotel. Guests in the pink-and-lime cottages have access to all the resort's amenities. The rest of Ramon's Village has retained much of its atmosphere. The cabanas are a bit too close together but are certainly comfortable. The best choices are the ones closest to the water. A small artificial reef near the 420-ft pier brings fish to snorkelers. A new pool is gorgeous, but it's smaller than it looks in the brochures. Ramon's has a well-regarded dive operation, sending out guests in seven dive boats. The resort's location, a five-minute stroll from town, can't be beat. Evening means margaritas at the poolside bar or a beach barbecue featuring live music. ⊠ *Coconut Dr.,* ☎ *226/2071; 800/624–4315 in the U.S.,* FAX *226/2214,* WEB *www.ramons.com. 61 rooms, 8 cottages. Restaurant, fans, some kitchens, cable TV, pool, beach, dive shop, dock, boating, snorkeling, bar, shop, laundry service, travel services. AE, MC, V.*

$$$ 🏨 **SunBreeze Beach Hotel.** This midsize resort at the southern edge of town has always enjoyed an unbeatable location. Under the no-nonsense hand of manager Julia Edwards, the place has truly blossomed. The rooms, surrounding a plant-filled courtyard, are quite large. Five deluxe rooms have whirlpool baths. All units are equipped for guests with disabilities. The hotel also has a small beach area (there's a seawall you must cross to reach the water), a shaded pool, and a dive shop. The Blue Water Grill serves Pan-Asian fare, including—a first for San Pedro—sushi. The first paved street on the island, a short strip of cobblestone put down in 1999, is just outside the front door. ⊠ *Coconut Dr.,* ☎ *226/2191,* FAX *226/2346,* WEB *www.sunbreeze.net. 36 rooms. Restaurant, some refrigerators, cable TV, pool, beach, dive shop, dock, laundry service, travel services. AE, MC, V.*

$$$ 🏨 **Caribbean Villas.** Mixing Caribbean and Spanish styles, these two
★   graceful villas are set on a lovely stretch of beach south of San Pedro. An intelligent and creative design—luggage hides beneath built-in sofas and spacious lofts sleep six—make these apartments feel larger than they are. A four-story bird-watching tower has made the place an oasis for birders, with as many as 100 species flitting about at any one time. This sanctuary was the brainchild of owner Susan Lala, an avid birder. A tiny artificial reef helps attract schools of fish. If relaxation by the sea is what you're seeking, few spots are better. There's no bar or restaurant, but a nice grocery store, Island Supermarket, is handy if you want to do your own cooking. ⊠ *Coconut Dr., 1 km (¾ mi) south of San Pedro,* ☎ *226/2715; 785/776–3738 in the U.S.,* FAX *226/2885,* WEB *www.caribbeanvillashotel.com. 10 suites. Fans, kitchenettes, outdoor hot tub, beach, dock, snorkeling, bicycles, travel services; no room phones, no TV in rooms. AE, MC, V.*

$$$ 🏨 **Xanadu Island Resort.** It's billed as the "world's first monolithic dome resort," a description that might appeal only to engineers. Happily, these domes look nicer than they sound. Owner Ivan Sheinbaum says construction is costly, but the result is a structure that can withstand winds of up to 300 mph. Covered with thatch, the buildings contain suites with bedrooms and baths on two levels. They are attractively furnished in earth tones and have all the modern amenities. There are a nice little stretch of beach, a 350-ft pier, and a pool. You also get free use of bikes, canoes, and kayaks. ⊠ *Coconut Dr., 2 km (1 mi) south of San Pedro,* ☎ *226/2814,* FAX *226/3409,* WEB *www.xanaduresort-belize.com. 10 suites. Fans, kitchens, cable TV, pool, beach, dock, snorkeling, travel services. AE, MC, V.*

$$–$$$ 🏨 **Banana Beach Resort.** Inspired by the architecture of the Mexican town of Mérida, this three-story resort is set on a sandy beach that happens to be one of the island's nicest. The expansive one-bedroom apartments surround a courtyard with a swimming pool and a breezeway leading to the sea. Many have balconies just feet from the sea, while others have ocean views. Ask for one of the corner units on the second and third floors. The rates are surprisingly low, considering the

quality. Flush with the success of Banana Beach, owner Tim Jeffers has added another 28 units next door, along with another pool, a restaurant, and dive shop. The staff, among the friendliest on the island, is glad to arrange diving and snorkeling trips, fishing excursions, and other activities. ⊠ *Coconut Dr., 3¼ km (2 mi) south of San Pedro,* ☎ *226/ 3890,* FAX *226/3891,* WEB *www.bananabeach.com. 63 suites. Restaurant, fans, kitchens, cable TV, 2 pools, beach, dive shop, dock, boating, bicycles, laundry service, travel services. AE, MC, V.*

$$ ▣ **Changes In Latitudes.** The sign out front, depicting an igloo melting under a tropical sun, is an in-joke about Canadian owner Lori Reed's decision to move south to run this little bed-and-breakfast. A relaxed spot, this inn is close to San Pedro's restaurants and bars. The rooms are all on the small side, but they're clean and have louvered windows to let in the ocean breezes. The three garden-side rooms get the most light; others face a concrete wall. A full breakfast is served in the common room, but you can also prepare your own meals and store beer upstairs in Lori's fridge. Diving, snorkeling, and boating trips are easy to arrange. ⊠ *Coconut Dr., ¼ mi south of San Pedro,* ☎ FAX *226/2986,* WEB *www.ambergriscaye.com/latitudes. 6 rooms. Fans, travel services; no room phones, no room TVs. AE, MC, V.*

$$ ▣ **Coconuts Caribbean Hotel.** Operated by the same folks who run Banana Beach, this inn by the ocean stays busy year-round thanks to low rates and a staff that always seems to be smiling. They are eager to arrange diving and snorkeling trips or help with restaurant selections. The two-story building has big, airy rooms, some with an L-shape sofa that unfolds into an extra bed. The bar on the sandy beach serves refreshing rum drinks. This is one of the best deals on the island, especially off-season. ⊠ *Coconut Dr., ¾ mi south of San Pedro,* ☎ *226/ 3500,* FAX *226/3501,* WEB *www.coconutshotel.com. 14 rooms. Snack bar, fans, beach, snorkeling, bicycles, bar, travel services; no TVs in some rooms. AE, MC, V.*

CONDOTELS

In addition to the Villas at Banyan Bay, Mayan Princess, and Banana Beach Resort, there are a number of other small condos on the island with units available for daily or weekly rental. Most don't have a restaurant or bar, and some don't have a pool, but they make up for it with extra room and fully equipped kitchens. Most have cable TV, fans, and air-conditioning. Because they are usually individually owned—the nonresident owners let local managers rent them out when they're not on vacation here—you won't find any cookie-cutter decor.

Belizean Reef Suites (⊠ Coconut Dr., ☎ 226/2582, WEB www. AmbergrisCaye.com/bzreef) is a six-unit oceanfront complex south of town. There's no pool, but you can soak up the sun on a small beach. **Belizean Shores** (☎ 226/3000, WEB www.belizeanshores.com), about 7 km (4 mi) north of San Pedro, has 12 buildings with sea views. The big pool is a beauty. **Corona del Mar** (☎ 226/2055), also known as Woody's Wharf, is a laid-back, comfortable complex south of town. The 12-unit **The Palms** (☎ 226/3322, WEB www.belizepalms.com) has a great location at the southern edge of town. **White Sands Cove** (☎ 800/887–2054 in the U.S., WEB www.whitesandscove.com) is a group of 16 condos about 5¾ km (3½ mi) north of San Pedro. **Sunset Beach Resort** (☎ 226/2373, WEB www.ambergriscaye.com/sunsetbeach), about 4 km (2½ mi) south of town, has large three-bedroom units and a pool.

VACATION HOMES

Ambergris Caye has dozens of homes that can be rented on a weekly basis. These range from simple two-bedroom cottages that go for

BZ$1,000–BZ$2,000 a week to luxurious four- or five-bedroom villas which can rent for BZ$5,000–BZ$10,000 or more weekly. In most cases credit cards are not accepted. **Caye Management** (☎ 226/3077, WEB www.cayemanagement.com) is the island's oldest and largest rental management company.

Outdoor Activities and Sports

BOATING

For sailing Belize will never rival the British Virgin Islands. The shallow water kicks up a lot of chop, and hidden coral heads and tidal currents pose a danger to even those who know the area. When you charter a boat you have to stay inside the barrier reef, but there's a lot of beautiful territory to explore. The top outfit here is **Tortola Marine Management** (✉ Coconut Dr., ☎ 226/3026, FAX 226/3072, WEB www.sailtmm.com), which has a small fleet of catamarans and a yacht with three staterooms. Rates vary, depending on the type of boat and time of year, but range from around BZ$5,000 to more than BZ$14,000 a week, not including provisions. Skippers and cooks are an additional BZ$200 per day each. Split among three to eight people, the prices are competitive with hotel rates.

SCUBA DIVING

Sensing that their future lay in tourism, the people of Ambergris Caye were the first to cater to those who wanted to witness Belize's undersea world. In number of dive shops, experience of dive masters, and range of equipment and facilities, Ambergris Caye remains ahead of the rest. San Pedro even has a hyperbaric chamber and an on-site doctor to tend to divers with the bends, paid for by contributions from all the dive shops.

Most dive masters are former fishermen, locals who began diving as a sideline and eventually began to do it fulltime. The best of them have an intimate knowledge of the reef and a superb eye for coral and marine life. They are also quite ecologically aware, knowing full well that the destruction of the reef would not only be a great tragedy in itself but would leave them without a way to support their families. It was a group of dive masters who fastened a network of buoys to the bedrock to prevent further destruction of the coral. In bad weather one anchor dragged across the bottom can destroy more coral than 1,000 divers.

Speedboats take divers out to their destinations. Power generally comes from two hefty outboards mounted on the back, and with the throttle open it's an exhilarating ride. If you don't want to get splashed, sit in the middle. Many boats are constructed from solid mahogany. As they represent the major investment of the dive companies, the boats are lovingly maintained.

Dives off Ambergris are usually single-tank dives at depths of 50 ft–80 ft, giving you approximately 35 minutes of bottom time. Most companies offer two single-tank dives per day, one in the morning and one in the afternoon. Snorkeling generally costs BZ$30–BZ$50 per person for two or three hours or BZ$70–BZ$100 for a day trip, including lunch. Diving trips run BZ$70–BZ$80 for a single-tank dive, BZ$100–BZ$130 for a double-tank dive, and BZ$300–BZ$380 for day trips with dives to Turneffe Atoll or Lighthouse Reef.

Amigos del Mar (✉ Off Barrier Reef Dr., near Mayan Princess Hotel, ☎ 226/2706, WEB amigosdive.com) is probably the most consistently recommended dive operation on the island. It offers a range of local dives as well as trips to Turneffe Atoll and Lighthouse Reef in a fast 42-ft dive boat. The well-regarded **Gaz Cooper's Dive Belize** (✉ 5 mi north of town at Playa Blanca Resort, ☎ 226/3202, WEB www.divebelize. com) boasts about having the smallest dive operation on the island, preferring to keep it exclusive. **Larry Parker's Reef Divers** (✉ Spindrift Hotel, Barrier Reef Dr., ☎ 226/3134, WEB www.reefdivers.com), a long-established company, offers a full range of dives and instruction. The owner has been diving in Belize since 1977. Among those offering atoll trips are **Blue Hole Dive Center** (✉ Barrier Reef Dr., San Pedro, Ambergris Caye, ☎ 226/2982, FAX 226/2810, bluehole@btl.net).

Nightlife

With live music most nights, **Barefoot Iguana** (✉ Coconut Dr., ¾ km south of town) is the loudest bar on the island. Known for its burgers, **BC's Beach Bar** (✉ South of SunBreeze Hotel) is a popular oceanfront bar that hosts all-you-can-eat barbecues on Sunday afternoon. **Big Daddy's** (✉ Barrier Reef Dr., north side of Central Park) is where the action is in downtown San Pedro. Since it's right on the water, there's a beachside barbecue some nights. The music and real boozing here don't usually get started until late, usually around 11. Across the street from Big Daddy's is **Jaguar** (✉ Barrier Reef Dr.), another popular San Pedro disco.

Shopping

At **Belizean Arts** (✉ Fido's Courtyard, off Barrier Reef Dr., ☎ 226/ 2638) you'll find a selection of works by local painters. Also on display are handicrafts from the region, including hand-painted animal figures from Mexico, masks and fabrics from Guatemala, and brilliantly colored tropical fish made of coconut wood. For clothing and such the best place to stop is **D&G Gift Shop** (✉ Angel Coral St., behind Elvi's, ☎ 226/2069). The store also sells custom-made jewelry. About 3 km (2 mi) south of town, **Hummingbird Rattan** (✉ Coconut Dr., at Mar de Tumbo, ☎ 226/2960) sells high-quality furniture. At **Sea Gal Boulique** (✉ Barrier Reef Dr., in Holiday Hotel, ☎ 226/2431) the owner has an artist's eye. Everything is beautiful, even the T-shirts.

Caye Caulker

❷ *8 km (5 mi) south of Ambergris Caye, 29 km (18 mi) northeast of Belize City.*

For many years Caye Caulker had a reputation as a haven for British "squaddies" looking for a fight and backpackers in search of a cheap place to crash. As more upscale lodgings begin to open, its charms are beginning to shine through. Brightly painted houses on stilts line the coral sand streets. Flowers outnumber cars ten to one (golf carts, bicycles, and bare feet are the preferred means of transportation). The living is easy, as you might guess from all the NO SHIRT, NO SHOES, NO PROBLEM signs at the bars. This is the kind of place where most of the listings in the telephone directory give addresses like "near football field."

A plethora of dive and snorkel operators offer reef tours (some of them are "cowboys," so make sure you use a reputable company). Plan on spending about BZ$25–BZ$40 for a snorkeling trip around the island or to Hol Chan Marine Reserve. If you run out of money, don't worry. One of the island's newer amenities is a bank.

Dining and Lodging

$$ ✕ **The Sandbox.** The names of regulars are carved on the backs of the chairs at this popular eatery. Whether outside under the palms or indoors under the lazily turning ceiling fans, you'll always have your feet in the sand here. Open from 7 AM to 9 PM, the Sandbox serves a lobster omelet for breakfast, a roast beef sandwich for lunch, and red snapper in a mango sauce for dinner. The chowders are very good, and the

conch fritters are suitably spicy. Prices are reasonable, and the portions are enormous. At night the bar gets very lively. ✉ *Front St. at public pier,* ☎ *226/0200. AE, MC, V.*

$$ ✕ **Sobre Las Olas.** The surf-and-turf specials are the reason to head to this beachfront barbecue spot. The cooks toss lobster or whatever other seafood is in season on the grill, along with steaks and chicken. All the seating is outdoors under a canopy, the better to enjoy the sea breezes. ✉ *Front St., near Rainbow Hotel,* ☎ *226/0243. No credit cards.*

$–$$ ✕ **CocoPlum Gardens.** It's a bit of a hike to this little restaurant at the south end of the island, but the breakfasts are worth the effort—enjoy wholesome breads, fresh-made granola, and homemade jams, all in a lovely garden setting (not surprising, as the owners also operate a nursery.) It's currently open only in the morning, but popular demand may convince them to start serving dinner. While you're here, browse the small gallery and gift shop with Belizean-made crafts. ✉ *South end of island, near airstrip,* ☎ *226–0226. MC, V. Closed Monday.*

$ ✕ **Glenda's.** Glenda's has been around for years, and it's as good as ever for cheap, filling breakfasts or lunches. The classic eye-opener is a cinnamon roll, johnnycake (ask for one, as they're not on the menu), and fresh-squeezed orange juice. You just have to order the tasty rice and beans for lunch. ✉ *Back St., toward south end of village,* ☎ *no phone. No credit cards. No dinner.*

$ ✕ **YooHoo Deli.** This is the best place to grab a Cuban sandwich and a Fanta before your afternoon snorkeling trip. It's open from 10 until around sunset. The place is standing room only, meaning there's no seating. ✉ *Front St. next to police station,* ☎ *226/0232. No credit cards.*

$$ ⊞ **Chocolate's.** Chocolate is a 70-something Belizean who rents out one of the best rooms on Caye Caulker—a romantic retreat with a four-poster bed, vaulted mahogany ceiling with fan, and a screened-in veranda that looks out to the sea. The tile bath has a very large shower (terry cloth robes are nearby). Halogen reading lamps, a refrigerator, and a coffeemaker are nice little extras. Chocolate's manatee-watching trips to Goff Caye and his alligator-spotting cruises in the coastal lagoons are terrific. Chocolate says he's planning on building a couple more rooms because the one he has stays full much of the time. ✉ *At north end of island, near the Split,* ☎ *226–0151. 1 room. Fans, refrigerator, shop, snorkeling; no air-conditioning, no room phone, no room TV. MC, V.*

$$ ⊞ **Iguana Reef Inn.** Far and away Caye Caulker's most upmarket lodging, Iguana Reef has just about everything but a concierge. The suites are colorfully furnished with handmade furniture and local artwork. Unusual for the island, all are air-conditioned. Upstairs suites have vaulted ceilings with skylights. The latest addition is a thatch-roof bar. Because the inn is on the lee side of the island, you have the benefit of sunset views from your veranda. Considering the amenities, the rates are quite reasonable. The manager is a wealth of information about the island. ✉ *Near end of Middle St., next to soccer field,* ☎ *226/0213,* FAX *226–0000,* WEB *www.iguanareefinn.com. 12 suites. Fans, refrigerator, snorkeling, fishing, bar, travel services; no room phones, no room TVs. AE, MC, V.*

$$ ⊞ **Seaside Cabanas.** Just to the left of the public pier is this cluster of thatch cabanas. Though a bit pricey for Caye Caulker, they've proven to be quite popular and often are full. All have private baths, and some have air-conditioning. Hummingbird Tours can arrange dive, snorkel, and sightseeing trips. ✉ *Near Front St., at public dock,* ☎ *226/0498,* WEB *www.seasidecabanas.com. 10 cabanas. Fans, refrigerators, cable TV, beach, dive shop, snorkeling, fishing, bar, travel services; no air-conditioning in some rooms, no room phones, no room TVs. MC, V.*

$$ ⊞ **Shirley's Guest House.** At the southernmost tip of the caye, this lit-tle inn has four green-trimmed wooden cottages raised up on stilts and a cabana with a covered veranda. All the rooms look out to sea. Shirley's place is quiet and safe because, according to her, she runs a tight ship and no one would mess with her. We have to agree. ⊠ *South end of is-land, on waterfront,* ☎ *226/2145,* FAX *226/0145,* WEB *www.geocities. com/shirleysguesthouse. 10 rooms. Fans, refrigerators, beach, laundry service; no air-conditioning, no room phones, no room TVs, no kids under 18. MC, V.*

$$ ⊞ **Lazy Iguana B&B.** This B&B may be the tallest structure on any of the cayes. The views of the sunsets from the rooftop terrace are ter-rific, though the hotel's location on the back side of the island means you may have to swat an occasional mosquito while you watch. The rooms are furnished with attractive wicker and tropical hardwood fur-niture. Feel free to make yourself at home in the common room—owner Mo Miller says no shoes are required. Breakfast is included in the rate. ⊠ *South of main public pier,* ☎ *226/0350,* FAX *226/0320,* WEB *www. lazyiguana.net. 4 rooms. Fans; no room phones, no in-room TVs. MC, V.*

$ ⊞ **Treetops.** Three miniature security guards—Jack Russell terriers—guard this comfortable hotel. The rooms are generously proportioned and so clean you could eat off the floor. Sporting probably the most unusual decor of any on the islands is the Premier Room, which has an East African theme, complete with authentic masks and spears (the owner was in Africa with the British armed forces). The white-sand garden lost much of its bougainvillea during Hurricane Keith, but it's still a peaceful place to curl up on a chaise lounge and read. The staff is happy to arrange water sports and tours. ⊠ *Caye Caulker,* ☎ *226/ 0008,* FAX *226/0115,* WEB *www.treetopsbelize.com. 4 rooms, 2 with bath. Fans, refrigerators, cable TV, beach, snorkeling, laundry service, travel services; no air-conditioning in some rooms, no room phones. MC, V.*

$ ⊞ **Trends Beachfront Hotel.** The first thing you see when you arrive at the pier is this little hotel, painted a tropical pink and green. Thanks to its location and its bright rooms, it stays full much of the time. TVs are available on request. ⊠ *Near Front St., at public dock,* ☎ *226/ 0094,* FAX *226/0097,* WEB *www.cayecaulker.com/trends.htm. 6 rooms. Fans, refrigerator; no air-conditioning, no room phones, no room TVs. MC, V.*

Outdoor Sports and Activities

If you're looking for someone to take you out to the reef, **Frenchie's Diving Services** (⊠ Front St., ☎ 226/0234) is a well-regarded local op-erator.

Shopping

Annie's Boutique (⊠ North end of island, near the Split, ☎ 226/0151) has the best women's and children's clothes in Belize. Here you'll find dresses and sarongs made with fabrics from Bali, some unique silver jewelry, and Guatemalan bags that somehow don't make you look like a backpacker. **Galleria Hicaco** (⊠ Front St., ☎ 226/0178) has Belizean arts and crafts, including jewelry, dolls, carvings, and pottery.

Caye Chapel

❸ *2 km (½ mi) south of Caye Caulker, 10 km (6 mi) south of Ambergris Caye.*

Not since the days of British colonialism has there been a real 18-hole golf course in Belize. But for traveling duffers, a new course opened on Caye Chapelin in late 1999. It's a beautiful par-72 course, flat but long, with four par-5 holes. Challenges include brisk prevailing winds and the occasional crocodile. If golf is your game, this is the best Belize has to offer (smaller 9-hole courses are also located near Altun Ha ruins on the Old Northern Highway and at Jaguar Reef Lodge near Hopkins). There has been considerable controversy over the construction of this course, as some environmentalists believe that a golf course—which typically requires large applications of fertilizer and pesticides—could pose an ecological danger to the nearby reef. However, the course uses a special hybrid grass that requires half the fertilizers, pesticides, and irrigation of ordinary grass.

Dining and Lodging

$$$$ 🏨 **Caye Chapel Golf Resort.** This resort was designed as a corporate retreat, but you can stay here if you've got the dough. The expansive villas, which stand at imperial attention along the seafront, are similar to what you might see in exclusive gated communities in Boca Raton, Florida. Inside you'll find every luxury—whirlpool baths, expansive wet bars, and kitchens with the latest German appliances. In 2002 a dozen "budget" casitas opened with a price tag that's significantly less than the villas. The golf course's clubhouse houses a restaurant with indoor and open-air dining and stunning views of the sea. ✉ *Caye Chapel,* ☎ *226/8250,* ℻ *226–8201,* 🌐 *www.belizegolf.cc. 8 villas, 12 casitas. Restaurant, fans, some in-room hot tubs, kitchens, cable TV, pool, gym, beach, dive shop, dock, boating, marina, fishing, basketball, tennis courts, marina, bar, laundry service, airstrip, travel services. AE, MC, V.*

St. George's Caye

❹ *15 km (9 mi) northeast of Belize City.*

Just a stone's throw from Belize City, this small caye is steeped in history. The state of Belize had its origins here, as St. George's Caye held the first capital of the original British settlement. Later the island was the site of a decisive battle with the Spanish. Islanders had a total of one sloop, while the Spanish had 31 ships. Their knowledge of the sea, however, helped them to defeat the invaders in two hours.

Getting to St. George's Caye couldn't be easier, as the boat trip from Belize City takes little more than 20 minutes. Although St. George's Caye has some great places to dive, many serious scuba enthusiasts choose to head out to the more pristine atolls.

Dining and Lodging

$$$$ 🏨 **St. George's Lodge.** In colonial days this long-established resort was a favorite with the British because of its proximity to Belize City. Today St. George's Caye is a favorite of divers, undoubtedly because of the diving program led by Fred Good. You have a choice of basic rooms in the main building or thatch cottages by the water. Electricity comes from the lodge's own windmills, and your shower water is heated by the sun. The lodge doesn't have a liquor license, but you can bring your own booze to the beautiful rosewood bar. The restaurant serves homemade bread and grilled snapper or grouper, and coffee is delivered to your door in the morning. Weekly dive packages start at around BZ$3,400 per person, including meals. ✉ *1604 Maple St., Nokomis, FL 34275,* ☎ *800/678–6871 in the U.S.,* ℻ *941/488–3953,* 🌐 *www.gooddiving.com. 6 cabanas, 10 rooms. Restaurant, fans, beach, dive shop, snorkeling, travel services; no air-conditioning, no room phones, no room TVs. AE, MC, V. AP.*

Turneffe Atoll

❺ *40 km (25 mi) east of Belize City.*

This chain of tiny islands and mangrove swamps makes up an atoll the size of Barbados. The largest of the three atolls, Turneffe Atoll is the closest to Belize City. It's one of the best spots for diving, thanks to several steep drop-offs. Only an hour from Lighthouse Reef and 45 minutes from the northern edge of Glover's Reef, Turneffe Atoll is a good base for exploring the atolls.

Turneffe Atoll's best-known attraction, and probably the most exciting wall dive in Belize, is the **Elbow,** at the southernmost tip of the atoll. You may encounter eagle rays swimming nearby. Sometimes as many as 50 flutter together, forming a rippling herd that will take your breath away. This is generally considered an advanced dive because of the strong currents, which sweep you toward the deep water beyond the reef.

Though it's most famous for its spectacular wall dives, the atoll has dives for every level. The atoll's leeward side, where the reef is wide and gently sloping, is a good place for shallower dives and snorkeling; you'll see large concentrations of tube sponges, soft corals such as forked sea feathers and sea fans, and plenty of fish. Also on the atoll's western side is the wreck of the *Sayonara*. No doubloons to be scooped up here—it was a small passenger and cargo boat that went down in 1985—but it's a good place to practice wreck diving.

Dining and Lodging

$$$$ ⊞ **Turneffe Flats.** The sound of the surf is the only thing you'll hear at these smart blue-and-white beachfront cabins. The rooms, fitted with elegant hardwoods, are a far cry from the bare-bones fishing camp that occupied this site in the early '80s. You can dive here—the reef is only 200 yards from the shore—but the ubiquitous fishing-pole racks suggest that snook, bonefish, and permit are still the dominant lure. If you don't love fishing, you may feel like a bit of an outsider, as 75% of the clientele comes expressly to fish. You pay a pretty penny to indulge your passion, however—a weekly fishing package for two is around BZ$10,000. ⊠ *Northern Bogue (Box 36, Deadwood, SD 57732),* ☎ *800/815–1304 or 605/578–1304,* FAX *605/578–7540,* WEB *www.tflats. com. 6 rooms. Restaurant, dive shop, snorkeling, fishing; no room phones, no TVs in rooms. No credit cards.*

$$$$ ⊞ **Turneffe Island Lodge.** White dive tanks serving as fence posts and
★ a rusty anchor from an 18th-century British warship set the tone at this shipshape resort at the south end of Turneffe Atoll. This was the first dive lodge on Turneffe Atoll, and it bagged the best spot a few hundred yards from the legendary Elbow. But if you came to Belize for the diving, this is an ideal base. The rooms, in palm-shaded cottages with views of the sea, have been refurbished without spoiling the cozy feeling created by the varnished hardwood fittings. For those who want more space, seven new beachfront cabanas were added in 2001. The two-story colonial-style house, which holds the bar and the dining room, glows from the original mahogany trim installed by Mennonite craftsmen in the early '60s. Late risers may not appreciate the early morning breakfast bell. ⊠ *Coco Tree Caye,* ☎ *713/313–4670 or 800/874–0118,* FAX *713/313–4671,* WEB *www.turneffelodge.com. 7 cabanas, 12 rooms. Restaurant, fans, dive shop, snorkeling, fishing, bar, travel services; no room phones, no room TVs. AE, MC, V.*

Lighthouse Reef Atoll

⑥ *80 km (50 mi) east of Belize City.*

If Robinson Crusoe had been a man of means, he would have repaired here for a break from his desert island. It's the most distant of Belize's atolls, but it's the closest you'll get to paradise. Lighthouse Reef is also the most accessible, thanks to an airstrip.

Lighthouse Reef is about 29 km (18 mi) long and less than 2 km (1 mi) wide and is surrounded by a seemingly endless stretch of coral. Here you'll find two of the country's five-star dives. From the air the **Blue Hole,** a breathtaking vertical chute that drops several hundred feet through the reef, looks like a dark blue eye in the center of the shallow lagoon. The Blue Hole was first dived by Jacques Cousteau in 1970 and has since become a diver's pilgrimage site. Just over 1,000 ft wide at the surface and dropping almost vertically to a depth of 412 ft, the Blue Hole is like swimming down a mine shaft. It is this excitement, rather than the marine life, that has led to the thousands of stickers reading, "I Dived the Blue Hole."

The best diving on Lighthouse Reef is at **Half Moon Caye.** A classic wall dive, Half Moon Caye begins at 35 ft and drops almost vertically to blue infinity. Floating out over the edge is a bit like free-fall parachuting. Magnificent spurs of coral jut out to the seaward side, looking like small tunnels; they're fascinating to explore and invariably full of fish. An exceptionally varied marine life hovers around this caye. On the gently sloping sand flats behind the coral spurs, a vast colony of garden eels stirs, their heads protruding from the sand like periscopes. Spotted eagle rays, sea turtles, and other underwater wonders frequent the drop-off.

Although difficult to reach and lacking accommodations, **Half Moon Caye National Monument,** Belize's easternmost island, offers one of the greatest wildlife encounters in Belize. Part of the Lighthouse Reef system, Half Moon Caye owes its protected status to the presence of the red-footed booby. The bird is here in such numbers that it's hard to believe it has only one other nesting ground in the entire Caribbean (on Tobago Island, off the coast of Venezuela). Some 4,000 of these birds hang their hats on Half Moon Caye, along with iguanas, lizards, and loggerhead turtles. The entire 40-acre island is a nature reserve, so you can either explore the beaches or head into the bush on the narrow nature trail. Above the trees at the center of the island is a small viewing platform—at the top you're suddenly in a sea of birds that will doubtless remind you of a certain Alfred Hitchcock movie. Several dive operators and resorts arrange day trips and overnight camping trips to Half Moon Caye.

Dining and Lodging

$$$$ 🏨 **Lighthouse Reef Resort.** Once a spartan dive camp, Lighthouse Reef
★   has gradually been transformed into one of the most exclusive resorts in Central America. You'll probably feel like you're the only person on the island. You have a choice of simple cabanas, suites with pine-plank floors, and handsome colonial-style villas with Queen Anne–style furnishings. The setting—palm trees lining the mint green ocean—is breathtaking, and the diving, under expert supervision, is as good as any in the world. Seven-night packages cost BZ$3,100–BZ$3,700 per person, including meals, dives, and air transfer from Belize City. ✉ *Northern Caye,* ☎ *800/423–3114 in the U.S.,* 𝖥𝖠𝖷 *941/439–2118 in the U.S.,* 𝖶𝖤𝖡 *www.scuba-dive-belize.com. 11 rooms. Restaurant, fans, some rooms with refrigerators, beach, dock, dive shop, fishing, travel services; no room phones, no room TVs. MC, V.*

South Water Caye

❼ *23 km (14 mi) southeast of Dangriga.*

The first island in the south to have been developed for tourism, tiny South Water Caye makes for good off-the-beaten-reef diving. The reef is only a short swim from shore. The nearby **Smithsonian Institution's Marine Research Laboratory** (✉ Carrie Bow Caye) welcomes visitors by appointment; contact the Blue Marlin Lodge for more information.

Dining and Lodging

$$$$ 🏨 **Blue Marlin Lodge.** This picturesque resort makes an excellent base for fishing, snorkeling, and diving trips, as the reef is only 50 yards away. World-class destinations such as Turneffe Atoll and Glover's Reef are easily accessible. The Belizean-run place is child-friendly, with activities to please everyone on your trip. Accommodations, which spread out over half the caye, range from thatch-roof cabanas to cabins perched on stilts to a trio of lemon-yellow concrete dome buildings. All rooms are close enough to the sea that the sound of the waves may lull you to sleep. A restaurant and bar are great places to swap stories with other travelers. The minimum stay is four days. ✉ *South Water Caye,* ☎ *522/2243; 800/798–1558 in the U.S.,* FAX *522/2296,* WEB *www.bluemarinlodge.com. 16 rooms. Restaurant, beach, dive shop, snorkeling, fishing, bar, baby-sitting, travel services; no air-conditioning in some rooms, no room phones, no room TVs. MC, V.*

$$$–$$$$ 🏨 **Pelican Beach Cottages.** If you like to snorkel, get thee to this former nunnery. Once a convent belonging to the Sisters of Mercy, this colonial-era house called Pelican's Pouch has five large rooms on the second floor. There are also two cottages; if you're with a group ask for the Osprey's Nest, a three-bedroom house with two large verandas. At the center of the island, at what's called "Pelicans' University," student groups can rent a large house with bunk beds. The resort has a great beach, where you can swim and snorkel to your heart's content. The fishing's good, too. You may occasionally have to combat sandflies and mosquitoes, so bring along strong repellent. ✉ *South Water Caye,* ☎ *522/2044,* FAX *522/2570,* WEB *www.pelicanbeachbelize.com. 5 rooms, 2 cottages, 1 dormitory. Restaurant, beach, dive shop, snorkeling, boating, fishing, travel services; no air-conditioning, no room phones, no room TVs. AE, MC, V.*

Tobacco Caye

❽ *18 km (11 mi) southeast of Dangriga.*

If you don't want to pay a lot for your place in the sun, Tobacco Caye may be for you. It's a tiny island—barely three acres—but it's right on the reef, so you can wade in and snorkel to your heart's delight. All the accommodations here are budget places, basically just rough wood cabins. Periodically they get blown away by storms but are rebuilt, usually a little nicer than they were before. But the prices remain low, around BZ$70–BZ$125 a day per person, including meals. Boats leave from Dangriga for the 30-minute trip to Tobacco Caye.

Dining and Lodging

$–$$ 🏨 **Tobacco Caye Lodge.** This little cluster of pastel blue cabins sits just feet from the turquoise sea. There's a bit more room here for stretching out than at the other lodges on the island, as the property extends from the sea to the lagoon. A thatch-roof bar is set away from the cabins, and three simple but filling meals are included in the rate. ✉ *Tobacco Caye,* ☎ *520/5033,* WEB *www.tclodgebelize.com. 6 cabins. Fans, beach, snorkeling, fishing, bar; no air-conditioning, no room phones, no room TVs. MC, V.*

Glover's Reef Atoll

⑨ *113 km (70 mi) southeast of Belize City.*

Named after the pirate John Glover, this coral necklace strung around a 208-square-km (80-square-mi) lagoon is the southernmost of Belize's three atolls. The diving rates as some of the best in Belize. Visitors to Glover's Reef are charged BZ$5 a day, paid to the Belize Fisheries Department.

Although most of the finest dive sites are along the atoll's southeastern side, one exception is **Emerald Forest Reef,** named for its masses of huge green elkhorn coral. Because the most exciting part of the reef is only 25 ft down, it's excellent for novice divers. **Long Caye Wall,** another exciting wall, has a dramatic drop-off hundreds of feet down. Overhangs covered in sheet and boulder coral make it a good place to spot turtles, rays, and barracuda.

Southwest Caye Wall is an underwater cliff that falls quickly to 130 ft. It's briefly interrupted by a narrow shelf, then continues its near-vertical descent to 350 ft. This dive gives you the exhilaration of flying in blue space, so it's easy to lose track of how deep you are going. Both ascent and descent require careful monitoring.

Dining and Lodging

$ 🏠 **Glover's Atoll Resort.** This little group of cabins is a lesson in laid-back living. Forget about electricity and running water and surrender to a life of nothing but fishing, diving, and cooking your own meals. You bring your tackle for the boat or shore fishing and your own food supplies (and anything else you'll need). This is as close as they come to a *Gilligan's Island*–style vacation spot. ⌧ *Box 563, Belize City,* ☎ *520/5016,* WEB *www.glovers.com.bz. MC, V.*

The Cayes and Atolls A to Z

To research prices, get advice from other travelers, and book travel arrangements, visit www.fodors.com.

AIR TRAVEL TO AND FROM THE CAYES AND ATOLLS

Maya Island Airways and Tropic Air operate flights to Ambergris Caye and Caye Caulker from both the municipal and international airports in Belize City. Each has hourly service every day to Ambergris Caye between 7:30 and 5:30. In high visitor season, additional flights are added to accommodate demand. Round-trip fares for the 20-minute flight are about BZ$104 (municipal) and BZ$188 (international).

The airstrip on Ambergris Caye is in San Pedro. You'll always find taxis waiting at the airstrip, and most hotels run shuttles. If you're proceeding on foot, it's about two minutes, around the edges of the soccer field, to the hotels in town. The airstrip on Caye Caulker is at the south end of the island. Hotels may send a golf cart to pick you up. Otherwise, you'll find that taxis are available.

There are no scheduled flights to the other cayes, although Lighthouse Reef and Caye Chapel both have airstrips where charter flights can land. ➤ AIRLINES AND CONTACTS: **Maya Island Airways** (⌧ Box 458, Belize City, ☎ 223/1403; 800/521–1247 in the U.S., WEB www.mayaairways.com). **Tropic Air** (⌧ Box 20, San Pedro, ☎ 226/2012; 800/422–3435 in the U.S., WEB www.tropicair.com).

BOAT AND FERRY TRAVEL

A variety of boats connect Belize City with Ambergris Caye. The cost is about BZ$25 one-way. The most dependable, operated by the Caye Caulker Water Taxi Association, leave from the Belize Marine Termi-

nal on North Front Street. The speedy open boats depart Belize City
at 9, noon, and 3 and return from San Pedro at 6 AM, 11.30 AM, and
2:30 PM. Caye Caulker Water Taxi Association boats bound for Caye
Caulker take 45 minutes and cost BZ$15 each way. Departures are every
90 minutes between 9 and 5, with return trips departing the Public Pier
in Caye Caulker between 6:30 and 3.

To reach the more remote cayes, you are left to your own devices. You
can charter boats in either San Pedro or Belize City, but they're not
cheap. The resorts on the atolls run their own flights or boats, but these
are not available to the general public. Ask your hotel if it provides
transportation. For the southern cayes, inquire about boats departing
from Dangriga. Dangriga's Pelican Beach Hotel sends a boat to its resort on South Water Caye. Several boats make the run from Dangriga
to Tobacco Caye for BZ$30 per person one-way. Check at the River-
side Restaurant in Dangriga or ask at your hotel on Tobacco Caye.
➤ CONTACTS: **Caye Caulker Water Taxi Association** (⊠ Marine Terminal, N. Front St. at Swing Bridge, Belize City, ☎ 223/1969).

EMERGENCIES
For medical care on Ambergris Caye try the Lions Club Clinic or Dr.
Lerida Rodriguez, who (as is often the case with physicians in Belize)
operates a pharmacy from her office. On Caye Caulker, the Caye
Caulker Health Center, usually staffed by a volunteer doctor, is open
weekdays 8–11:30 and 1–4:30. For dental care or serious ailments you
need to go to Belize City.
➤ DOCTORS: **Lerida Rodriguez** (⊠ Galleria Bldg., San Pedro, ☎ 226/
3197).
➤ HOSPITALS: **Lions Clinic** (⊠ Near airstrip, San Pedro, ☎ 226/2073).
Caye Caulker Health Center (⊠ Front Street, near Lena's Hotel, Caye
Caulker, ☎ 226/0166).

HEALTH
Visiting Ambergris Caye is like a vacation in Florida—you'll face few
health concerns worse than sunburn. San Pedro's water, from a treated
municipal water supply, is safe to drink. On Caye Caulker, the water,
usually from brackish shallow wells, often smells of sulfur. To be safe,
drink only bottled water. On other remote cayes the water usually comes
from cisterns. You'll want to stick to the bottled stuff.

MAIL AND SHIPPING
On Ambergris Caye the post office in San Pedro is open weekdays 8–
noon and 1–5. On Caye Caulker the post office is on Back Street on
the south side of town. It is open 9–noon and 2–5 weekdays and 9–
noon Saturday.
➤ POST OFFICES: **Caye Caulker** (⊠ Back St., ☎ 226/0325). **San Pedro**
(⊠ Barrier Reef Dr., ☎ 226/2250).

MONEY MATTERS
Atlantic Bank, on Barrier Reef Drive in San Pedro, is open Monday,
Tuesday, Thursday, and Friday 8–noon and 1–3, Wednesday 8–1, and
Saturday 8:30–noon. Belize Bank, on Barrier Reef Drive in San Pedro,
is open Monday–Thursday 8–1 and Friday 8–1 and 3–6. There is just
one bank on Caye Caulker, Atlantic Bank on Back Street, south of Chan's
Market. It is open weekdays 9–1. Although all these banks have ATMs,
they don't accept cards issued outside Belize. Cash advances on your
Visa or MasterCard are available at these banks.
➤ BANKS: **Atlantic Bank** (⊠ Barrier Reef Dr., San Pedro, ☎ 226/2195;
⊠ Back St., Caye Caulker, ☎ 226/0207). **Belize Bank** (⊠ 49 Barrier
Reef Dr., San Pedro, ☎ 226/2482).

TOUR OPERATORS

All tour guides in San Pedro and on Caye Caulker should be members of their respective associations—if in doubt, ask to see identification. Among the top tour operators in San Pedro are Tanisha Tours, which offers excellent trips to Altun Ha and Lamanai, and SEAduced by Belize, which is unmatched for its nature and kayak tours. On Caye Caulker, Chocolate is the best-known guide and tour operator and is known for his full-day manatee trips.

➤ TOUR COMPANIES: **Chocolate Tours** (✉ Front St., Caye Caulker, ☎ 226/0151). **SEAduced by Belize** (✉ Tarpon St., San Pedro, ☎ 226/2254). **Tanisha Tours** (✉ San Pedro, ☎ 226/2314).

VISITOR INFORMATION

Ambergris Caye, Caye Caulker, and the other cayes are in some ways stepchildren of Belize's official tourist industry. Though these islands draw more visitors than any other area, the Belize Tourist Board and Belize Industry Tourist Association seem to give short shrift to the cayes. There may or may not be an official tourist information office open in San Pedro when you're there, and there isn't one on Caye Caulker. In any case, by far the best source of information on the island is online. The Web site www.AmbergrisCaye.com, operated by Marty Casado, has more than 6,000 pages of facts and figures on San Pedro, along with a good bit of information on Caye Caulker and other parts of the country.

NORTHERN AND CENTRAL BELIZE

Because Belize is so small, much of the country is accessible from Belize City. This is especially true of the north, where the Northern Highway treats travelers much better than many of the circuitous routes and badly maintained roads of the south. The landscape is mostly flat—this is sugarcane country—and although the north sees fewer travelers than the Cayo, it holds some of Belize's most interesting Maya sites as well as several first-class resorts.

Numbers in the margin correspond to points of interest on the Northern and Central Belize map.

Río Bravo Conservation Area

❶ *3½ hrs west of Belize City.*

The Río Bravo Conservation Area, created with the help of distinguished British naturalist Gerald Durrell, covers 250,000 acres near the spot where Belize, Guatemala, and Mexico meet. The four-hour drive here from Belize City takes you through deep bush where you might encounter a troupe of spider monkeys, wildcats, flocks of oscellated turkeys, a dense shower of butterflies—anything but another vehicle.

Within the borders of the reserve are more than 60 Maya sites, most of which have yet to be explored. The most important is **La Milpa,** the largest site in Belize besides Caracol and Lamanai.

Dining and Lodging

$$$–$$$$ 🖼 **Chan Chich Lodge.** Maybe one day the spirit of Smoking Shell or
   ★   another fierce Maya ruler will take revenge on Barry Bowen for erecting a group of cabanas in the middle of a Maya archaeological site. Until then, Chan Chich remains one of the best jungle lodges in all of Central America. Former U.S. president Jimmy Carter is among the many illustrious guests who have stayed at this magnificent property. Excellent tour guides lead you on wildlife excursions into the several

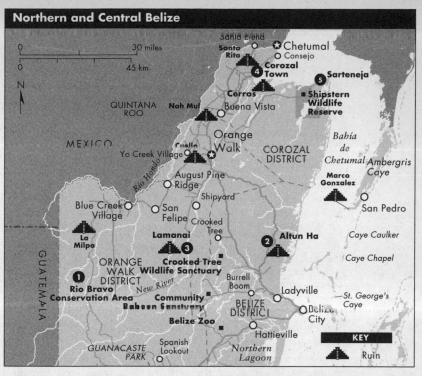

Northern and Central Belize

hundred thousand acres of surrounding bush. You are more likely to see the elusive jaguar here than anywhere else outside the Belize Zoo, as the lodge averages about one sighting a week. Other tours include canoe trips on the river, bird-watching treks (some 350 species have been identified here), and horseback rides to Maya ruins that have *not* been disturbed. Each of the dozen thatch-roof cabanas has a wraparound veranda. A gorgeous pool is screened to keep out insects. ⊠ *Box 37, Belize City,* ☎ *223–4419; 800/451–8017 in the U.S.,* FAX *223–4419,* WEB *www.chanchich.com. 12 cabanas. Restaurant, fans, pool, lake, horseback riding, bar, library, shop, laundry service, travel services; no air-conditioning, no room phones, no room TVs. AE, MC, V.*

Altun Ha

❷ *45 km (28 mi) north of Belize City.*

If you've never visited an ancient Maya city, make a trip to Altun Ha. It's not the most dramatic site in Belize—Caracol takes that award—but it is the most thoroughly excavated and the most accessible. People resided here for nearly two millennia; the first inhabitants settled here before 900 BC, and their descendants finally abandoned the site around AD 900. At its height the city was home to 10,000 people.

A team from the Royal Ontario Museum that first excavated the site in the mid-1960s found 250 structures spread over more than 1,000 square yards. At Plaza B, in the Temple of the Masonry Altars, the archaeologists found the grandest and most valuable piece of Maya art ever discovered—the head of the sun god Kinich Ahau. Weighing nearly 10 pounds, it was carved from a solid block of green jade. As there's no national museum, the head is kept in a solid steel vault in the central branch of the Bank of Belize. ☎ *No phone.* ⊠ *BZ$5.* ☉ *Daily 9–5.*

Lamanai

★ ❸ *About 39 km (24 mi) south of Orange Walk Town.*

Lamanai ("submerged insect" in Maya, often mistranslated as "submerged crocodile") was the longest-occupied Maya site in Belize, inhabited until well after Christopher Columbus discovered the New World in 1492. In fact, archaeologists have found signs of continuous occupation from 1500 BC until AD 1700.

The people of Lamanai carried on a way of life that was passed down for millennia, until the Spanish missionaries arrived. You can still see the ruins of the church the missionaries built in the nearby village of Indian Church. The same village also has an abandoned 19th-century sugar mill. With its immense drive wheel and steam engine—on which you can still read the name of the manufacturer, Leeds Foundry of New Orleans—swathed in strangler vines and creepers, it's a haunting sight.

In all, 50 or 60 Maya structures were spread over what is now a 950-acre archaeological reserve. The most impressive of these is the largest Preclassic structure in Belize—a massive, stepped temple built into the hillside overlooking the river. Many structures at Lamanai have been only superficially excavated. Trees and vines grow from the tops of the temples, the sides of one pyramid are covered with vegetation, and another pyramid rises abruptly from the forest floor. There are no tour buses or cold-drink stands here—just ruins and the slowly advancing forest.

There are several ways to get here. One option is to drive on the well-maintained unpaved road from Orange Walk Town. From here head west to Yo Creek, then southwest to San Felipe village, a total of 39 km (24 mi). In San Felipe go straight (the road to Chan Chich turns to the right) for another 19 km (12 mi) to reach the ruins. It's about a 1½-hour drive. The best way to approach the ruins, however, is by boat, which takes just a little longer. Boats leave from the New River Park Hotel, about 10 km (6 mi) south of Orange Walk. You can also take a charter plane from Belize City for the 15-minute trip.

On the grounds of the site you'll find Belize's only archaeological museum, where caretakers will be glad to show you a 2,500-year progression of pottery, carvings, and small statues. ✉ *South of Orange Walk.* 🕾 *BZ$5.* ⊙ *Daily 9–5.*

Dining and Lodging

$$–$$$ 🔝 **Lamanai Outpost Lodge.** Perched on a low hillside, Lamanai Outpost Lodge has a great view of the beautiful New River Lagoon. The lodge is home to the Lamanai Field Research Center, where you'll find resident naturalists, archaeologists, and ornithologists. This is a popular spot for anyone with a love of nature, and guests range from groups of children to seniors on Elderhostel programs. Even when you sneak off to the bar lounge, the Digger's Roost, you'll find archaeological memorabilia and a full-size reproduction of a Lamanai stela showing Lord Smoking Shell. A dock extends 130 ft into the lagoon and is a good place for swimming—just keep an eye out for ol' Mr. Croc. Bird-watching is superb, with at least 370 species identified within a 3-km (2-mi) radius of the lodge. The thatch cabanas, set among lovely gardens, all have porches with lagoon views. The Lamanai ruins are within walking distance, as is a small butterfly farm called Xochil Ku. ✉ *Indian Church,* ☎ *223/3578; 888–733/7864 in the U.S.,* FAX *727/864–4062 in the U.S.,* WEB *www.lamanai.com. 16 cabins. Restaurant, fans, lake, boating, bar, library, laundry service, travel services; no air-conditioning, no room phones, no room TVs. AE, MC, V. Closed Sept.*

Corozal

① *153 km (95 mi) north of Belize City.*

The last town before you reach Río Hondo, the river that separates Belize from Mexico, Corozal was originally settled by refugees from the Yucatán during the 19th-century caste wars. Though thoroughly ignored by today's visitors, this friendly town is a great place to enjoy a few days of easy living by the turquoise waters of Corozal Bay. It's hard not to fall into the laid-back spirit of life here—a sign at the entrance of Reyes Grocery advertises STRONG RUM, 55 BELIZE DOLLARS A GALLON. The climate is unequivocally appealing, with less rain than almost anywhere else in Belize. The sunny disposition of residents—mestizos, Creoles, Maya, and even North Americans—is compelling.

That said, sleepy Corozal may soon be rudely awakened. The Corozal Free Zone, just south of the Santa Elena border crossing, is starting to be known as a place where businesses can escape the high import duties of the rest of Belize. One casino is planned for the area, but in typically Belizean fashion the only evidence is a big bulletin board fading in the subtropical sun.

Though English is the official language, Spanish is just as common here. The town has been largely rebuilt since Hurricane Janet nearly destroyed it in 1955, so it's neat and modern. Many houses are clapboard, built on wooden piles, though a growing clan of expats, especially in the Consejo Shores area north of town, are putting up new houses that would not look out of place in Florida. One of the few remaining colonial-era buildings is a portion of the old fort in the center of town. The history of Corozal, including a graphic depiction of the brutality of colonial rule on the indigenous people, is depicted in a strikingly beautiful mural by Manuel Villamar Reyes on the wall of Town Hall.

In a landmark 100-year-old building near the market, the **Corozal Cultural Center,** now a museum and tourist information center, once served as a lighthouse. You can still see the spiral staircase and parts of the original beacon. Also on display are hand-blown rum bottles and a traditional Maya thatch hut. ⊠ *Off 1st Ave., at edge of Corozal Bay,* ☎ *422–3176.* 🎫 *BZ$3.* ☉ *Tues.–Sat. 9–noon and 1–4:30.*

Not far from Corozal are several Maya sites. The closest, **Santa Rita,** is a short walk from the center of the town. Only a few of its structures have been excavated, so it takes some imagination to picture this settlement, founded in 1500 BC, as one of the major trading centers in the district. ⊠ *Corozal,* ☎ *no phone.* 🎫 *BZ$5.* ☉ *Daily 8–4.*

Cerros, a late Preclassic center, is south of Corozal on the coast. As at Santa Rita, little has been excavated, but the site, which dates from about 2000 BC, includes a ball court, several tombs, and a large temple. The setting, on a peninsula in the Bay of Chetumal, is beautiful. The best way to get here is by boat from Corozal, around BZ$120 to BZ$160 for up to four people. ⊠ *Corozal,* ☎ *no phone.* 🎫 *BZ$10.* ☉ *Daily 8–4.*

Dining and Lodging

$$ ✗ **Le Café Kelá.** The last place you'd expect to find good French food is probably Corozal, but this café consisting of five tables under a cozy palapa near the bay is proof that in Belize anything is possible. Everything here is delicious, from the savory crepes to grouper sautéed with herbs. And the prices? *Mais oui,* it's hard to spend more than a few dollars a person. The fresh-squeezed fruit juices are heavenly, and the pizzas are the best in town. ⊠ *37 1st Ave., about 2 blocks north of Corozal Cultural Center,* ☎ *422/2833. No credit cards.*

$ ✕ **Cactus Plaza.** Ready for a bargain? Grab a seat at the counter or at one of the outdoor tables under a canvas awning and order a plateful of tacos, tostadas, *salbutes* (stuffed tortillas), and other Mexican finger foods. You won't be stuck with a big check, as most entrées are under BZ$2. Everything is freshly made and tasty. ✉ *6 6th St. S, 2 blocks west of bay,* ☎ *422/2004. No credit cards.*

$$ 🏨 **Casablanca by the Sea.** It's worth a short trip to Consejo, about 18 km (8 mi) northeast of Corozal Town, just to see the hand-carved mahogany doors gracing the entrance of each room at this inn. Once here, you'll want to stay. Consejo, a tiny village across the bay from Chetumal, is one of those off-the-beaten-path places that could easily steal your heart. Beverly Temte, an expat from New England, bought a building near the customs office to create this charming small hotel. The best rooms in the house are the three second-floor suites that face the bay. The other rooms, all on the small side, have tile floors and walls trimmed with native hardwoods. The first-floor restaurant, which often caters to groups, serves tasty Belizean and American food. ✉ *Consejo, 18 km (8 mi) northeast of Corozal Town,* ☎ *423–1018,* FAX *423–1003,* WEB *www.cbbythesea.com. 7 rooms, 3 suites. Restaurant, fans, cable TV, dock, bar, meeting rooms, travel services; no room phones. AE, MC, V.*

$$ 🏨 **Tony's Inn.** For almost 30 years Tony and Donna Castillo's little motel has been a popular stop for those arriving from Mexico. A new bar and grill that replaced the venerable bayside bar (somebody ought to put up a historic marker in memory of that Belikin-soaked spot) serves seafood, ribs, and burgers in a breezy setting on the water. The motel has a marina where you can arrange fishing trips. The hotel claims a beach, although it's really more of a patch of ground with imported sand. The more expensive digs on the second floor are the way go to here—they have some of the coldest air-conditioning in Belize. ✉ *Northern Hwy., south of 10th St.,* ☎ *422/2055,* FAX *422/2829,* WEB *www. tonysinn.com. 24 rooms. Restaurant, cable TV, beach, dock, marina, fishing, bar, laundry service, travel services. AE, MC, V.*

$ 🏨 **Hok'ol K'in Guesthouse.** This motel, named for a Yuacatec Maya phrase for welcoming the rising sun, is set across the street from Corozal Bay. Thanks to the stiff breezes, guest rooms are naturally cooled. They're a bit crowded by two queen beds, but verandas with hammocks give you a little more space. The best views are from the second-floor rooms. One room is wheelchair accessible. The restaurant serves breakfasts, snacks, and the best burgers in town. Inexpensive and interesting tours, including one to local schools, are available. ✉ *1 block south of the market,* ☎ *422/3329,* FAX *422/3569, maya@btl.net. 9 rooms. Restaurant, fans, bar, travel services; no air-conditioning, no room phones, no room TVs. AE, MC, V.*

$ 🏨 **International Cozy Corners Guesthouse.** This inn, which opened in late 2001, is a good value. The owners, an American expat and her Mexican husband, renovated a large yellow-concrete house at the north edge of town, turning the first floor into three good-size guest rooms with tile floors. At the front is a tiny swimming pool, while in the back the attractively landscaped gardens adjoin a small bar and restaurant. ✉ *2nd St. N,* ☎ *422/0150, blperse@btl.net. 3 rooms. Restaurant, fans, pool, bar; no room phones, no room TVs. MC, V.*

Sarteneja

❺ *67 km (40 mi) from Corozal.*

This small community of mestizo people makes a living from lobster fishing and pineapple farming. Sarteneja also is a center for building wooden boats. Although Sarteneja has traditionally had more in common with nearby Mexican villages than with the rest of Belize, this is changing with improvements on the road to Orange Walk.

The 81 square km (31 square mi) of tropical forest that now form the **Shipstern Wildlife Reserve** are, like the Crooked Tree Wildlife Sanctuary, a paradise for bird-watchers. Look for egrets (there are 13 species here), American coots, keel-billed toucans, flycatchers, warblers, and several species of parrots. Mammals are in healthy supply as well, including peccaries, pumas, jaguars, and raccoons. The butterfly farm next to the visitor center used to export pupae but is now only a small education area with a few adults left flitting about. For overnight stays cabins on the reserve may be rented for BZ$20 a night. Sarteneja village has a couple of guest houses—ask in the village what's available. ✉ *Sarteneja*, ☎ 223/4533, FAX 223/4985, WEB *www.belizeaudubon.org* 🖃 *BZ$10.*

Northern and Central Belize A to Z

To research prices, get advice from other travelers, and book travel arrangements, visit www.fodors.com.

AIR TRAVEL TO AND FROM NORTHERN AND CENTRAL BELIZE

Tropic Air and Maya Island Air each have three flights daily between Ambergris Caye and the airstrip at Corozal, about 3 km (2 mi) south of town off the Northern Highway. The journey takes 20 minutes and costs about BZ$70 one-way.

➤ AIRLINES AND CONTACTS: **Tropic Air** (✉ Northern Hwy., ☎ 422/0356). **Maya Island Air** (✉ South End, ☎ 422/2874).

BUS TRAVEL TO AND FROM NORTHERN AND CENTRAL BELIZE

Novelo's makes the three-hour journey between Belize City and Corozal several times a day. The cost is about BZ$8. Buses also continue on to Chetumal, Mexico.

➤ BUS INFORMATION: **Novelo's** (✉ 13 4th Ave., Corozal, ☎ 422/3034).

BOAT AND FERRY TRAVEL

An old sugar barge ferries passengers and cars across the New River from just south of Corozal Town to the road to Copper Bank, Cerros, and the Shipstern peninsula. It operates free from 6 AM to 9 PM daily. To get to the ferry from Corozal, take the Northern Highway toward Orange Walk Town to just south of Jal's Travel and Paula's Gift Shop. Turn left and follow the road for 4 km (2½ mi) to the ferry landing.

Two ferries between Corozal Town and Ambergris Caye began operations in 2001. The *Thunderbolt* departs Corozal from the pier near Reunion Park at 3 PM and returns from San Pedro, leaving from the Thunderbolt dock on the back side of the island, at 7 AM. Fare is US$20 one-way, US$40 round-trip. Thunderbolt has three 250-horsepower outboards, a canopy cover with sliding windows, and bus-style seats. The *Lady Lowe* departs from the pier at Corozal Bay Inn and Tony's at 6 AM, arriving at the Texaco dock on the back side of Ambergris Caye. It returns from San Pedro at 4 PM. Fare is US$17.50 one-way, US$32.50 round-trip. The open boat, with two 200-horsepower outboard motors, carries up to 40 passengers. Some hotels in Corozal and San Pedro sell tickets, or you can purchase them at the departure piers. These ferries may have reduced schedules from May to November.

➤ CONTACTS: **Lady Lowe Ferry** (✉ Corozal Bay Inn, Corozal Bay Rd., Corozal Town, ☎ 422/2691). **Thunderbolt** (✉ San Pedro Town, ☎ 226/ 2217).

CAR RENTAL

Car-rental agencies in Belize City will deliver vehicles to Corozal for a small fee. Corozal police enthusiastically ticket cars from other parts of Belize for minor violations such as parking the wrong way on a one-way street, so be especially cautious.

CAR TRAVEL

From Belize City Corozal is the last stop on the Northern Highway before you hit Mexico. The 153-km (95-mi) journey will probably take you a good 2–3 hours.

EMERGENCIES

For dental and medical care many residents of Corozal go to Chetumal, Mexico. In Corozal call John Drummer if you need medical care or Glenda Major if you require a dentist. The Corozal Hospital is on the Northern Highway.

➤ DOCTORS AND DENTISTS: **John Drummer** (✉ Santa Rita Rd., ☎ 422/2129). **Dr. Glenda Major, Dental Clinic** (✉ 12 1st St. S, ☎ 422/2837).
➤ HOSPITALS: **Corozal Hospital** (✉ Northern Hwy., ☎ 422/2076).
➤ PHARMACIES: **V-Mart Pharmacy** (✉ 4th Ave. and 1st St. N, ☎ 422/2597).

HEALTH

Health and hygiene standards are high in Corozal and in most of northern Belize. Around Cerros and Sarteneja be prepared for lots of mosquitoes, some of which may carry malaria or dengue fever. Bring plenty of strong insect repellent.

MAIL AND SHIPPING

The Corozal post office, on the west side of the main town plaza, is open 8:30–noon and 1–4:30.
➤ POST OFFICES: **Corozal** (✉ 5th Ave., ☎ 422/2462).

MONEY MATTERS

Although American dollars are accepted everywhere in Corozal, money changers at the Mexico border exchange Belize dollars for U.S. and Mexican currency, usually for better rates than in banks. The three banks in Corozal have ATMs, but these don't accept cards issued outside Belize. You can cross the border to Chetumal and use the ATMs there, although you will get your money in pesos.
➤ BANKS: **Atlantic Bank** (✉ Park St. S, ☎ 422/3473). **Bank of Nova Scotia** (✉ 4th Ave., ☎ 422/2046). **Belize Bank** (✉ 5th Ave. at 1st St. N, ☎ 422/2087).

SAFETY

Corozal is one of the safest areas of Belize. Petty theft and burglaries are not uncommon, however, so use common sense when traveling through the area.

TAXIS

To get around Corozal, call the Taxi Association or ask your hotel to arrange for transportation.
➤ TAXI COMPANIES: **Taxi Association** (✉ 1st St. S, ☎ 422/2035).

TOUR OPERATORS

Stephan Moerman, a French biologist, provides excellent tours of Cerros and other local archaeological sites. Henry Menzies arranges trips to Mexico as well as to sites around Corozal.
➤ CONTACTS: **Stephan Moerman** (✉ 37 1st. Ave., ☎ 422/2833). **Henry Menzies** (✉ Caribbean Village, South End, ☎ 422/3415).

VISITOR INFORMATION
Brochures and visitor information are available in the Corozal Cultural Center, on 1st Avenue near the market. The best source of on-line information about Corozal is www.corozal.com, a Web site put together by students at a local community college.

➤ TOURIST INFORMATION: **Corozal Cultural Center** (✉ 1st Ave., ☎ 422/3176.

THE CAYO

When the first jungle lodges opened in the Cayo, not many people thought this wild district on the country's western border would become a magnet for travelers. The region was too remote, the weather too unpredictable. Today more than half of those touring Belize visit the Cayo sometime during their trip, making this the country's second most popular destination. Comprising more than 5,200 square km (2,000 square mi) but with fewer than 15,000 inhabitants, the mountainous region is both Belize's largest district and one of its least populated.

You'll know you are entering the Cayo a few miles west of Belmopan. Having run along the Belize River for miles, the road winds out of the valley and heads into a series of sharp bends. In a few minutes you'll see cattle grazing on steep hillsides and horses flicking their tails. If it weren't for the Fanta orange sunsets and palm trees, this could be the Auvergne.

Other things change as you enter the Cayo. The heavyset Creole people who live along the coast give way to light-footed Maya; English is replaced by Spanish as the predominant language; and four-wheel-drive vehicles become a necessity. The lost world of the Maya begins to come alive through majestic, haunting ruins. And the Indiana Jones in you can now hike through the jungle, ride horseback, canoe down the Macal or Mopan rivers, and explore incredible caves.

Most wildlife featured on Belize's currency lives in the Cayo—the mountain lion, the jaguar and its diminutive cousin the ocelot, and the even smaller margay. Ornithologists in search of the country's 400-plus avian species carry telescopes, cameras, and tape recorders with microphones the size of Larry King's, but for most people a pair of binoculars will do. Even if you've never been bird-watching, setting off through the jungle in search of motmots, masked tityras, violaceous trogons, and scaly throated leaf-tossers as the sun begins to burn off the early morning mist will soon have you hooked.

National Geographic filmed *Journey to the Underworld* in the Cayo's Caves Branch River area, where fascinating limestone caves are found in lush tropical forests. Many of these caverns, hung with glistening white stalactites, have barely been explored. Resorts such as Caves Branch, Pook's Hill, and Jaguar Paw are arranging more and more expeditions for guests who want to see the caves from an inner tube or a boat. Serious spelunkers can even explore with scuba gear. Before trying either, though, inquire about histoplasmosis, a fungal infection of the lungs that can threaten explorers who venture into caves containing large numbers of bats.

As for lodging, you may be out in the bush, but you won't be roughing it. The Cayo has some of the country's finest accommodations, from simple cabanas to beautifully landscaped resorts. All place special emphasis on ecotourism, and most are on what might be called "safari strip"—the Western Highway heading from San Ignacio toward Guatemala.

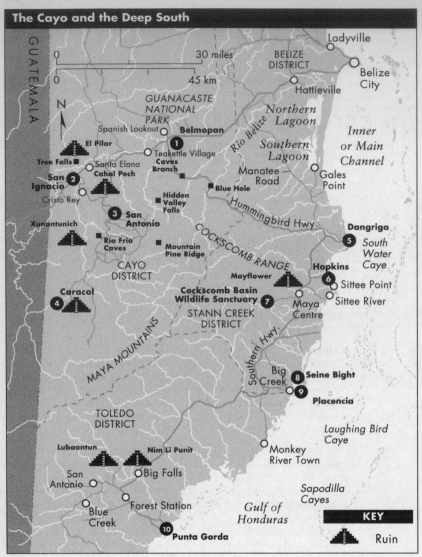

The Cayo and the Deep South

Numbers in the margin correspond to points of interest on the Cayo and the Deep South map.

Belmopan

❶ *80 km (50 mi) southwest of Belize City.*

The best way to see Belize's capital is through the rearview mirror as you head toward the Cayo. The brainchild of Belize's longest-serving prime minister, George Price, Belmopan was to be Belize's answer to Brasilia and Canberra—a resplendent, modern capital city. Instead, it's a dreary cluster of concrete office buildings plunked down in the middle of nowhere, proving that cities cannot be created overnight but must come into being over centuries. It's a great shame because that money could have been spent on revamping the seaside town of Belize City, which could have been greatly transformed.

Worth a quick visit on the way out of Belmopan is Belize's small nature reserve, **Guanacaste National Park,** named for the huge guanacaste trees that grow here. Also called monkey's ear tree because of their oddly shaped seedpods, the trees tower to more than 100 ft. Locals use them for dugout canoes called dorries. The 50-acre park has a rich population of tropical birds, including smoky brown woodpeckers, black-headed trogons, red-lored parrots, and white-breasted wood wrens. You can try one of the eight hourly tours every day, or you can also wander around on your own. ☉ *Daily, tours every hr 8:30–3:30.* ☞ *BZ$5.*

The small hilltop village of **Spanish Lookout,** about 19 km (12 mi) north of the Western Highway, is one of the centers of the Mennonite community in Belize. At first the village's blond-haired, blue-eyed residents seem out of place in this tropical country. In fact, they are thriving. Carpenters and dairy farmers, they build nearly all the resorts in the area, and most of the eggs and milk you'll consume during your stay will have come from their farms. The women dress in cotton frocks and head scarves, and the men wear straw hats, suspenders, and dark trousers. Many still travel in horse-drawn buggies. The cafés and small shops in Spanish Lookout offer a unique opportunity to mingle with these world-wary people, but note that they do not appreciate being gawked at or photographed any more than you do.

Less than half an hour south of Belmopan, **Blue Hole** is a natural turquoise pool surrounded by mosses and lush vegetation, excellent for a cool dip. The Blue Hole is actually part of an underground river system. On the other side of the hill is St. Herman's Cave, once inhabited by the Maya. A path leads up from the highway, right near the Blue Hole, but it's quite steep and difficult to climb unless the ground is dry. To explore the cave, it's best to wear sturdy shoes and bring a flashlight. Some years ago there were some unfortunate incidents at the site, with tourists robbed and, in one case, raped. A full-time attendant was subsequently appointed to patrol the area. ⊠ *Hummingbird Hwy.* ☞ *BZ$8*

Dining and Lodging

$$$$ ☒ **Jaguar Paw.** Although this lodge is down a long dirt road, it's any-
★ thing but rustic. Inside the massive structure you're struck by the eye-popping Maya murals painted by American Pam Braun. Each room has a theme—the Victorian Room, with a country armoire and sheer curtains; the Pioneer Room, with a pebble-lined shower and rough-hewn wooden bed; and others. There's 24-hour air-conditioning, thanks to Big Gennie the generator. Surrounding all of this is 215 acres of jungle that contains caves that you (and day-trippers from Ambergris Caye) can float through on an inner tube. It's not unheard of to clamber into one of these caves with a flashlight (watch out for bats) and to find a 1,000-year-old clay pot cradled in a crevice. Several jaguars have also been spotted here—hence, the name. ⊠ *Off Western Hwy., turn south at Mile 37 and follow dirt road 11 km (7 mi),* ☎ *888/775–8645 in the U.S.,* ⩌ *www.jaguarpaw.com. 16 rooms. Restaurant, fans, pool, fishing, hiking, bar, travel services; no room phones, no room TVs. AE, DC, MC, V.*

$$–$$$ ☒ **Banana Bank Ranch.** This isn't the most luxurious of the jungle lodges,
★ but it's one of the best values. It's also one of the best spots for families with kids. Riding enthusiasts of all skill levels can choose from 50 fine horses. Owners John and Carolyn Carr, both American expats, arrange canoeing, bird-watching, and other trips. A hand-pulled ferry takes you across the Belize River to the lodge. Several domesticated animals live on the property, including a monkey named Simon and a ravishingly beautiful jaguar named Tika. The newly restored century-old house, called the Headquarters, serves as a café and lounge. The thatch cabanas, with their curving walls, are simple but pleasant. ⊠

Off Western Hwy., turn north at Mile 48, ☎ *820/2020,* FAX *820/2026,* WEB *www.bananabank.com. 7 cabanas, 3 rooms. Restaurant, air-conditioning in some rooms, fans, horseback riding, bar, travel services; no room phones, no room TVs. MC, V.*

$–$$$ ⛺ ⚠ **Caves Branch Adventure Co. & Jungle Camp.** Those with Indi-
★ ana Jones fantasies should look no farther than this 58,000-acre pri-
vate reserve. The most intrepid will head to the bunkhouse, while
those in search of creature comforts will appreciate the cabanas of ma-
hogany and bamboo. Owner Ian Anderson offers more than a dozen
different wilderness adventures. On the tubing expedition to Footprint
Cave you'll spend hours floating around underground lakes and crawl-
ing past stalagmites into dry chambers. Unbelievable Maya relics are
scattered about, seemingly ignored by archaeologists. Just when you
think you've left your world behind, your guide will unpack a lunch
that you'll eat where Maya performed bloodletting rituals. Cold Be-
likins await you when you return, followed by a delicious family-style
meal. Don't fill up on the fresh-baked bread, though, as at least two
entrées are sure to follow. For real masochists there are "Bad Ass" ex-
peditions into the jungle that last 7 to 9 days. ⊠ *19½ km (12 mi) south
of Belmopan at Mile 41½ of Hummingbird Hwy.,* ☎ FAX *822/2800,* WEB
*www.cavesbranch.com. 12 cabanas, 6 with bath; 8 beds in bunkhouse;
camping. Restaurant, fans, hiking, caving, bar, travel services; no air-
conditioning, no room phones, no room TVs. No credit cards.*

$$$ ⛺ **Pook's Hill.** When the lamps are lighted each night on the polished
★ rosewood veranda, this low-key jungle lodge is one of the most pleas-
ant places in the Cayo. Owners Vicki and Ray Snaddon used to be bee-
keepers, but when African bees wiped out their hives, they decided to
become hoteliers. Their stone-and-thatch cabanas are laid out on a grassy
clearing around a small Maya site. The circular ones at the top are smaller,
but they make up for it with treetop views. The larger ones below sit
on a grassy terrace facing the jungle. During the day you can swim,
ride horses through a 6,800-acre reserve teeming with wildlife, or boat
up the Roaring River to a series of caves, many of which contain
Maya burial sites. ⊠ *At Mile 52 of Western Hwy., head south for 8
km (5 mi),* ☎ FAX *820/4017,* WEB *www.pookshillbelize.com. 9 cabanas.
Restaurant, hiking, bar; no air-conditioning, no room phones, no
room TVs. MC, V.*

$$ ⛺ **Warrie Head Ranch & Lodge.** On arrival you're greeted with fresh-
fruit punch served by Miss Lydia, the personable Creole woman who
manages this peaceful lodge. The elegant grounds, with seemingly
every tree and shrub ablaze with color, have the look of a botanical
garden. It's a short walk across the property to a small waterfall on
Warrie Head Creek and to the beautiful Old Belize River. A monstrous
steam tractor, once used to drag mahogany logs to the river, a horse-
drawn sugar mill, and several old chicle pots enhance the historic
atmosphere of this former logging camp. Owners John and Bia Searle
have stocked the cozy rooms with 18th-century antiques. Dinner is spe-
cial at Warrie Head, with guests lining up at the buffet to enjoy big
helpings of Miss Lydia's tasty home-style cooking, which draws on cre-
ole, Spanish, and North American recipes. ⊠ *Western Hwy.,* ☎ *227/
0755,* FAX *227/5213,* WEB *www.warriehead.com. 10 rooms. Restaurant,
fans, hiking, bar, travel services; no air-conditioning, no room phones,
no room TVs. AE, MC, V.*

San Ignacio

❷ *37 km (23 mi) southwest of Belmopan.*

When you hear the incredible commotion made by grackles in the trees
of the town square, you'll know that you've arrived at San Ignacio,

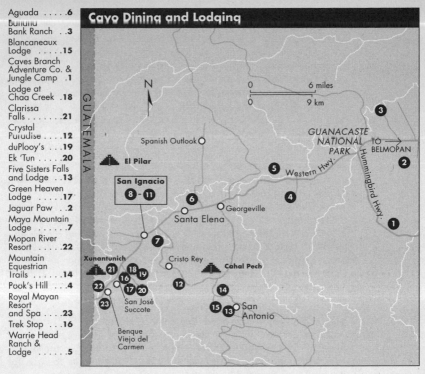

Cayo Dining and Lodging

the hub of the Cayo district. It's worth coming here at sunset to listen to the eerily beautiful sound made by these iridescent birds.

With its well-preserved wooden structures, dusty little San Ignacio is one of the few Belizean towns where you might wish to linger. Evenings are cool and mosquito free, and the colonial-era streets are lined with a few funky bars and restaurants. The location, in a pretty valley nestled between the Macal and Mopan rivers, makes San Ignacio an excellent base for exploring western Belize. Nearby are three Maya ruins, as well as a few national parks and a cluster of butterfly farms.

★ After crossing the Mopan River near the village of San José Succotz on a hand-pulled ferry—ask to work the crank yourself, if you'd like— you'll reach the archaeological site of **Xunantunich** (pronounced *zoo-nan-too-nitch*), which means "stone maiden." As you hike through the profusion of maidenhair ferns to the ruins, you'll encounter numerous butterflies flitting through the air. A magnificent avenue of cohune palms announces your arrival at an important ceremonial center from the Maya Classic Period. Drinks and snacks are available at a visitor center that provides the the history of the site. El Castillo, the massive 120-ft-high main pyramid, was built on a leveled hilltop. Though it's not as excavated as Altun Ha, the pyramid furnishes a spectacular 360-degree panorama of the Mopan River valley. On the eastern wall is a reproduction of one of the finest Maya sculptures in Belize, a frieze decorated with jaguar heads, human faces, and abstract geometric patterns that tells the story of the Moon's affair with Morning Light. *Southwest of San Ignacio.* ⊠ *BZ$5.* ⊙ *Weekdays 8–5, weekends 8–4.*

El Pilar, a less frequented archaeological site, is still being excavated under the direction of Anabel Ford, a professor at the University of California. Excavations of Maya ruins have traditionally concentrated on public buildings, but at El Pilar the emphasis has been on domestic architecture—everything from reconstructing houses to replanting gardens with crops used by the Maya. El Pilar, occupied from 700 to 1000, shows evidence of sentry posts in some areas, suggesting that this was a community of high-ranking officials surrounded by a hostile population. Two well-marked trails take you around the site. Because the structures have not been stripped of vegetation, you may feel like you're walking through a series of shady orchards. Don't forget your binoculars: in the 5,000-acre nature reserve there's some terrific bird-watching. Behind the main plaza a lookout grants a spectacular view across the jungle to El Pilar's sister city, Pilar Poniente, on the Guatemalan border. ⊠ *13 km (8 mi) west of Bullet Tree Falls.*

Just outside San Ignacio is a third major Maya ruin, the unfortunately named **Cahal Pech** (meaning "place of the ticks"). It was occupied from around 900 BC to AD 1100. At its peak, around AD 600, Cahal Pech was a medium-size settlement with some three dozen structures huddled around seven plazas. It is thought that it functioned as a kind of guard post, standing watch over the nearby confluence of the Mopan and Macal rivers. It may be somewhat less compelling than the area's other ruins, but it's really no less mysterious, given that these structures mark the presence of a civilization we still know so little about. You can try to get some answers at the small museum. *South of San Ignacio.* 🗺 *BZ$5.* ☉ *Tues.–Sat. 9–noon and 1–4:30, Sun. 9–noon.*

The **Ix Chel Tropical Research Center,** founded by Rosita Arvigo, is a center for traditional Maya medicine. Arvigo met Don Elijio Pantí, a Belizean shaman, and in 1985 became his apprentice by promising to preserve traditional healing practices. The center, run by Arvigo and her husband, has established itself as a special botanical garden: the beautiful Rainforest Medicine Trail takes you on a short, self-guided walk through the rain forest, providing you with a chance to study the symbiotic nature of its plant life. Learn about the healing properties of such indigenous plants as gumbo-limbo and man vine and see some of the endangered medicinal plants that Arvigo and her colleagues have rescued. The center has sent about 3,000 species of Belizean plants to the U.S. National Institutes of Health for analysis. The shop here sells Maya medicinal products like Belly Be Good and Flu Away, as well as Arvigo's excellent books. Arvigo and her staff offer aromatherapy and herbal and mineral-water therapies, as well as Maya massage, manicures, and pedicures. ⊠ *Next to Chaa Creek,* ☎ *824/3870,* WEB *www. rainforestremedies.com.* 🗺 *BZ$12 for Rainforest Medicine Trail.*

The **Chaa Creek Natural History Center** is a small but always expanding museum of Belize's flora and fauna. It has a tiny library and lots of displays of everything from butterflies to snakes (thankfully pickled in jars). Just outside is a screened-in blue morpho butterfly breeding center. If you haven't encountered blue morphos in the wild, you can see them up close here and even peer at their slumbering pupae, which resemble jade earrings. Once you're inside the double doors, the blue beauties, which look boringly brown when their wings are closed, flit about or remain perfectly still, sometimes on your shoulder or head, and open and close their wings to what seems like an innate rhythm akin to inhaling and exhaling. Hourly tours are led by a team of naturalists. ⊠ *The Lodge at Chaa Creek,* ☎ *824/2037,* FAX *824–2501,* WEB *www.chaacreek.com.* 🗺 *BZ$10.* ☉ *Daily 9–4.*

The life's work of Ken duPlooy, an ornithologist who died in 2001, and the personable Judy duPlooy is the 45-acre **Belize Botanical Gardens,** a collection of hundreds of trees, plants, and flowers from all over Central America. Enlightening tours are given by local Maya who can tell you the names of the plants in Mayan, Spanish, and English and explain their varied medicinal uses. An orchid house holds the duPlooys' collection of 180 orchid species. ⊠ *duPlooy's, San Ignacio, head 7½ km (4¾) mi west on Benque Rd., turn left on Chial Rd.,* ☎ *824/3101,* FAX *824/3301,* WEB *www.duplooys.com.* ☑ *BZ$10.*

Besides thoughtful displays on Cayo flora and fauna, **Tropical Wings,** a little nature center, raises 20 species of butterfly including the blue morpho, owl, giant swallowtail, and monarch varieties. The facility, at the Trek Stop, has a small restaurant and gift shop. ⊠ *10 km (6 mi) west of San Ignacio,* ☎ *823/2265.* ☑ *BZ$5.*

Dining and Lodging
IN SAN IGNACIO

$$ ✕ **Sanny's Grill.** Belizean basics such as chicken or pork chops are the staple here, but they are transformed into something wonderful with a hot grill and equally hot spices. Try the champagne shrimp or lime-thyme red snapper, served with the tastiest, spiciest rice and beans in the Cayo. You can enjoy them outside on a covered deck or inside in a casual dining room. And the prices? The restaurant's democratic motto proclaims: PRICES ANYONE CAN AFFORD. In a residential area off Benque Road, Sanny's can be hard to find after dark. ⊠ *23rd St., heading west of San Ignacio, look for a sign just beyond the Texaco station,* ☎ *824–2988. No credit cards. No lunch Sun.*

$ ✕ **Eva's.** Not just a bustling café and bar, Eva's is a Cayo institution—it's an Internet café, bulletin board, information center, trading post, and meeting place all in one. The food is honest-to-goodness Belizean fare, with some bacon and eggs, omelets, and sandwiches thrown in for good measure. Mugs of wickedly strong black tea are always available. No one is in much of a hurry, making this an excellent place to write postcards, catch up on your journal, or just soak up some authentic Belizean atmosphere. Presiding over the colorful chaos is Bob Jones, a garrulous British ex-serviceman, who can tell you everything from where to rent a canoe to what to do if you get bitten by a fer-de-lance to where to find a room. You can use Eva's computers to catch up on your e-mail. ⊠ *22 Burns Ave.,* ☎ *824–2267,* WEB *www.evasonline.com. No credit cards.*

$$$ ▥ **San Ignacio Resort Hotel.** Queen Elizabeth stayed here when she visited the Cayo in 1994. If you want a hotel in San Ignacio itself, this could be the place for you. It doesn't look like much from the road, but the large and comfortable rooms have verandas facing the jungle. There are a small pool and an iguana hatchery. The Running W restaurant specializes in steak, and the bar is big and usually busy. The staff can arrange birding and other excursions. Next door is a small casino packed with video poker machines, one-armed bandits, and a few live tables. ⊠ *Buena Vista Rd., San Ignacio,* ☎ *824/2034,* FAX *824/2134,* WEB *www.sanignaciobelize.com. 25 rooms. Restaurant, cable TV, pool, bar, casino, laundry service, meeting rooms, travel services. AE, MC, V.*

$$ ▥ **Windy Hill Resort.** You don't have to drive for hours to get to this lodge—it's on 100 acres just south of San Ignacio. The cabanas, all with private verandas, are perched on a low hill across the landscaped grounds. Furnishings are custom-made from local hardwoods, and decorations include handwoven Guatemalan rugs. Each is cooled by a lazily turning ceiling fan. The resort runs many tours to Tikal (a favorite here), Caracol, and other destinations. It recently added a popular night jungle-walk tour. ⊠ *Benque Rd., 1½ km (1 mi) west of San Ignacio,* ☎ *824/2017; 800/946–3995 in the U.S.,* FAX *824/3080,* WEB *www.windyhillresort.com. 25 cabanas. Restaurant, fans, minibars, pool, horseback riding, travel services; no air-conditioning, no room phones, no room TVs. AE, MC, V.*

60

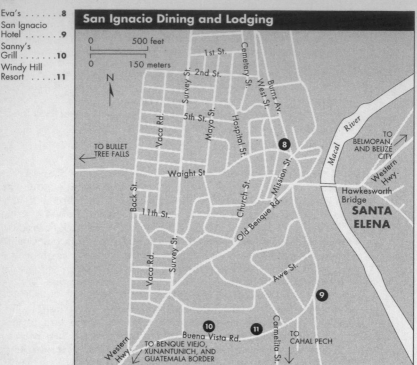

San Ignacio Dining and Lodging

NEAR SAN IGNACIO

$$$$ 🏨 🐾 **The Lodge at Chaa Creek.** This is the queen of jungle resorts.
★   Everything about the place, from the beautiful hardwood furniture to
the friendly staff of 70, is simply better than anywhere else. The setting, on 330 acres of rolling hills above the Macal River, is magnificent. The whitewashed stone cottages manage to be both extremely
simple and extremely elegant. Surrendering to progress, electricity has
been installed throughout. For the budget traveler Chaa Creek has the
Macal River Safari Camp in a clearing above the Macal River. Small
A-frame rooms are set up on individual wooden platforms. The resort's
new spa, on a hill above the lodge, has an unspeakably gorgeous view
of the Mayan Mountains and is by far the best-equipped facility in Belize. Treatments include mud and herbal body wraps, scrubs, massages,
and facials. As if all this weren't enough, Chaa Creek's safari-style tours
are among the finest in the country. ⊠ *West of San Ignacio, drive 7½
km (4¾) mi on Benque Rd., turn left on Chial Rd.,* ☎ *824/2037,* FAX
824/2501, WEB *www.chaacreek.com. 20 rooms, 2 suites, 10 casitas.
Restaurant, room service, fans, hiking, horseback riding, spa, laundry
service, meeting rooms, travel services; no air-conditioning, no room
phones, no room TVs. AE, DC, MC, V.*

$$$$ 🏨 **Ek 'Tun.** Imagine water as blue as a sapphire gushing from a natu-
★   ral mineral spring. Imagine a pool constructed not of concrete but of
limestone and other natural materials set among towering palms. Then
imagine being here in complete solitude—even going skinny-dipping,
if you like—with only the howler monkeys for company. With only
two cottages, Ek 'Tun is more of a bed-and-breakfast in the jungle than
a traditional lodge. After arriving on a river skiff, you step onto the
600-acre grounds, which have giant ceiba trees and flowering shrubs.
Both cabanas are constructed of thatch and hardwood poles, with rough-
hewn staircases leading up to the sleeping lofts. On the extensive net-

work of trails you can spot orange-breasted falcons and toucans. You can also explore several of Belize's most interesting caves. The excellent meals, included in the price, are served in a stucco-and-thatch dining room overlooking the river. ⊠ *On Macal River,* ☎ *820/3002; 303/442–6150 in the U.S.,* WEB *www.ektunbelize.com. 2 cabanas. Restaurant, river beach, pool, hiking, horseback riding, caving, bar, travel services; no air-conditioning, no room phones, no room TVs. MC, V.*

$$$$ 🏨 **Mopan River Resort.** Belize's first true all-inclusive resort includes everything from meals to tours to lodging in one reasonably priced package. Once you've taken the short ferry trip across the Mopan River to the resort's manicured palm-studded grounds, you're in your own private bit of paradise. The facades of the cabanas look traditional, but inside are amenities like cable TVs and minibars stocked with complimentary soft drinks and beer. Birders will enjoy the new 20-ft-tall bird-watching tower. Owner Jay Picon is affable and well traveled. Over drinks or a barbecue, Jay will regale you with tales of his days as a pilot and corporate executive. Dinners are often Thai themed, with recipes his wife picked up from cooking courses taken in Bangkok. ⊠ *Benque Viejo del Carmen,* ☎ *823–2047,* FAX *823/3272,* WEB *www. mopanriverresort.com. 12 cabanas. Restaurant, refrigerators, minibars, some kitchens, cable TV, pool, laundry service, travel services; no air-conditioning, no room phones, no smoking in cabanas. D, MC, V. All-inclusive. Closed July–Oct.*

$$–$$$$ 🏨 **duPlooy's.** High above a bend in the Macal River called Big Eddy is the spectacular location of this resort. From the deck, 30 ft above the forest floor, you look straight out to a dramatic sweep of limestone cliffs. From the sandy beach below you can swim and dive off the rocks. Bungalows are filled with hardwood furnishings. A new two-story cottage has wraparound porches, king-size beds, whirlpool bath, fridge, and great views. There are less expensive rooms in the jungle lodge. The food is terrific, and there's always a vegetarian option. On the premises is the 45-acre Belize Botanical Gardens. By canoe this resort is only a few minutes upstream from Chaa Creek; by car it's a 15 minute-drive over a bumpy track. ⊠ *San Ignacio, head 7½ km (4¾) mi west on Benque Rd., turn left on Chial Rd.;* ☎ *824/3101,* FAX *824/3301,* WEB *www.duplooys.com. 8 rooms, 2 with bath. Restaurant, fans, hiking, horseback riding, laundry service, travel services; no air-conditioning, no room phones, no room TVs. MC, V.*

$$$ 🏨 **Royal Mayan Resort & Spa.** If you can get up the stupendously steep hill and ignore the closet-size guest rooms, you might enjoy this alternative to the region's jungle lodges. The view—from the top of that darn hill—is nothing short of breathtaking. The hotel, owned by the same well-connected people who developed Fort Point Tourist Village in Belize City, has a gorgeous pool and two outdoor hot tubs (one overlooking the ruins of Xunantunich). The staff at the spa delivers a range of soothing services, including massages. Guest rooms are nicely furnished, with custom-made cabinets and designer linens that give the rooms an upscale atmosphere. ⊠ *Benque Viejo del Carmen,* ☎ *888/271–3483 in the U.S.,* FAX *305/969–7946 in the U.S.,* WEB *www.royalmayan.com. Restaurant, cable TV, fans, pool, gym, spa, travel services.*

$$ 🏨 **Green Heaven Lodge.** What's a nice young couple from the south of France doing in Belize? Dominique Agius and Anne-Karine Chappaz say one day they were looking for the Costa Rican consulate but stumbled upon the Belize consulate instead. That led to a trip to a country they knew almost nothing about. They now provide personal attention to their guests, who are usually outnumbered by the staff. Scattered around a low hill are four yellow-stucco cabins with red-tin roofs, all modestly appointed with Belizean-made furniture. Take a dip

in one of the nicest pools in the Cayo, or relax in the hammocks under the poolside palapa. Dominique runs the restaurant, La Vie En Rose, serving French classics like beef bourguignon. It's open daily from 7 AM to 10 PM. ✉ *Chial Rd., 8 km (4¼ mi) west of San Ignacio,* ☎ *820/ 2034; 800/889–1512 in the U.S.,* WEB *www.ghlodgebelize.com. 4 cabins. Restaurant, fans, pool, volleyball, bar, travel services; no air-conditioning, no room phones, no room TVs. AE, MC, V.*

$$ 🏨 **Maya Mountain Lodge.** This hilltop lodge is not luxurious, but that's not its intention. In recent years the lodge has focused on family-oriented activities. Owner Suzi Mickler, who has a master's degree in curriculum management, is the lodge's "headmistress." In addition to designing the nature trails (one trail passes 150 species of edible jungle plants, the other concentrates on ornamentals), she has created a host of courses at different levels, particularly for children, covering everything from Belizean history to ornithology. The lodgings are whitewashed cottages with private patio. A large wooden building has rooms for budget-conscious travelers. A pleasant open-air dining room serves up food that is tasty and plentiful. The staff is agreeable, and the grounds are thriving thanks to more than a decade of tender loving care. ✉ *Cristo Rey Rd., outside San Ignacio,* ☎ *824/2164,* FAX *824/ 2029,* WEB *www.mayamountain.com. 8 cottages, 6 rooms with shared baths. Restaurant, fans, pool, hiking, laundry service, travel services; no air-conditioning in some rooms, no room phones, no room TVs. AE, MC, V.*

$–$$ 🏨 **Clarissa Falls.** The rumbling low falls are the first and last sounds of the day at Clarissa Falls. It's a well-known place among Belizeans, who head here for tasty meals of enchiladas and black bean soup served under the open-air palapa overlooking the Mopan River. Chena Galvez, the charming owner, and her sister Anna create the simple, delicious food the friendly staff serves in copious quantities. This is their family ranch, a rolling 900-acre expanse of grassy pasture. Chena has spent her life on the ranch, and over the years she has built a small colony of homey thatch cabanas with electricity and private baths. Two are big enough for large families. The pet parrot, Larry, enjoys drinking coffee. ✉ *Western Hwy., 9 km (5½ mi) west of San Ignacio,* ☎ FAX *824/3916, clarifalls@btl.net. 11 cabanas, 9 with bath. Restaurant, bar, hiking; no air-conditioning, no room phones, no room TVs. MC, V.*

$ 🏨 **Aguada.** When you can get a room in a clean, attractive hotel that's this cheap, go for it. This hotel in Santa Elena, a low-key town near San Ignacio, has proved so popular that the owners, an American man and his Belizean wife, have added more rooms overlooking the pool. The hotel has a friendly restaurant serving Belizean dishes as well as American standards like burgers. The large common room has a television and games. If you're carless, the hotel is within walking distance of downtown San Ignacio. There are also a real London taxi cab, used for trips around the Cayo, and vans that run to and from the airports in Belize City. ✉ *Santa Elena,* ☎ *824/3609,* WEB *www.aguada.com. 14 rooms. Restaurant, pool, travel services; no room phones, no room TVs. MC, V.*

$ ✗🏨 ♨ **The Trek Stop.** A cold Belikin and filling Mexican and Belizean dishes await you when you return to this cluster of neat-as-a-pin cabins. Tents or just campsites are also available, as is a common kitchen for cooking your own grub. American expats Judy and John Yaeger and their Belizean partners opened this spot on top of a hill near San José Succotz in 1998. It's a fine find, particularly for budget travelers. *San José Succotz, 9⁹⁄₁₀ km (6 mi) west of San Ignacio,* ☎ *823/2265,* WEB *www.tbcnet.com/dyaeger/susa/trekstop.htm. 6 cabins without bath. Restaurant, bar, travel services; no air-conditioning, no room phones, no room TVs. MC, V.*

Outdoor Activities and Sports

CANOEING

The Cayo's many rivers, especially the Mopan and Macal, make it an excellent place for canoeing. Most of the larger resorts, like Chaa Creek and duPlooy's, have canoes. You can easily rent canoes in San Ignacio from **Toni Canoes** (☎ 824/3292).

CAVING

Over the millennia, as dozens of swift-flowing rivers bored through the soft limestone, the Maya Mountains became pitted with miles of caves. The Maya used them as burial sites and, according to one theory, as subterranean waterways that linked the Cayo with communities as far north as the Yucatán. Then the caves fell into a 1,000-year slumber, disturbed only by the nightly flutter of bats. In recent years the caves have been rediscovered by spelunkers. First on the scene was Ian Anderson, owner of **Caves Branch Adventure Co. & Jungle Camp** (⊠ 19½ km [12 mi] south of Belmopan, ☎ FAX 822/2800, WEB www.cavesbranch.com). He and his friendly staff of trained guides run exhilarating Indiana Jones–style caving, tubing, and hiking trips from a tiki-torchlighted jungle camp just south of Belmopan. David Simson, of **David's Adventure Tours** (⊠ San Ignacio, ☎ 824/3674, WEB www.belizex.com/davidstours.htm) was the first to do tours of the now-popular Barton Creek Cave. **Mayawalk Adventures** (⊠ San Ignacio, ☎ 824/3070, WEB www.mayawalk.com) specializes in tours to the spectacular, and spooky, cave of Actun Tunichil Muknal.

HORSEBACK RIDING

When it comes to horseback riding adventures, the undisputed local experts are found at the lodges of Mountain Equestrian Trails and Chaa Creek. **Easy Rider** (⊠ Collins Ave., San Ignacio, ☎ 824/3734) also runs equestrian tours of the Maya ruins and other points of interest in the region.

Shopping

Caesar's Place (⊠ Western Hwy., east of San Ignacio, ☎ 824/2341) has T-shirts, hammocks, postcards, and jewelry for last-minute shoppers. Don't expect a deal, though.

San Antonio

❸ *27 km (17 mi) south of San Ignacio.*

Heading southeast from San Ignacio, the road winds up from the Macal Valley through fertile farming country where corn, peanuts, and beans grow in small roadside clearings. A few miles beyond the village of Cristo Rey, the vegetation gets wilder as the road swings south and southeast away from the river. Cohune palms, trumpet trees, wild papayas, and strangler vines grow in profusion, while here and there a crop of bananas or corn cuts into the hillside. Shortly before the village of San Antonio, you emerge onto a plateau with fine views of the Maya Mountains. With its sheep, goats, and orange trees, San Antonio's cluster of brightly painted wooden houses clinging to the hillside at 1,000 ft looks like a tropical version of a Greek hilltop community.

A rugged dome of granite and limestone containing some of the most ancient rocks in Central America, the 780-square-km (300-square-mi) ★ **Mountain Pine Ridge Forest Reserve** is a highlight of any journey to Belize and an adventure to reach. Along with the Cockscomb Basin Wildlife Sanctuary and the Maya ruins at Lamanai, it's one of the sights no visitor should miss.

As you leave the lush tropical forest, the road circles the western slopes of the mountains. Baldy Beacon, at just over 3,000 ft, lies to the east. After the heat and humidity of lowland Belize, the cooler air is enormously refreshing. Unfortunately, much of the savanna here is marked by dead trees. A southern pine beetle infestation in 2000 and 2001 killed thousands of acres of mountain pines. The dead pines, besides being an eyesore, are also potential fuel for the forest fires common in this region during the dry season, from around February or March through May.

But there is more to see in Mountain Pine Ridge than pines. You'll see lilac-color mimosa, St. John's wort, and occasionally a garish red flower known as hotlips. There's also a huge variety of ferns, ranging from the tiny maidenhair fern to giants the size of coconut palms, and a fair selection of Belize's 154 species of orchids. Look out, too, for a wild tree called craboo, whose berries are used for making a brandylike liqueur believed to have aphrodisiac properties. Birds love this fruit, too, so any craboo is a good place to look for orioles and woodpeckers.

The roads—there are about 2,400 km (1,500 mi) of them—were built by the British army, which, with U.S. and Belize forces, still uses this area for training in jungle warfare. Some roads have names, but most have numerical monikers, like A10. Of course, the best way to see this area is on a mountain bike or by the power of your own feet, not bouncing around in an Isuzu Trooper. The village of Augustine is home to the headquarters of the forest reserve. It's the only place in the area where you're allowed to camp.

Inside Mountain Pine Ridge Forest Reserve is **Hidden Valley Falls.** Also known as the Thousand Foot Falls (although in fact it drops nearly 1,600 ft), it's the highest in Central America. A thin plume of spray plummets over the edge of a rock face into a seemingly bottomless gorge below. All this isn't as appealing as it sounds, as the viewing area is some distance from the falls. To climb closer requires a major commitment. A shelter, some benches, and a public rest room provide creature comforts. The nearby **Río On** has flat granite boulders on which to sunbathe and a series of crystal-clear pools and waterfalls in which to dunk yourself.

Just outside the reserve proper are the **Río Frío Caves.** They're only a few miles down a steep track, but ecologically speaking these caves are a different world. In the course of a few hundred yards, you drop from pine savanna to tropical forest. Nothing else in Belize illustrates the country's extraordinary geological variety so clearly as this startling transition. A river runs right through the center and over the centuries has carved the rock into fantastic shapes. Swallows fill the place, and at night ocelots and margays pad silently across the cold floor in search of slumbering prey. Seen from the dark interior, the light-filled world outside seems more intense and beautiful than ever. Rising vertically through the mouth of the cave is a giant hardwood tree, *Pterocarpus officialis,* its massive paddle-shape roots anchored in the sandy soil of the riverbank and its green crown straining toward the blue sky.

More than 30,000 pupae are raised each year at this facility, the largest of Belize's six butterfly farms. if you want to get a closer look at the creatures, **Green Hills Butterfly Farm** hosts about 30 butterfly species in a 2,700-square-ft flight area. Jan Meerman, who has published a book on the butterflies of Belize, runs the place with Dutch partner Tineke Boomsma. ⊠ *Mile 8, Pine Ridge Rd.,* ☎ FAX *820/4034.* ⌦ *BZ$8.* ☉ *Daily 8–4:30.*

The newly established **Elijio Panti National Park,** created in 2001 and named after the famed Guatemala-born herbal healer who died in

Cayo in 1996 at the age of 106, is a wonderful addition to the already extensive Belize national parks system. It comprises 100,000 acres of land around the villages of San Antonio, Cristo Rey, and El Progreso. The hope is that the elimination of hunting in this park will encourage the return of more wildlife to western Belize. At this early stage the park boundaries are as yet ill-defined, no admission fee is charged, an official welcome center and other park formalities are absent.

Dining and Lodging

$$$$ ⊡ **Blancaneaux Lodge.** You may detect a whiff of Beverly Hills as you
★ sweep down the hibiscus- and palm-lined driveway of this upscale Mountain Pine Ridge resort and pass a well-groomed croquet lawn. This is hardly surprising, as Blancaneaux Lodge is owned by Francis Ford Coppola. Laid out on a hillside above the Privassion River, the lodge's five villas have been featured in *Architectural Digest*. They have soaring thatch ceilings, Japanese-style tile baths, and screened porches overlooking the river. The filmmaker's own villa, one of the finest Cayo residences, is available when he's not here. A fleet of Land Rovers takes you to remote Maya ruins or on shopping trips to Guatemala. Bring your plane, as this resort has its own landing strip. ⊠ *Near San Antonio,* ☎ 824/3878; 800/746–3743 *in the U.S.,* FAX *824/3919,* WEB *www. blancaneauxlodge.com. 7 cabanas, 5 villas. Restaurant, fans, hiking, horseback riding, bar, laundry service, airstrip, travel services; no air-conditioning, no room phones, no room TVs. AE, MC, V.*

$$$ ⊡ ⚠ **Mountain Equestrian Trails.** Even if you don't ride, Mountain Equestrian Trails is a gorgeous place to stay. The setting, in the bottom of a lush valley with views of the jungle-covered flanks of the Mountain Pine Ridge, is second to none. Owners Jim and Marguerite Bevis, back in the saddle after a stint in the United States, have expanded the lodge to include 10 Spanish-style cabanas with lighting from kerosene lamps. Budget travelers like the tents, each built on a permanent wooden platform. Home-style meals are served in the "cantina," which doubles as a bar and reception area. Surefooted Texas quarter horses pick their way over the resort's 97 km (60 mi) of jungle trails, some of which wind up and down quite precipitous slopes. Nearby is Green Hills Butterfly Ranch. ⊠ *Mountain Pine Ridge Rd., off Western Hwy.,* ☎ 800/838–3918 *in the U.S.,* FAX *941/488–3953 in the U.S.,* WEB *www. metbelize.com. 10 cabanas, 8 tents. Restaurant, hiking, horseback riding, bar; no air-conditioning, no room phones, no room TVs. MC, V.*

$$–$$$ ⊡ **Five Sisters Falls & Lodge.** It's unfair to call this place a poor man's Blancaneaux Lodge. This resort, run by retired Belizean customs officer Carlos Javier Popper, has its own laid-back style, and the setting is possibly even more dramatic than that of its neighbor. Perched on a steep hill, it looks down on the waterfall that gives the place its name. Accommodations are in thatch cabanas with screened porches, as well as in boxy rooms in the main building. A tram will take you down to the river if you don't fancy walking down the 286 steps. After your swim the thatch-roof bar is a great place to unwind. The restaurant, with a beautiful view of the falls, serves Belizean food. ⊠ *Near San Antonio,* ☎ 800/447–2931 *in the U.S.,* ☎ FAX *820/4005,* WEB *www. fivesisterslodge.com. 8 cabanas, 7 rooms, 5 with bath. Restaurant, fans, hiking, bar, meeting room; no air-conditioning, no room phones, no room TVs. AE, MC, V.*

$$ ⊡ **Crystal Paradise.** In the village of Cristo Rey, this resort is one of the area's few Belizean-owned family operations. And what a family this is! The Tuts, an equal mix of Creole, Maya, and Spanish cultures, have 10 children. Eldest son Jeronie can identify more than 200 bird species and is an expert on medicinal plants; younger brother Evrald knows the surrounding jungle of the beautiful Mountain Pine Ridge area about as well as anyone. The Tuts have a good variety of very reasonably priced tours, including jungle camping, river excursions, and horseback riding. The whitewashed cabanas have Guatemalan bedspreads and other nice touches. ⊠ *Cristo Rey Rd., 6¼ km (4 mi) from San Ignacio,* ☎ FAX *824/2772,* WEB *www.crystalparadise.com. 8 cabanas, 12 rooms. Restaurant, fans, hiking, horseback riding; no airconditioning, no room phones, no room TVs. MC, V.*

Shopping

The village of San Antonio is home to the **Tanah Art Museum** (⊠ San Antonio, ☎ 824/3310), run by four sisters with clever hands and great heads for business. Look for the eye-catching slate carvings. At the other end of the village is the Magana family's arts-and-crafts shop, **Magana Zaac-tunich Art Gallery** (⊠ San Antonio, ☎ no phone), which specializes in wood carvings.

Caracol

★ ❹ *65 km (40 mi) south of San Ignacio, a 3-hr journey by road.*

Caracol (Spanish for "snail") is the most spectacular Maya site in Belize, as well as one of the most impressive in Central America. It was once home to as many as 200,000 people, nearly the population of modern-day Belize. It was a Maya Manhattan, a metropolis with five plazas and 32 large structures covering nearly a square mile. Once Caracol has been fully excavated it may dwarf even the great city of Tikal, which lies only a few dozen miles away. The latest evidence suggests that Caracol won a crushing victory over Tikal in the mid-6th century, a theory that Guatemalan scholars have not quite accepted. Until a group of *chicleros* (collectors of gum base) stumbled on the site in 1936, Caracol was buried under the jungle of the remote Vaca Plateau. It's hard to believe it could have been lost for centuries, as the great pyramid of Canaa is the tallest structure in Belize. The road to Caracol is decent, but if you want to drive on your own, be sure to inquire about road conditions first. A visitor center has opened here. ⊠ *From Mountain Pine Forest Ridge reserve entrance, head south 23 km (14 mi) to village of Douglas De Silva; turn left and go 58 km (36 mi).* ☒ *BZ$10.* ☉ *Daily 8–4.*

The Cayo A to Z

To research prices, get advice from other travelers, and book travel arrangements, visit www.fodors.com.

AIRPORTS AND TRANSFERS

Most people bound for the Cayo fly into Belize City. Discovery Expeditions, with a location at the international airport, picks up Cayo-bound passengers at both the international and municipal airports. Many resorts provide transportation to the Cayo from both airports in Belize City for about BZ$70 each way. Several hotels in San Ignacio, including Aguada, also run shuttles to and from Belize City and San Ignacio, for around BZ$50 a person. Call ahead for reservations.

➤ AIRLINES AND CONTACTS: **Discovery Expeditions** (⊠ 126 Freetown Rd., Belize City, ☎ 223/0748, FAX 223/0750).

BUS TRAVEL TO AND FROM THE CAYO

Novelo's has frequent service between Belize City and San Ignacio. The journey on the Western Highway takes about three hours and costs BZ$5–BZ$6, depending on whether the bus is a local or express.

➤ BUS INFORMATION: **Novelo's** (⊠ 1 Wyatt St., San Ignacio, ☎ 824/2508).

CAR RENTAL

Safe Tours Belize is a well-regarded rental agency in Santa Elena, just east of San Ignacio.

➤ LOCAL AGENCIES: **Safe Tours Belize** (✉ Western Hwy., Santa Elena, ☎ 824/3731, WEB www.belizex.com/safetours.htm).

CAR TRAVEL

To get to the Cayo, simply follow the Western Highway from Belize City. The Western Highway is a well-maintained two-lane highway. Watch out for "sleeping policemen" (speed bumps) near villages along the way.

EMERGENCIES

In case of emergency you'll find La Loma Luz Hospital, in Santa Elena, just east of San Ignacio.

➤ HOSPITALS: **La Loma Luz Hospital** (✉ Western Hwy., Santa Elena, ☎ 824/3253).

➤ HOT LINES: **Police** (☎ 824/2111).

➤ PHARMACIES: **The Pharmacy** (✉ 24 West. St., San Ignacio, ☎ 824/2510).

HEALTH

Health standards in the Cayo are fairly high. The water in San Ignacio and Santa Elena comes from a treated municipal system, so it's safe to drink. Resorts in the region have their own safe water systems. There are relatively few mosquitoes or other insects in the Cayo, as the porous limestone terrain means that rain does not stand in puddles. Some cases of dengue fever and malaria have been reported in the Cayo, however, so you may want to slather yourself with repellent that contains DEET.

MAIL AND SHIPPING

The San Ignacio post office is on Hudson Street. It's open weekdays 8–noon and 1–4:30 and Saturday 8–noon.

➤ POST OFFICES: **San Ignacio** (✉ Hudson St., San Ignacio, ☎ 824/2049).

MONEY MATTERS

Although American dollars are accepted everywhere, you can exchange money at the border crossing in Benque Viejo del Carmen. Banks in San Ignacio include Atlantic, Belize Bank, and Bank of Nova Scotia. They are all downtown on Burns Avenue. All have ATMs, but none accepts cards issued outside the country.

➤ BANKS: **Atlantic Bank** (✉ 17 Burns Ave., San Ignacio, ☎ 824/2596). **Bank of Nova Scotia** (✉ Burns Ave. at Riverside St., San Ignacio, ☎ 824/4190). **Belize Bank** (✉ 16 Burns Ave., San Ignacio, ☎ 824/2031).

SAFETY

Being close to the El Petén region of Guatemala, thousands of Cayo visitors make short trips over the border to see the fantastic ruins of Tikal. It's proximity to this tourist attraction is a boon for the Cayo but also a burden, as the poverty-stricken population of northern Guatemala spills over the border into relatively affluent Belize. Armed gangs from Guatemala have on several occasions robbed tourists around San Ignacio. But despite these events, the Cayo has comparatively little crime. As a visitor, you are unlikely to encounter any problems.

TOUR OPERATORS

Most jungle lodges offer a full range of day trips. Among the largest and best lodge-affiliated tour operations are Chaa Creek Expeditions and Windy Hill Tour Company. For cave tours, David's Adventure Tours, Mayawalk Adventures, and Caves Branch Adventure Company are the best. International Archeological Tours runs good expeditions to Maya sites in Belize and Guatemala. Toni's River Adventures is the leading operator for canoe trips.

➤ TOUR COMPANIES: **Chaa Creek Expeditions** (✉ 77 Burns Ave., San Ignacio, ☎ 824/2037, WEB www.chaacreek.com). **Caves Branch Adventure Company** (✉ Mile 41½, Hummingbird Hwy., Belmopan, ☎ 824/2800, WEB www.cavesbranch.com). **David's Adventure Tours** (✉ Savannah St., San Ignacio, ☎ 824/3674, WEB www.belizex.com/davidstours.htm). **International Archeological Tours** (✉ West St., San Ignacio, ☎ 824/3391). **Windy Hill Tour Company** (✉ Western Hwy., San Ignacio, ☎ 824/2017, WEB www.windyhillresort.com).

VISITOR INFORMATION

There is a Belize Tourist Industry Association office at the Cahal Pech ruins, but the best way to find out what's happening is to stop by Eva's in San Ignacio, a café that doubles as an unofficial visitor center. Owner Bob Jones, a tattooed ex-British soldier, knows the Cayo like the back of his hand. You can also contact local tour operators.

➤ TOURIST INFORMATION: **Belize Tourist Industry Association** (✉ Cahal Pech, San Ignacio, ☎ 824/4236). **Eva's** (✉ 22 Burns Ave., San Ignacio, ☎ 824/2267).

PLACENCIA AND ENVIRONS

As always in Belize, the transition from one landscape to another is swift and startling. When you approach Placencia, the lush, mountainous terrain of the north gives way to flat plains bristling with orange trees. The Stann Creek Valley is Belize's San Fernando Valley, the place where most of its fruit is grown. Bananas were the original bumper crop here, and banana plantations are still an important industry today. Equally startling is the cultural segue: whereas San Ignacio has a Spanish feeling, this area is strongly Afro-Caribbean.

Tourist dollars, the staple of contemporary Belize, have largely slipped passed Dangriga, but they are rapidly transforming Placencia, the region's most picturesque spot. Several years ago there were only three small resorts north of town. Now there are about 20, stretching up to the village of Seine Bight and beyond. The paving of the Southern Highway from Dangriga to the turnoff for Placencia and the construction of an airstrip north of Placencia have made the region more accessible (once you arrive, however, most roads consist of red dirt and potholes). Real estate sales are a driving force here. A section of the road down the peninsula was moved west in 1999 so that more land would be on the valuable side facing the sea. Much of the land north of Placencia has been divided up into lots awaiting development; if things continue at this pace, the area will one day rival Ambergris Caye as Belize's top beach destination.

Tourism in Placencia and elsewhere in southern Belize suffered a major blow in October 2001, when Hurricane Iris slammed the region with 140 mph winds and a 10-ft storm surge. The villages of Seine Bight, Placencia, and Monkey River were badly hit, with more than 95% of the homes here either destroyed or badly damaged. No lives were lost on the peninsula, but at Big Creek 20 people—three Belizeans and 17 Americans—died when a live-aboard dive boat called *Wave Dancer* capsized, throwing passengers and crew into the swirling black waters. After the storm it took several months for water, electricity, and other services to be restored. Many hotels and restaurants were closed for months, and some older places, such as Sonny's and Mother Ocean, shuttered for good. Larger resorts north of Placencia, such as Kitty's

Place, Nautical Inn, Rum Point Inn, and the Inn at Robert's Grove, were able to reopen by late 2001. Coconut palms mostly rode out the storm, and some plants, such as the scarlet-flowered hibiscus, seemed to thrive from the saltwater infusion. Some visitors to the region today may not even be able to tell that there was a major hurricane.

Numbers in the margin correspond to bullets on the Cayo and the Deep South map.

Dangriga

❺ *160 km (99 mi) southeast of Belmopan.*

With a population of 8,800, Dangriga is the largest town in the south and the home of the Garífuna (or Black Caribs, as they are also known). They are perhaps the most unusual of the many ethnic groups that have found a home in this tiny country. The Garífunas' story is a bizarre and moving one, an odyssey of exile and dispossession in the wake of the confusion wrought in the New World by the Old. They are descended from a group of Nigerian slaves who were shipwrecked on the island of St. Vincent in 1635. At first the Caribs, St. Vincent's indigenous population, fiercely resisted the outsiders, but they soon overcame their initial distrust.

In the eyes of the British colonial authorities, the new ethnic group that developed after years of intermarriage was an illegitimate and troublesome presence. Worse still, the Garífuna sided with, and were succored by, the French. After nearly two centuries of guerrilla warfare, the British decided that the best way to solve the problem was to deport them en masse. After a circuitous and tragic journey across the Caribbean, during which thousands perished of disease and hunger, the exiles arrived in Belize.

That the Garífuna have managed to preserve their cultural identity is one more example of Belize's extraordinary ability to maintain rather than suppress diversity. They have their own religion, a potent mixture of ancestor worship and Catholicism; their own language, which, like Carib, has separate male and female dialects; their own music, a percussion-oriented sound known as punta rock; and their own social structure, which dissuades young people from marrying outside their own community. In writer Marcella Lewis, universally known as Auntie Madé, they also had their own poet laureate.

For the traveler there's not much to keep you in Dangriga. But for one day each year, November 19, the town is all color and exuberance—this is Garífuna Settlement Day, when these proud people celebrate their arrival in Belize and remember their roots. Dangriga then cuts loose with a week of Carnival-style celebrations.

Dining and Lodging

$$ 🏠 **Mama Noots Backabush Resort.** Being environmentally aware doesn't mean you can't also be comfy. Instead of a diesel motor behind your cabana, here you have a combination solar, wind, and hydro system to generate electricity. Most produce served in the open-air dining room is grown on the grounds. Rooms, in thatch cabanas or a modern concrete building, have views of the rugged Maya Mountains. Because the resort is *backabush* (in the forest), owners Kevin and Nanette Denny advise guests to bring lightweight "jungle clothing," along with a poncho, plenty of insect repellent, and an adventuresome spirit. Nearby is the Mayflower archeological site, where a long-awaited excavation and restoration have begun, and miles of jungle trails and waterfalls. Wildlife spotting and birding here are excellent.

⊠ *Near Mayflower archeological site,* ☎ *520/2050,* WEB *www.ma-manoots.com. 6 rooms, 2 dorm rooms. Restaurant, fans, hiking, bar; no air-conditioning, no room phones, no room TVs. AE.*

$$ 🏨 **Pelican Beach Resort.** It has linoleum floors and thin wood walls, but this waterfront hotel outside Dangriga is the best the town has to offer. There are a dock and a little beach area, but you won't find the water appealing for swimming. You are close to boats to the southern cayes and Cockscomb Basin Wildlife Sanctuary. The staff is knowledgeable and friendly. Most rooms are in a two-story colonial-style building with a veranda. Some have porches with sea views, and all have real tubs rather than showers. The restaurant is a bit pricey for what you get, but the food and service are dependable. The resort has an annex on Southwater Caye, 20 minutes away by boat. ⊠ *Northeast of Dangriga,* ☎ *522/2044,* FAX *522/2570,* WEB *www.pelicanbeachbelize.com. 20 rooms. Restaurant, fans, dock, boating, bar, laundry service, meeting rooms, travel services; no air-conditioning in some rooms, no phones in some rooms, no TVs in some rooms. AE, MC, V.*

Hopkins

❻ *17 km (10 mi) south of Dangriga on the Southern Hwy., then 3½ km (2 mi) east on a dirt road.*

Hopkins is an interesting Garífuna village on the coast about halfway between Dangriga and Placencia. Garífuna culture is more accessible here than in Dangriga. Hopkins has the same toast-color beaches as those you'll find in Placencia, and a number of new resorts have opened to take advantage of them. Americans, Canadians, and Europeans are snapping up beachfront land here at prices lower than in Placencia or on Ambergris Caye, but so far only a few vacation homes have been built. If there's a downside to the area, it is the sandflies, which can be vicious here.

Dining and Lodging

$$$$ 🏨 **Kanantik Reef & Jungle Resort.** Are you looking to experience the
★   barrier reef and the jungle without having to make decisions more difficult than whether to have the fish or the steak for dinner? Intent on frolicking on a palm-lined private beach? Want an active vacation with all the snorkeling, sailing, kayaking, and fishing that you can handle? Then this luxurious all-inclusive resort that opened in early 2002 may be your place. Kanantik—a Mopan Maya word meaning "to take care"—has air-conditioned cabanas hidden away on 300 acres just south of Hopkins. The large and luxuriously outfitted cabanas, echoing African themes, are striking round structures with conical roofs. The resort took years to build; construction included bulldozing a lengthy road and building an airstrip. Rates are at the top end of the Belize spectrum, at BZ$1,200 a day double. ⊠ *Southern Hwy., 23 km (14 mi) south of Dangriga,* ☎ *520/8048; 800/965–9689 in the U.S.,* WEB *www.kanantik.com. 25 cabanas. Restaurant, fans, refrigerators, pool, beach, dive shop, dock, snorkeling, boating, fishing, horseback riding, bar, laundry service, airstrip, travel services. All-inclusive. AE, MC, V.*

$$$$ 🏨 **Jaguar Reef Lodge.** At night, with a row of torches burning on the beach and the thatch-covered dining room glowing in the lamplight, this lodge has an East African feel. Nestled on the coast, it has views over the water in one direction and of the green slopes of the Maya Mountains in the other. Cottages of whitewashed stone have soaring pitched ceilings with exposed wooden beams. Inside you'll find Mexican-tile baths with mahogany-encased basins. Even those items that are less essential, like the mahogany-and-canvas beach umbrellas, are

held to the same high standards. The resort can arrange dive trips, cruises on the nearby Sittee River, or excursions to nearby wildlife reserves. The beach is only so-so for swimming, but there's a seaside pool. About the last thing you'd expect to find in this area is a golf course, but 9 holes will be completed in 2002. The food is good, served in a waterside dining room with indoor and outdoor seating. The Garífuna staff is polite and easygoing. ⊠ *Hopkins,* ☎ *800/289–5756 in the U.S.,* WEB *www.jaguarreef.com. 12 rooms, 4 suites. Restaurant, fans, refrigerators, 9-hole golf course, pool, beach, dive shop, dock, snorkeling, fishing, bar, laundry service, travel services. AE, MC, V.*

$$$–$$$$ 🛏 **Hamanasi.** With a name that is Garífuna for "almond," Hamanasi has quickly become one of the top beach resorts in Belize. The hotel looks unprepossessing from the dirt road, but once you arrive, you see the manicured grounds and the lobby lined with original art. The "zero effect" pool that seems to stretch to infinity is one of the most appealing in Belize. Choose from regular rooms, gorgeous suites with king-size four-poster beds of barba jolote wood, and "tree houses" raised on stilts. Diving is why most people come to the resort—owners Dana and David Krauskopf have dived all over the world, from Bali to Zanzibar—but you won't feel out of place here if you want to snorkel or just laze around the pool. The restaurant serves delicious seafood and an eclectic blend of American and Belizean dishes. ⊠ *Hopkins,* ☎ *520/7073; 877/552–3483 in the U.S.,* WEB *www.hamanasi.com. 8 rooms, 8 suites. Restaurant, fans, refrigerators, pool, beach, dive shop, dock, boating, fishing, bar, travel services. MC, V.*

$$$–$$$$ 🛏 **Lillpat Sittee River Lodge.** This lodge, on 50 acres near the Sittee River, is devoted to a single passion. The fishing—on the river, on the flats, or out at Glover's Reef—is superb. The staff takes you where the bonefish, tarpon, permit, and snook are biting. You get a lot more than a fishing shack, as native hardwoods and Guatemalan furnishings are used throughout the lodge. The curved mahogany table in the dining room, where you eat family-style meals, is a thing of beauty. If you just want to relax, there's a beautiful new pool. If you don't fish, the lodge can also arrange bird-watching and snorkeling trips. ⊠ *Sittee River,* ☎ FAX *520/7019,* WEB *www.lillpat.com. 4 rooms. Restaurant, fans, cable TV, pool, boating, fishing, hiking, bar, travel services. AE, MC, V.*

$$ 🛏 **Beaches and Dreams.** New hotels are popping up all around the region, but Beaches and Dreams has managed to secure one of the area's nicest tan-color stretches of shoreline. Like many other innkeepers in the area, Sharon and Dave Helgesen left their jobs behind to build a beachside bungalow in Belize. Their tiny B&B, completed in late 1998, has two octagonal cottages, each with a vaulted ceiling, rattan furnishings, and a small veranda just a few feet from the sea. The pub-style restaurant serves some of the best food and coldest drinks in Hopkins. Try the seafood-and-fruit kebabs or the Cajun chicken pizza. Diving trips can be arranged. ⊠ *Sittee Point,* ☎ FAX *523/7078,* WEB *www. beachesanddreams.com. 4 rooms. Restaurant, fans, beach, bar, travel services; no air-conditioning, no room phone, no room TVs. MC, V.*

$ 🛏 **Tipple Tree Beya Inn.** Tiny Tipple Tree Beya Inn provides a comfortable alternative to the upmarket resorts along the coast. Here you can relax on the beach or kick back in a hammock. Run by a friendly British woman, the inn has three rooms that are simple but shiny clean, as well as a separate private cabin with a kitchenette. You can even pitch a tent on the beach. Bicycles and kayaks are available for rent. Tipple Tree also operates a small lodge in nearby Sittee River village, where you can relax by the river under the jungle canopy. You might even see a jaguar. ⊠ *Hopkins,* ☎ *520/7006,* WEB *www.tippletree. net. 1 cabin, 3 rooms without bath. Beach, snorkeling, camping; no air-conditioning, no room phone, no room TVs. MC, V.*

$ ⌨ **Toucan Sittee.** Neville Collins used to run a store in San Ignacio, before he retired here to a 20-acre farm where he grows 10 varieties of mangoes. He and his wife, Yoli, also run this retreat on the Sittee River. Each of the four cottages on stilts has living and dining rooms and one or two bedrooms. Collins can arrange all kinds of activities (canoeing, hiking, bird-watching) if you tire of just hanging around in a peaceful place filled with birds flying among the ginger plants. Delicious meals use organic ingredients grown on the farm. Like all lodges in these parts, this one can get a bit buggy, so bring repellent. ⌧ *Sittee River,* ☎ *523/ 7039,* ⓦ *www.freespace.virgin.net/david.griggs. 3 apartments, 2 rooms without bath. Fishing, camping; no air-conditioning, no room phone, no room TVs. No credit cards.*

Shopping
Jaguar Reef Resort (⌧ Hopkins, ☎ 800/289–5756 in the U.S.) has a fine little gift shop filled with pottery and embroidery as well as Garífuna crafts. The store also carries Marie Sharp's superb hot sauces, New Age music, and drugstore items like sunscreen and the very necessary no-see-um repellent.

Outdoor Activities
The best diving operation in the area is at **Hamanasi** (⌧ Hopkins, ☎ 520/7073). Here you'll find the newest equipment and the biggest boats. **Second Nature Divers** ⌧ Sittee River, ☎ FAX 523/7038, ⓦ www. belizenet.com/divers.html) has a good reputation.

Cockscomb Basin Wildlife Sanctuary

★ ❼   *48 km (30 mi) southwest of Dangriga.*

The mighty jaguar, once the undisputed king of the Central and South American jungles, is now endangered. But it has a haven in the Cockscomb Basin Wildlife Sanctuary, which covers 102,000 acres of lush rain forest in the Cockscomb Range of the Maya Mountains. Because of this reserve, as well as other protected areas around the country, Belize has the highest concentration of jaguars in the world.

Jaguars are shy, nocturnal animals that prefer to keep their distance from humans, so the possibility of sighting one in the wild is small. The jaguar, or *el tigre,* as it's known in Spanish, is nature's great loner, a supremely free creature that shuns even the company of its own kind. Except during a brief mating period and the six short months the female spends with her cubs before turning them loose, jaguars live alone, roaming the rain forest in splendid isolation. At certain times of year, however, jaguars are routinely spotted here. In November 2001 visitors saw jaguars, including mothers with cubs, nearly every day of the month on the road to the visitor center. They had to get up early, as the sightings occurred between 5:30 and 6.

In the 1980s, in a misguided attempt by an American naturalist to track their movements, seven jaguars were tagged with radio collars. Special steel cages were built to catch them because they had smashed several wooden ones to pieces. A jaguar would enter a cage, trip a door behind it, and find itself captive. What followed was a conflagration of fur and fury of almost unbelievable proportions. The captured jaguars were so powerful that in their desperate attempts to escape they threw the 300-pound cages around like matchboxes. They sheared off most of their teeth as they tried to bite through the steel. Within a year all seven had died.

Other conservation efforts have been more successful. Today there are an estimated 25–30 jaguars—8–10 adult males, 9–10 adult females, and the rest young animals—spread over about 400 square km (154 square mi). This is the world's largest jaguar population. In contrast, the jaguar was hunted to extinction in the United States by the late 1940s.

Cockscomb Basin has a wonderful array of Belize's wildlife other than jaguars. You might see other cats—pumas, margays, and ocelots—plus coatis, kinkajous, deer, peccaries, and, last but not least, tapirs. Also known as the mountain cow, this shy, curious creature appears to be half horse, half hippo, with a bit of cow and elephant thrown in. Nearly 300 species of birds have been identified in the Cockscomb Basin, including the keel-billed toucan, the king vulture, several species of hawks, and the scarlet macaw.

The reserve boasts Belize's best-maintained system of jungle and mountain trails, most of which lead to at least one outstanding swimming hole. The sanctuary also offers spectacular views of Victoria Peak and the Cockscomb Range. Bring some serious bug spray with you—the reserve is alive with mosquitoes and tiny biting flies called no-see-ums, and wear long-sleeve shirts and long pants. The best times to hike anywhere in Belize are early morning, late afternoon, and early evening, when temperatures are lower and more animals are on the prowl.

You have to register in a hut by the entrance before proceeding several miles to the visitor center. The road winds through dense vegetation—splendid cahune palms, purple mimosas, orchids, and big-leaf plantains—and as you go higher. The marvelous sound of tropical birds, often resembling strange windup toys, grows stronger and stronger. This is definitely four-wheel-drive terrain. You may have to ford several small rivers as well as negotiate deep, muddy ruts. At the end, in a clearing with hibiscus and bougainvillea bushes, you'll find a little office where you can buy maps of the nature trails, along with rest rooms, several picnic tables, cabins, and a campground.

You're not likely to see jaguars here, as they have an exceptionally good senses of smell and hearing. But walking along these 12 well-marked nature trails is a good way to get to know the region. Most are loops of 1–2 km (½–1½ mi), so you can do several in a day. The most strenuous trail takes you up a steep hill, from the top of which there is a magnificent view of the entire Cockscomb Basin. ⊠ *Outside Maya Centre,* ☎ *227/7369.* ☜ *BZ$10.* ☉ *Daily 8–5.*

Dining and Lodging

You can camp in the reserve for BZ$10 a night per person, or for a little more money you can stay in pleasant new rooms in cabins with solar-generated electricity for BZ$44 per person. Book in Belize City through Belize Audubon Society (☎ 223/5004).

$ ⊡ **Tutzil Nah Cottages.** Gregoria Chun and his family, Mopan Maya people who have lived in this area for generations, provide accommodations in simple thatch cabanas. Meals also are available, and the Chuns provide a range of tours to Cockscomb and to Maya sites. ⊠ *Near Maya Centre, Km 13 ½, Southern Hwy.,* ☎ *520/3044,* WEB *www. mayacenter.com. 5 cabanas. No air-conditioning, no room phone, no room TVs. No credit cards.*

Seine Bight

❽ *44 km (27 mi) south of Dangriga.*

Like Placencia, its Creole neighbor to the south, Seine Bight is a sleepy coastal fishing village. It may not be like this for long, though, as Placencia's resorts are stretching north to this Garífuna community. The beach is among the best in Belize, even though garbage sometimes mars the view. Hotels do rake and clean their beachfronts, and several community cleanups have been held to try to solve this problem. All the businesses catering to tourists are off the main road (actually, it's the only road) that leads to Placencia. Like Placencia village, Seine Bight was devastated by Hurricane Iris in October 2001, and many of the simple wooden homes in the village were destroyed. Maya Beach, to the north of Seine Bight, is a collection of homes and hotels along the shore.

Dining and Lodging

$–$$ ✕ **Mango of Maya Beach.** Owner and chef Chris Duffy, a painter from Connecticut, serves something different every day in her tiny thatch-top restaurant. All the entrées are sophisticated by Belizean standards—field greens with Dijon vinaigrette, lobster scampi, and tropical fruit fondue are often on the menu. Lunch and dinner are served daily, but she appreciates your letting her know you're coming. ✉ *Maya Beach, 2 km (1 mi) north of Seine Bight, on main road,* ☎ *614/7023. No credit cards.*

$$$$ ⌂ **Inn at Robert's Grove.** Imagine that you've met an energetic New
★   York couple named Bob and Risa Frackman, and they invite you to stay at their place on a palm-lined stretch of beach. You can play a few games of tennis and swim in one of the beachside pools or in the sea. Their chef, Frank Da Silva, will cook you large breakfasts, pack picnic lunches for boat rides to deserted cayes, and serve dinner in the seaside dining room. This personal attention is what you get at this resort, often full in season. The choicest digs are the suites, featuring verandas overlooking the ocean. On the roof of each building is a whirlpool, also with a view. You can even work out in the new gym. The hotel has its own dive center, with three boats, and a private caye for picnics. ✉ *1 km (½ mi) south of Seine Bight,* ☎ *523/3565; 800/ 565–9757 in the U.S.,* FAX *523/3567,* WEB *www.robertsgrove.com. 20 rooms, 12 suites. Restaurant, fans, some rooms with refrigerators, 2 pools, gym, beach, dive shop, dock, snorkeling, windsurfing, boating, fishing, 2 tennis courts, bars, gift shop, laundry service, travel services. AE, MC, V.*

$$$–$$$$ ✕⌂ **Luba Hati.** From the widow's walk above the central wing of the
★   two-story main house there's a great view of the lagoon in one direction and the ocean in the other. The red-tile roofs and tree-filled courtyard below feel a bit like Umbria—no accident, as owners Franco and Mariuccia Gentile are originally from Italy. No thatch-covered huts here—accommodations are in substantial structures of stone and mortar. Creative touches include staircases supported by giant tree trunks. Each room is decorated with African and Guatemalan fabrics. New beachfront cottages are the most popular digs. You'll eat well here, too; Franco is an excellent chef, and his selection of classic Italian dishes and wines has brought a touch of the dolce vita to Placencia. The staff is happy to arrange tours and other activities. ✉ *1 km (½ mi) south of Seine Bight village,* ☎ *523/3402,* FAX *523/3403,* WEB *www.lubahati.com. 3 cottages, 8 rooms. Restaurant, fans, saltwater pool, beach, dock, snorkeling, fishing, laundry service; no air-conditioning in some rooms, no room TVs. AE, MC, V.*

$$$ ⌂ **Green Parrot.** This cluster of Mennonite-built cottages on a pretty beach is great for families with small kids, as each has a dining area and a fully stocked kitchenette. The sleeping quarters are upstairs in a loftlike space with a pitched wooden roof. One nifty feature is an octagonal-shape wall panel, operated by pulleys, that can be opened for a bedside view of the ocean. Two thatch cabanas have outdoor showers. The beachfront restaurant and bar are decorated with high-back chairs of varnished cane that were made by local craftspeople. It's best if you have a car here, as it's an expensive cab ride from Placencia. ✉

Maya Beach, 6½ km (4 mi) north of Seine Bight, ☎ *523/8009,* FAX *523/ 2488,* WEB *www.greenparrot-belize.com. 6 cabins, 2 cabanas. Restaurant, fans, beach, dock, snorkeling, bar; no air-conditioning, no room phone, no room TVs. AE, MC, V.*

$$$ 🖫 **Nautical Inn.** "It's not for campers" is how owner Ben Ruoti describes this inn, which consists of two-tier octagonal cottages brought here from North Carolina. He and his wife, Janie, are proud of their American-style fixtures, such as firm mattresses and glass-wall showers. The Oar House restaurant serves good Belizean home cooking as well as barbecues right on the beach. The pool is one of the nicest on the peninsula. The inn has some canoes as well as a dive boat to get you to the reef. If you just want to hang out, a pretty beach awaits. Janie will show you her baby iguanas, which she raises and releases. On Wednesday evening the hotel hosts Garífuna drummers and coconut bowling. There's nothing like a milk-filled ball to throw off your game. ✉ *Seine Bight,* ☎ *523–3595; 800/688–0377 in the U.S.,* FAX *523/3594,* WEB *www.nauticalinnbelize.com. 12 rooms. Restaurant, fans, pool, beach, dock, dive shop; no room phones, no TVs in some rooms. AE, MC, V. FAP.*

$$$ 🖫 **Singing Sands.** The six wood-and-thatch cabanas here are small and simply decorated with Guatemalan needlecrafts. They were relocated after Hurricane Iris and now have better views. Singing Sands has its own 25-ft boat for snorkeling, a treat of a beach, a dock with a nice area for swimming, and a pool for those who'd rather take a dip in freshwater. ✉ *Seine Bight,* ☎ *800/649–3007 in U.S.,* WEB *www. singingsands.com. 6 cabanas. Restaurant, fans, refrigerators, pool, beach, dock, dive shop, bar, travel services; no air-conditioning, no room phones, no room TVs. AE, MC, V.*

$$ 🖫 **Barnacle Bill's.** If you're the independent type, this property on Maya Beach has a pair of wooden cottages set among the palm trees about 60 ft from the surf. Each cottage has fully equipped kitchen where you can make your own meals and a private deck. ✉ *23 Maya Beach Way,* ☎ FAX *523/8010,* WEB *www.gotobelize.com/barnacle. 2 cottages. Fans, beach, snorkeling, fishing; no air-conditioning, no room phones, no room TVs. MC, V.*

Shopping

Painter and writer Lola Delgado moved to Seine Bight from Belize City in the late 1980s. Her workshop, **Lola's Art,** displays her cheerful acrylic paintings of local scenes (BZ$100 and up). She also sells hand-painted cards and some of her husband's wood carvings. Espresso and pastries are available. Open 9 AM–10 PM, the workshop is up a flight of steps in a tiny wooden house off the main street, behind the football field.

Placencia

❾ *8 km (5 mi) south of Seine Bight, 52 km (32 mi) south of Dangriga.*

Set in a sheltered half-moon bay with crystal-clear water and almost 5 km (3 mi) of palm-dotted white sand, this fishing village is straight out of a Robert Louis Stevenson novel. Founded by pirates, the community is now inhabited by an extraordinary mélange of peoples. To the west the Cockscomb Range ruffles the tropical sky with its jagged peaks; to the east a line of uninhabited cayes grazes the horizon. From here you can dive along the reef, hike into the jungle, explore the Maya ruins at Lubantuun, or treat yourself to some of the best sportfishing in the country. Once you arrive, you'll probably just want to lie in a hammock with a good book, perhaps getting up long enough to cool off in the waves.

Placencia is so small that it doesn't even have a main street—it has a concrete path just wide enough for two people. Setting off purposefully from the southern end of town, the path meanders through everyone's backyard, passes wooden cottages on stilts overrun with bougainvillea and festooned with laundry, then, as if it had forgotten where it was headed in the first place, peters out abruptly in a little clearing filled with lovely white morning glories. Stroll along the sidewalk, and you've seen the town. If you don't mind it being a little rough around the edges, you'll be utterly enchanted by this rustic village, where the palm trees rustle, the waves lap the shore, and no one is in a hurry.

Along the path are most of the village's quaint inns and palapa-covered cafés, which serve mainly burgers, rice and beans, and a bit of seafood. With the opening of more and more small resorts up the peninsula, Placencia is beginning to compete with Ambergris Caye in the dining category.

The biggest change of all was due to a mean lady named Iris, the hurricane that blasted the peninsula in 2001. The eye came ashore right at Placencia. Few homes or hotels were spared, and many of the old frame structures, especially on the sea side, were blown down or washed away forever. Many little restaurants and businesses, including Omar's and Rasta Pasta, were destroyed. As this chapter was being written, the village was well on its way to rebuilding. In some ways it looks better than ever, but for those who have known it for many years, it will never be quite the same.

Blancaneaux's Turtle Inn, one of the region's top hotels, was completely destroyed by Hurricane Iris. Owner Francis Ford Coppola, who also operates Blancaneaux Lodge in Mountain Pine Ridge, hopes to reopen the seaside inn in late 2002. Reservations may be made through Blancaneaux Lodge.

Dining and Lodging

$$–$$$ ✕ **Pickled Parrot Bar & Grill.** This popular feet-in-the-sand restaurant and bar is in the heart of Placencia. Fresh seafood is the main draw, but owner Wende Bryan also offers pizza on Friday and American-style burgers every day. She has converted the Barracuda and Jaguar Inn to long-term rentals. ⊠ *Off main road, behind Wallen's Market,* ☎ *523/ 3330. AE, MC, V.*

$$$ 🏨 **Rum Point Inn.** When they first came to Placencia, George and
★ Coral Bevier had to cut their way through the undergrowth to find the old colonial-style house they'd bought. Today this beachfront inn is one of southern Belize's best-known resorts. The domelike original buildings—a bit like flying saucers—are all about space and light. Each has a unique set of windows—some are portholes, others geometric patterns cut into the walls. A cluster of two-story buildings have four high-ceilinged rooms with baths equipped with double sinks and Japanese-style tubs. The library has one of Belize's best collections of books on the Maya, piles of novels and magazines, and a raft of CDs and videos. The *Auriga,* the inn's jet-powered dive boat, can anchor beside the most remote caye. Tours and activities abound, including a splendid trip up the Monkey River. ⊠ *2½ km (1½ mi) north of Placencia,* ☎ *523/3239; 800/747–1381 in the U.S.,* FAX *523/3240,* WEB *www.rumpoint.com. 22 rooms. Restaurant, pool, dock, dive shop, snorkeling, travel services; no air-conditioning in some rooms, no room phones, no room TVs. AE, DC, MC, V. FAP, MAP.*

$$–$$$ 🏨 **Kitty's Place.** Kitty's has stood the test of time. It's not the fanciest resort on the peninsula, but it has a barefoot feel that the newer places can't duplicate. On the same beautiful stretch of soft sand as Rum Point Inn, it offers a mixed bag of accommodations, from single rooms to

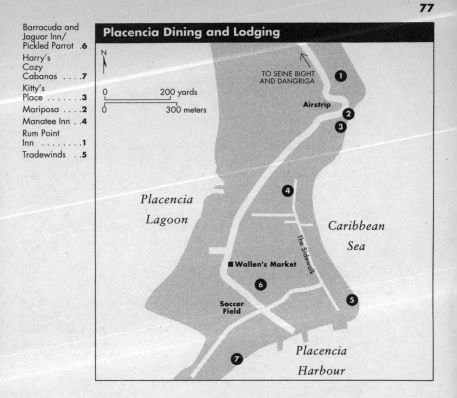

studios. Three newer cottages face the sea, but some of the nicest rooms are in the colonial-style house. The upstairs restaurant, decorated with Bob Marley posters, is lively and serves good local fare. The gift shop sells everything from suntan lotion to Guatemalan crafts. If you need to check your e-mail, Kitty's has one of the village's two Internet cafés. Sea kayaking, diving, and fishing are popular activities, and for BZ$100 per person Kitty will pack you off to a remote caye for the night. ✉ *2½ km (1½ mi) north of Placencia,* ☎ *523/3227,* FAX *523/3226,* WEB *www.kittysplace.com. 3 cabanas, 8 rooms. Restaurant, beach, dive shop, boating, gift shop, travel services; no air-conditioning, no room phones, no room TVs. AE, MC, V.*

$$$ 🖼 **Mariposa.** No sign marks the entrance to this brace of oceanfront suites in a private home just north of Placencia. You only know you're at Mariposa (Spanish for "butterfly") when you see all the wings painted on posts and doorways along the driveway. Low-key is the catchword here. Owners Peter and Marcia Fox let you lounge in your own palapa near the private beach or relax on your secluded veranda. If you like, they'll stock your kitchen with all the groceries you need. Mariposa is quite the opposite of a big full-service beach resort, but it's an appealing spot if you are searching for a home away from home. ✉ *2½ km (1½ mi) north of Placencia,* ☎ *523/4069,* FAX *523/4076,* WEB *www. mariposabelize.com. 2 suites. Fans, beach. D, MC, V.*

$$ 🖼 **Harry's Cozy Cabanas.** Harry Eiler's three varnished-wood cabanas with screened porches are as nice as Harry is, though they don't have quite as much character. Each has a kitchenette with a fridge. The location is quieter than the main part of the village. ✉ *Placencia Harbor, just south of Tentacles,* ☎ *523/3155, harbaks@yahoo.com. Fans, kitchenettes; no air-conditioning, no room phones, no room TVs. No credit cards.*

$–$$ ⊡ **Tradewinds.** If you're yearning for a secluded cottage directly on
★   the beach but don't want to pay a lot of money, then this little colony
        is for you. Five cabins, painted in Caribbean pastels, are small but pleas-
        ant. Rebuilt after Hurricane Iris, they enjoy just about the best loca-
        tion in the village, off to themselves on the beach at the south point of
        the peninsula. The owner is the village's former postmistress, Janice
        Leslie. ⊠ *South Point, Placencia,* ☎ *523/3122. 5 cabins. Fans, refrig-*
        erators, beach, snorkeling; no air-conditioning, no room phones, no
        room TVs. MC, V.

$ ⊡ **Manatee Inn.** Run by a friendly young Czech couple, the Manatee
        Inn offers top value for your money. The rooms on the second floor
        of this wood-frame two-story lodge, new in 2001, are simply fur-
        nished but extremely clean and have hardwood floors and private
        baths. Larger apartments, perfect for families, are on the first floor. The
        hotel isn't on the beach, but it has a freshwater pool. ⊠ *At north end*
        of village, ☎ FAX *523/4083,* WEB *www.manateeinn.com. 6 rooms, 2 apart-*
        ments. Fans, pool; no air-conditioning, no room phones, no TVs in some
        rooms. AE, MC, V.

Outdoor Activities and Sports

FISHING

The fly-fishing on the flats off the cayes east of Placencia is some of
Belize's best. You'll encounter plentiful tarpon—they flurry 10 deep
in the water at times—as well as permit, bonefish, and snook. Most
of the better hotels can arrange guides. If you want a local guide, call
Kevin Modera (☎ 523/3243, WEB www.kevinmodera.com). He has
great information about fishing in Placencia.

SAILING

In late 2001, **Moorings** (⊠ Placencia Harbor, Placencia, ☎ 888/952–
8420 in the U.S.) opened a branch in Placencia. It offers bareboat catamaran charters, with a week's sailing going for around BZ$9,000.

SCUBA DIVING

By the time you get this far south, the reef is as much as 33 km (20
mi) offshore, necessitating boat rides of at least 45 minutes to reach
dive sites. Because this part of the reef has fewer cuts and channels,
it's also more difficult to get out to the seaward side, where you'll find
the best diving. As a result, most diving in this region is done from the
offshore cayes, which have small reefs around them, usually with gently sloping drop-offs of about 80–100 ft. If you want spectacular wall
dives, this isn't the place; you're better off staying in the north or heading out to the atolls. If you want a unique experience, Placencia might
be the place for you. Near Moho Caye, southeast of Placencia, you'll
find brilliant red and yellow corals and sponges that rarely appear elsewhere in Belize.

Diving costs a little more in Placencia than elsewhere. All-day trips,
including two-tank dives and lunch, run BZ$130, including all gear.
Snorkeling is about BZ$80 for a trip that lasts much of the day.

Most of the larger resorts, like Nautical Inn, Inn at Robert's Grove,
and Rum Point Inn, have good dive shops. For been-there-done-that
divers, Rum Point also has a new program that lets you take part in a
marine wildlife survey run out of Key Largo. Divers are asked to fill
out survey forms listing the number of bar-fin blennies or mimic
triplefins they spot, and the information is forwarded to Florida for
cataloging. Brian Young runs the **Seahorse Dive Shop** (☎ 523/3166),
which has a good reputation. For snorkeling trips and gear there's **Ocean
Motion** (☎ 523/3363), near the grocery store.

Placencia and Environs A to Z

To research prices, get advice from other travelers, and book travel arrangements, visit www.fodors.com.

AIR TRAVEL TO AND FROM PLACENCIA AND ENVIRONS
Both Tropic Air and Maya Island Air have regular service to Placencia from Belize City (BZ$118 from the municipal airport, BZ$140 from the international one). You can purchase tickets at some of the region's resorts, such as Kitty's and Inn at Robert's Grove. The airstrip is about 3 km (2 mi) north of the center of Placencia, so you'll probably want to take a taxi (BZ$10 from the center of town) if your hotel doesn't provide a shuttle.
➤ AIRLINES AND CONTACTS: **Maya Island Air** (✉ Placencia airstrip, ☎ 523/3475, WEB www.mayaairways.com). **Tropic Air** (✉ Placencia airstrip, ☎ 523/3410, WEB www.tropicair.com).

BUS TRAVEL TO AND FROM PLACENCIA AND ENVIRONS
For routes south to Belmopan, Dangriga, and Punta Gorda, try Southern Transport, a successor to Z-Line. The main bus stop in Placencia is near the Shell station. The bus station in Dangriga is seven blocks south of town on the main road, near the Texaco and Shell stations.
➤ BUS INFORMATION: **Southern Transport** (✉ 3 Havana St., Dangriga, ☎ 522/2160).

CAR RENTAL
Budget and other rental agencies in Belize City will deliver a car to Placencia for a fee of around BZ$130.

CAR TRAVEL
To get to Placencia, head southeast from Belmopan on the Hummingbird Highway. Once a potholed nightmare, the thoroughfare is now the best road in Belize, if not in all of Central America. It's also the most scenic route in Belize. On your right rise the jungle-covered Maya Mountains, largely free of signs of human habitation except for the occasional field of corn or beans.

If you want to drive directly from Belize City to Placencia, take the turnoff at Mile 30 on the Western Highway for Dangriga and the south. The 60-km (36-mi) Manatee Road is unpaved—dusty in dry weather, sometimes flooded after rains—but it saves about an hour on the drive south. The Southern Highway is now beautifully paved from Dangriga to Independence south of Placencia, and another 42 km (25 mi) is paved from Punta Gorda north. Eventually the 50 km (30 mi) of remaining dirt on the Southern Highway will be paved, according to the Belize government. From the Southern Highway to Placencia most of the 42 km (25 mi) is unpaved and can be treacherous after rains, even for four-wheel-drive vehicles.

EMERGENCIES
Although Placencia now has a nurse, an acupuncturist, a part-time chiropractor, and a natural healer, for serious medical attention you should go to Dangriga or Independence.
➤ HOSPITALS: **Dangriga Regional Hospital** (✉ Stann Creek District Hwy., Dangriga, ☎ 52/2078). **John Price Memorial Clinic** (✉ Independence, ☎ 62/2167).

HEALTH
Malaria and dengue fever are present in the region's more remote reaches. The water supply in Dangriga is not dependable, so make sure to drink bottled water. Placencia and Hopkins have safe, treated water.

MAIL AND SHIPPING

The Placencia post office is on the second floor of a wooden building at the south end of the sidewalk. It is usually open 8:30–noon and 1–4 weekdays.

➤ POST OFFICES: **Placencia** (✉ South end of sidewalk, ☎ 62/3104).

MONEY MATTERS

In Placencia, Atlantic Bank is open weekdays 8–noon. There are no ATMs in town that accept foreign-issued cards in Placencia. Amazingly, the Barclays Bank in Dangriga has an ATM that (usually) accepts foreign cards.

➤ BANKS: **Atlantic Bank** (✉ at end of main road, Placencia, ☎ 523/3386). **Barclays Bank** (✉ Commerce St., Dangriga, ☎ 522/2015).

TAXIS

If you need a ride to the airport in Dangriga, call Neal's Taxi. Fare from downtown to the airstrip at the north end of town should be about BZ$6. In Placencia taxis are more expensive, given the relatively short distances involved. It's BZ$30–BZ$40 one way from Placencia to Maya Beach, BZ$10 from downtown to the airstrip.

➤ TAXI COMPANIES: **Neal's Taxi** (✉ 1 St. Vincent St., Dangriga, ☎ 522/3309).

TOUR OPERATORS

Many tour guides and operators offer dive and snorkel trips to Laughing Bird, Ranguana, or other cayes, wildlife tours to Monkey River, and excursions to Maya ruins such as Nim Li Punit or Lubaantun. For the more adventurous traveler, Toadal Adventures has excellent biking, hiking, and kayaking tours.

➤ TOUR COMPANIES: **Toadal Adventures Belize** (✉ Point Placencia, Placencia, ☎ 253/3207, debanddave@btl.net).

VISITOR INFORMATION

The Placencia office of the Belize Tourism Industry Association is in a building near the gas station at the south end of the village. The agency publishes the *Placencia Breeze,* an informative monthly newspaper. Placencia has a very helpful Web site listing all accommodations, restaurants, and bars, www.placencia.com. Hopkins has an interesting Web site put together by local people, www.hopkinsbelize.com.

➤ TOURIST INFORMATION: **Belize Tourism Industry Association** (✉ Point Placencia, Placencia, ☎ 523/4045).

TOLEDO AND THE DEEP SOUTH

For many years ill-maintained roads, spotty communications, and the country's highest annual rainfall—as much as 160 inches—kept Belize's southernmost region off-limits to all but the most adventurous of travelers. The precipitation hasn't changed (you'll need boots and an umbrella in the rainy season), but with improvements to the Southern Highway—the 40 km (24 mi) from Dangriga south to Independence have been paved—and the opening of new lodges and hotels, the riches of the Toledo district are finally becoming accessible. It's rather like the Cayo district was 10 years ago, except that the flora and fauna are even more dramatic.

Toledo is the only part of Belize that has what can truly be described as a rain forest, and the canopy of trees hides a plethora of wildlife, including jaguars, margays, and tapirs, as well as a wide variety of tropical birds. The area's rich Maya heritage is only just being unearthed, including a major site currently being excavated by a team from the

National Geographic Foundation with help from the Royal Engineers. By all accounts, it dwarfs even Caracol.

Toledo does not have good beaches: the waters of the Gulf of Honduras are invariably muddy from silt deposited by the numerous rivers flowing down from the Maya Mountains. But the cayes off the coast are well worth exploring. The closest are the Snake cayes; farther out are the Sapadilla cayes, the largest of which is Hunting Caye. A horseshoe-shape bay at the eastern end of the caye has beaches of white coral where turtles nest in late summer.

Hurricane Iris swept across Toledo in 2001. It did little damage to Punta Gorda, but it wreaked havoc on the thatch homes of Maya villages in southern Toledo, leaving 13,000 people homeless. The storm destroyed an estimated 16,000 acres of bananas, rice, corn, and other crops and blew down tens of thousands of trees, including many mature tropical hardwoods. With government and private help, Toledo residents have rebuilt their homes, and the tropical climate of southern Belize quickly regenerated the vegetation. Visitors today may not even notice that one of the worst storms in the country's history blew through here.

Punta Gorda

10 *164 km (102 mi) south of Placencia.*

Most journeys south begin in the region's administrative center, Punta Gorda. Founded in 1867 by immigrants from the United States and settled by missionaries, Punta Gorda once boasted 12 sugar estates, each with its own mill. By 1910, however, the town had almost been swallowed by the jungle. Its fortunes revived after World War II, when Britain built an important military base here, but when that closed in 1994, the linchpin of the local economy had been yanked out. With tourist dollars starting to flow, P.G. (as it's affectionately known) is starting to pick up again, but the town maintains a frontier atmosphere. Don't expect many tourist services, either. When you ask at your hotel for ice, you may get a blank stare. Restaurant food ranges from fair to truly awful. In keeping with its evangelical origins, many of the visitors you see are missionaries who vie for the souls of the Maya by offering them free dentistry or medicine. But on market days, Wednesday and Saturday, the town comes to life with Guatemalan vendors, who pack the downtown area with colorful fruit and vegetable stands.

Dining and Lodging

$—$$ ✕ **Punta Caliente.** This is definitely the place for hearty local fare. The cheerfully homey restaurant has Garífuna relics mounted on the walls—the owner is a scholar of Garífuna customs—and the blue plate specials are the typical Belizean mix of fish and chicken dishes, heavy on the rice and beans. They're prepared by Garífuna grannies who really know how to make your mouth water. In good weather you can sit at one of the two tables outside. ⊠ *108 José Marina Nuñez St., at Victoria St.,* ☎ *722/2561. No credit cards.*

$–$$ ✕ **Exile 360.** Fill up on fried chicken, grilled fish, beans and rice, and other Belizean dishes at this restaurant and bar in a thatch palapa. It's on the north side of town just before the Joe Taylor Bridge. ⊠ *Front St., north of Seafront Inn,* ☎ *722/2718. No credit cards.*

$$ 🏠 **Sea Front Inn.** The opening of this four-story lodging helped draw tourism to Punta Gorda. With its pitched roofs and stone-and-wood facade, it looks like a ski lodge in the Swiss Alps. It looks directly over the Gulf of Honduras, with the green humps of the Saddle Back Mountains as a backdrop, so the top floors command especially fine views.

Inside are a dozen single and double rooms and two suites with kitch-enettes. Each is unique, furnished with Belizean hardwoods. A third-floor restaurant (now open only for breakfast) has a roof supported by rosewood tree trunks etched with Maya carvings. At the end of the din-ing room are windows lined with stools where you can sit with a drink and look out to sea. If you're lucky, you'll spot a pod of passing por-poises. ✉ *Front St., Punta Gorda,* ☎ ℻ *722/2682,* 𝚆𝙴𝙱 *www.belizenet. com. 12 rooms, 2 suites, 4 apartments. Restaurant, fans, snorkeling, travel services; no room phones. MC, V.*

$ 🏠 **Nature's Way Guest House.** An assortment of rooms for travelers on a budget are found in this ramshackle house near the water. Like a hostel, it's a meeting place for travelers exploring the frontier or head-ing on to Guatemala or Honduras. Choose from one of the very, very simple rooms or a bunk in one of the dorm-style rooms. The break-fast-only menu includes tofu, yogurt, and granola. The owner has been in P.G. for quite a while and is glad to share his strong opinions on Toledo and just about anything else. ✉ *83 Front St., Punta Gorda,* ☎ *722/2119. 17 rooms without bath. Restaurant, travel services; no air-conditioning, no room phones, no room TVs. No credit cards.*

$ 🏠 **T.E.A.** The Toledo Ecotourism Association arranges stays in one of 10 participating Maya and Q'eqchí villages. You stay in a simple but clean guest house, then visit Maya homes for breakfast, lunch, and din-ner. The English-speaking staff will arrange vegetarian or special meals. During the day there are walks to the nearby ruins or to waterfalls that empty into shimmering pools. For some this is a rare opportunity to learn about a culture. For others chickens running in and out may be a bit too authentic an experience. ✉ *Front St., Punta Gorda,* ☎ *722/ 2096,* ℻ *722/2199, ttea@btl.net. Hiking; no air-conditioning, no room phones, no room TVs. No credit cards.*

Outdoor Activities and Sports

FISHING

For bonefish and tarpon head to the estuary flats at the end of the Río Grande. **Fish & Fun** (☎ 722/2670), operated by George Coleman and Ovel Leonardo, runs snorkeling and fly-fishing trips to nearby rivers and to the cayes. The **Sea Front Inn** (☎ ℻ 722/2682) can provide good local guides.

SCUBA DIVING

This far south the reef has pretty much broken up, but individual cayes have their own small reef systems. The best of the bunch is at the Sapodilla cayes, which have great wall dives. The only drawback is that they are 64 km (40 mi) off the coast: a day's dive trip will cost BZ$350 per person. **Sea Hunt Adventures** (☎ 722/2467) can arrange diving, snorkeling, and fishing trips.

The Maya Heartland

Drive a few miles out of town, and you'll find yourself in the heart-land of the Maya people. Half the population of Toledo is Maya, a far higher proportion than any other region, and you'll find the people here are more cohesive and more political than anywhere else in Belize. The Toledo Maya Cultural Council has created an ambitious network of Maya-run guest houses, and in 1995 it initiated the Mayan Mapping Project. By collating oral history and evidence of ancient Maya settle-ments, the project hopes to secure rights to land that the Maya have occupied for centuries but that the Belizean government has seen fit to cede to multinational logging companies.

The Maya divide into two groups: Mopan Maya and Q'eqchí-speak-ing peoples from the Guatemalan highlands. Most of the latter are re cent arrivals, refugees from repression and overpopulation. Each group tends to keep to itself, living in separate villages and preserving unique traditions. The village of **San Antonio,** a market town 56 km (35 mi) west of Punta Gorda, is the second-largest town in Toledo. It was settled by people from the Guatemalan village of San Luis, who revere their former patron saint. The village church, built of stones carted off from surrounding Maya ruins, has a stained-glass window donated by another city with a connection to the saint: St. Louis, Missouri. The people of San Antonio have not forgotten their ancient heritage, though, and each year on June 13 they take to the streets for a festival that dates back to pre-Columbian times. Like other parts of Toledo, San Antonio lost many of its homes and other buildings to the winds of Hurricane Iris in 2001.

A little farther west is the Q'eqchí village of **San Pedro Columbia,** a cheerful cluster of brightly painted buildings and thatch houses. One of the most eye-catching is a raspberry-red grocery called the People Little Store. On the way to San Pedro Columbia, don't miss **Blue Creek,** a beautiful stretch of river dotted with turquoise swimming holes. Unfortunately, many of the mature hardwood trees were felled by Hurricane Iris. A path up the riverbank leads to a series of dramatic caves. The Hokeb Ha Cave is fairly easy to explore on your own, but others should be visited only with a local guide. International Zoological Expeditions, a Connecticut-based student travel organization, has established a **jungle lodge** (✉ 210 Washington St., Sherborn, MA 01770, ☎ 508/655–1461; 800/548–5843 in the U.S., FAX 508/655–4445) at Blue Creek, with seven rustic cabanas and a restaurant. Don't swim in the river at night—a poisonous snake called the fer-de-lance likes to take nocturnal dips.

Three of Toledo's major Maya sites have already been excavated: Nim Li Punit, Uxbenka, and Lubaantun. **Nim Li Punit,** a late-classic site, was discovered in 1976. Twenty-five stelae were unearthed, including one 30 ft tall, the largest ever found in Belize. In 1986 a royal tomb was excavated. Sadly, few of these artifacts remain. There's an informative visitor center on the premises. ✉ *37 km (22 mi) northwest of Punta Gorda,* ✺ *BZ$5.*

Lubaantun, which lies beyond the village of San Pedro Columbia, is also a late-classic site. It was discovered in 1924 by German archaeologist Thomas Gann, who gave it a name that means "place of fallen stones." Lubaantun must have been an awe-inspiring sight: on top of a conical hill, with views to the sea in one direction and the Maya Mountains in the other, its stepped layers of white-plaster stone would have towered above the jungle like a wedding cake. No one knows exactly what function the structures served, but the large number of miniature masks and whistles found here suggests it was a center of ceramic production. The trio of ball courts and the central plaza with tiered seating for 10,000 spectators give rise to images of a Maya Madison Square Garden.

In the last century, Lubaantun became the scene of the biggest hoax in modern archaeology. After it was excavated in the 1920s, a British adventurer named F. A. Mitchell-Hedges claimed to have stumbled on what became known as the Crystal Skull. Mitchell-Hedges described the incident in a potboiler, *Danger, My Ally,* in 1951. According to the book, the Crystal Skull was found under an altar at Lubaantun by his daughter Anna. Mitchell-Hedges portrayed himself as a serious archaeologist and explorer: in truth, he was a magazine hack who was later exposed in England as a fraud and a grave robber. The Crystal Skull made good copy. Also known as the Skull of Doom, it was supposedly used by Maya high priests to zap anyone they did not care for. Mitchell-Hedges claimed it was 3,600 years old and had taken 150 years to fashion by rubbing a block of pure rock crystal with sand. A similar skull, in the possession of the British Museum, shows signs of having been manufactured with a dentist's drill. Anna Mitchell-Hedges, who today lives in Ontario, has promised to one day reveal the secret. So far, she has adamantly refused to allow the Crystal Skull to be tested and has denied all requests by the Belizean government to return it. ⊠ *Northwest of Punta Gorda,* ⊡ *BZ$5.*

Dining and Lodging

$$$ ⊞ **Fallen Stones Butterfly Ranch & Jungle Resort.** The view from the
★   hardwood terrace behind the restaurant at this excellent lodge is one of the best in Belize: a 360-degree treetop panorama across the jungle to the inky outline of the Maya Mountains. The accommodations, in cabanas laid out on a steep hillside swathed in heliconia, are not quite so spectacular, but the surroundings are so breathtaking it doesn't much matter. The rooms are on the small side, and the baths are modest. Two cabanas have small verandas. Owner Ray Halberd, a delightfully whimsical Welshman who breaks into song at the slightest provocation, spent his life working as an agricultural botanist in such remote corners of the empire as the Gilbert and Ellis islands. His lifelong dream was to breed butterflies, and Fallen Stones, which opened in 1992, was where he achieved it. There are often as many as 3,000 blue morphos on hand, creating a kaleidoscope of flashing neon blue. From the lodge you can arrange trips to nearby Lubaantun or head off on a three-hour jungle trek. Then it's back to the lamplighted restaurant for spicy beef stew with dumplings, chicken soufflé, or coconut blancmange with prune sauce. ⊠ *Between San Pedro Columbia and San Miguel,* ☎ ⒻⒶⓍ *722/2167,* ⓌⒺⒷ *www.global-travel.co.uk/fallen.htm. 8 rooms. Restaurant, hiking, bar; no air-conditioning, no room phones, no room TVs. MC, V.*

Toledo and the Deep South A to Z

To research prices, get advice from other travelers, and book travel arrangements, visit www.fodors.com.

AIR TRAVEL TO AND FROM TOLEDO AND THE DEEP SOUTH

Both Maya Island Air and Tropic Air fly south to Punta Gorda from both the municipal (BZ$152 one-way) and international (BZ$177 one-way) airports. The Punta Gorda airstrip is on the west side of town; from the town square, walk four blocks west on Prince Street.

➤ AIRLINES AND CONTACTS: **Maya Island Air** (⊠ Punta Gorda airstrip, ☎ 722/2856). **Tropic Air** (⊠ Prince St., ☎ 722/2008).

BOAT AND FERRY TRAVEL

Several water taxi services, including Requena, provide daily boats, usually departing around 9 AM from Punta Gorda, to Puerto Barrios and Livingston, Guatemala. Fares are BZ$20–BZ$25.

➤ CONTACTS: **Requena** (⊠ 12 Front St., Punta Gorda, ☎ 722/2070).

BUS TRAVEL TO AND FROM TOLEDO AND THE DEEP SOUTH

For routes south to Dangriga, Placencia, and Punta Gorda, try Southern Transport. To Punta Gorda it's a nine-hour ride that costs around BZ$22. Road conditions are unpredictable in the rainy season, which runs from June to September.

➤ BUS INFORMATION: **Southern Transport** (⊠ Main St., Punta Gorda, ☎ 522/2160).

CAR TRAVEL

The journey to Punta Gorda via the Hummingbird and Southern highways used to be a chiropractor's nightmare: a bone-shuddering marathon via Belmopan, Dangriga, and Big Creek across some of the worst roads in Belize. The completion of paving of the Hummingbird Highway and improvements to the Southern Highway have made the trip much shorter and much more pleasant. At press time the Southern Highway sections from Punta Gorda to Big Falls, at the south end, and from Dangriga to Independence and Big Creek, at the north end, are paved, with work continuing on the remain 50 km (30 mi).

EMERGENCIES

➤ HOSPITALS: **Punta Gorda Hospital** (✉ Main St. at south end of town, ☎ 722/2026).

HEALTH

Malaria is a problem in southern Belize. If you are going to spend any time in the bush, discuss with your physician whether to use chloroquine or other malaria prophylaxes. The municipal water supply in Punta Gorda is treated and is safe to drink. In rural areas the water is often from community wells; here you should drink bottled water.

MAIL AND SHIPPING

The Punta Gorda post office is on Front Street across from the ferry dock. Hours are 8:30–noon and 1–4:30 weekdays.
➤ POST OFFICES: **Punta Gorda post office** (✉ Front St., ☎ 722/2087).

SAFETY

Punta Gorda is a safe, friendly town. Using the normal precautions, you should have no problem walking around town, even after dark. The nearby Maya villages are also relatively free of crime. Guatemala's Caribbean coast, just a short bus or boat ride away, has a reputation for lawlessness, which occasionally can spill over into Toledo.

TOUR OPERATORS

Operating out of Punta Gorda, Clive Genus is an incredibly pleasant tour operator with whom you'll enjoy jostling around on bumpy roads leading to the ancient ruins.
➤ TOUR COMPANIES: **Clive Genus** (✉ 30 Wahima Alley, Punta Gorda, ☎ 722/2068).

VISITOR INFORMATION

The office of the Belize Tourism Industry Association on Front St., near the ferry dock, is open Tuesday–Saturday 9–noon and 1–4:30, Sunday 9–noon. It has brochures and information on local hotels, tours, and bus schedules.
➤ TOURIST INFORMATION: **Belize Tourism Information Center** (✉ Front St., ☎ 722/2531).

BELIZE A TO Z

To research prices, get advice from other travelers, and book travel arrangements, visit www.fodors.com.

AIR TRAVEL TO AND FROM BELIZE

The main airlines serving Belize from the United States are American, with daily flights from Miami and Dallas–Fort Worth; Continental, which has daily nonstop flights from Houston; and Taca, which has nonstop flights from Houston. It is often cheaper to fly into the Mexican city of Cancún, but the journey to Belize will take a full day away from each end of your Belize vacation. AeroCaribe no longer flies to Belize City from Cancún.

Planes on domestic routes are usually single- or twin-engine island hoppers. Depending on where you depart, you may endure several take-offs and landings (a flight from Punta Gorda to San Pedro, for example, will likely include three stops.) Most domestic flights leave from the municipal airport, near the center of Belize City, which is easier to reach than the international airport. Domestic flights from the municipal airport tend to be cheaper than from the international one. The main carriers are Tropic Air and Maya Island Air, both of which fly to Ambergris Caye and Caye Caulker, as well as Dangriga, Placencia, Corozal, and Punta Gorda, and Santa Elena in Guatemala.

➤ AIRLINES AND CONTACTS: **Maya Island Airways** (✉ Belize Municipal Airport, Belize City, ☎ 226–3838, 800/225–6732 in the U.S., WEB www.mayaairways.com). **Tropic Air** (✉ San Pedro, ☎ 226/2012, 800/ 422–3435 in the U.S., WEB www.tropicair.com).

AIRPORTS AND TRANSFERS
Philip S. W. Goldson International Airport is 14 km (9 mi) north of the city. Taxis to town cost BZ$35. The Belize City Municipal Airport has flights to San Pedro and down the coast to Dangriga, Placencia, and Punta Gorda.

➤ AIRPORTS: **Belize City Municipal Airport** (✉ North of Belize City). **Philip S. W. Goldson International Airport** (✉ Ladyville).

BUS TRAVEL TO AND FROM BELIZE
There is daily bus service from the Guatemalan and Mexican borders. Buses cross from Chetumal, Mexico, and stop in Corozal, Belize, where you can catch another bus to Belize City or a plane to San Pedro. Buses from Guatemala (via Flores) stop in the border town of Melchor de Mencos. Cross the border and take a bus or taxi to San Ignacio, 13 km (8 mi) away, or continue on the bus to Belize City.

BUS TRAVEL WITHIN BELIZE
Although there is no rail system in Belize, there is fairly extensive bus service by private companies. The quality of the buses and the roads on which they travel vary considerably. Novelo's, the dominant carrier in the country, especially on the Western and Northern highways, has acquired several competing companies. Because of consolidations in the industry that created Novelo's and other companies, you'll find that schedules are in flux. However, buses are still extremely cheap (about BZ$5–BZ$22 from Belize City to other points in the country) and remain an excellent way to experience Belize as the Belizeans do. Outside the cities you can flag them down like cabs, and the driver will let you off whenever you want. Expect to ride on old U.S. school buses or retired Greyhound buses. On the Northern and Western highways there are a few express buses with air-conditioning and other comforts; these cost a few dollars more.

Novelo's buses stop in Corozal, Belmopan, and San Ignacio and go north to Orange Walk and Corozal, while Southern Transport covers Dangriga and Punta Gorda.

➤ BUS INFORMATION: **Novelo's** (✉ W. Collet Canal, Belize City, ☎ 227/ 2025, novelo@btl.net). **Southern Transport** (✉ 3 Havana St., Dangriga, ☎ 522/2211).

CAR RENTAL
Belize City now has branches of most international car-rental agencies, as well as several local operators. Prices vary from company to com-

pany, but all are high by U.S. standards (BZ$120–BZ$230 per day). Some cars rented out by the local operators—V-8 gas-guzzlers driven down from Texas—will cost you dearly for gas alone, whereas the international agencies have modern, dependable fleets. A four-wheel-drive Suzuki with unlimited mileage from Budget costs about BZ$150 per day. Off-season rates are lower. For serious safaris a four-wheel-drive vehicle (preferably a Land Rover or an Isuzu Trooper) is invaluable. Some major hotels offer all-terrain vehicles with guides for about BZ$400 per day.

CAR TRAVEL

Belize is one of the few countries left in the Americas where off-road conditions are still the norm on many of the major roads. Getting somewhere is never a question of simply going from A to B; there are always a bit of adventure involved and a few detours to Y and Z.

Only the Northern Highway (to Orange Walk and Corozal), the Western Highway (to Belmopan and San Ignacio), and the Hummingbird Highway (from Belmopan to Dangriga) are fully paved. The Southern Highway is now about three-fourths of the way along, with only about 50 km (30 mi) still unpaved. Once you get off the main highways, distances don't mean that much—it's time that counts. You might have only 20 km (12½ mi) to go, but it can take you a grueling 90 minutes. If you bring your own car, you'll need to buy insurance in Belize.

GASOLINE

Unleaded premium gasoline costs around BZ$5.50 per gallon. There are modern service stations, even a few open 24 hours, in Belize City and in most of the north and west. In remote areas fill up whenever you see a gas station.

EMBASSIES AND CONSULATES

There are no Australian or New Zealand embassies or consulates in Central America.
➤ CONTACTS: **British High Commission** (✉ Embassy Square, Belmopan, ☎ 822/2146). **Canadian Consulate** (✉ 29 Southern Foreshore, Belize City, ☎ 223/1060). **U.S. Embassy** (✉ 29 Gabourel La., Belize City, ☎ 227/7161).

MONEY MATTERS

The greenback is accepted everywhere in Belize, so if you are carrying U.S. dollars you do not need to exchange money. Other currencies, including Canadian dollars, are generally not accepted in Belize. If you need to exchange another currency, you can do so at one of the five banks operating in Belize—Alliance Bank, Atlantic Bank, Bank of Nova Scotia, Barclays, and Belize Bank. Most banks have their main offices on Albert Street in Belize City, with branches in larger towns around the country. Should you exchange U.S. dollars at a bank, expect to be charged a 1%–2% fee.

The money exchange situation in Belize is in a state of flux. In early 2002 there was a minor currency crisis because of a shortage of U.S. dollars. Businesses in Belize had a difficult time getting greenbacks to pay for their imported goods, and there was talk of devaluation of the Belize dollar. The Belize government also was considering authorizing private money exchange offices. As of this writing, only banks are supposed to exchange currency, although private money changers have traditionally operated in Belize, especially at border areas. These entrepreneurs deal for the most part in U.S. and Belize dollars and either Mexican pesos or Guatemalan quetzales, not Canadian or European currencies. They often offer better rates than the usual BZ$2 for each U.S. dollar. In the recent past this gray-market rate has ranged from around BZ$2.05 to BZ$2.30 to the U.S. dollar.

TOUR OPERATORS

Many tour companies stick to their local area, but several venture farther afield. One of the best is Discovery Expeditions, which has several offices in Belize City hotels. The staff is friendly and well informed and can help you arrange expeditions virtually anywhere in the country. Maya Travel Services, in Belize City, is knowledgeable about the country and can book hotels, tours, and transportation. S&L Travel Services, in Belize City, is also reputable. Amigo Travel, the largest tour company on Ambergris Caye, offers both mainland and island tours and snorkeling excursions.

➤ TOUR COMPANIES: **Amigo Travel** (✉ Barrier Reef Dr., San Pedro, ☎ 226/2180). **Discovery Expeditions** (✉ 5916 Manatee Dr., Buttonwood Bay, Belize City, ☎ 223/0748, FAX 23/0750). **Maya Travel Services** (✉ Belize City Municipal Airport, Belize City, ☎ 223/1623). **S&L Travel Services** (✉ 91 N. Front St., Belize City, ☎ 227/7593).

3 GUATEMALA

With incomparable ancient ruins, graceful colonial churches, and colorful highland markets, Guatemala is the center of the Maya heartland. This landscape is known for its rushing white-water rivers and expansive stretches of rain forest that hide spider monkeys, toucans, and iguanas among massive mahogany trees draped with mosses, ferns, and rare orchids.

Updated by
Gregory
Benchwick

C APTIVATING TRAVELERS FOR CENTURIES, Guatemala has lost none of its charm. From conquistador Pedro de Alvarado, who stopped between battles to marvel at the beauty of Lago Atitlán, to writer Aldous Huxley, who waxed poetic on the same lake's shores centuries later, this intricate jewel of a country has intrigued and inspired its share of foreigners. In a matter of days you can walk the cobblestone streets of a colonial capital, barter with indigenous people who still worship the gods of the ancient Maya, and explore the meandering trails of a tropical rain forest.

Perched at the top of the Central American isthmus, Guatemala is divided into a number of distinct regions: the Pacific Lowlands, the Western Highlands, the central Verapaces, the Caribbean Lowlands, and the northern jungle region of El Petén. With a territory of just 108,900 square km (42,046 square mi), Guatemala has 19 ecosystems encompassing palm-lined beaches, luxuriant cloud forests, rugged mountain ranges, scrubby desert valleys, and rain forests chock-full of tropical flora and fauna.

Guatemala's landscape may be fascinating, but its population of more than 12.5 million people is even more compelling. Half are of indigenous descent, and though they have adopted some of the European customs forced on their ancestors, they remain some of the region's most dedicated protectors of ancient culture.

All the indigenous peoples are Maya, but they comprise at least 22 ethnicities, differentiated by sometimes subtle distinctions in language, dress, and customs. The other half of the population is divided among mestizos (Spanish-speaking descendants of Spaniards and Indians), Garífunas (descendents of escaped African slaves), and those of predominantly Spanish ancestry who have maintained their imported bloodline and their lease on power. Though Spanish is Guatemala's official language, it's the mother tongue of only about half the population. Many people in the highlands speak one of the many indigenous languages, while some people along the coast speak Garífuna.

Guatemala's recent history has largely been the story of a struggle for land and political equality in the face of military rule. In 1944 Jorge Ubico, the last of the old-time strongmen, was deposed in a peaceful revolution. Elected in his place was schoolteacher Juan José Arévalo, who promised education and agrarian reform. Arévalo was succeeded by Jacobo Arbenz, who dared to expropriate a small part of the vast holdings of the United Fruit Company. The United States, anxious to protect national interests, sponsored a successful coup in 1954. The move effectively closed the door on democratic elections for nearly 30 years.

By the late 1970s guerrilla groups had begun to tap into the long-held grievances of Guatemala's indigenous peoples. The right-wing government unleashed a brutal campaign not just against the guerrillas, but against civilians. During the worst years of the violence—the "scorched-earth" campaigns of the early 1980s—some 100,000 people were tortured and killed as the military razed hundreds of villages in an effort to flush out a handful of guerrillas. Negotiations between the government and the guerrillas, monitored by the United Nations, began in 1990. A peace accord finally put an end to the 36-year civil war in 1996.

Guatemala has entered a period of slow recovery. With peace has come increased international investment, and evidence of this economic growth appears throughout the country in the form of new roads, better communication systems, and more electrical power reaching isolated regions. All these improvements have made the country much more attractive to visitors. There are still problems to overcome, such as a rise in robberies and other violent crimes. But despite its troubles, Guatemala is clearly moving in the right direction.

Pleasures and Pastimes

Archaeological Treasures

The department of El Petén, much of which is covered with tropical rain forest, was the heart of the ancient Maya empire. Only a fraction of the estimated 1,500 ruins have been explored, and even those that have been excavated remain surrounded, if not actually covered, by vegetation. Aside from Tikal, traveling to the archaeological sites often involves maneuvering a four-wheel-drive vehicle down muddy roads. More isolated sites require taking a boat, riding a mule, or hacking your way through the trees. No matter how you get there, it's likely to be an adventure.

Caving

An awesome selection of caves awaits subterranean explorers. Aktun Kan, in El Petén, is very easy to reach. In Naj Tunich, near Poptún, you'll find carbon frescoes painted by the ancient Maya. The Candelaria River, in Alta Verapaz, passes through a series of caverns only accessible by water a few months of the year. Many other caves remain largely unexplored.

Dining

The basis of Guatemalan food is corn, usually eaten as a tortilla, as a tamale, or on the cob. Black beans accompany most meals, either whole beans cooked in a broth or mashed and refried. Meats are often served in *caldos* (stews) or cooked in a spicy chili sauce. Thin and tender *lomito,* a popular cut of beef, is on the menu in most restaurants. In rural areas you might also see *venado* (venison) and *tepezcuintle* (a large rodent) on the menu. The most popular fish is the delicious *robálo,* known elsewhere as snook. Along the coast you'll find *tapado,* a coconut stew made with plantains, shrimp, crab, and fish. The *queso fundido* (melted cheese with condiments and tortillas), which is sometimes served as an appetizer, is a good choice for light eaters.

CATEGORY	COST*
$$$$	over 100 quetzales (over US$13)
$$$	70 quetzales–100 quetzales (US$9–US$13)
$$	40 quetzales–70 quetzales (US$5–US$9)
$	under 40 quetzales (under US$5)

per person for a main course at dinner

Lodging

Guatemala now has a wide range of lodging options, from suites at luxurious high-rises to stark rooms in budget hotels. Guatemala City has the most options, but the much more appealing city of Antigua is a better base for exploring the country. Rooms often fill up on weekends, so make reservations well in advance. Panajachel has the widest selection of accommodations in the highlands, and Chichicastenango and Quetzaltenango can claim some creditable lodgings. Most remote villages offer only spartan lodgings, if any at all.

CATEGORY	COST*
$$$$	over 600 quetzales (over US$77)
$$$	360 quetzales–600 quetzales (US$46–US$77)
$$	160 quetzales–360 quetzales (US$20–US$46)
$	under 160 quetzales (under US$20)

All prices are for a standard double room, excluding tax.

Guatemala

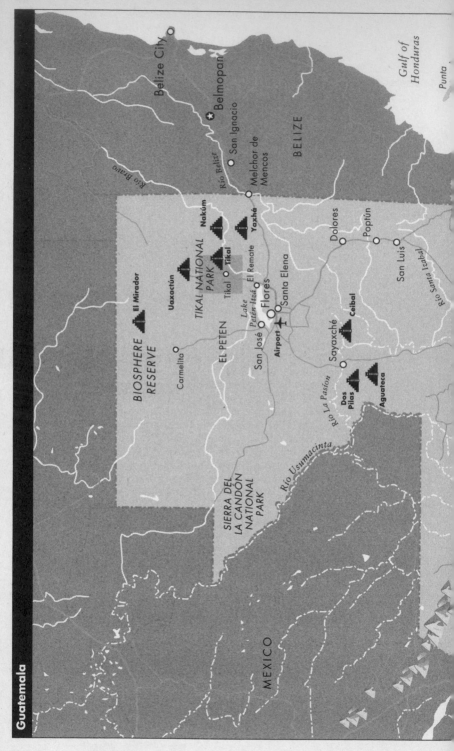

Belize City

Belmopan

San Ignacio

Río Belize

Melchor de Mencos

BELIZE

Gulf of Honduras

Punta

Río Bravo

Dolores

Poptún

San Luis

Río Santa Izabal

Nakúm

Yaxhá

Tikal

TIKAL NATIONAL PARK

El Remate

Tikal

Uaxactún

Santa Elena

El Mirador

BIOSPHERE RESERVE

EL PETÉN

Lake Petén Itzá

Flores

San José

Airport

Ceibal

Carmelita

Sayaxché

Río La Pasión

Dos Pilas

Aguateca

SIERRA DEL LA CANDÓN NATIONAL PARK

Río Usumacinta

MEXICO

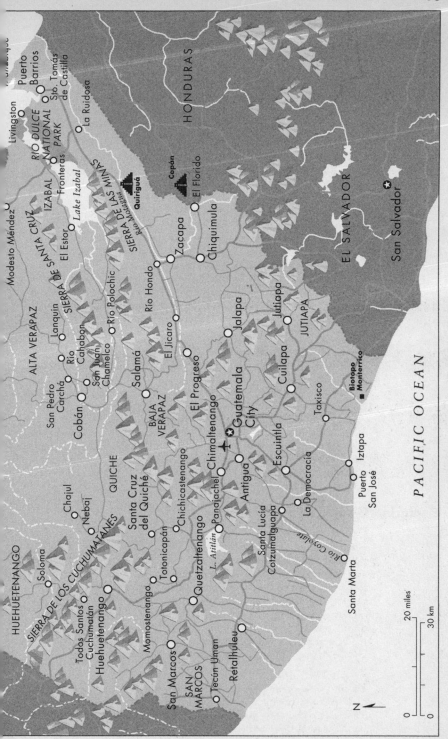

Shopping

Nearly all of Guatemala's handicrafts come from the highlands, so it's no surprise that this region is a shopper's paradise. Most famous are the handwoven fabrics—in every highland village you'll see women weaving traditional patterns. But Guatemala's indigenous population creates countless other kinds of handicrafts; just as each region has its traditional fabrics, it has other specialties, such as ceramics, baskets, toys, statues, bags, or hats. Don't worry if you forget to buy that souvenir in Sololá, as most of these items are also available in the markets of Antigua and Guatemala City.

Guatemala's markets are a wonderful way to witness the everyday lives of the population. Vendors lining a jumble of narrow passages hawk everything from fruits and vegetables to clothing and toiletries. On Monday markets are held in Antigua, Chimaltenango, and Zunil. Sololá has a market on Tuesday, while Chimaltenango has one on Wednesday. Thursday is a popular day for buying and selling, with markets in Antigua, Chichicastenango, Nebaj, Quetzaltenango, San Juan Atitlán, San Lucas Tolimán, Santa Cruz del Quiché, and Todos Santos Cuchumatán. Friday finds vendors in Chimaltenango, Sololá, and San Francisco El Alto, while Saturday is market day in Antigua and Totonicapán. Sunday markets are everyone's favorite, and some of the most colorful are in Antigua, Chichicastenango, Momostenango, Nebaj, San Lucas Tolimán, Quetzaltenango, and Todos Santos Cuchumatán.

White-water Rafting

Guatemala is filled with raging rivers waiting to be explored. Adding to the adventure, most flow through lush tropical forests where you'll see plenty of wildlife. Some moderately difficult rivers include Río Chiquibul, a smooth ride traversing tall limestone canyons, and Río Naranjo, an exhilarating plunge through the jungle. Adventure of a more challenging nature can be had on Río Los Esclavos, which takes you through a narrow canyon with high waterfalls, and Río Candelaria, which passes through virgin forests and caves. You can also rent *kayukos* (canoes fashioned from tree trunks) at Río Dulce and Río El Boqueron for a more leisurely trip.

Exploring Guatemala

Great Itineraries

Guatemala is a rugged country where major roads are few and far between and highways are nonexistent. But because there are only two airports—one in Guatemala City, the other in Flores—you're forced to do most of your travel by land. All but the hardiest travelers will want to stay in the larger towns and explore the more isolated regions on day trips. A trip to Guatemala should last no less than five days, during which you can take in the most popular sights and still get off the beaten path. Eight days allow a better look at Tikal and El Petén, and 10 days could add a trip to the Caribbean coast.

IF YOU HAVE 5 DAYS

Fly into **Guatemala City,** departing immediately for the colonial city of ⊞ **Antigua.** Spend at least two nights here. If you're in Antigua on Thursday or Sunday, plan an early morning excursion to the mountain village of **Chichicastenango,** where the region's best handicrafts are found at a lively market. On your fourth day take an early morning plane to **Flores,** a pastel-painted town in El Petén. Head straight to the ruins at nearby **Tikal.** Depending on your schedule, you may choose to spend the night either here so you can see the ruins in the morning (a must for birders) or in Flores so you'll be closer to the airport for your flight back to Guatemala City.

Spend your first day in **Guatemala City,** visiting the museums and dining in Zona Viva. On day two head for **Antigua** so you can tour the remarkable ruins of 16th-, 17th-, and 18th-century monasteries and cónvents. Spend two nights here, and then head for **Panajachel.** Spend day five visiting the villages surrounding picture-perfect Lago Atitlán or head to the renowned market in the colonial village of **Chichicaste-nango.** On day six fly north to **Flores,** where you can spend the afternoon shopping, strolling, and sipping cappuccino. Make arrangements for a taxi to pick you up at your hotel the next morning—you'll want to leave before dawn for the breathtaking ruins of **Tikal.** Climb the rustic ladder to the top of the tallest temple, then watch the sunrise over the rain forest that engulfs the ancient city. Spend your last morning hiking the terrific trails of the **Biotopo Cerro Cahuí** before returning to Guatemala City.

Those who've come for relaxation should follow the seven-day itinerary, adding additional days to explore the highland markets, tour the villages around Lago Atitlán, or climb Volcán Pacayá. More energetic types should travel east to **Río Dulce,** once an important trading river for the Maya. The next day take an early-morning boat ride to the **Biotopo Chocón Machacas,** then continue onward to the colorful Garífuna community of **Livingston.** On the last morning take a ferry to the banana port of **Puerto Barrios,** where you can swim or explore the waterfront. By early afternoon head back to Guatemala City.

When to Tour Guatemala

Most come to Guatemala from June to August and from January to April. The busiest time of year is *Semana Santa,* the week from Palm Sunday to Easter Sunday. Hotels in Antigua, Panajachel, and Chichicastenango are booked months ahead for this holiday. The rainy season runs from May to November, with a few dry spells in July and August. A typical day in the rainy season is sunny in the morning, cloudy at midday, and pouring throughout the afternoon and evening. Guatemala's climate depends more on altitude than season. The coasts and El Petén are hot, while the mountains enjoy warm days and cool nights.

GUATEMALA CITY

Once hailed as the "jewel of Central America," Guatemala City has certainly lost its luster. The country's capital, a tangle of streets and alleyways, retains little of its colonial charm. With few of the country's most popular attractions—no ancient ruins, flamboyant markets, or spectacular mountains—there's little reason to stay longer than necessary. But as it's the country's transportation hub, you're likely to end up here. Fortunately, the city has some decent restaurants and hotels, as well as several excellent museums and a lively nightlife.

The sprawling metropolis can be intimidating, as it is divided between the Old City and the New City as well as into 21 different *zonas.* But there is virtually no reason to stray from the four central zones, which makes getting around—and getting your bearings—quite manageable. The Old City covers Zona 1, in the north, and the New City spans Zona 9 and Zona 10, in the south. Between them is Zona 4, notable only because it contains the bus terminals. Otherwise, this seedy section is best avoided.

In the Old and New cities, numbered *avenidas* (avenues) run south to north, while *calles* (streets) run west to east. Addresses are usually given as a numbered avenida or calle followed by two numbers separated by a dash: the first number is a nearby cross street or avenue and the second is a specific building. The building numbers increase as they approach the higher-numbered cross streets and then start over at the next block, so 9 Avenida 5–22 is on 9 Avenida near 5 Calle, and 9 Avenida 5–74 is on the same block, only closer to 6 Calle. A word of warning: make sure you're in the right zone. Different zones often contain identical addresses.

The city's major arteries are 6 and 10 avenidas: 6 Avenida runs from Zona 1 to Zona 4 to Zona 9, passing three series of identically numbered calles; 10 Avenida runs through Zonas 1 and 4 before becoming Avenida La Reforma in Zona 10. Comfort seekers tend to stick to the New City, while those interested in bargain shopping head for the Old City.

Numbers in the text correspond to numbers in the margin and on the Guatemala City map.

The New City

Whereas the Old City is the real Guatemala, the New City's modern look and pace are reminiscent of upscale districts in North American cities. This is especially the case in Zona Viva, the posh center of Zona 10, where dozens of smart restaurants, bars, and clubs stay open long after the rest of the city goes to bed. During the day the New City's museums and cultural sites draw an equally affluent and savvy crowd.

Avenida La Reforma splits the New City down the middle, with Zona 9 to the west, and Zona 10 to the east. To save confusion, always check which zone your destination is in before heading there.

A Good Tour

Begin at the **Museo Nacional de Arqueología y Etnología** ① for a crash course in Maya history. Next door, the **Museo Nacional de Arte Moderno** ② will ricochet you into the present with exhibitions of contemporary Guatemalan art. Taxi over to **Zona Viva** ③ for lunch at one of the several terrific restaurants. Afterward, head downhill on 6 Calle past 6 Avenida to the **Museo Ixchel** ④, arguably the city's best museum, where you'll learn about traditional Maya textiles. Next door is the **Museo Popol Vuh** ⑤, which holds a collection of remarkable archeological objects. From here the **Jardines Botánico** ⑥ is about seven blocks away: walk north on 6 Avenida and turn left on 1 Calle. Strolling here is a great way to wind up your afternoon before heading back to your hotel to rest before dinner.

TIMING

If you visit all the museums and stop for lunch, this tour will easily fill a day. Because the Zona 13 museums are somewhat far from the rest of the attractions in the Zona 10 environs, you'll likely want to get a lift. A taxi is about 40 quetzales.

Sights to See

⑥ **Jardines Botánico.** At the northern end of Zona 10, the small but lovely Botanical Gardens contain an impressive collection of plants and a little natural history museum. ⊠ *Calle Mariscal Cruz, near Av. La Reforma, Zona 10,* ☎ *331–0904.* ⊙ *Weekdays 8–4.*

★ ④ **Museo Ixchel.** The city's best museum focuses on textiles of Guatemala's indigenous community. An impressive array of handwoven fabrics from 120 highland communities, some of which date from the 19th

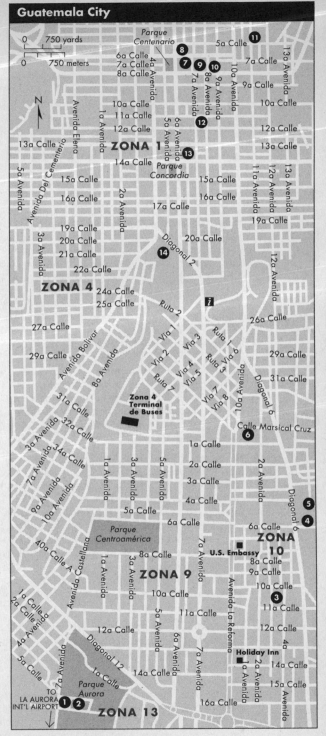

Guatemala City

century, is displayed here. You'll also find sculptures, photographs, and paintings, including work by Andres Curruchich, an important and influential Guatemalan folk painter. Multimedia and interactive weaving displays make it engaging for all ages, and there are a café, a bookstore, and a terrific gift shop. The only drawback is its location—at the bottom of a long hill at the Universidad Francisco Marroquín. ⊠ *End of 6 Calle, at 6 Av., Zona 10,* ☎ *331–3739.* ⊠ *Q20.* ⊙ *Weekdays 8:30–5:50, Sat. 9–1.*

OFF THE   **KAMINALJUYÚ –** From 300 BC to AD 900, an early Maya city of some
BEATEN PATH   50,000 people flourished in what is now the heart of Zona 7. Though
                 most of this city is buried beneath today's urban sprawl, this impressive
                 site, which includes the bases of several pyramids, offers a glimpse of
                 the area's history. Some of the objects found here are on display at
                 Museo Popol Vuh.

★ ❶ **Museo Nacional de Arqueología y Etnología.** Dedicated to the ancient and modern Maya, the National Museum of Archaeology and Ethnology has a large and excellent collection of Maya pottery, jewelry, masks, and costumes, as well as models of the ancient cities themselves. ⊠ *Edificio 5, La Aurora Park, Zona 13,* ☎ *472–0478.* ⊠ *Q40.* ⊙ *Tues.–Sun. 9–4.*

NEED A   Satisfy your sweet tooth on the porch of **Café Zurich** (⊠ 6 Av. 12–58,
BREAK?   Zona 10, ☎ 334–2781), a former colonial home. The menu has spe-
                 cialty coffees as well as chocolate, chocolate, and more chocolate.

❷ **Museo Nacional de Arte Moderno.** Surrealism and multimedia work are among the wide range of styles represented at the National Museum of Modern Art. Many of Guatemala's most distinguished artists are represented here, including Efraín Recinos and Zipacna de León. ⊠ *Edificio 6, La Aurora Park, Zona 13,* ☎ *472–0467.* ⊠ *Q16.* ⊙ *Tues.–Fri. 9–4.*

★ ❺ **Museo Popol Vuh.** Though much smaller than the city's other museums, Popol Vuh has an interesting display of stone carvings from the Preclassic period, with the earliest pieces dating from 1500 BC. Religious figures, animals, and mythological half-animal–half-man creatures all have stolid eyes, hawkish noses, and fierce poses. These are well preserved, with the details surprisingly intact. Statues range widely in size, but some are quite big, which is particularly impressive given that they were each cut from a single stone. Also look for the "painted books," which were historical records kept by the Maya. The most famous is the museum's namesake, the Popol Vuh, which was lost (and later recovered) after it was translated into Spanish. ⊠ *Calle 6 at 6 Av., Zona 10,* ☎ *361–2301.* ⊠ *Q20.* ⊙ *Weekdays 9–5, Sat. 9–1.*

❸ **Zona Viva.** Upscale restaurants and nightclubs have popped up here around the office towers and high-rise hotels. Undoubtedly the most cosmopolitan area of town, Zona Viva is filled with well-dressed people flaunting their electronics (cell phones and handheld computers are ubiquitous). The daytime crowd is mostly business executives, but at night a livelier bunch takes over. Avenues accommodate pedestrians overflowing from the narrow sidewalks on which restaurants have somehow introduced outdoor seating. Lines extend from popular discos and bars, where the thumping music sometimes gets people dancing in the streets. Although the shopping mall called Los Proceres is nearby, you won't find the boutiques that characterize San Salvador's Zona Viva. Things seem to be headed in that direction, however. ⊠ *Zona 10.*

The Old City

Older and grittier than the New City, the Old City has the hustle and bustle of many Central American capitals. But walking around the area, especially around the Plaza de las Armas, is quite pleasant.

A Good Walk

Start at the **Plaza Mayor** ⑦, the heart of the Old City. Clustered around the square are some of the city's oldest landmarks, including the **Palacio Nacional** ⑧ and **Catedral Metropolitano** ⑨. A block east is the **Mercado Central** ⑩, an underground maze of stalls selling goods from the highlands. Walk two blocks east to 11 Avenida, then head north until you reach **La Merced** ⑪. The tiny church is worth a look for its ornate interior.

Three blocks south of Plaza Mayor is the **Edificio de Correos Central** ⑫, a lovely colonial structure that houses the main post office. Two blocks farther is a lovely old church, the **Iglesia de San Francisco** ⑬. History buffs will want to continue south to the **Centro Cultural Miguel Ángel Asturias** ⑭.

TIMING

A few hours should suffice to see the Old City sights.

Sights to See

⑨ **Catedral Metropolitano.** Built between 1782 and 1868, Metropolitan Cathedral is a rare example of colonial architecture in the Old City. Standing steadfast on the eastern end of Plaza Mayor, it is one of the city's most enduring landmarks. The ornate altars hold outstanding examples of colonial religious art, including an image of the Virgen de la Asunción, the city's patron saint. ⊠ *8 Calle and 7 Av.,* ☎ *no phone.* 🎟 *Free.* 🕑 *Daily 8–6.*

⑭ **Centro Cultural Miguel Ángel Asturias.** The imposing Teatro Nacional and the Teatro del Aire Libre are parts of this cluster of buildings named for Guatemala's Nobel Prize–winning novelist. Asturias opposed the dictatorship and therefore spent much of his life in exile. ⊠ *24 Calle 3–81, Centro Cívico,* ☎ *232–4041.* 🎟 *Free.* 🕑 *Weekdays 10–4.*

⑫ **Edificio de Correos Central.** You can mail packages from your hotel, but it's far more fun to come to the main post office, housed in a cantaloupe-color structure dating from the colonial era. ⊠ *7 Av. 12–11,* ☎ *332–6101.* 🕑 *Weekdays 8–7, Sat. 8–3.*

OFF THE BEATEN PATH	**MAPA EN RELIEVE DE GUATEMALA –** This relief map depicting Guatemala's precipitous topography is so immense you have to view it from an observation tower. What makes it amazing is that it was built in 1904, before satellite or even aerial topography. ⊠ *Minerva Park, at end of Av. Simon Cañas, Zona 2,* ☎ *254–1114.* 🎟 *Q16.* 🕑 *Daily 9–5.*

⑬ **Iglesia de San Francisco.** Built between 1800 and 1851, the Church of St. Francis is known for its ornate wooden altar. Here you'll find a small museum explaining the church's history. ⊠ *6 Av. and 13 Calle.*

⑩ **Mercado Central.** A seemingly endless maze of underground passages is home to the Mercado Central, where handicrafts from the highlands are hawked from overstocked stalls. It's not as appealing as the open-air markets in Antigua or Chichicastenango, but the leather goods, wooden masks, and woolen blankets found here are often cheaper. The fruit and vegetable stands on the first floor are full of wonder smells. There are skilled pickpockets in the market, so keep an eye on your purse or wallet. ⊠ *8 Calle and 8 Av.,* ☎ *no phone.* 🕑 *Mon.–Sat. 9–6, Sun. 9–noon.*

⑪ **La Merced.** If religious iconography is one of the reasons you're in Guatemala, step inside this lovely church dating from 1813 to see its baroque interior. Many of the elaborate paintings and sculptures found in the baroque structure originally adorned La Merced in Antigua but were moved here after earthquakes devastated that city. ⊠ *5 Calle and 11 Av.* ⊙ *Daily 6 AM–7 PM.*

⑧ **Palacio Nacional.** Built between 1939 and 1944, the grandiose National Palace was built to satisfy the monumental ego of President Jorge Ubico Castañeda. It once held the offices of the president and his ministers, but now its 320 rooms house an art museum. The collection of paintings and sculptures by well-known Guatemalan artists was moved here from Antigua after that city's devastating earthquakes. Look for Alfredo Gálvez Suárez's murals illustrating the history of the city above the entry. The palace's ornate stairways and stained-glass windows are a pleasant contrast to the gritty city outside its walls. The guards will lead you to the presidential balcony off the banquet room for a *propina* (tip). ⊠ *6 Calle and 7 Av.,* ☎ *no phone.* 🎟 *Free.* ⊙ *Daily 9–noon and 2–5:30.*

⑦ **Plaza Mayor.** Clustered around this historic square are landmarks that survived the 19th century's earthquakes. In the center of the park is a fountain where children sometimes splash, always within sight of their parents on the nearby benches. ⊠ *Between 6 and 8 calles and 6 and 7 avenidas.*

Dining

The New City

Guatemala City has the varied cuisine you'd expect in a major city, with the finer restaurants clustered in the New City, particularly the Zona Viva. Virtually every street here has two or more tempting restaurants, making it almost impossible to choose. Some tried-and-true favorites are listed below. Fortunately, the Zona Viva is small enough that you can stroll around until you find that perfect place.

CONTEMPORARY

$$$–$$$$ ✕ **Jake's.** If you only have one meal in Guatemala City, head to this
★ excellent eatery. Jake Denburg, a painter-turned-restaurateur, has used his creative talents to produce dishes ranging from handmade smoked chicken tortellini to robálo in a green-pepper sauce. The crowning achievement is the robálo *Venecia royal* (with a creamy shrimp sauce over a bed of spinach). These carefully prepared meals are served in a beautiful converted farmhouse with hardwood ceilings and tile floors. The wine list is quite possibly the best in Central America. ⊠ *17 Calle 10–40, Zona 10,* ☎ *368–0351,* 🖷 *363–0115. AE, DC, MC, V. Mon.– Sat. noon–3 and 7–10:30, Sun. noon–4.*

$$–$$$ ✕ **Siriacos.** Modern art adorns the walls of this cheerful bistro, which serves excellent pasta in a vaguely art deco setting. Take a seat in one of the black high-back chairs and enjoy the tasty Caesar salad. ⊠ *1 Av. 12–12, Zona 10,* ☎ *334–6316. AE, DC, MC, V. Closed Sun. No lunch Sat.*

$$ ✕ **Tamarindos.** Guatemala City's best new restaurant, Tamarindos
★ serves up innovative, decidedly eclectic fare ranging from duck in tamarind sauce to Thai-style curries. Curlicue lamps and whimsical sofas that seem straight out of *Alice in Wonderland* lend the place a postmodern ambience. It's an exhilarating destination for dinner, but the reasonably-priced menu also makes this an excellent choice for lunch. The excellent wine list includes choices from around the globe. ⊠ *11 Calle 2–19A, Zona 10,* ☎ *360–2815,* 🖷 *360–2853. AE, DC, MC, V. Weekdays noon–3 and 7–10:30, Sat. 7–10:30.*

GUATEMALAN

$$$–$$$$ ✕ **Hacienda Real.** Small stone pedestals containing hot coals warm the
★ dining room, so even on a chilly day you needn't pass up this charm-
ing restaurant serving authentic Guatemalan fare. Choose from plat-
ters of róbalo, steak, or pork, all served with a variety of savory
condiments like fresh salsa, pickled carrots, and jalapeños. The atten-
tive servers bring endless baskets of warm tortillas, but try not to eat
every last one—the truly incomparable caramel flan shouldn't be
missed. ⊠ *13 Calle 1–10, Zona 10,* ☎ *335–5409. AE, MC, V.*

$$$–$$$$ ✕ **Los Ranchos.** A pretty blue colonial facade with big picture windows
★ welcomes you to Guatemala's best steak house. Most meat, including
the rib-eye and chateaubriand, comes from the United States, but the
specialty of the house, a skirt steak called the *churrasco los ranchos,*
is a hearty cut that hails from Argentina. Ask your server to recom-
mend one of the excellent wines from Chile and France. Save room for
the desserts, which range from tiramisu to *tres leches,* a type of cake
injected with sweetened condensed milk, evaporated milk, and cream.
Every Saturday there's a ceviche lunch buffet with shrimp, clams, crab,
squid, and black conch. ⊠ *2 Av. 14–06, Zona 10,* ☎ *363–5028. AE,
DC, MC, V.*

$$$–$$$$ ✕ **Romanello's.** As the name suggests, Italian influences creep into the
★ cooking at this Zona Viva eatery. There's no set menu, but you can
usually choose from tenderloin, lobster, and róbalo. There's always a
pasta dish that can be prepared with a variety of sauces. The decor is
simple but elegant, with a few antiques set here and there. One table
in the back overlooks a small garden. There is no sign outside, but it's
next door to De Mario. ⊠ *1 Av. 12–70, Zona 10,* ☎ *361–1116. AE,
DC, MC, V. Closed Sun.*

$$–$$$$ ✕ **Hacienda de los Sanchez.** This Zona Viva steak house is known for
its quality cuts of beef, yet the atmosphere has won over more than
one vegetarian. The brick-floored dining room calls to mind the American West, with such touches as sturdy wooden tables and old saddles.
Eat inside or on the plant-filled patio. Grilled and barbecued meats dominate the menu, but you can also order chicken and seafood. There's
a decent wine list. ⊠ *12 Calle 2–25, Zona 10,* ☎ *334–8448. AE, DC,
MC, V.*

ITALIAN

$$–$$$ ✕ **Jake's Tomato Pies.** Serving up the best pizza this side of the Río
Grande, this place is a winner. The recipe hails from New Jersey, which
the eponymous owner claims is where the best pizza in the world is
made. Here you'll be able to find tried-and-true favorites, or you can
go out on a limb and try a duck-sausage-and-pepper or shrimp-and-
pesto pizza. ⊠ *13 Calle and Av. Reforma, Zona 10,* ☎ *367–1760. AE,
DC, MC, V. Closed Sun.*

$$ ✕ **Tre Fratelli.** Run by three hip Guatemalans, this bustling restaurant
caters to the city's young professionals. The food is definitely Italian,
but there are plenty of local touches. Favorites like fettuccine *frutti di
mare* (with seafood), ravioli *alla Bolognese* (with a variety of meats),
and the *quattro stagione* (four-season) pizza are all served with freshly
baked bread. Top your meal off with chocolate mousse, homemade ice
cream, or a cappuccino or espresso brewed in real Italian coffee urns.
⊠ *2 Av. 13–25, Zona 10,* ☎ *366–2678. AE, MC, V. No dinner Sun.*

MIDDLE EASTERN

$$–$$$ ✕ **Olivadda.** An ideal lunch spot, this cozy eatery in the Hotel Santa
Clara serves up tasty Mediterranean fare. Take a table on the tranquil
patio, where a melodic fountain is surrounded by flowers filled with
hummingbirds. Start with traditional Middle Eastern appetizers such
as tabbouleh, *baba ghanouj,* and falafel, then move on to *kafta* (deli-

cately spiced beef patties served in pita bread with tahini). The chicken-breast sandwich with cumin dressing is also delicious. Finish your meal with an orange-and-honey baked apple stuffed with almonds and cinnamon. ⊠ *12 Calle 4–21, Zona 10,* ☎ *339–1811. AE, DC, MC, V.*

SPANISH

$$$–$$$$ ✕ **De Mario.** The cuisine at this Zona Viva favorite is firmly rooted in Spanish traditions, so you can enjoy such entrées as paella and roast suckling pig. But the menu here is one of the country's most original, combining flavors from both sides of the Atlantic. Entrées like robálo with mushroom sauce are standouts. The fine service continues to live up to its reputation. ⊠ *1 Av. 12–98, Zona 10,* ☎ *339–2329. AE, DC, MC, V. No dinner Sun..*

The Old City

AMERICAN

$ ✕ **Europa Bar & Restaurante.** Judy Strong, a native of Oregon, opened this long-standing hangout for American expatriates. Expect comfort food like hamburgers, mashed potatoes, and chili, as well as diner-style breakfasts of eggs, bacon, and hash browns. In the second-floor bar you can play a game of backgammon or watch football on cable TV. ⊠ *11 Calle 5–16, Zona 1,* ☎ *253–4929. No credit cards. Closed Sun.*

GUATEMALAN

$$ ✕ **Arrin Cuan.** Ask locals to recommend a place to eat in the Old City, and chances are they will send you to this spirited Guatemalan favorite. The decor couldn't be simpler—wooden masks adorn the walls and soda-bottle flower vases add a touch of color to each table. The flavorful cuisine, typical of the Cobán region, includes *kak-ik* (a spicy turkey stew), *gallo en chicha* (chicken in a slightly sweet sauce), and *sopa de tortuga* (turtle soup). More adventurous types will want to sample the roasted tepezcuintle. On Friday and Saturday nights you'll dine to live marimba music. ⊠ *5 Av. 3–27, Zona 1,* ☎ *238–0784 or 238–0242. AE, DC, MC, V.*

MEXICAN

$$–$$$ ✕ **Los Cebollines.** The decor is nothing special, but the attraction here is the delicious Mexican food. Sangria or beer is the typical accompaniment to traditional tacos, burritos, fajitas, and, less predictably, *caldo tlalpeño de pollo* (a chicken stew with chickpeas and avocado). There's another in Zona 10. ⊠ *6 Av. 9–75, Zona 1,* ☎ *232–7750;* ⊠ *1 Av. 13–42, Zona 10,* ☎ *368–0663. AE, DC, MC, V.*

$–$$ ✕ **El Gran Pavo.** You can't miss this restaurant—it's housed in a pink building with a gaudy neon sign on top. Inside is just as flashy. Bright colors dazzle you as you walk past hats, blankets, and other Mexican kitsch. The standard tacos and enchiladas are on the menu, but you'll also run across items like *aujas norteñas* (grilled beef strips covered with a red sauce and surrounded by avocado slices) and *camarones siempre joven* (shrimp in a spicy black chili sauce). Open past midnight, the restaurant is the domain of a mariachi band that will perform private concerts for a small fee. ⊠ *13 Calle 4–41, Zona 1,* ☎ *232–9912. AE, DC, MC, V.*

SPANISH

$$–$$$ ✕ **Altuna.** A few blocks south of Plaza Mayor, this popular restaurant
★   serves Spanish and Basque cuisine in a pleasantly bustling atmosphere. Waiters in white jackets and ties move briskly around the covered courtyard that serves as the main dining room. If you want a bit more privacy, ask to be seated in one of several adjacent rooms decorated with Iberian paintings, photographs, and posters. The menu is fairly limited; consider the calamari, paella, or filet mignon with mushroom sauce.

✉ *5 Av. 12–31, Zona 1,* ☎ *251-7185 or 232-0669. AE, DC, MC, V. Closed Mon.*

$$ ✗ **El Mesón de Don Quijote.** In the heart of the Old City, this colorful restaurant serves respectable cuisine from northern Spain (Asturias, to be exact). Popular with old-timers, it's a favorite late-night spot because it's open until 1 AM. The long bar adjoining several dining rooms hosts live musicians who play under a flashy painting of a flamenco dancer. The extensive menu is filled with such palate pleasers as seafood casserole, sliced Spanish ham, lentils with sausage, and paella big enough for four people. On weekdays people head here for the four-course executive lunch. ✉ *11 Calle 5–27, Zona 1,* ☎ *232-1741. AE, DC, MC, V. Closed Sun.*

Lodging

Guatemala City has the country's widest range of accommodations. Upscale hotels are found in the New City, while more moderately priced accommodations are clustered in the Old City.

The New City

$$$$ ⊡ **Camino Real.** With every imaginable amenity and a staff that aims
★ to please, it isn't surprising that the immense Camino Real has hosted everyone from rock stars to heads of state. The spacious reception area lies just beyond a long foyer lined with comfortably overstuffed leather chairs. Stately rooms are furnished with carved French provincial–style pieces. Executive floors hold spacious suites with room for business travelers to spread out. French doors provide views of the nearby volcanoes. ✉ *14 Calle and Av. La Reforma, Zona 10,* ☎ *333–4633; 800/ 228–3000 in the U.S.,* FAX *337–4313,* WEB *www.westin.com. 388 rooms. 2 restaurants, in-room safes, minibars, cable TV, 2 pools, spa, 2 tennis courts, 3 bars, 8 shops, concierge, business services, meeting rooms, travel services. AE, DC, MC, V.*

$$$$ ⊡ **Guatemala City Marriott.** Although its facade won't win any awards, this hotel does earn points for its excellent location not far from the Zona Viva. The lovely lounge offers rest to the weary; relax with a cocktail in one of the comfortable armchairs as you listen to jazz. You can always head to the Cabaña Club, a spacious spa and sports facility. Rooms are nicely furnished, with desks designed for business travelers. Each has a small balcony with a view of the city. ✉ *7 Av. 15–45, Zona 9,* ☎ *339–7777; 800/228–9290 in the U.S.,* FAX *332–1877,* WEB *www.marriotthotels.com. 385 rooms. 3 restaurants, minibars, cable TV, pool, spa, health club, bar, meeting room, travel services. AE, DC, MC, V.*

$$$$ ⊡ **Hotel Santa Clara.** This colonial house has character that most other hotels can't match. Ivy-covered walls give way to a cozy reception area. Some rooms surround a breezy courtyard overflowing with potted plants, while others share a balcony reached by a spiral staircase. The softly lighted rooms have wooden paneling and tile floors, as well as elegant touches like dried flowers. The Middle Eastern restaurant is recommended. ✉ *12 Calle 4–51, Zona 10,* ☎ *339–1811,* FAX *332–0775,* WEB *www.hotelcasasantaclara.com 14 rooms. Restaurant, room service. AE, DC, MC, V.*

$$$$ ⊡ **Mansión San Carlos.** Formerly the owner's own home, this modest colonial structure puts a little space between you and the bustling Zona Viva. Floor-to-ceiling windows in the reception area look out onto a sunny courtyard dotted with statues. Sloping stairs lead up to the individually decorated rooms, where hardwood floors add lots of character. Other rooms in an annex are newer, but they lack the charm of those in the main house. ✉ *Av. La Reforma 7–89, Zona 10,* ☎ *362–*

9077, FAX 331–6411. 21 rooms. Restaurant, bar, business services. AE, DC, MC, V.

$$$$ 🏨 **Meliá Guatemala.** Giant glass elevators in the atrium-style lobby ascend to a dizzying view of the city. With 22 meeting rooms and 16 ballrooms, the hotel is designed to accommodate large conventions. Executives can also take advantage of the array of business services available. Rooms on the south side have the most impressive views of the surrounding volcanoes—even the health club overlooks these soaring peaks. The hotel is convenient to the airport, but it's quite a distance from the Zona Viva. ✉ *Av. Las Américas 9–08, Zona 13, ☎ 339–0666; 800/339–3542 in the U.S., FAX 339–0690, WEB www.solmelia.com. 194 rooms, 2 suites. 2 restaurants, minibars, cable TV, health club, sauna, spa, bar, business services, convention center, meeting rooms, car rental. AE, DC, MC, V.*

$$$$ 🏨 **Real Inter-Continental.** In the center of the Zona Viva, the towering Inter-Continental has a decidedly modern feel. A giant statue of bartering Mayas greets you at the entrance, where massive columns of rough stone rise majestically. On either side are sweeping staircases. The comfortable rooms, where modern art adorns the walls, follow this theme. The very good French restaurant imported its chef from Paris. Other restaurants, as well as shops and boutiques, are within walking distance. ✉ *14 Calle 2–51, Zona 10, ☎ 379–4446, FAX 379–4447, WEB www.interconti.com. 239 rooms. Restaurant, café, minibars, pool, spa, bar, meeting room, travel services. AE, DC, MC, V.*

$$$ 🏨 **La Casa Grande.** This stately hotel, housed in a former residence, is one of the best lodging options in the New City. You enter through iron gates, then step into a small reception area that leads to a comfortable lounge with a fireplace to keep out the chill. The restaurant spills out into the courtyard; its cast-iron chairs are surrounded by arches covered with dangling philodendrons. Traditional tile floors grace the rooms, which are furnished with antiques. Rooms in the front open onto a balcony, but those in the back are quieter. ✉ *Av. La Reforma 7–67, Zona 10, ☎ FAX 332–0914. 28 rooms. Restaurant, bar. AE, DC, MC, V.*

$$$ 🏨 **Stofella.** For those who feel more at home in smaller hotels, Stofella is a real find. A short staircase leads to a flower-filled reception area. Charming rooms have small sitting areas that afford a bit of privacy. Ask for one of the original rooms, as those added during a recent renovation lack character. If you're feeling social, join the other guests in the cozy bar. ✉ *2 Av. 12–28, Zona 10, ☎ 334–6191, FAX 331–0823. 102 rooms. Gym, bar, laundry service, business services. AE, DC, MC, V.*

$$$ 🏨 **Cortijo Reforma.** Don't be put off by its drab exterior—this high-rise is perfect for an extended stay in the capital. The staff here is experienced and friendly. The suites, with 1970s-era decor, easily sleep four. Each has a full kitchen, and most have two baths. Some have views of the nearby volcanoes, while others overlook the Torre del Reformador, a scaled-down version of the Eiffel Tower that lights up at night. ✉ *Av. La Reforma 2–18, Zona 9, ☎ 332–0712; 800/344–1212 in the U.S.; FAX 331–8876, WEB www.goldentulip.com. 150 suites. Restaurant, minibars, shop, hair salon, bar, meeting room, travel services. AE, DC, MC, V.*

The Old City

$$$$ 🏨 **Hotel Royal Palace.** A diamond in the rough, this classy hotel is a welcome retreat from the frantic pace of the streets outside. The hotel has a great sense of style—a tile fountain reminiscent of Andalusia graces the central courtyard. The rooms are slightly musty but are nevertheless comfortable and quiet. Ask for one with a view of 6 Avenida—it's a great way to view the action without having to fight the crowds. ✉ *6 Av. 12–*

66, Zona 1, ☎ *220–8970,* FAX *238–3715,* WEB *www.hotelroyalpalace.com 74 rooms. Restaurant, gym, sauna, concierge, travel services, airport shuttle. AE, DC, MC, V.*

$$$ ☆ 🏨 **Pan American.** The grande dame of downtown hotels, the Pan American was for many years the most luxurious lodging in town. To step into the lobby of this former mansion is to leave the confusion of the city behind. A covered courtyard with attractive wrought-iron chandeliers spills out from the restaurant, whose servers wear traditional highland dress. The rooms are small but attractive, with tile floors, handmade rugs and bedspreads, and walls adorned with traditional paintings. ✉ *9 Calle 5–63, Zona 1,* ☎ *251–8713; 800/418–8355 in the U.S.,* FAX *232–6402,* WEB *www.hotelpanamerican.com. 56 rooms. Restaurant, concierge, travel services, airport shuttle. AE, DC, MC, V.*

$$ 🏨 **Chalet Suizo.** This quiet hotel has been popular with budget travelers for more than 40 years. An attractive central courtyard behind the reception area is a great place to relax. Facing a series of smaller courtyards, the rooms are all fairly plain. The staff is friendly and will happily store your extra luggage while you travel around the country. ✉ *14 Calle 6–82, Zona 1,* ☎ *251–3786,* FAX *232–0429. 51 rooms, 15 with bath. Restaurant, travel services. No credit cards.*

$$ 🏨 **Fortuna Royal.** This hotel has succeeded where few others have by offering stylish accommodations for a reasonable rate. The marble-floor lobby gives way to rooms with plush carpeting and cheery floral wallpaper. To top it off, everything is immaculately clean. ✉ *12 Calle 8–42, Zona 1,* ☎ *230–3378,* FAX *251–2215,* WEB *www.telcom.net/ hotelroyal. 20 rooms. Restaurant, room service. AE, DC, MC, V.*

$$ 🏨 **Hotel Colonial.** It occupies a lovely 19th-century house, but this hotel isn't quite as charming inside. The reception area overlooks an enclosed patio overflowing with potted plants, and the lounge is furnished with reproductions of antiques. The rooms all have colonial-style decor. A few are exceptional—some of the larger ones have very nice views. ✉ *7 Av. 14–19, Zona 1,* ☎ *232–6722 or 232–2955,* FAX *232–8671. colonial@ infovia.com.gt. 42 rooms. Breakfast room. AE, DC, MC, V.*

$$ 🏨 **Hotel Spring.** Most rooms in this colonial-style hotel face a pleasant courtyard with cast-iron tables and chairs and lots of greenery. Several on the second floor share a balcony that overlooks the avenue. A small café behind the courtyard is a great place to relax after a day of exploring the city. Next door is a refuge for street children, so keep your eyes open for those tempted to pickpocket a less-than-alert tourist. ✉ *8 Av. 12–65, Zona 1,* ☎ *232–6637,* FAX *232–0107. 40 rooms, 22 with bath. AE, DC, MC, V.*

$$ ☆ 🏨 **Posada Belén.** This little bed-and-breakfast on a quiet side street is exceptional, thanks to the couple that runs it. Built in 1873, the family's former home has been renovated just enough to combine old-world charm with modern comfort. Rooms have tile floors, handwoven bedspreads, and walls decorated with Guatemalan paintings and weavings. A small but impressive collection of Mayan artifacts graces the dining room. Family-style meals are made to order by the owners, who are also a font of information about the city. ✉ *13 Calle A 10–30, Zona 1,* ☎ *232–9226 or 254–5430,* FAX *251–3478,* WEB *www.guatemalaweb. com. 10 rooms. Dining room, library, travel services, airport shuttle. AE, DC, MC, V.*

$ 🏨 **Hotel Ajau.** This slightly faded hotel has an interior courtyard and three floors of balconied rooms. The rooms are clean, with tile floors and a few pieces of wooden furniture. Rooms facing away from the street are quieter. ✉ *8 Av. 15–62, Zona 1,* ☎ *232–0488,* FAX *251–8097. 43 rooms, 23 with bath. No credit cards.*

Nightlife and the Arts

The Zona Viva is the city's nightlife center, offering everything from sedate bars to noisy discos. Strolling the streets is especially entertaining, as people come here to see and be seen. Dress codes have been implemented by many dance clubs, which generally means men must wear sports jackets to be admitted. Expect lines around the block at the most popular places.

Old City nightspots have more character than those in the New City, so they shouldn't be passed up just because the area isn't the greatest. Walking alone at night isn't a good idea, especially south of 15 Calle. At night it's always best to take a cab for any destination more than a few blocks away.

The New City

The **Brass Beer Company** (⊠ 3 Av. 12–48, Zona 10) serves a variety of excellent microbrews to a mellow crowd. **Giuseppe Verdi** (⊠ 14 Calle at Av. La Reforma, Zona 9) is an upscale bar that caters mostly to tourists. Attracting an international crowd, **Sesto Senso** (⊠ 2 Av. 12–81, Zona 10) offers live music ranging from Guatemalan folk to American pop. A longtime favorite, **El Establo** (⊠ Av. La Reforma 10–31, Zona 9) has been playing rock and roll for more than two decades.

Discos come and go, but the place to be right now is **Q** (⊠ 4 Av. 15–53, Zona 10). **Rich and Famous** (⊠ Los Proceres Mall, Av. La Reforma and Blvd. de los Proceres, Zona 9) is a decent club in a mall. A fun crowd heads to **Salambo** (⊠ 1 Av. 13–70, Zona 10), where the ambience is decadently camp.

The Old City

Drawing an intellectual crowd, **La Bodeguita del Centro** (⊠ 2 Calle 3–55, Zona 1) hosts live music and poetry readings. If you feel like dancing, go to **El Gazabo** (⊠ 6 Calle at 3 Av., Zona 1).

Outdoor Activities and Sports

Fishing

Guatemala's southern coast is arguably one of the best billfishing spots in the world, especially during fall and spring. Several world records have been recorded here. The targets are sailfish that can reach 150 pounds, but enormous yellow tuna and blue marlin are often caught in the outer waters. **Artmarina** (⊠ Iztapa, ☎ 881–4035, WEB www.artmarina. com) offers outings on well-equipped vessels. **Villas del Pacifico** (⊠ Iztapa, ☎ 316–1741) is one of the best companies in the area, offering a variety of excursions from the Iztapa area.

White-Water Rafting

On an exhilarating white-water rafting trip down the Río Coyolate, offered June through October, you'll pass iguanas sunning themselves, toucans resting on overhanging branches, and flitting morpho butterflies. Take a break from paddling to enjoy the warm waterfalls. **Area Verde Expeditions** ⊠ 4 Av. Sur 8, Antigua, ☎ 832–3863) offers trips that range from easy to challenging. **Clark Tours** (⊠ 6 Diagonal 10–01, 7th floor, Zona 10, ☎ 339–2888) offers a range of trips.

Shopping

With the exception of the big market in the Old City, shop hours are weekdays 10–1 and 3–7, Saturday 10–1.

Art

Works by contemporary Guatemalan painters are on display at **El Ático** (⊠ 4 Av. 15–45, Zona 14). **Galería Ríos** (⊠ Calle Montúfar 0–85, Zona 9), in the Centro Comercial Plaza, has a good selection of works by local artists. **Sol de Río** (⊠ 5 Av. 10–22, Zona 9) is small gallery with a selection that makes it well worth a visit.

Books

In the Zona Viva, **Sophos** (⊠ Av. La Reforma 13–89, Zona 10) is one of the best places in the city to find books in English (as well as German and French). You can even grab a cup of coffee while you peruse the shelves. Nor far from Sophos is **Etc. Ediciones** (⊠ 6 Av. 13–35, Zona 10), which also has a decent selection of books. **Geminis** (⊠ 3 Av. 17–05, Zona 14) sells recent titles in English. Used English-language paperbacks (including, for some reason, lots of westerns) can be bought or borrowed at **El Establo** (⊠ Av. La Reforma 10–31, Zona 9).

The gift shop at **Museo Popol Vuh** (⊠ 6 Calle at 6 Av., Zona 10) has an interesting collection of books on art, archaeology, and history. The **Instituto Guatemalteco Americano** (⊠ 1 Ruta 4–05, Zona 4, ☎ 331–0022) has an extensive lending library of English-language titles.

Handicrafts

If you're in the market for *típica,* a term that roughly translates as "typical goods," head to **Mercado Central** (⊠ 8 Calle and 8 Av.). There's also a **Mercado de Artesanías** (⊠ 6 Calle in La Aurora Park, Zona 13), where you can find goods made by highland artisans.

A number of stores east of Avenida La Reforma sell handmade goods. It's small, but **El Gran Jaguar** (⊠ 14 Calle 7–49, Zona 9) has a decent selection. The spacious **San Remo** (⊠ 14 Calle 7–60, Zona 9) has a wide variety of handcrafted items. **Típicos Reforma Utatlán** (⊠ 14 Calle 7–77, Zona 13) has an excellent selection of textiles made in highland villages.

Across Avenida La Reforma is a cluster of souvenir shops. In addition to *artesanía,* **Coleccion 21** (⊠ 15 Calle 2–64, Zona 10) has an art gallery featuring works by local painters. **Topis** (⊠ Calle 12 and Diagonal 6, Zona 10) has a fine selection of pottery by artists from Antigua. The elegant **Casa Solares** (⊠ Av. La Reforma 11–07, Zona 10) is pricey, but you can be certain that you are buying the best-quality goods. **In Nola** (⊠ 18 Calle 21–31, Zona 10) specializes in textiles, but you will also find items in leather and wool. It's your best bet if you only have time to pop into one shop.

In the Old City, **Lin Canola** (⊠ 5 Calle 9–60, Zona 1) has an excellent selection of típica and other goods. The prices are often inexpensive.

Jewelry

Esmeralda (⊠ Hotel Camino Real, 14 Calle and Av. La Reforma, Zona 10) specializes in settings of the precious green stone. **Jades** (⊠ Hotel Camino Real, 14 Calle and Av. La Reforma, Zona 10) is a branch of the well-known jewelry shop in Antigua. **Joyería el Sol** (⊠ 13 Calle 2–75, Zona 10) is one of the city's best-known jewelers. **L'Elegance** (⊠ Camino Real, 14 Calle and Av. La Reforma, Zona 10) sells exquisitely crafted silver trays, vases, jewelry boxes, and place settings by the Italian Camusso family.

Leather

Arpiel (⊠ Av. La Reforma 15–54, Zona 9; Av. Las Américas 7–20, Zona 13) has reasonably priced leather goods. **Principe de Gales** (⊠ 2 Calle 16–28, Zona 15) sells clothing, including hand-tailored leather items.

In the Old City, **Piel Kabal** (⊠ 10 Av. 16–24) sells custom-made leather jackets.

Side Trips from Guatemala City

Biotopo Monterrico
48 km south of Guatemala City.

The Biotopo Monterrico encompasses 6,916 acres along Guatemala's Pacific coast that include everything from mangrove swamps to dense tropical forests. This is a haven for ornithologists, as the reserve is home to more than 100 species of migratory and indigenous birds. Turtles swim ashore from July to February, and you can often see them digging nests for their eggs at night. The nearby village of Monterrico even has a decent beach, but be careful about the rough current. ⊠ *South of the village of Monterrico,* ☎ *no phone.* ☞ *Free.*

Copán
238 km (147½ mi) northeast of Guatemala City.

Lying in the jungles of western Honduras, the ancient city of Copán is considered one of the pinnacles of Maya achievement. The powerful pyramids, the stately stelae depicting various rulers, and other relics left by this highly advanced civilization make this a must-see. Remarkably well preserved, the ornate ruins are arranged around an expansive, neatly groomed central plaza.

Copán reached its apex during the 8th century, when it controlled much of the southern reaches of the Maya empire. It was then home to more than 20,000 people. For more than 100 years archaeologists have been excavating the ancient city, but significant discoveries have only been made in the last 25 years. What researchers do know comes from hieroglyphics carved when the city was at its peak. The tales still visible today tell of kings, gods, and bloody battles.

The most fascinating artifact here is the Hieroglyphic Stairway, a massive structure that contains the single largest collection of glyphs in the world. Erected by King Smoke Shell, the 63 steps immortalize Copán's kings. The carving pays special attention to King Smoke Jaguar, who ruled over the city at the height of its power. Once placed chronologically, the history can no longer be read because an earthquake knocked many steps free and archaeologists replaced them out of order. All may not be lost, however, as experts have located an early photograph of the stairway that may prove the key to unlocking the proper sequence. The museum near the ruins is well worth a visit. The **Museo de Escultura Maya,** near the entrance, contains facades of a ball court and several temples. Some of the sculptures, such as the leering skulls on the tombs, are amazingly detailed. The main draw is a model of the Rosalila Temple, which archaeologists found buried nearly intact beneath another structure. ⊠ *Copán Ruinas, Honduras,* ☎ *no phone,* WEB *www.copanruins.com.* ☞ *$10.* ◐ *Daily 9–5.*

Guatemala City A to Z

To research prices, get advice from other travelers, and book travel arrangements, visit www.fodors.com.

AIR TRAVEL TO AND FROM GUATEMALA CITY
Most international flights into Guatemala head to Aeropuerto Internacional La Aurora, an unusually friendly airport where a marimba band often greets you as you step off the plane. The international airlines serving the airport are American, Aviateca, Continental, Copa, Iberia, KLM, Mexicana, Taca, Tapsa, and United.

Domestic carriers fly between the capital and Flores/Santa Elena, in El Petén; Puerto Barrios and Río Dulce, on the Atlantic coast; and Quetzaltenango and Huehuetenango, in the highlands. Serving these routes are Aeroquetzal, Aerovias, and Tikal Jets.

➤ DOMESTIC CARRIERS: **Aeroquetzal** (☎ 334–7689). **Aerovias** (☎ 332–7470 or 332–5686). **Tikal Jets** (☎ 334–5568).

➤ INTERNATIONAL CARRIERS: **Aerovias** (☎ 332–7470 or 332–5686). **American** (☎ 334–7379). **Continental** (☎ 366–9985). **Copa** (☎ 361–1577). **Iberia** (☎ 332–0911). **KLM** (☎ 367–6179). **Mexicana** (☎ 333–6001). **Taca** (☎ 331–8222). **Tapsa** (☎ 331–9180). **United** (☎ 336–9900).

AIRPORTS AND TRANSFERS

Less than a mile from the New City, Aeropuerto Internacional La Aurora is a bit too close for comfort. A taxi to the airport from downtown runs $6–$8.

➤ AIRPORTS: **Aeropuerto Internacional La Aurora** (☎ 332–6084 or 332–6085).

BUS TRAVEL TO AND FROM GUATEMALA CITY

The *terminal de buses,* or main bus station, is in Zona 4. From here you can catch a bus to almost anywhere in the country. Autobuses de Oriente has service to the Atlantic Lowlands, Las Verapaces, and El Petén. Transgalgos travels to the highlands.

Some companies run small minivans, which are a much more comfortable way to travel. Atitrans, Turansa, and Vision Travel offer shuttle service to most cities.

➤ BUS INFORMATION: **Atitrans** (☎ 832–0644). **Autobuses de Oriente** (☎ 238–3894). **Transgalgos** (☎ 253–4868). **Turansa** (☎ 832–2928). **Vision Travel** (☎ 832–3293).

BUS TRAVEL WITHIN GUATEMALA CITY

The bus system can be quite confusing, but locals are usually happy to point you to the one you need. After a while you'll get to know the system. Buses that serve La Reforma say REFORMA on the windshield; likewise, buses that say TERMINAL all pass by the main bus station in Zona 4. Only the buses marked AEROPUERTO go to the airport. Bus service pretty much ends at 8 PM. Watch your belongings at the bus station, as well as while boarding, riding, and exiting the bus.

CAR RENTAL

If you're not intimidated by Guatemala City's winding mountain roads, renting a car is a great way to see the countryside. There are several international agencies at Aeropuerto Internacional La Aurora and dozens in the New City. Reputable local companies include Tabarini and Tikal.

➤ LOCAL AGENCIES: **Avis** (✉ 6 Av. 11–24, Zona 9, ☎ 332–7744). **Budget** (✉ Av. Hincapié 11–01, Zona 13, ☎ 332–2024). **Hertz** (✉ 7 Av. 14–76, Zona 9, ☎ 332–2242). **National** (✉ 12 Calle Montúfar 7-69, Zona 9, ☎ 360–2030, WEB national@intelnet.net.gt). **Tabarini** (✉ 2 Calle A 7–30, Zona 10, ☎ 331–9814). **Tikal** (✉ 2 Calle 6–56, Zona 10, ☎ 361–0257)

CAR TRAVEL

Driving in Guatemala City is a headache. You can expect narrow streets jammed with traffic at just about any time of day. Things get better once you move out of the center of the city. Drives to nearby destinations like Antigua, for example, can be quite pleasant.

Breaking into cars is common in the capital, so it's best to park in a
guarded lot. All expensive and most moderate hotels have protected
parking areas. Avoid leaving anything of value in the car.

EMERGENCIES

If you're a little out of sorts, there's no reason to leave your hotel because Farmacias Klee delivers 24 hours a day. El Sauce Las Americas,
with branches in the Old City and the New City, is open 24 hours a
day. Osco and Meykos also have reputable pharmacies in the New City's
Zona 10.

➤ EMERGENCY SERVICES: **Ambulance** (☎ 128). **Fire** (☎ 122 or 123).
Police (☎ 110 or 120).

➤ HOSPITALS: **Centro Médico** (✉ 6 Av. 3–47, Zona 10, ☎ 332–3555).
Hospital Herrera Llerandí (✉ 6 Av. 8–71, Zona 10, ☎ 334–5959 or
332–5455).

➤ PHARMACIES: **El Sauce Las Americas** (✉ Calle 23 and Av. Las Américas, Zona 13, ☎ 331–5996; ✉ 4 Av. and 16 Calle, Zona 1, ☎ no phone).
Osco (✉ 16 Calle and 4 Av., Zona 10, ☎ 337–1566). **Meykos** (✉ Blvd.
Los Próceres, Zona 10, ☎ 363–5903; ✉ 6 Av. 5–01, Zona 9, ☎ 334–
1962). **Farmacias Klee** (☎ 360–8383).

MAIL AND SHIPPING

To ship important packages, use Federal Express or United Parcel Service. Both have offices in the New City. You can also send packages
from the Correos Central.

➤ OVERNIGHT SERVICES: **United Parcel Service** (✉ 12 Calle 5–53, Zona
10, ☎ 360–6460).**Federal Express** (✉ Av. 7–12, Bodega 20, Zona 14,
☎ 80/472–2222 in the U.S.).

➤ POST OFFICES: **Correos Central** (✉ 7 Av. 12–11, Zona 1, ☎ 332–6101).

MONEY MATTERS

You can exchange currency at almost any bank in Guatemala City. Bancared, one of the most popular banks, has 150 ATMs around the city.
Many hotels even have ATMs on the premises.

➤ BANKS: **Bancared** (✉ 7 Av. 15–45, Zona 9). **Banco Industrial** (✉ 7
Av. 5–10, Zona 4, Guatemala City).

SAFETY

Guatemala City is no more dangerous than any other large city. To avoid
being preyed upon by pickpockets and other unsavory characters,
leave expensive jewelry and watches at home, carry purses and camera bags close to the body, and take along only as much cash as you'll
need. At night stick to well-lighted areas.

TAXIS

Taxis can be found waiting at hotels and intersections or can be flagged
down on the street. Most do not have meters, so negotiate a price before getting in. Within a single zone, a ride should cost Q16–Q24; between zones expect to pay Q32–Q48. Taxis Intercontinental is a
reputable firm.

➤ TAXI COMPANIES: **Taxis Intercontinental** (☎ 336–9624 or 202–
09800).

TOUR OPERATORS

Many major tour operators offer half- and full-day tours of the capital as well as day trips outside the city. Area Verde offers white-water
rafting and kayaking trips. Other reputable companies are Clark Tours,
Jaguar Tours, Tropical Tours, Turansa, and Unitours.

➤ TOUR COMPANIES: **Clark Tours** (✉ 6 Diagonal 10–01, 7th floor, Zona
10, ☎ 339–2888, info@clarktours.com.gt). **Jaguar Tours** (✉ 13 Calle

3–40, Edificio Atlantis, 3rd floor, Zona 10, ☎ 363–2640, jaguar-tours@c.net.gt). **Maya Expeditions** (✉ 15 Calle 1–91, Zona 10, ☎ 363–4955; 800/733–3350 in the U.S., WEB www.mayaexpeditions.com). **Tropical Tours** (✉ 3 Calle A 3–22, Zona 10, ☎ 339–3662, tropical-tour@guate.net). **Turansa** (✉ Km 15 Carretera Roosevelt, Zona 11, locale 69, ☎ 595–3575, info@turansa.com). **Unitours** (✉ 12 Calle 9–35, Edificio Ermita, Zona 1, ☎ 230–0696, unitours@infovia.com.gt).

VISITOR INFORMATION

Inguat, Guatemala's ever-helpful government tourism office, is open weekdays 8–4 and Saturday 8–1.

➤ TOURIST INFORMATION: **Inguat** (✉ 7 Av. 1–17, Zona 4, ☎ 331–1333 or 331–1334, WEB www.guatemala.travel.com).

ANTIGUA

45 km (28 mi) west of Guatemala City.

Filled with vestiges of its colonial past—cobblestone streets, enchanting squares, and deserted convents—Antigua instantly transports you back hundreds of years to when the Spanish ruled this land. Founded in 1543, the city was initially called Santiago de los Caballeros de Guatemala after the patron saint of the conquistadors. For 200 years it was the capital of a region that included what is now Central America and part of Mexico. Along with Lima and Mexico City, it was one of the greatest cities of the Americas.

By the late 18th century the city had been destroyed by earthquakes several times. Because it was a major political, religious, and intellectual center—it had 32 churches, 18 convents and monasteries, seven colleges, five hospitals, and a university—it was always rebuilt. Powerful tremors struck again in late 1773, reducing much of the city's painstakingly restored elegance to rubble. The government reluctantly relocated to a safer site in the Ermita Valley, 45 km (28 mi) east, where Guatemala City now stands.

Ironically, it is because Antigua was abandoned that it retains so much of its colonial character. Only the poorest inhabitants stayed put after the capital was moved, and being of limited means, they could only repair the old structures, not tear them down or build new ones. In the 1960s laws took effect that limited commercial development and required all development to remain in keeping with the city's colonial character. The National Council for the Protection of Antigua Guatemala was formed in 1972 to restore the ruins, maintain the monuments, and rid the city of such modern intrusions as billboards and neon signs. Restoration projects, both private and public, have transformed Antigua into a captivating destination.

Today you'll find a mountainside enclave that is vastly more pleasant than Guatemala City. An ever-increasing influx of visitors has brought in some of the country's finest hotels and restaurants, a collection of boutiques and galleries, and several dozen Spanish-language schools that attract students from all over the world. Antigua is also a favored escape for wealthy Guatemalans. Its higher prices mean that many people cannot afford to live here, so they travel to the city each day to sell their wares.

The most spectacular time to be in Antigua is Semana Santa, which brings a series of vigils, processions, and reenactments of Christ's last days in Jerusalem. You'll see Roman centurions charging through the streets on horseback, boulevards carpeted with colored sawdust and flowers, and immense hand-carried floats wending their way through throngs of onlookers.

Numbers in the text correspond to numbers in the margin and on the Antigua map.

A Good Walk

Any tour of Antigua must start at **Plaza Mayor** ①, the tree-shaded central park. As in most other Central American communities, this is a place that always buzzes with activity. On the north side of the square stands the **Palacio del Ayuntamiento** ②, an imposing structure that once served as the city hall. Facing it is the **Palacio de los Capitanes Generales** ③. The most impressive building on the square is the **Catedral de San José** ④, one of the loveliest of the city's many churches. Across 5 Calle Oriente from the cathedral is the **Museo de Arte Colonial** ⑤, where you'll find religious art dating from the 17th century. Between 2 and 4 you can visit **Casa Popenoe** ⑥, a private residence and a restored and beautifully furnished colonial mansion, two blocks east. Close by are the ruins of **Convento Santa Clara** ⑦, with hidden passages and mysterious underground rooms, and the **Monasterio San Francisco** ⑧, where you can knock on the tomb of Friar Pedro de San José de Betancur to have your prayers answered.

Head north on 2 Avenida to reach the labyrinthine ruins of the **Convento de las Capuchinas** ⑨. Two blocks east, spanning 5 Avenida Norte, is the graceful **Arco de Santa Catalina** ⑩. Half a block north is the **Nuestra Señora de La Merced** ⑪, an ornate church painted the same brilliant yellow as the arch. Walk west to walk around the impressive ruins of **La Recolección** ⑫. Just to the south is a covered market called **Mercado Central** ⑬. Women from nearby villages come here to sell fruits and vegetables.

TIMING

As you wander Antigua's ancient avenues you will be continually surprised by its peaceful atmosphere. As you explore the picturesque streets, take breaks in places that have views of the volcanoes. This tour, taken at a leisurely pace, can fill a day. Remember that most sights close promptly at 5 PM and that some ruins are closed on Sunday and Monday.

Sights to See

★ ⑩ **Arco de Santa Catalina.** The only remnant of the once-enormous Convent of St. Catherine is this beautiful yellow arch that spans 5 Avenida Norte, a street locals call Calle de Santa Catalina. The convent was founded in 1613 with only four nuns, but by 1693 its growing numbers forced it to expand across the street. The arch was built to allow the sisters to pass from one side to the other unseen. ⊠ *5 Av. Norte and 2 Calle Poniente,* ☎ *832–0184.* ⌨ *Q30.*

....

NEED A   Near the Arco de Santa Catalina you'll find the **Posada Don Rodrigo**
BREAK?   (⊠ 5 Av. Norte 17), a colonial mansion that has been transformed into
             a hotel. Wander around the courtyards and gardens, listen to the musi-
             cians play the marimba, and indulge in a serving of Antiguan flan, a
             desert layered with figs and sweet potatoes. You'll want to come back
             for dinner.

....

Casa K'Ojom. K'Ojom means "music" in three indigenous languages, and this very modest museum highlights the musical traditions of Guatemala's vastly diverse indigenous population. An interesting 15-minute documentary film is a good introduction for the newcomer touring the collection of musical instruments and other artifacts. A gift shop

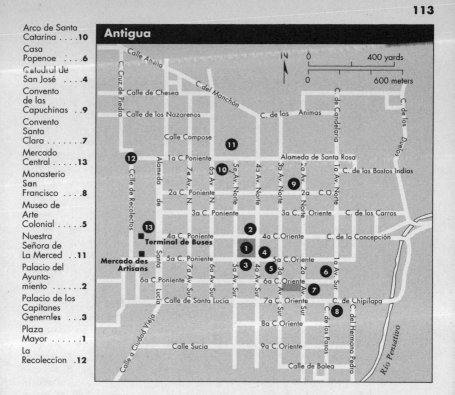

sells locally made crafts, simple instruments, and recordings of
Guatemalan music. While you're here, learn about harvesting and
roasting coffee beans at the adjacent coffee plantation. Here you'll find
a working mill dating from 1883. The museum is in the village of Jocotenango, 4 km (2 mi) from Antigua. Taxis from Antigua run 20–25
quetzales. ⊠ *Calle del Cemetario Final, Jocotenango,* ☎ *832–0907.*
WEB *www.centroazotea.com.gt.* ≡ *Q25.* ☉ *Weekdays 8:30–4, Sat.*
8:30–2.

6 **Casa Popenoe.** A short loop through this beautifully restored colonial
mansion takes you through courtyards and several rooms containing
decorative items, including original oil paintings, fine ceramic dishes,
and other items that have been in the house since its original construction
in 1636. An English-speaking guide is usually available. Since this is
a private home, hours are limited. ⊠ *1 Av. Sur at 5 Calle Oriente,* ☎
no phone. ≡ *Q10.* ☉ *Mon.–Sat. 2–4.*

4 **Catedral de San José.** Only two chapels remain in what was once the
city's main house of worship. The lovely white cathedral was completed
in 1680 but destroyed in an earthquake less than 100 years later. As
in most other Latin American churches, the cross and altar are toward
the east so that worshipers face the Holy Land. ⊠ *4 Av. Sur, east side*
of Plaza Mayor, ☎ *no phone.* ≡ *Q3.*

★ **9** **Convento de las Capuchinas.** Antigua's largest convent was built by
the Capuchins nuns, whose number had swelled because they, unlike
other sisterhoods, did not require young women to pay dowries to un-
dertake the religious life. They constructed the mammoth structure in
1736, just a decade after the first of their order arrived from Madrid.
The convent was abandoned after the earthquake of 1773, even though
damage to the structure was relatively light. In the 1940s the convent
was restored and opened to the public. The ruins, which are quite well

preserved, include several lovely courtyards and gardens, the former bathing halls, and a round tower lined with the nuns' cells—two of which illustrate cloistered life with rather eerie mannequins. Climb to the roof for a memorable view of the surrounding landscape. ⊠ *2 Av. Norte at 2 Calle Oriente,* ☎ *832–0184.* ⌨ *Q30.* ⊙ *Daily 9–5.*

⑦ Convento Santa Clara. Shortly after it was founded in 1699, the Convent of St. Clara grew to be a rather elaborate complex housing nearly 50 nuns. When it was destroyed by an earthquake in 1717, the sisters quickly rebuilt it with the intention of having it exceed its former glory. It was struck by violent tremors again in 1773, and the site was finally abandoned. The remaining arches and courtyards make a pleasant place to roam. Keep an eye out for hidden passages and underground rooms. ⊠ *2 Av. Sur at 6 Calle Oriente,* ☎ *832–0184.* ⌨ *Q30.* ⊙ *Daily 9–5.*

⑬ Mercado Central. The smell of fresh fruits and vegetables will lead you to this unassuming market. Women in colorful skirts sell huge piles of produce from their own gardens. Their husbands are nearby, chatting with friends or watching a soccer match. ⊠ *Between Amaeda de Santa Lucia and Calle de Recolectos.*

⑧ Monasterio San Francisco. Pedro de San José de Betancur, a friar who lived in the 17th and 18th centuries, was beatified by Pope John Paul II for his good works, which has made his tomb at the Monastery of St. Francis an important local landmark. Many miracles are ascribed to Friar Pedro, who until recently answered all the prayers of petitioners, who had only to knock gently on his casket. His remains have since been moved to a more finely rendered receptacle to the left of the main altar, but those in need of his assistance still cover the original tomb with letters, photos, and plaques. The remainder of the ruins, dating from 1579, is worth a visit for the views of the surrounding areas from the upper floor. Enter through a small path near the rear corner of the church. ⊠ *7 Calle Oriente and 1 Av. Sur,* ☎ *no phone.* ⌨ *Q2.* ⊙ *Daily 9–5.*

⑤ Museo de Arte Colonial. On the former site of the University of San Carlos, the Museum of Colonial Art, its cloisters left largely intact through the shakier centuries, holds a collection of mostly 17th-century religious paintings and statues commissioned by the Castilians. There's also a display of photographs of Semana Santa celebrations. ⊠ *Calle de la Universidad and 4 Av. Sur,* ☎ *832–0429.* ⌨ *Q25.* ⊙ *Tues.–Fri. 9–4, weekends 9–noon and 2–4.*

NEED A BREAK?   Wander over to **Cookies, Etc.** (⊠ 4 Calle Oriente and 3 Av. Norte), a four-table café and pastry shop serving 15 kinds of homemade cookies filled with nuts, chocolate, coconut, oatmeal, and spices.

★ **⑪ Nuestra Señora de La Merced.** Our Lady of Mercy is one of Antigua's most eye-catching attractions, known far and wide for its fanciful yellow stucco facade. The church was built in 1548, only to be destroyed by an earthquake in 1717. It was finally rebuilt 1767, six years before a second massive earthquake forced the city to be abandoned. Architect Juan Luis de Dios Estrada wisely designed the church to be earthquake resistant. The squat shape, thick walls, and small, high windows are responsible for La Merced surviving the 1773 quake with barely a crack. The attached monastery, which has an immense stone fountain in the central courtyard, has excellent views of surrounding volcanoes. There are remnants of unfinished restoration projects here and there, and the fountain never seems to flow, but this doesn't interfere with the church's beauty, particularly when the bougainvillea are in bloom. ⊠ *1 Calle Poniente and 6 Av. Norte,* ☎ *no phone.* ⌐ *Q2.* ⊙ *Daily 9–noon and 3–6.*

② Palacio del Ayuntamiento. As in colonial times, the City Hall continues to serve as the seat of government. Today it also houses two museums, the Museo de Santiago (Museum of St. James) and Museo del Libro Antiguo (Museum of Antique Books). The former, which adjoins what was once the city jail, displays colonial art and artifacts; Central America's first printing press is displayed in the latter, along with a collection of ancient manuscripts. ⊠ *4 Calle Poniente, north side of Plaza Mayor,* ☎ *832–5511.* ⌐ *Q10.* ⊙ *Tues.–Fri. 9–4, weekends 9–noon and 2–4.*

❸ Palacio de los Capitanes Generales. Although it has not yet been fully restored, the Palace of the Captains General is easily recognized by its stately archways. It houses the city's tourism office and other governmental agencies. ⊠ *5 Calle Poniente, south side of Plaza Mayor.*

OFF THE
BEATEN PATH
ANTIGUA SPA RESORT – About 3 km (2 mi) from Antigua in the village of San Pedro El Panorama, this spa is a perfect getaway for those who want to be pampered. Massages, facials, and a variety of other treatments are available. Free transportation to and from Antigua is provided. ⊠ *3 Av. 8–66, Zona 14,* ☎ *333–4620,* FAX *337–3418,* WEB *www.antiguaspa.com.*

❶ Plaza Mayor. Surrounded by old colonial buildings, this tree-lined square is where locals and travelers alike pass quiet afternoons on shady benches listening to the trickling fountain. ⊠ *4 Calle Poniente and 5 Av. Norte.*

⑫ La Recolección. Despite opposition from the city council, which felt the town already had plenty of monasteries, La Recolección was inaugurated in 1717, the same year it was destroyed by an earthquake. Like many others, it was quickly rebuilt but shaken to the ground again in 1773. A stone arch still graces the church stairway, but the ceiling did not fare so well—it lies in huge jumbled blocks within the nave's crumbling walls. The monastery is in better shape though, with spacious courtyards lined with low arches. Enter by a small path to the left of the church. ⊠ *1 Calle Poniente at Calle de Recolectos,* ☎ *no phone.* ⌐ *Q30.* ⊙ *Daily 9–5.*

Dining and Lodging

$$$$ ✕ **Welten.** You feel like a guest in a private home when you arrive at
★ this restaurant—you even have to knock to get in. Take your pick of tables, which are set on a patio with cascading orchids, by a small pool in the rear garden, or in one of the elegantly appointed dining rooms. The menu includes homemade pasta dishes, such as semi-circular *anolini* served with a creamy pepper-and-cognac sauce, as well as fish and meat dishes served with a variety of sauces. All the vegetables are organic, and the bread is made right on the premises. Save room for the tasty desserts. ⊠ *4 Calle Oriente 21,* ☎ *832–0630. AE, DC, MC, V. Closed Tues.*

$$–$$$ ✕ **Café Letras.** With its stark white walls and modern lines, Café Letras calls to mind the cool minimalism of northern Europe. The only color in the restaurant comes from the blue of the striped tablecloths and the red of the roaring fire. The menu, like the ambience, is spare, featuring such Scandinavian favorites as Swedish meatballs. The excellent salmon should not to be missed. There is also an extensive, well-thought-out wine list. ⊠ *1 Calle Poniente 3,* ☎ *832–0277. V. Closed Tues.*

$$–$$$ ✕ **La Casserole.** The chef at this restaurant serves up classic French fare with subtle Guatemalan influences, incorporating local flavors and colors into classic dishes. Although the menu changes every week or so, there are a few constants—-seafood bouillabaisse cooked in a slightly spicy tomato sauce and steak tenderloin with a salsa made from spicy *chiltepe* peppers are two standouts. The restaurant and an adjacent art gallery called El Picarón are housed in a renovated colonial mansion. The peach-and-gold walls are lined with rotating exhibits of paintings and photographs. ⊠ *Callejón de la Concepción 7,* ☎ *832–0219. AE, DC, MC, V. Closed Mon. No dinner Sun.*

$$–$$$ ✕ **Fonda de la Calle Real.** An old Antigua favorite, this place now has two locations serving the same Guatemalan and Mexican fare. The original restaurant, on 5 Avenida Norte near Plaza Mayor, has pleasant views from the second floor. It tends to be a bit cramped, however. The newer space, around the corner on 3 Calle, is in a colonial home spacious enough to offer both indoor and outdoor seating. Musicians stroll about on weekends. The menu includes queso fundido and a famous *caldo real* (a hearty chicken soup). ⊠ *3 Calle Poniente 7, at 6 Av. Norte,* ☎ *832–0507.* ☾ *Daily noon–10;* ⊠ *5 Av. Norte 5, at 4 Calle Poniente,* ☎ *832–2696.* ☾ *Daily 7:30 AM–9:30 PM. AE, DC, MC, V.*

$$ ✕ **Café Flor.** Once this homey restaurant switched from Mexican to Asian cuisine, it never looked back. The friendly proprietors serve a menu that includes Thai curries, Chinese noodles, and Indian vegetable dishes. Be careful—some of the dishes, especially the curries, are quite spicy. Asian food aficionados will find the food not at all like the real thing, but Antigua is, after all, about as far from the source as you can get. On weekends the restaurant is open until midnight. ⊠ *4 Av. Sur 1, at 5 Calle Oriente,* ☎ *832–5274. AE, MC, V.*

$$ ✕ **El Mediterraneo.** Step into this tiny restaurant and you're transported
★ to northern Italy. Delicious antipasti, delicate homemade pastas, and other favorites are among the best Italian dishes in the city. Wash it all down with a selection from the affordable wine list. The atmosphere and decor are low-key, but the service is first rate. ⊠ *6 Calle Poniente 6-A,* ☎ *832–7180. V. Closed Tues.*

$$ ✕ **Quesos y Vino.** This small Italian restaurant serves up homemade pastas, pizzas from a wood-burning oven, and a variety of home-baked breads. Choose from an impressive selection of cheeses and wines sold by the bottle. ⊠ *5 Av. Norte 32, near Arco de Santa Catalina,* ☎ *832–7785. No credit cards. Closed Tues.*

$$ ✕ **Restaurante Don Martín.** For old-world charm, head to this intimate restaurant in a restored colonial home. The spare menu features local and international favorites, including a variety of salads and desserts— the mango salad and five-pepper steak are highly recommended. The service is always impeccable, and the food is delicious. ⊠ *4 Av. Norte 27,* ☎ *832–1063. V.*

$–$$ ✕ **Frida's.** Looking for a place where you and your friends can knock back a few margaritas? At this festive cantina the whole group can fill up on classic Mexican fare, including *taquitos,* enchiladas, and burros, the diminutive siblings of the American-style burrito. Things really get going when the mariachi band shows up. Fans of Frida Kahlo and Diego Rivera will find a great selection of prints from these veritable masters— the menu even bears Frida's signature portrait. ⊠ *5 Av. Norte 29, near Arco de Santa Catalina,* ☎ *832–0504. AE, DC, MC, V.*

$ ✕ **Café Condesa.** Homemade pies and pastries make this a popular spot. Beginning at 6:45 AM, breakfast is known for daily specials such as toast topped with strawberries, papaya, or mango and sprinkled with sugar, and omelets made with fresh vegetables. For lunch try the quiche or the brie plate. You can eat in the café's airy dining room or grab a cap-

When you pack your MCI Calling Card, it's like packing your loved ones along too.

Your MCI Calling Card is the easy way to stay in touch when you travel. Use it to call to and from over 125 countries. Plus, every time you call, you can earn frequent flier miles. So wherever your travels take you, call home with your MCI Calling Card. It's even easy to get one. Just visit **www.mci.com/worldphone** or **www.mci.com/partners.**

EASY TO CALL WORLDWIDE

1. Just enter the WorldPhone® access number of the country you're calling from.
2. Enter or give the operator your MCI Calling Card number.
3. Enter or give the number you're calling.

Argentina	0800-222-6249
Belize	815
Brazil	0800-890-0012

Chile	800-207-300
Colombia ◆	01-8009-160-001
Costa Rica ◆	0800-012-2222
Ecuador ⋮	999-170
El Salvador	800-1567
Guatemala ◆	14-59-189
Honduras ⋮	8000-122
Mexico	01-800-021-8000
Nicaragua	166
Panama	00800-001-0108
Venezuela ◆ ⋮	0-800-100-1131

◆ Public phones may require deposit of coin or phone card for dial tone.   ⋮ Limited availability.

EARN FREQUENT FLIER MILES

Find America *with a Compass*

Written by local authors and illustrated throughout with spectacular color images, Compass American Guides reveal the character and culture of more than 40 of America's most fascinating destinations. Perfect for residents who want to explore their own backyards and for visitors who want an insider's perspective on the history, heritage, and all there is to see and do.

Fodor's COMPASS AMERICAN GUIDES

At bookstores everywhere.

puccino and a sweet roll at Café Condesa Express next door. ⊠ *5 Av. Norte, west side of Plaza Mayor,* ☎ *832–0038. MC, V.*

$ ✕ **Café de la Fuente.** This popular vegetarian eatery takes over the courtyard of La Fuente, a classy collection of shops in a renovated colonial estate. Classical music creates a peaceful atmosphere. The international breakfasts, served until 11 AM, range from New York-style bagels and cream cheese to Mexican-style tofu *ranchero*. La Fuente also makes one of the best desserts in town—a decadently rich chocolate brownie topped with coffee ice cream and chocolate syrup. ⊠ *4 Calle Oriente 14, at 2 Av. Norte,* ☎ *832–4520. No credit cards.*

$ ✕ **Doña Luisa Xicotencatl.** Named after the mistress of Spanish con-
★ quistador Pedro de Alvarado, Doña Luisa Xicotencatl is something of a local institution. A multitude of tables are scattered throughout a dozen rooms and on the balcony and terrace of this former colonial residence, but it's still not easy to get a seat. Early morning specialties include fruit salad, pancakes, and very fresh bread (the bakery is right downstairs). Sandwiches and other light fare make for ample lunch and dinner options. The service can be slow, but the eclectic decor makes the wait pleasant. The bulletin board downstairs is an excellent source of information for travelers. ⊠ *4 Calle Oriente 12, at 3 Av. Norte,* ☎ *832–2578. MC, V, DC.*

$$$$ ✕⊞ **Hotel Posada de Don Rodrigo.** A night in this restored colonial mansion, some 250 years old, is a journey back in time. All the rooms, with soaring ceilings and gorgeous tile floors, are set around two large courtyards and several smaller gardens. A tile fountain trickles in the dining room, which is set on a garden terrace. To the side a woman with a piping hot grill prepares the tortillas for your traditional Guatemalan meal. Light sleepers, beware: the lively marimba band can sometimes play long into the night. The staff will be happy to arrange transportation to a sister hotel in Panajachel. ⊠ *5 Av. Norte 17,* ☎ *832–0291,* WEB *posadadedonrodrigo.centroamerica.com. 35 rooms. Restaurant, bar. AE, DC, MC, V.*

$$–$$$ ✕⊞ **Mesón Panza Verde.** A beautiful courtyard with a fountain sur-
★ rounded by colorful gardens welcomes you to this restful retreat. The elegant rooms downstairs open onto small gardens, while the romantic suites upstairs have four-poster beds piled high with down comforters and terraces where hammocks swing in the breeze. The rooftop patio is wonderful in late afternoon or early morning, and the restaurant is one of the best in town. The meat dishes are particularly good, such as the *lomito* bourguignonne with escargot. Leave room for the scrumptious desserts. ⊠ *5 Av. Sur 19,* ☎ FAX *832–2925. 3 rooms, 3 suites. Restaurant. AE, DC, MC, V.*

$$$$ ⊞ **Casa Azul.** Not many hotels have guest books filled with recommendations for specific rooms, but those on the second floor are so good that people want to share them with others. The upstairs rooms with views of the volcanoes are more expensive, but they are also larger and brighter. All are painted in washes of red and, of course, blue. With sitting rooms that open onto a pleasant courtyard, centrally located Casa Azul has a serene atmosphere. Breakfast is served beside the small pool. ⊠ *4 Av. Norte 5,* ☎ *832–0961 or 832–0962,* FAX *832–0944,* WEB *www.casazul.guate.com. 10 rooms. Pool, hot tub, sauna, bar. AE, DC, MC, V.*

$$$$ ⊞ **Casa de Los Sueños.** This stunning colonial mansion, recently converted into an elegant bed-and-breakfast, may truly be the house of your dreams. With a lovely patio surrounded on all sides by hanging plants, this little inn is a perfect romantic getaway. A joyful antique hobbyhorse and a square grand piano add character to the sitting room. Tastefully decorated with antiques, the rooms are painted the washed-out hues that typify Antigua. A pool out back is a refreshing retreat. ⊠ *1 Av. Sur*

1, ☎ FAX 832–0802 or 832–2177, WEB www.lacasadelossuenos.com. 8 rooms. Pool. AE, DC, MC, V.

$$$$ ⊞ **Casa Santo Domingo.** This elegant hotel was built around the ruins
★ of the ancient Monasterio Santo Domingo, taking advantage of its long
passageways and snug little courtyards. Dark carved-wood furniture,
yellow stucco walls, and iron sconces preserve the monastic atmosphere.
Luxurious amenities abound, such as private hot tubs in the baths, but
these do not detract from the historical feel. The food at the restaurant, however, is considerably less inspiring. A small museum is housed
in the hotel. ⊠ *3 Calle Oriente 28,* ☎ *832–0140,* FAX *832–4155,* WEB
*www.casasantodomingo.com.gt. 97 rooms. Restaurant, pool, mas-
sage, sauna, spa, bar, concierge. AE, DC, MC, V.*

$$$$ ⊞ **Hotel Antigua.** As a tasteful combination of colonial elegance and
modern comfort, Hotel Antigua is one of the city's most popular lodgings. The sparkling pool, set amid lush gardens, is a treat after a day
exploring the dusty city streets. Standard rooms have plenty of space
for two, while one- and two-level suites can house a whole family quite
comfortably. The oldest part of the hotel is a colonial-style building
with a restaurant, bar, and a beautiful sitting room. Weddings are
sometimes held in a sunny esplanade overlooking the ruins of Iglesia
de San José. ⊠ *8 Calle Poniente 1, at 5 Av. Sur,* ☎ *832–0288 or 832–
0331,* FAX *832–2807,* WEB *www.hotelantigua.com.gt. 60 rooms. 2 restaurants, bar, pool, playground, convention center. AE, DC, MC, V.*

$$$$ ⊞ **Posada del Ángel.** You'd never know from the unassuming wooden
★ gate that you're at the threshold of Antigua's most beautiful lodging.
It's all part of the ruse at this truly angelic inn. Large corner fireplaces
warm the rooms, each of which is decorated with well-chosen antiques.
Those on the main floor look out onto a plant-filled courtyard, while
the one above has a private rooftop terrace. Early morning light
bounces off the long reflecting pool and into the windows of the cozy
breakfast room. The library and sitting room are full of charm. The
staff has catered to presidents and prime ministers, but you'll receive
the same fine service. ⊠ *4 Av. Sur 24A,* ☎ *832–5303; 800/934–0065
in the U.S.,* WEB *www.posadadelangel.com. 5 rooms. Dining room, room
service, bar, library, concierge, airport shuttle. AE, DC, MC, V.*

$$$ ⊞ **Hotel Aurora.** This genteel inn, still run by the same family that opened
it in 1923, has an unbeatable location in the heart of the city. The dimly
lighted colonial-style rooms face a beautifully tended garden. You can
relax on a tiled portico strewn with plenty of comfortable rattan chairs.
Rooms have wooden furniture and old-fashioned armoires. Breakfast
is included. ⊠ *4 Calle Oriente 16,* ☎ FAX *832–0217/5515. 16 rooms.
AE, MC, V.*

$$$ ⊞ **Hotel Convento.** This hotel was built among the ruins of an old con-
★ vent where only the often-photographed Arco de Santa Catalina re-
mains. The spacious rooms, all a bit dimly lighted, are tastefully
decorated with handicrafts and handwoven bedspreads. Most face a
verdant courtyard where a smattering of tables and chairs encourages
you to venture out with a good book. The modern rooms in the annex
are brighter and have kitchenettes. ⊠ *5 Av. Norte 28, at 2 Calle
Poniente,* ☎ *832–3879,* FAX *832–3079,* WEB *www.convento.com. 18
rooms. Restaurant, some kitchenettes, Internet, shop. No credit cards.*

$$$ **Quinta de las Flores.** With view of three volcanoes from the well-
★ tended gardens and the open-air dining room, this luxury hotel takes
advantage of its location southeast of the city. It's great for those in search
of peace and quiet. This 19th-century hacienda combines colonial com-
fort with a sense of whimsy—the decor includes modern takes on tra-
ditional crafts. All the high-ceilinged rooms have fireplaces to keep you
cozy on chilly evenings. The quaint bungalows, which sleep as many
as five, even have small kitchenettes. ⊠ *Calle del Hermano Pedro 6,*

☎ 832–3721 or 832–3722, FAX 832–3726, WEB *www.quintadelasflores. com. 9 rooms, 5 bungalows. Restaurant, some kitchenettes, minibars, pool, bar, playground. AE, DC, MC, V.*

$$ 🔟 **Posada Asjemenou.** There are plenty of charming hotels in colonial mansions, but the difference here is that you won't pay through the nose. The rooms are clean and comfortable, and the staff is friendly and eager. The small café serves breakfast and snacks. If you hanker for more substantial fare, head to the nearby pizzeria run by the same family. ⊠ *5 Av. Norte 31, at 1 Calle Poniente,* ☎ FAX *832–2670,* WEB *www.antiguacolonial.com/asjemenou.htm. 12 rooms, 9 with bath. Café. AE, DC, MC, V.*

$$ 🔟 **Posada Los Bucaros.** The pretty fountain that gives this hotel its name, set against a wall in the courtyard, is just one of little touches that make this hotel special. The rooms have red-tile floors and wrought-iron furnishings. The owner and staff are extremely friendly. ⊠ *7 Av. Norte 94,* ☎ FAX *832–2346. 12 rooms. Breakfast room. No credit cards.*

Nightlife and the Arts

You won't have trouble finding a bar in Antigua, as the city is filled with watering holes. Many of these you'll find within a few blocks of Plaza Mayor are favored by young people studying Spanish at one of the many language schools. Head a bit farther afield and you can raise a glass with the locals.

Bars

Locals swear that the place to be is **Ricky's** (⊠ 4 Av. Norte 4). The conversation is convivial and the cocktails are inexpensive. Homesick Brits should head to **Hogshead** (⊠ 1 Calle Poniente 23), where pub food is served in a relaxed atmosphere. The staff is warm and attentive. Upstairs from Frida's is **El Atico** (⊠ 5 Av. Norte 29), a popular local hangout. The pool table is free as long as you're drinking.

For live music, seek out **Jazz Gruta** (⊠ Calzada de Santa Lucía Norte 17), an intimate club where local groups perform every night except Sunday. Root for your favorite team at **Monoloco** (⊠ 2 Av. Norte 6B), where soccer matches are always on the television. Wash down one of the giant burritos with a pint of one of the micro-brews. Head to **Tacool** (⊠ 5 Av. Norte 30A) for late-night snacks.

Dance Clubs

The ever popular **Chimenea** (⊠ 4 Calle Poniente and 7 Av. Sur) caters to students who crowd the small dance floor. If you want to dance the night away, **Casbah** (⊠ 5 Av. Norte 45) is Antigua's only real disco. Latin rhythms make the place popular.

Outdoor Activities and Sports

From mountain biking to white-water rafting, Antigua has plenty of activities for those who want to explore the great outdoors. Don't just head out solo, however. Some of the most popular destinations have been the sites of robberies. Choose a knowledgeable tour operator who will set you up with a guide who knows the area. The most reputable ones will even refund your money if the trip doesn't go as planned. Don't count on having the same luck with the freelance tour operators who approach you in Plaza Mayor.

Biking

The rolling hills that surround Antigua make for great mountain biking. Local agencies rent bikes as well as equipment like helmets and water bottles. **Mayan Bike Tours** (⊠ 3 Calle Poniente and 7 Av. Norte, ☎ 832–3743, WEB www.mayanadventures.com) offers trips ranging from easy rides in a morning or afternoon to more challenging treks lasting several days. **Old Town Outfitters** (⊠ 5 Av. Sur 12, ☎ 832–4171, WEB www.bikeguatemala.com) caters to a backpacker crowd, but its trips are suitable for people of all ages.

Hiking

Hikers head to the volcanoes surrounding Antigua. Of the four reachable from Antigua, only Volcán Pacayá is still active (although Volcán Fuego smokes fairly often). Volcán Pacayá erupts with some frequency, so always ask about conditions before you sign up for a tour. The crater is awhirl with sulfur gas emanating from the lava you'll see deep inside. The vapors smell terrible, so bring along a handkerchief to cover your nose. It's also a good idea to bring a sweater, as it gets cold on the summit as the sun begins to set. You'll want to stay a while to enjoy the view. Do not wear sandals to climb any of these monoliths, as the volcanic rock can be razor sharp.

Antigua's best volcano expeditions are offered by **Eco-Tours Chejos** (⊠ 3 Calle Poniente 24, ☎ 832–5464), whose friendly owner has climbed Volcán Pacaya more than 1,800 times. The prices are higher than most, but there are usually fewer people. **Sin Fronteras** (⊠ 3 Calle Poniente 12, ☎ 832–1017) will take you on a one-day trip to Pacayá or a two-day trip to Fuego or Acatenango. **Voyageur** (⊠ 4 Calle Oriente 14, ☎ 832–4237) is another reputable outfitter.

Shopping

Antigua is a shopper's paradise. The single largest concentration of shops can be found in the **Mercado de Artisanías** (⊠ 4 Calle Poniente and Alameda de Santa Lucía), but stroll down any street and you'll find boutiques selling everything from finely embroidered blouses to beautiful ceramics.

Books

Thanks to its sizable expatriate population, Antigua has Guatemala's best selection of English-language reading material. **Casa Andinista** (⊠ 4 Calle Oriente 5) sells some hard-to-find titles, as well as note cards and other items. Facing Plaza Mayor, **Casa del Conde** (⊠ 5 Av. Norte 4) has a good selection of books. Along with new and used books, **Hamlin & White** (⊠ 4 Calle Oriente 12A) sells newspapers and magazines. **Libreria Pensativo** (⊠ 5 Av. Norte 29) has a huge selection of used books. **Un Poco de Todo** (⊠ 5 Av. Sur 10) has a decent selection of English titles.

Clothing

A 10-minute drive southwest of Antigua brings you to San Antonio Aguas Calientes, a dusty little village built around a hot springs. It's worth a special trip here to visit **Artesanías Unidas** (⊠ San Antonio Aguas Calientes, ☎ 831–5950) known for its incomparable selection of handwoven fabrics. In Antigua, **Nim Po't** (⊠ 5 Av. Norte 29) is a self-proclaimed *centro de textiles tradicionales*. Here you'll find a large selection of fabrics from a few dozen neighboring villages.

Pues Si Tu (⊠ 5 Calle Norte 27A) is a little shop that carries a variety of clothing in traditional patterns. **Manos de Hoy, Arte de Ayer** (⊠ 6 Av. 11) offers a hodgepodge of handmade items including embroidered blouses.

Galleries

El Sitio (⊠ 5 Calle Poniente 15) is a small gallery that also occasionally screens films and hosts concerts. **Galería Estilo de Vida** (⊠ 4 Calle Oriente 23) displays art and furniture. An excellent selection of primitivist paintings is on display at **Wer Art Gallery** (⊠ 4 Calle Oriente 27).

La Antigua Galería de Arte (⊠ 4 Calle Oriente 15) features works from the 19th and 20th centuries. **La Salamandra** (⊠ 6 Calle Oriente 3A) has a small collection of modern art.

Handicrafts

With a wide selection of *artisanía,* **Casa de Artes** (⊠ 4 Av. Sur 11) is a nice place to browse. **Casa de los Gigantes** (⊠ 7 Calle Oriente 18) has a good selection of quality items, including genuine antique festival masks. For hand-painted pottery by local artisans, try **Topis** (⊠ 5 Av. Norte 20B).

Menage (⊠ 3 Av. Sur 8) carries everything from colorful ceramics to hand-blown glassware. **Angelina** (⊠ 4 Calle Oriente 22) sells surreal items made of carved wood.

Jewelry

Jade is mined all over the country, but it is fashioned into jewelry almost exclusively in Antigua. Most of the jade shops offer free tours of their facilities, so you can see how the stones are selected, cut, and polished. The craftsmanship is beautiful, and many pieces are quite affordable by U.S. standards. Perhaps the best place to watch artisans carving the green stone is at **Jades** (⊠ 4 Calle Oriente 34, ☎ 832–3841). Former U.S. president Bill Clinton bought a necklace here for his daughter, Chelsea. With a small in-house workshop, **Jades Imperio Maya** (⊠ 5 Calle Oriente 2) has an extremely friendly staff. **Casa del Jade** (⊠ 4 Calle Oriente 10) is small but nice. The **Jade Kingdom** (⊠ 5 Av. Norte 28) also has tours through its factory.

Tired of green stones? **Joyería del Angel** (⊠ 4 Calle Oriente 5A) has a fine selection of 100% jade-free jewelry. **Platería Típica Maya** (⊠ 7 Calle Oriente 9) is a top-notch jewelry retailer.

Antigua A to Z

To research prices, get advice from other travelers, and book travel arrangements, visit www.fodors.com.

AIR TRAVEL TO AND FROM ANTIGUA

The nearest airport is Guatemala City's Aeropuerto Internacional La Aurora, a little less than an hour's drive away. If your hotel does not offer a transfer from the airport, there are plenty of shuttle buses that run this route.

BUS TRAVEL TO AND FROM ANTIGUA

A variety of companies run frequent shuttle buses between Guatemala City and Antigua. Transportes Turisticos Atitrans and Turansa are both reputable companies. Buses leave every 15 minutes from 18 Calle and 4 Avenida in Zona 1 in Guatemala City. They depart on a similar schedule from the bus station in Antigua. It's best to call ahead for reservations, but you can also purchase tickets on board.

Transportes Turisticos Atitrans and Turansa also offer service to the Western Highlands, with the cost ranging from 100 quetzales for Chichicastenango and Panajachel to 200 quetzales for Quetzaltenango. You can also catch a public bus at the terminal, which is cheaper but much less comfortable. There are one or two direct buses to Panajachel and Quetzaltenango each day, as well as five or six bound for Chichicastenango. Tickets cost about 16 quetzales.

➤ BUS COMPANIES: **Transportes Turisticos Atitrans** (⊠ 6 Av. Sur 8, ☎ 832–1381). **Turansa** (⊠ 5 Calle Poniente 11B, ☎ 832–4691).

➤ Bus Stations: **Terminal de Buses** (✉ Alameda Santa Lucía at 4 Calle Poniente).

CAR RENTAL

If you want to rent a car to explore the Antigua, it's a good idea to do so in Guatemala City's Aeropuerto Internacional La Aurora. In Antigua a reputable local agency is Tabarini Rent-A-Car.
➤ Local Agencies: **Tabarini Rent-A-Car** (✉ 2 Calle Poniente 19A, ☎ FAX 832–3091).

CAR TRAVEL

The roads around Antigua are mostly well paved, so drives through the countryside can be quite pleasant. Keep on your guard, though, as other vehicles may ignore traffic laws and common sense. As one jovial man behind the wheel of a bus recently said, "All drivers in Guatemala are crazy."

To reach Antigua, drive west out of Guatemala City via the Calzada Roosevelt, which becomes the Pan-American Highway. At San Lucas turn right off the highway and drive south to Antigua. If you're coming from the Western Highlands, head south near Chimaltenango.

EMERGENCIES

For all emergencies call the police department. Contact the tourist police for free escorts, information, and minor matters.
➤ Emergency Services: **Police** (✉ 5 Calle Poniente, west end of Palacio del Capitán, ☎ 832–0251). **Tourist police** (✉ 4 Av. Norte, Palacio del Ayuntamiento, ☎ 832–7290 or 832–0532).
➤ Hospitals: **Pedro de Betancourt Hospital** (✉ Calle de Los Peregrinos and 4 Av. Sur, ☎ 831–1319).
➤ Pharmacies: **Farmacia Roca** (✉ 4 Calle Poniente 11, ☎ 832–0612).

INTERNET

With its sizable population of expatriates, Antigua has a good supply of Internet cafés. The competition is fierce, so expect very low prices. Enlaces and Enlinea have conveniently located offices. Antigua Post also has a scanner, so you can send photos to friends and family back home.
➤ Internet Cafés: **Enlaces** (✉ 6 Av. Norte 1). **Enlinea** (✉ 1 Calle Poniente 9; 1 Av. Sur 17; 5 Av. Sur 12). **Antigua Post** (✉ 6 Av. Sur 12).

MAIL AND SHIPPING

Antigua's main post office is across from the bus station. You can drop off your letters here, or ask the staff at your hotel to mail them for you. For packages try Envios Etc.
➤ Overnight Services: **Envios Etc.** (✉ 3 Av. Norte 26).
➤ Post Offices: **Correos Central** (✉ 4 Calle Poniente and Alameda Santa Lucía).

MONEY MATTERS

You won't have a problem finding ATMs in Antigua. Bancared, near Plaza Mayor, has one that accepts cards issued in the United States.
➤ Banks: **Bancared** (✉ 4 Calle Poniente 22).

SAFETY

Antigua is one of Guatemala's safest cities, as the streets around Plaza Mayor are patrolled by the tourist police. Farther from the square you should walk in groups or take taxis after the sun goes down. Be careful in the countryside, where there have been some robberies. If you plan to tackle one of the nearby volcanoes, hire a reputable guide.

TAXIS

A taxi between Guatemala City and Antigua should cost about 200 quetzales. Many run between Aeropuerto Internacional La Aurora and Antigua. Mijandos has a good reputation.

➤ TAXI COMPANIES: **Mijandos** (☎ 832–5051 or 832–5049).

TOUR OPERATORS

There are a number of travel agencies that can book you on trips around the region and throughout the country. Among the better known are Rainbow Travel Center, Vision Travel, and Turansa. One of the best is Antigua Tours, run by independent guide Elizabeth Bell. It offers all sorts of personalized trips, from walking tours of Antigua to excursions to Tikal.

A number of *fincas* (farms) in the hills around Antigua offer tours. Finca Los Nietos, a coffee plantation, and Finca Valhalla, a macadamia farm, are both southwest of the city.

➤ TOUR COMPANIES: **Antigua Tours** (✉ 3 Calle Oriente 28, in the Hotel Casa Santo Domingo, ☎ 832–5821, WEB www.antiguatours.net). **Finca Los Nietos** (✉ 6 km [4 mi] from Antigua, ☎ 831–5438). **Finca Valhalla** (✉ 7 km southwest of Antigua, ☎ 831–5799). **Rainbow Travel Center** (✉ 7 Av. Sur 8, ☎ 832–4202). **Turansa** (✉ 5 Calle Poniente 11B, ☎ 832–4691). **Vision Travel** (✉ 3 Av. Norte 3, ☎ 832–3293, WEB www.guatemalainfo.com).

VISITOR INFORMATION

Inguat, the national tourism agency, has an office in the Palacio de los Capitanes Generales, on the south side of Plaza Mayor. It is open daily 8–noon and 2–5.

➤ TOURIST INFORMATION: **Inguat** (✉ 5 Calle Poniente, Palacio de los Capitanes Generales, ☎ 832–0763).

THE WESTERN HIGHLANDS

Beginning near the colonial capital of Antigua, the Western Highlands run all the way to the border of Mexico. This is a spectacular landscape where grumbling volcanoes rise above broad alpine lakes and narrow river ravines, lush tropical valleys and misty cloud forests, pine-draped hillsides and wide pastoral plains. Many people come to the Western Highlands to experience its natural beauty, and few are disappointed.

This region is home to the majority of Guatemalan's indigenous people, most of whom live in small villages you'll find nestled in the valleys and perched on the hillsides. Most are descendants of the Maya, and they proudly hold onto their heritage. Many of the 23 distinct ethnic groups continue to speak their own languages, such as Cakchiquel, Mam, and Tzutuhil. Some still follow the ancient 260-day Tzolkin Maya calendar, one of the most accurate ever invented. And although Christianity has been practiced here for 500 years, it still has only a tentative hold. In Chichicastenango, Maya ceremonies unfold on the steps of the local church. Maximón, the smoking and drinking saint, hears prayers and receives symbolic offerings of cigars and whiskey from faithful believers in the lakeside village of Santiago Atitlán.

Village life, for the most part, consists of backbreaking work in the fields. Most survive on subsistence farming, selling what little is left over. Entire families pack fruits, vegetables, and whatever else they have onto their backs and head to market. Market day, held at least once a week in most communities, is as much a social gathering as anything else. Activity starts in the wee hours, when there is still a chill in the air. Bargaining and selling are carried out in hushed, amicable tones. The momentum wanes around late afternoon as the crowds depart, eager to head home before the sun sinks behind the mountains.

Highland markets were once a local affair, but in the past decade or so they have began to attract the attention of the rest of the world. The market for Guatemalan textiles has grown by leaps and bounds, and many villages have benefited. Unfortunately, many of the finer points of the weaving tradition are being left by the wayside to accommodate the frenzied shoppers. The traditional back-strap looms are speedily being replaced with gleaming sewing machines so garments can be churned out faster. Fewer people make the handmade *huipiles*, the embroidered blouses that sometimes take as long as six months to weave. The patterns that once relayed information such as what village the wearer was from are now abandoned for those favored by tourists. But you can still witness some symbols that speak volumes about the culture: if a woman's apron is finished with jagged edges, for example, it means she is from the mountains.

Much of the country's 36-year civil war was fought in the Western Highlands. During the "scorched-earth" campaigns of the early 1980s, entire towns were burned to the ground and tens of thousands of people were tortured and killed by paramilitary forces. The violence was designed to terrify the indigenous peoples so they would be too afraid to assist the rebel guerrillas with so much as a loaf of bread. And terrify them it did. Thousands fled into the mountains or across the border into Mexico or Belize. Although many issues remain unresolved, the people of the Western Highlands are now weary of fighting, and most, regardless of their wartime sympathies, say that they simply want peace.

The heart of the Western Highlands is undoubtedly Lago Atitlán. At the foot of three massive dormant volcanoes—San Pedro (9,920 ft), Tolimán (10,340 ft), and Atitlán (11,560 ft)—the lake is one of the loveliest spots in Guatemala. More than a dozen communities are found along its shores. Early in the morning and on calm nights the lake's water is as smooth as glass, capturing the huge volcanic cones in its reflection. But in the early afternoon a wind known as the *xochomil* blows across the lake, and the surface turns choppy and defiant. Another curiosity of the lake is its lack of outlets, as the water drains through underwater fissures. In 1976, when an earthquake broke open a gigantic underwater chamber, the surface level to drop a whopping 6 ft in a matter of hours.

To the north of Lago Atitlán is the charming village of Chichicastenango. Quiet for most of the week, it explodes with activity on Thursday and Sunday, when a sprawling open-air market takes over its main square and the surrounding streets. West of Lago Atitlán lies Quetzaltenango, Guatemala's second-largest city. The Sierra de Chuacús, a string of active and dormant volcanoes just outside the city limits, makes this an ideal place for outdoor activities. It also has a number of Spanish schools, attracting students who want an alternative to the crowded classes in Antigua.

Guatemala has been dubbed the "land of eternal spring," and this region's warm afternoons and cool evenings fit the bill. But Quetzaltenango and other high-altitude towns can get downright cold at night, especially in the winter. There's no need to overpack, but a sweater or jacket is essential.

Numbers in the text correspond to numbers in the margin and on the Lago Atitlán map and the Western Highlands map.

Lago Atitlán

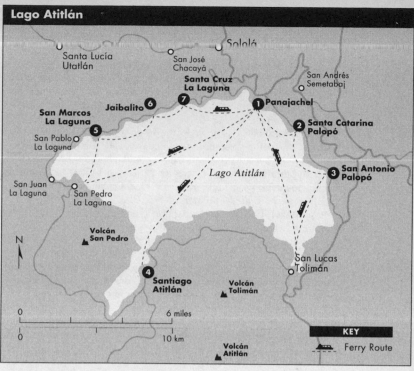

Santa Lucía
Utatlán

San José
Chacayá

Sololá

**Santa Cruz
La Laguna**

San Andrés
Semetabaj

Jaibalito ⑥   ⑦

① Panajachel

**San Marcos
La Laguna**

⑤

② **Santa Catarina
Palopó**

San Pablo
La Laguna

Lago Atitlán

③ **San Antonio
Palopó**

San Juan
La Laguna

San Pedro
La Laguna

N

**Volcán
San Pedro**

San Lucas
Tolimán

④ **Santiago
Atitlán**

**Volcán
Tolimán**

0 ⊢———⊣ 6 miles

0 ⊢———⊣ 10 km

**Volcán
Atitlán**

KEY

🚢 Ferry Route

Panajachel

① *110 km (68 mi) northwest of Antigua.*

A few decades ago Panajachel was just a quiet Cakchiquel village on the northern shore of Lago Atitlán, but it has since grown into a hang-out for foreigners who came here and loved the region so much that they never left. And who can blame them? Bordered by three volcanoes that drop off into the crystalline waters of Lago Atitlán, Panajachel's setting could hardly be more dramatic. In the past few years Panajachel has become an extremely popular destination for international travelers, so it's no surprise that the town has earned the nickname Gringotenango. But the old part of town hasn't lost its charm, and on market day Panajachel looks pretty much like any other highland village.

The **Reserva Natural Atitlán** (⊠ 2 km [1 mi] west of Panajachel, ☎ 762–2565) has a walking trail that loops through a small river canyon, crossing suspension bridges and passing a butterfly atrium and enclosures of spider monkeys and coatimundis. There's also a private beach for a bit of posteducational relaxation. Campsites are available in the park.

Dining and Lodging

$$$–$$$$ ✗ **Casablanca.** Panajachel's most elegant restaurant, Casablanca has a white-walled dining room with windows overlooking the main street. The handful of tables on the upper level is much more intimate. The menu is ample, if a bit overpriced, and includes a few seafood standouts such as lobster. Musicians occasionally entertain. ⊠ *Calle Principal 0–93, at Calle Santander,* ☎ 762–1015, **FAX** 762–2025. *AE, DC, MC, V.*

$–$$ ✕ **El Bistro.** Hummingbirds dart among flowering vines at this ro-
★   mantic eatery on the shores of Lago Atitlán. Enter though an iron gate
       that leads into a garden hidden behind a low wall. Eat at one of the
       tables outside or choose between the pair of intimate dining rooms.
       All the delicious Italian food, from the tasty bread to the fresh pasta,
       is homemade. Two standout specialties are the fettuccine *arrabiata* (with
       a slightly spicy tomato sauce) and the steak au poivre (cooked in a wine
       sauce and black pepper) that is served with fresh vegetables. ⊠ *End
       of Calle Santander,* ☎ *762–0508. AE, MC, V. Closed Tues.*

$–$$ ✕ **El Patio.** Although it's known by the outdoor patio that gives the place
       its name, most of the restaurant's tables are inside a large dining room
       with little ambience. Nevertheless, it's a popular spot for breakfast. The
       lunch and dinner menus offer greater variety, including such items as
       filet mignon, roast pork, and chicken à la king. On Sunday the staff serves
       up barbecue. ⊠ *Calle Santander,* ☎ *762–2041. AE, DC, MC, V.*

$ ✕ **Pájaro Azul.** Tired of *frijoles* for breakfast? There isn't a single bean
★   to be found at this pastel-hue café, which serves up outstanding crepes.
       Choose from a small but creative menu of savory dinner crepes and
       sweet dessert crepes, or pick and choose among your favorite ingre-
       dients. While you wait you can thumb through a pile of back-issue mag-
       azines (including, oddly enough, the *New Yorker*). ⊠ *Calle Santander,
       next to the post office,* ☎ *762–2596. No credit cards.*

$$$$ ✕▦ **Hotel Atitlán.** In a quiet cove east of Panajachel, this Spanish-style
★   inn consists of a main building flanked by two-story wings that sur-
       round a pool. The extensive grounds border on a long stretch of shore-
       line and the Reserva Natural Atitlán, a wooded reserve crossed by
       footpaths and hanging bridges. The tile-floor rooms, each with carved
       wooden furniture and handwoven bedspreads, have balconies over-
       looking the gardens or the lake. Even if you don't stay here, stop by
       for views of the lake at sunset. The menu is reliable, if a bit overpriced,
       offering entrées such as baked chicken. ⊠ *2 km (1 mi) west of Pana-
       jachel,* ☎ *762–0048 in Panajachel; 360–8405 in Guatemala City.* WEB
       *www.hotelatitlan.com. 64 rooms. Restaurant, pool, beach tennis court,
       bar, shop. AE, DC, MC, V.*

$$$ ✕▦ **Cacique Inn.** A collection of little buildings about a block from
       the main street, Cacique Inn is a relaxing retreat. Spacious, if sparsely
       furnished, rooms have sliding-glass doors that open onto the lovely gar-
       den. The rooms may seem a bit cool because of the tile floors, but they
       have fireplaces that warm you up in a snap. The grounds are surrounded
       by a wall, which makes the terraces by the pool a private place to sun-
       bathe. The restaurant is one of the best in town, serving an wide se-
       lection of Guatemalan dishes. The agreeable chefs will sometimes even
       prepare dishes to order. ⊠ *Calle del Embarcadero, near Calle Princi-
       pal,* ☎ FAX *762–1205 or 762–2053. 35 rooms. Restaurant, pool, bar.
       AE, DC, MC, V.*

$$$$ ▦ **Hotel Posada de Don Rodrigo.** At the end of Calle Santander, this
       excellent hotel possesses some of the best views of the lake (they would
       be even better if the giant waterslide wasn't in the way). The nicely
       decorated rooms make use of handwoven fabric from the local com-
       munities. Ask for one of the newer rooms, which have better views.
       The restaurant, which serves good standard fare, never seems crowded.
       Relax by the pool or in one of the hammocks hung along a breezy cor-
       ridor. ⊠ *End of Calle Santander,* ☎ *762–2326 or 762–2329,* FAX *331–
       6838.* WEB *posadadedonrodrigo.centroamerica.com. 39 rooms. Restau-
       rant, pool, sauna, squash. AE, DC, MC, V.*

$$$$ ▦ **Porta Hotel del Lago.** Panajachel's biggest hotel, the Porta Hotel del
       Lago also has the most amenities. Although it lacks the character of
       smaller hotels, it's comfortable and conveniently located and has top-
       notch service. Rooms have balconies overlooking the public beach on

Lago Atitlán. The huge restaurant next door looks out onto the pool. ⊠ *End of Calle Rancho Grande, at Calle Buenas Nuevas,* ☎ *762–1555,* FAX *762–1562,* WEB *www.portahotels.com. 100 rooms. Restaurant, cable TV, pool, gym, hot tub, massage, sauna, bar, meeting room. AE, DC, MC, V.*

$$$ 🏨 **Hotel Dos Mundos.** Set amid colorful gardens, this hotel gives you comfortable accommodations without the hefty price tag of more deluxe digs. The medium-size rooms are simply and tastefully furnished. Most open onto the pool area, where you can spend your afternoon on a lounge chair with a cocktail. The restaurant has a certain elegance, with tables set beneath a soaring thatch roof. The menu includes well-made pasta dishes and lots of wine. ⊠ *Calle Santander 4–72,* ☎ *762–2078 or 762–2140,* FAX *762–0127, dosmundos@atitlan.com. 21 rooms. Restaurant, pool, travel services. AE, DC, MC, V.* WEB *www.atitlan.com.*

$$$ 🏨 **Rancho Grande Inn.** A German immigrant by the name of Milly Schleisier opened this string of bungalows back in the 1940s. In so doing, she created what is still one of the most charming of Panajachel's accommodations, melding the designs of country houses in her homeland with the colorful culture of her adopted country. Each of the bungalows is unique, but all have king-size beds covered with locally woven spreads. The largest bungalow, which can sleep up to five, also has a fireplace. Breakfast is served family style every morning. ⊠ *Calle Rancho Grande,* ☎ *762–1554,* FAX *762–2247,* WEB *www.travellog.com. 11 bungalows, 1 bungalow suite. Breakfast room. AE, DC, MC, V.*

$$ 🏨 **Müllers Guest House.** On the quiet street parallel to Calle Santander, this little inn is set in a pretty garden. The rooms call to mind a European bed-and-breakfast with their honey-hued wood floors and pastel walls. Breakfast is in the homey sitting room, the same place where you will enjoy wine and cheese in the late afternoon. Reserve well in advance in high season. ⊠ *Calle Rancho Grande 1–82,* ☎ *762–2442 or 762–2392,* FAX *337–0656, htmuller@amigo.net.gt 3 rooms, 1 bungalow. MC, V.*

$ 🏨 **Hotel Galindo.** Separate sitting rooms with fireplaces make the suites at this budget-minded hotel worth the money. They surround a courtyard filled with greenery. The restaurant is breezy and attractive. ⊠ *Calle Principal,* ☎ *762–1168 or 762–2071. 14 rooms, 4 suites. Restaurant. No credit cards.*

Nightlife and the Arts

Because Panajachel is a resort town, it probably has the liveliest nightlife in the highlands. Most bars are clustered near the intersection of Avenida de los Arboles and Calle Principal. The **Circus Bar** (⊠ Av. de los Arboles, ☎ 762–2056) is a popular spot for locals and travelers alike. There's often live music. The dimly lighted **Chapiteau Disco** (⊠ Av. de los Arboles) plays mostly rock.

A cluster of other bars less frequented by backpackers is in the same area. You can enjoy good Mexican food at the aptly named **Sunset Café** (⊠ Calle Santander). There's live music almost every night. The **Grapevine** (⊠ Calle Santander) hosts a popular happy hour from 7 to 9.

Outdoor Activities and Sports

Water sports are becoming more popular at Lago Atitlán, giving the lake a Club Med feel. You can rent a canoe from **Diversiones Acuáticas Balom** (⊠ on the public beach near ferry terminals, ☎ 762–2242). It's best to get out early and be back by noon, as the afternoon winds can be fierce. The company also offers tours of the lake.

For exploring the countryside you can rent a mountain bike at **Moto Servicio Quiché** (⊠ Av. de los Arboles at Calle Principal) and pedal over to nearby villages.

Shopping

Calle Santander is one long open-air market, lined on both sides with vendors who hang their wares from fences and makeshift stalls. Examine the items carefully, as goods purchased here are often not the best quality. An outdoor market called **Tinimit Maya** (⊠ Calle Santander) is easily the best place for reasonably priced artesanía. **El Guipil** (⊠ Calle Santander) is a large boutique with a varied selection of handmade items from highland villages. **Ojalá Antiques** (⊠ Av. de los Arboles) has a small but excellent selection of antiques.

Santa Catarina Palopó

② *4 km (2½ mi) east of Panajachel.*

You'll be surrounded by the brilliant blues and greens of huipiles worn by local women as you walk down the cobblestone streets of this picturesque town. From here you'll be treated to magical views of the trio of volcanoes that loom over the lake. In Santa Catarina you'll see ramshackle homes standing within sight of luxury chalets whose owners arrive as often by helicopter as they do by car.

Dining and Lodging

$$$ ✕🖫 **Villa Santa Catarina.** In a long yellow building with an adobe-tile roof, Villa Santa Catarina has magical views. Rooms are small, but each has a private balcony overlooking the lake. The restaurant serves typical Guatemalan dishes such as *pepian de pollo* (chicken in a spicy sauce). You can relax in the pool or head to a series of natural hot springs that are only a few hundred feet away. ⊠ *Calle de la Playa,* ☎ FAX *334–8136. 36 rooms. Restaurant, bar, pool, waterskiing. AE, DC, MC, V.*

$$$$ 🖫 **Casa Palopó.** By far the best B&B on the lake, luxurious Casa
★   Palopó has an almost mystical atmosphere. Each of the six rooms, decorated with religious-themed artworks from around the world, offers incredible views of the volcanoes. Muted blues run throughout this former villa, mirroring the colors of the lake. Most baths have giant tubs perfect for soaking. ⊠ *South of Santa Catarina Palopó,* ☎ 762–2270, FAX *762–2721.* WEB *www.casapalopo.com. 2 rooms, 2 suites. Restaurant, pool, library, Internet, no kids under 15. AE, DC, MC, V.*

San Antonio Palopó

❸ *6½ km (4 mi) east of Santa Catarina Palopó.*

Slightly larger than neighboring Santa Catarina Palopó, San Antonio Palopó is a quiet farming village. Most people have tiny plots of land where they grow green onions, which you may see them cleaning down by the lake. This is one of only a handful of regions in Latin America where men still dress in traditional costumes on a daily basis. Their pants have geometric motifs and calf-length woolen wraparounds fastened by leather belts or red sashes. Women go about their business wearing white blouses with red stripes.

The beautiful adobe **Iglesia de San Antonio Palopó** stands in a stone plaza that marks the center of town. The interior is particularly peaceful. During the day the steps are a meeting place where all passersby are sure to stop for a while. The Cakchiquel people still hold many of their Maya beliefs. For instance, infants here don't see the light of day for the first year of life, as their faces are kept covered to ward off evil spirits.

Lodging

$$ ⊞ **Terrazas del Lago.** This charming hotel overlooking the lake is notable for its floral-pattern stone tiles. Simply decorated rooms have wooden tables and iron candlesticks. Those in front have patios with great vistas. A small restaurant serves simple breakfasts and lunches, while several terraces are perfect for a quiet cup of afternoon tea. ⊠ *Calle de la Playa,* ☎ *762–0157,* FAX *762–0037. 12 rooms. No credit cards.*

Shopping

On the main street, not far from the church, is an excellent women's textile cooperative, where you see master weavers in action. The process is fascinating to watch, and the finished fabrics are stunning. There's a small shop on site where the proceeds help sustain the cooperative.

Santiago Atitlán

★ ❹ *21 km (13 mi) west of San Antonio Palopó.*

Across the lake from Panajachel, Santiago Atitlán has a fascinating history. With a population of about 48,000, this capital of the proud and independent Tzutuhil people is one of the largest indigenous communities in Guatemala. They resisted political domination during the country's civil war, which meant that many residents were murdered by the military. After a 1990 massacre in which 12 people were killed, the villagers protested the presence of the army in their town. To everyone's surprise, the army actually left, and Santiago Atitlán became a model for other highland towns fighting governmental oppression.

A road that leads up from the dock is lined on both sides with shops selling artesanía—take a good look at the huipiles embroidered with elaborate depictions of fruits, birds, and spirits. Many local women wear a "halo," which is a 12-yard-long band wrapped around their forehead. Older men also wear traditional dress, sporting black-and-white-stripe calf-length pants with detailed embroidery below the knee.

The main road leads to the squat white **Iglesia de Santiago Atitlán,** the church where Tzutuhil deities can be seen in the woodwork around the pulpit. It was on this very pulpit that Father Stanley Francis Rother was assassinated by right-wing death squads in July 1981 for his outspoken support of the Tzutuhil cause. Beloved by the local parishioners, he is remembered with a plaque near the door.

As you get off the boat, small children may offer to lead you to the **Casa de Maximón** in exchange for a few quetzales. Santiago Atitlán one of the few places where people actively worship Guatemala's cigar-smoking Maximón, a local deity who also goes by the name San Simón. Every year a different member of the local *cofrade* (religious society) houses the wooden idol and accommodates his many faithful followers. When you locate the right house, you'll be ushered inside to see the shrine. If you haven't brought a cigar to leave is his collection plate, a few quetzales will do just fine.

On the road west to San Pedro, **Parque de la Paz** commemorates a dozen Tzutuhil people, including several children, who were killed when the army open fired on a peaceful demonstration that protested the military presence here. The massacre drew national outrage, and President Serrano Elías himself apologized and withdrew military forces from Santiago. The memorial is a sober reminder of Guatemala's tortured past.

Dining and Lodging

$$ ✕⚏ **Bambú.** Run by a Spanish expatriate with a penchant for fine food, Bambú is known for its excellent restaurant. You'll be served Spanish fare in an A-frame dining room warmed by a crackling stone fireplace. On the beautifully tended grounds are a string of thatch-roof bungalows with private patios overlooking the lake. Immaculate stone pathways loop through a series of taxonomically arranged gardens (cacti in one, flowers in the next, and so on), while most of the restaurant's fruits, vegetables, and herbs are cultivated out back. Canoes are available for paddling around. ⊠ *1 km (½ mi) east of town,* ☎ 721–7332, ⬛ 721–7197. *5 bungalows. Restaurant, boating, bar. AE, DC, MC, V.*

$$ ✕⚏ **Posada de Santiago.** This longtime favorite has deluxe accom-
★ modations in private bungalows with volcano views. Pass through the carved-wood doors into the stone-walls bungalows and you'll find fireplaces and thick wool blankets piled high on the beds. The restaurant serves exquisite food, such as smoked chicken píbil in a tangy red sauce and Thai coconut shrimp. The wine list is surprisingly extensive. On the premises is a small store where you can rent canoes and mountain bikes. ⊠ *1 km (½ mi) south of town,* ☎ 410–2444, ⬛ 721–7167, ⬛ *www.atitlan.com. 12 bungalows. Restaurant, boating, mountain bikes, shop. AE, DC, MC, V.*

Outdoor Activities and Sports

Horseback riding around the lake is arranged by Americans Jim and Nancy Mattisson at **Aventura en Atitlán** (⊠ 10 km [6 mi] from town, ☎ 201–5527). Various rides, including an exhilarating torchlighted nighttime outing, wind through lush lowlands and spectacular cloud forests. A terrific meal at the ranch awaits the end of every ride. The prices here are significantly higher than at other outfitters, but the trips are immeasurably better. Reservations are recommended.

San Marcos La Laguna

❺ *15 minute boat trip from Panajachel.*

San Marcos is a tiny village catering mostly to tourists. From the dock you can reach the center of the village by walking uphill along a narrow cobblestone path. The village itself has one or two stores and a restaurant around the central square. If you plan on staying in San Marcos you should remember to bring a flashlight, as most of the town does not have electricity.

Lodging

$$ ⚏ **Posada Schumann.** Full of old-fashioned charm, this little inn has bungalows set along a narrow swath of garden stretching down to the lake. Exposed stonework and unfinished wood paneling lend the place a slightly rustic feel, but the rooms are enlivened by the festive colors from local weaving. The hot water can be unreliable. ⊠ *San Marcos La Laguna,* ☎ 202–2216. *4 rooms without bath, 3 bungalows. Restaurant. No credit cards.*

$ ⚏ **Hotel Jinava.** Set in a secluded cove, the small hotel is a great place to get away from it all. Each of the bungalows, shaded by avocado and papaya trees, has excellent views of the volcanoes. Ask the friendly German owner to make you a tropical drink, one of his favorite pastimes. If piña coladas are not your thing, then request a massage—he is rumored to be the best masseur on the lake. The restaurant serves up great curries and other international dishes. ⊠ *San Marcos La Laguna,* ☎ 705–6035, 406–5986. ⬛ *www.jinava.de 5 bungalows. Restaurant, massage. No credit cards.*

$ ⊞ **Las Pirámides.** The tranquillity of the lake provides the perfect setting for this yoga retreat, which offers day-, week-, and monthlong courses. The price includes accommodations, classes, and use of the sauna and other facilities. ⊠ *San Marcos La Laguna,* ☎ *205–7151 or 205–7302. 5 rooms. Sauna. No credit cards.*

Jaibalito

➏ *10-min boat trip west of Panajachel.*

So small that it rarely appears on maps of the region, Jaibalito is the most undisturbed of the villages surrounding Lago Atitlán. Santa Cruz La Laguna is a short walk away, but otherwise Jaibalito is quite isolated. There is no boat service after 6 PM, so this village is only for those seeking peace and quiet.

Dining and Lodging

$–$$ ✕⊞ **Vulcano Lodge.** Set on a coffee plantation, this lodge has well-tended gardens with hammocks that make nice retreats in the afternoon. The tastefully decorated rooms are on the small side, but they all have private terraces. Alas, there are no views of the lake. The restaurant serves up international favorites. ⊠ *Jaibalito,* ☎ *410–2237. 5 rooms, 1 suite. Restaurant. No credit cards.*

$$ ✕⊞ **Casa del Mundo.** Built atop a cliff overlooking the azure waters, this gorgeous inn has unquestionably the best vantage point for gazing at Lago Atitlán. All the rooms have views, but those from Number 1 and Number 3 are the most breathtaking. If you can tear yourself away from the windows you'll notice the beautifully decorated rooms have wood-beam ceilings, red-tile floors, and stucco-and-stone walls hung with local handicrafts. If you want to get a closer look at the lake, kayaks are available. Meals are served family style in the cozy restaurant. ⊠ *Jaibalito dock,* ☎ *204–5558,* WEB *www.virtualguatemala.com/ casadelmundo. 8 rooms, 4 with bath. Restaurant, boating. No credit cards.*

Santa Cruz La Laguna

➐ *10-min boat ride west of Panajachel.*

It's a steep walk to the hillside village of Santa Cruz La Laguna, but the hale and hearty are rewarded with a stroll through a community that most travelers overlook. The square adobe house are positioned precariously on the slopes, looking as if they might be washed away by the next heavy rain. A highlight of this little village is a squat adobe **church** in the main plaza. Make sure to look inside at where the walls are lined with carved wooden saints.

Dining and Lodging

$$ ✕⊞ **Arca de Noé.** Magnificent views are the big draw at this rustic retreat. Housed in several bungalows constructed of wood and stone, the rooms are small but neat. The delicious home cooking is served family style in the main building, which resembles a New England farmhouse. The menu changes constantly, but each meal comes with fresh vegetables and bread hot out of the oven. Electricity is solar-generated, so there is no hot water. ⊠ *Santa Cruz La Laguna,* ☎ *306–4352. 10 rooms, 6 with bath. Restaurant, boating. No credit cards.*

$ ✕⊞ **La Iguana Perdida.** Part hotel and part summer camp, the Lost Iguana is brimming with character. There are no electricity and no hot water, and the toilets are about as basic as they come. The restaurant serves up good family-style meals, and the dorm-style rooms can hold up to eight of your traveling companions. For a bit more privacy choose one of the thatch-roof bungalows lighted with kerosene lamps.

Guests tend to be fairly young, as most come for scuba-diving courses. ✉ *Santa Cruz La Laguna,* ☎ FAX *762–2621. 3 cabins, 14 rooms, 2 dorm-style rooms. Restaurant, sauna, dive shop. No credit cards.*

Outdoor Activities and Sports

There are plenty of opportunities for hiking in the hills around Santa Cruz. It is the starting point of a scenic four-hour walk to San Marcos de La Laguna. The trail passes through several tiny villages and over gusty bluffs overlooking the lake.

Lago Atitlán's wealth of underwater wonders draws divers from around the world. **ATI Divers** (✉ Iguana Perdida, ☎ 762–2621) is a certified diving school that offers courses for all levels, from basic certification to dive master.

Chichicastenango

★ *37 km (23 mi) north of Panajachel, 108 km (67 mi) northwest of Antigua.*

Perched on a hillside, Chichicastenango is in many ways a typical highland town. The narrow cobblestone streets converge on a wide plaza where most days you'll find a few old men passing the time. You'd hardly recognize the place Thursday and Sunday, when row after row of colorful stalls fill the square and overflow into the adjoining alleys. There's a dizzying array of handmade items, from wooden masks to woolen blankets to woven baskets. Much of the artesanía is produced for tourists, but walk a few blocks in any direction and you'll find where the locals do their shopping. South of the square you'll see a narrow street where stern-faced women sell chickens. To the east you might run across a family trying to to coax a just-purchased pig up a rather steep hill.

Try to get to Chichicastenango at dawn, when the early morning mist swirls around the vendors as they set up shop. Better yet, come late in the day on Wednesday or Saturday. Not only will you get better deals before the tourists arrive, but you'll witness the town's amazing trans formation. Arriving by bus or by foot, the people of the surrounding villages come with what they have to sell strapped to their backs. Men balance heavy wooden tables across their shoulders, while old women bend over under the weight of wrought-iron machines for making shaved ice. Even little children help, balancing bundles bigger than they are.

With a little luck you'll visit Chichicastenango during an elaborate procession marking a saint's day for one of the equally elaborate Maya rituals. The biggest celebration is Día de Santo Tomás, when the city explodes with parades and dances. During the festivities, held December 13–21, the *cofrades* (city leaders) wear elegant silver costumes and carry staffs topped by magnificent sun medallions.

A Good Walk

Any tour of Chichicastenango begins in the tranquil **Parque Central** ⑧, which is transformed twice each week when hundreds of vendors arrive from villages near and far. Don't forget to wander along the neighboring streets, as the market long ago outgrew the square. Presiding over Parque Central is the gleaming white **Iglesia de Santo Tomás** ⑨, where Christian ceremonies and Maya mysticism intertwine. Across the square is the smaller but no less lovely **Capilla de Calvario** ⑩. On the south side of the square is **Museo Regional** ⑪, which provides a look at the culture of the region before the arrival of the Spanish. Head west down a street hill to the colorful **cementerio** ⑫, just outside town. You'll be treated to wonderful views of the city's red rooftops. If you're intrigued by the evidence of ancient rituals found in the cemetery, head south of town to the Maya shrine of **Pascual Abaj** ⑬, which is still used today. If you're lucky, you might see locals praying before the stone head.

TIMING

After a morning wandering around the market, you can see the rest of the sights in this little town in the course of an afternoon. Wear comfortable shoes, as the walk uphill to Pascual Abaj can be challenging.

Sights to See

⑩ **Capilla de Calvario.** Across from the Iglesia de Santo Tomás is this squat little chapel. It doesn't attract the attention that its much larger neighbor does, but from its steep steps you'll have a nice view of the market. ⊠ *West end of Plaza Mayor.*

⑫ **Cementerio.** Filled with mausoleums painted brilliant shades of teal, yellow, and orange, the town's cemetery is one of the most colorful in the Western Highlands. In the midst of headstones topped with crosses you'll doubtless find candles and incense—evidence of Maya rituals. ⊠ *West end of 8 Calle.*

⑨ **Iglesia de Santo Tomás.** Standing watch over the square is this gleaming white church, busy with worshipers all day and late into the night. Enter through a door on the right side. The church was built in 1540 on the site of an ancient temple, and locals say a block of stone near the massive front doors is all that remains of the altar. The Quiché people still consider Chichicastenango their holy city. Church officials look the other way as Maya ceremonies are still practiced here today. Some worshipers wave around pungent incense during the day, while at night others toss rose petals and pine needles into a raging fire right on the steps of the church. ⊠ *East end of Plaza Mayor.*

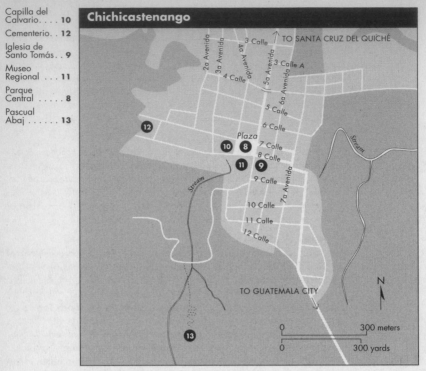

⑪ **Museo Regional.** If you want to learn more about the history of Chichicastenango, this little colonial-era building displays pre-Columbian artifacts that came from the private collection of a local priest. ✉ *Next
to Iglesia de Santo Tomás.*

⑧ **Parque Central.** As in most colonial villages, the heart of Chichicastenango is its central square. All the major sights are either here or on
the nearby streets. Three blocks north is Arco Gucumatz, an arch over
5 Avenida where you watch vendors heading to the square. ✉ *5 Av.
and 7 Calle.*

⑬ **Pascual Abaj.** This ancient Maya shrine, perched on a hilltop south of
town, is often vandalized by overzealous Christians. The elongated stone
face of the waist-high idol is always restored so that believers can return to their daily prayers. *Brujos,* the local shamans, lead villagers in
special rites that occasionally include slaughtered chickens. Because it's
one of the most accessible of the highland shrines, Pascual Abaj often
attracts travelers eager to see these rituals firsthand. To see the shrine,
follow 9 Calle until you see the signs for the narrow footpath up the
hill. Boys hanging around Plaza Mayor will guide you to the shrine
for a small fee and can tell you when the rituals will take place. ✉ *South
of Chichicastenango.*

Dining and Lodging

$–$$ ✕ **Las Brasas.** An eclectic collection of local handicrafts brightens the
walls of this excellent second-floor steak house. The chef, formerly of
Hotel Santo Tomás, grills up a great steak, but there are plenty of other
options, including a delicious *longaniza* (a spicy sausage similar to
chorizo). Music and a full bar keep things lively, but not intrusively
so. ✉ *6 Calle 4–52, second level,* ☎ *756–2226. AE, DC, MC, V.*

$–$$ ✕ **La Villa de los Cofrades.** With two locations within a block of each
other, it's hard to miss this longtime favorite. The smaller of the two
has patio seating right on Plaza Mayor, where you can watch the ven-

dors setting up their stalls while you feast on Belgian waffles or sip one of the finest cappuccinos in the country. If you're in a hurry to get to the market, remember that the service here can be miserably slow. The other location, a block away on 5 Calle, has a less hectic atmosphere. ✉ *7 Calle and 5 Av., 5 Calle and 6 Av.,* ☎ *756–1643. AE, MC, V.*

$–$$ ✕ **La Fonda del Tzijolaj.** This restaurant's second-story balcony overlooking Plaza Mayor is a great place to watch the vendors set up on the eve of the market. The *pollo chimichurri* (chicken in an herb sauce) is one of the best choices from the mostly traditional menu. There are also a few surprises, such as spinach gnocchi. ✉ *7 Calle and 4 Av.,* ☎ *756–1013. AE, DC, MC, V.*

$$$$ ✕⊞ **Hotel Santo Tomás.** Built in the Spanish style around a central courtyard, Hotel Santo Tomás is one of the town's best lodgings. Breezy passageways in which hundreds of plants spring from rustic clay pots lead past two trickling fountains. Spacious rooms are decorated with traditional textiles and antique reproductions. Each has a fireplace to warm you when the sun goes down. The back of the hotel is quieter and has views of the surrounding countryside. The large restaurant serves an excellent lunch buffet on market days. Attendants wearing traditional garb leave you to your own devices unless you call upon them. ✉ *7 Av. 5–32,* ☎ *756–1316 or 756–1061,* ℻ *756–1306. 43 rooms. Restaurant, pool, gym, hot tub, sauna, bar. AE, DC, MC, V.*

$$$ ✕⊞ **Mayan Inn.** Intricate woodwork and solid adobe construction make
★ the luxurious Mayan Inn one of the country's loveliest hotels. Run by the Clark family since 1932, the Mayan Inn is regarded by locals as a town treasure. A tour is highly recommended, even if you're staying elsewhere. Rooms with corner fireplaces surround a series of beautifully maintained garden courtyards. Most have wide windows overlooking the pine-covered hills. The service is excellent—an attendant in traditional costume is assigned to each room and does everything from lighting fires to serving dinner. Meals are taken in stately old dining halls, with a set menu that changes daily. The restaurant is open from 7 AM to 9 AM, noon to 2 PM, and 7 PM to 9 PM. ✉ *3 Av. at 8 Calle, 1 block west of plaza,* ☎ *756–1179; 339–2888 in Guatemala City,* ℻ *756–1212; 339–2909 in Guatemala City. 30 rooms. Restaurant, bar. AE, DC, MC, V.*

$$ ✕⊞ **Hotel Chugüila.** In an older building a few blocks north of the plaza, this hotel has a variety of rooms facing a nice cobblestone courtyard. The plant-filled portico leading to most rooms is scattered with inviting chairs and tables. Rooms are simply furnished, and a few have fireplaces. The oddly shaped and warmly lighted dining room is perhaps the hotel's best feature, especially since its windows look out onto the main street. Lunch and dinner menus offer standard Guatemalan fare. ✉ *5 Av. 5–24,* ☎ ℻ *756–1134. 25 rooms, 20 with bath, 2 suites. Restaurant. AE, DC, MC, V.*

$ ⊞ **Hospedaje Salvador.** Looking like something out of the game Chutes and Ladders, this colorful mishmash of a hotel is a favorite among budget travelers. Rooms are aligned along three and four levels of incongruously curved breezeways, with steep stairs zigzagging all about. In the middle of it all is a cobblestone courtyard decorated with statues. Facing the entrance is a small shrine shared by the Virgin Mary and a Maya deity. Though the rooms are a bit musty, the beds are a bit lumpy, and hot water is available only for a couple of hours in the morning, what the hotel lacks in comfort it compensates for with lots of character. ✉ *10 Calle at 5 Av., 3 blocks south of the plaza,* ☎ *756–1329. 46 rooms, 10 with bath. No credit cards.*

$ ⊞ **Hotel Chalet.** The Alps are nowhere to be seen, but the sun-splashed breakfast room at the heart of this cozy little hotel somehow makes the name work. The rooms are smallish but not cramped. Wooden masks and other handicrafts adorn the walls. A pleasant terrace is a great place for relaxing after a taxing day of shopping. The hotel is down a small unpaved road near 7 Avenida. ⊠ *3 Calle C 7–44,* ☎ FAX *756–1360. 7 rooms. AE, DC, MC, V.*

$ 🏨 **Posada El Arco.** This great little hotel has a distinctly homey feel. The spacious rooms, with their slightly corny decor, are happily reminiscent of the '70s. All rooms have fireplaces for the chilly evenings. To get here, climb up the stairs to the top of the arch that crosses 5 Avenida and turn left. ⊠ *4 Calle 4–36,* ☎ *756–1255. 7 rooms. Laundry facilities. No credit cards.*

Nightlife and the Arts

Nightlife is limited in hard-working Chichicastenango, although there are many tiny bars along the streets surrounding the plaza where you can join the locals for a beer. **Las Brasas** (⊠ 6 Calle 4–52, ☎ 756–2226) occasionally has live music.

Santa Cruz del Quiché

⑭ *19 km (12 mi) north of Chichicastenango.*

Adventurous travelers may want to continue north from Chichicastenango for further glimpses of the region called El Quiché, where you'll find traditional villages set on the pine-covered hills. A half hour north of Chichicastenango lies the provincial capital of Santa Cruz del Quiché, which serves as a base for exploring the area. Quiché, as the town is commonly called, is known for its pretty white church on the east side of the Parque Central. It was built from the stones taken from a Maya temple destroyed by the Spanish.

North of town is **K'umarcaaj,** the ancient capital of the Quiché kingdom. This once-magnificent site was destroyed by Spanish conquistadors in 1524. The ruins haven't been restored, but they are frequently used for Maya rituals. A taxi to and from the ruins should cost less than 60 quetzales. You can also walk the pleasant 3-km (2-mi) route without much difficulty. Follow 10 Calle out of town, where it becomes a dirt road. A tight S curve is the halfway point. The road forks at the bottom of a hill; take the road to the right.

Dining and Lodging

$ ✕ **Comedor Flipper.** A cage of lively birds lends a cheerful atmosphere to this small eatery, which serves good Guatemalan fare. The *avena* (a warm wheat beverage) is delicious, especially on a cold morning. There is no sign of the restaurant's trusty cetaceous namesake, though a ceramic sailfish atop the refrigerator comes close. ⊠ *1 Av. 7–31, around the corner from Hotel San Pasqual,* ☎ *no phone. No credit cards.*

$ 🏨 **Hotel San Pasqual.** This little hotel has a definite charm, most of it emanating from the engaging couple that runs it. The simple rooms, with handwoven bedspreads, surround a sunny courtyard. Clotheslines full of the day's laundry stretch to the roof next door. The shared baths are clean, but hot water is available only in the morning. ⊠ *7 Calle 0–43, Zona 1,* ☎ *755–1107. 37 rooms, 11 with bath. No credit cards.*

Nebaj

⑮ *95 km (59 mi) north of Santa Cruz del Quiché.*

An interesting although somewhat inaccessible part of the Western Highlands is a region called the Ixil Triangle. The Ixil Triangle is home to the indigenous Ixiles, a proud people who speak a unique language and preserve a rich culture.

Close-Up

I, RIGOBERTA MENCHÚ. . . MOSTLY

IN 1992 THE NOBEL PEACE PRIZE was awarded to Guatemalan writer Rigoberta Menchú, raised in the tiny highland village of San Miguel Uspantán. Menchú was born in 1959, just before a string of military dictators usurped control of Guatemala for 43 war-filled years. She grew up as dozens of opposition and guerrilla groups rose to resist them. Along with many of her family members, Menchú opposed the dictatorship with peaceful demonstrations that included peasants from various regions. When she was eventually forced into exile, she continued her opposition to Guatemala's military rule by drawing international attention to the repressive regime. She even addressed the United Nations numerous times, telling the world her harrowing tale.

In 1983 she published her testimonial, *I, Rigoberta Menchú: An Indian Woman in Guatemala,* and the plight of Guatemala's indigenous people—and the brutality of the military regime—was revealed in wrenching detail. In her book Menchú described losing two brothers to malnutrition on a coffee plantation and the razing of her village by wealthy land prospectors. Most disturbingly, Menchú related the story of a third brother, who was kidnapped by the army, tortured, and then burned alive in the plaza of a nearby town.

In 1999 American anthropologist David Stoll challenged Menchú's account with the publication of *Rigoberta Menchú and the Story of All Poor Guatemalans.* His research suggested that the conflict over the lands of Menchú's village was actually a long-running dispute between her father and his in-laws and that although Menchú's brother was unquestionably kidnapped, tortured, and murdered by the military, it was probably not carried out in the manner that Menchú had suggested. Although still a potent symbol of indigenous rights, Menchú—and the cause of native peoples by association—is now viewed by some with incredulity. More than a few have called for her Nobel Prize to be revoked.

Whether or not Menchú personally witnessed the events she describes, it is indisputable that hundreds of indigenous workers, particularly children, died of disease, malnutrition, or outright abuse on the plantations. It is also clear that the military committed innumerable acts of brutality, including public executions, in villages all across the country. In 1998 the Guatemalan Truth Commission sponsored by the United Nations denounced the military's actions during the civil war as genocide. Some argue that if Menchú's account wasn't wholly her own, but included incidents suffered by other indigenous men and women, that it doesn't detract from the horror of what occurred. If she included the experiences of others to draw attention to a conflict the international community had ignored for more than 20 years, they argue, can anyone really blame her?

Stoll himself admits Menchú is fundamentally right about the army's brutality, though he downplays it considerably, no doubt to bolster his own book's more dubious claim: that it was the guerrillas, not the ruling generals, who were responsible for igniting political violence in the highlands. But it is the debunking of Rigoberta Menchú that he will be remembered for and that will forever endear him to Guatemala's war criminals, many of whom remain in public life. Stoll may claim he's playing the devil's advocate, but in this case, the devil really doesn't need his help.

— *Gary Chandler*

The main town in this region is Nebaj, where cobblestone streets lead to a central plaza with a large colonial church. On Thursday and Sunday the town swells with people who come from the surrounding villages to sell their distinctive weavings. Besides shopping, hiking in the surrounding mountains is the main draw for tourists.

Lodging

$ 🔟 **Hotel Ixil.** Nebaj doesn't have much in the way of lodging. The best is this friendly hotel set around two courtyards. Some of the spacious rooms overlook the garden. ⊠ *Nebaj,* ☎ *no phone. 12 rooms. No credit cards.*

Quetzaltenango

91 km (56 mi) southwest of Chichicastenango.

Originally part of the Maya empire, Quetzaltenango was captured in the 14th century by the Quiché people, who called it Xelajú. It remained part of the Quiché kingdom until 1524, when Spaniard Pedro de Alvarado defeated the great warrior Tecún Umán at a battle here in 1524. The conquistador destroyed the city and used the stones for a new city called Quetzaltenango, which means "place of many quetzals." Locals have never gotten used to the name and still refer to Quetzaltenango as Xelajú, or simply Xela.

In a valley guarded by Volcán Santa María, Quetzaltenango has long had an economy based on agriculture. The rolling hills are particularly good for growing coffee. More recently, it has begun to attract travelers, who come here to purchase the intricate weavings from the surrounding villages. The first Sunday of each month is the main market day, and the central square is filled with women selling their wares.

Quetzaltenango is also a choice place to study Spanish, as here you'll find several excellent programs widely considered more rigorous than those in Antigua. Word spreads fast, however, and the city has recently seen a sharp rise in the number of students. Quetzaltenango is no longer the place to visit if you really want to avoid speaking English.

A Good Walk

Begin your stroll aroun Quetzaltenango in the beautiful **Parque Centroamérica** ⑯, pausing to admire the facade of the colonial-era **Catedral del Espíritu Santo** ⑰. Be sure to visit the **Museo de Historia Natural** ⑱ and the **Museo del Arte** ⑲. Save your ticket stub for an afternoon visit to the **Museo del Ferrocarril de los Altos** ⑳. From the central plaza head north, stopping along the way at Mercado La Democracia for a little shopping. Two blocks north is the shady **Parque Benito Juarez** ㉑. Enjoy an ice cream cone in this lovely park, then check out the **Iglesia de San Nicolás** ㉒.

TIMING

Quetzaltenango is fairly compact, so it's possible to see the major sights in a sunny afternoon. Remember that while most sights are in Zona 1, Parque Benito Juarez is to the north in Zona 3.

Sights to See

Almolonga. In this charming village you'll find women wearing bright orange huipiles and beautiful headbands. At the busy Wednesday and Saturday markets you can buy fruits cultivated in the area. A few kilometers beyond the town are several hot springs where you can relax for a few quetzales. ⊠ *5 km (3 mi) south of Quetzaltenango.*

 Catedral del Espíritu Santo. On the southeastern corner of Parque Centroamérica, this cathedral dates from 1535. The crumbling facade, which

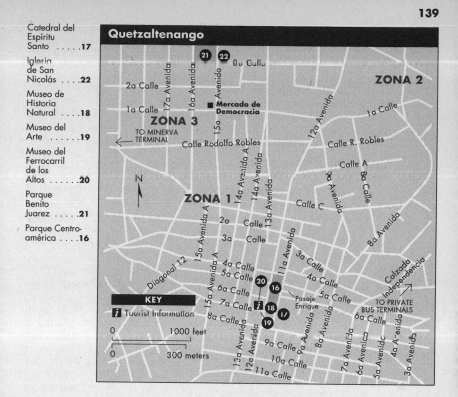

Quetzaltenango

features life-size saints that look down upon those headed here to pray, is currently undergoing reconstruction. ⊠ *11 Av. and 7 Calle, Zona 1.*

㉒ Iglesia de San Nicolás. This blueish church, on the east side of Parque Benito Juarez, is known for its unusual baroque design. Although lovely, it looks a bit out of place in the town's mix of Greek and colonial structures. ⊠ *15 Av. and 3 Calle, Zona 3.*

⑱ Museo de Historia Natural. To the south of Parque Centroamérica, the Museum of Natural History is an interesting mainly for its neoclassic flourishes. Inside are some mildly interesting examples of pre-Columbian pottery. ⊠ *7 Calle and 11 Av., Zona 1,* ☎ *761–6427.*

NEED A
BREAK?
The inexpensive **Café Baviera** (⊠ 5 Calle and 12 Av.), just off Parque Centroamérica, has an ample selection of excellent coffees and fresh pastries.

⑲ Museo del Arte. On the southwest corner of the main square is the Museum of Art, whose eclectic collection ranges from realist oils to abstract and multimedia works. The building also houses a school of art. ⊠ *12 Av. and 7 Calle, Zona 1,* ☎ *no phone.*

★ **⑳ Museo del Ferrocarril de Los Altos.** In the same building that houses the Museum of Art, the Los Altos Railroad Museum tells the history of the railroad that once connected Quetzaltenango with other towns in the Western Highlands. ⊠ *12 Av. and 7 Calle, Zona 1,* ☎ *no phone.*

㉑ Parque Benito Juarez. About 10 blocks north of Parque Centroamérica is this palm-lined park where many families spend their Sunday afternoons. Ice cream stands are in glorious abundance. ⊠ *15 Av. and 3 Calle, Zona 3.*

⓰ **Parque Centroamérica.** The central plaza in Quetzaltenango is one of the most beautiful in Central America. It's surrounded by architectural masterpieces, such as the magnificent building called Pasaje Enríquez. ✉ *12 Av. and 4 Calle, Zona 1.*

San Miguel Totonicapán. This traditional highland village is famous for its wooden toys. The community is full of workshops where a wide variety of handicrafts are actually produced. Come on Saturday for the market day, when you can find hand-loomed textiles, wax figures, and painted and glazed ceramics. ✉ *5 km (3 mi) south of Quetzaltenango.*

Dining and Lodging

$$ ✕ **Da Valentino.** White walls sparsely adorned with watercolor paintings provide a subdued setting for this Italian eatery. This lets the food do all the talking, and the handmade egg noodles and delicious gnocchi covered with rich sauces speak volumes. Da Valentino advertises its "high-quality slow food," and for good reason: expect to wait a while for the steaming platters of pasta to arrive. ✉ *14 Av. A 1–37, Zona 1,* ☎ *761–4494. No credit cards. Closed Mon.*

$–$$ ✕ **Royal Paris.** This bistro caters to the foreign students who have come to Quetzaltenango to study Spanish, so it offers a wide selection of dishes. Some aren't the least bit Parisian, such as the succulent chicken curry. It's all prepared with flair, however. The ambience is definitely imported, with a slightly bohemian feeling courtesy of the paintings of cabaret scenes on the walls. There's also a bar with an extensive wine list. ✉ *Calle 14A 3–06, Zona 1,* ☎ *761–1942. AE, DC, MC, V.*

$ ✕ **El Kopetin.** Good food, attentive service, and reasonable prices make this place popular with the locals, so it can be tough to get a table later in the evening. It couldn't be described as fancy, but this restaurant's long polished bar and wood paneling give it a comforting atmosphere. The menu has a number of delicious appetizers, including traditional queso fundido and a selection of meat and seafood dishes that are smothered in rich sauces. ✉ *14 Av. 3–51, Zona 1,* ☎ *761–8381. AE, DC, MC, V.*

$$$ ✕🏠 **Hotel Villa Real Plaza.** Surrounding a covered courtyard illuminated by skylights, the spacious rooms at Hotel Villa Real Plaza all have fireplaces that you'll appreciate on cool evenings. Those in a newer wing are superior to those in the dimly lighted older section. Ask for a room away from the bar, as the crowd can be noisy as the night winds down. The restaurant has an interesting menu whose offerings range from chicken cordon bleu to a variety of meaty stews. There is also a large bar. ✉ *4 Calle 12–22, Zona 1,* ☎ *761–6270,* 🗚 *761–6780. 58 rooms. Restaurant, bar. AE, DC, MC, V.*

$$$ ✕🏠 **Pensión Bonifáz.** Don't let the name fool you into thinking this is a modest establishment—Pensión Bonifáz is Quetzaltenango's most upscale hotel. Housed in a stately old building at the central plaza's northeast corner, it has a modern interior that doesn't quite live up to its exterior. Still, it is a comfortable, well-run establishment. The nicest rooms are in the older building, where small balconies offer nice views of the plaza. The rooftop garden makes a nice spot to take a book to in the afternoon. A small café serves light fare for lunch, while the larger restaurant has a Continental menu; both share a devilishly tempting pastry cart. ✉ *4 Calle 10–50, Zona 1,* ☎ *761–4241 or 761–2182,* 🗚 *763–0671. bonifaz@guate.net 74 rooms. Restaurant, café, pool, hot tub, bar. AE, DC, MC, V.*

$$$ 🏠 **Casa Mañen.** West of the central plaza, this romantic little B&B blends colonial comforts with modern conveniences. The rooms are spacious and homey, with handmade wall hangings and throw rugs and the occasional rocking chair. On the roof is a two-level terrace with a fan-

tastic view of the city. Breakfast is served in a small dining room downstairs. The staff is incredibly friendly and will be happy to help you with travel plans. ⊠ *9 Av. 4–11, Zona 1,* ☎ *765–0786,* FAX *765–0678,* WEB *www.comeseeit.com. 9 rooms. AE, DC, MC, V.*

$$ ☎ **Hotel Modelo.** Founded in 1892, this family-run establishment is run by a wizened man who was actually born on the premises. Over the years the distinguished hotel has maintained its tradition of good service. The wood-floor rooms, furnished with antiques, surround a few small courtyards leading off the lobby. Dinner is served in a fine colonial-style restaurant. ⊠ *14 Av. A 2–31, Zona 1,* ☎ *761–2529,* ☎ FAX *763–1376. 24 rooms. Restaurant. AE, DC, MC, V.*

$ ☎ **Casa Kaehler.** A few blocks off the plaza, this slightly ramshackle hotel is a popular spot with travelers on a budget. Rooms on two floors of a converted residence face a small courtyard overflowing with plants. Though simple, they are clean and comfortable. There's a separate lounge where you can chat with other guests. ⊠ *13 Av. 3–33, Zona 1,* ☎ *761–2091. 7 rooms, 1 with bath. No credit cards.*

Nightlife

Aside from the lounges in the big hotels, there are only a few nightspots in Xela. Right off the central square, **Salon Tecún** (⊠ Pasaje Enrique, Zona 1) is a small pub that is popular with students. Catering to the university crowd, **El Duende** (⊠ 14 Av. between 1 Calle and 2 Calle, Zona 1) is the place to go dancing on the weekends. There's also dancing at **Cuba Disco** (⊠ Blvd. Minerva, Zona 3).

For a taste of Xela's bohemian scene, head to the oh-so-funky **La Luna** (⊠ 8 Av. 4–1, Zona 1). **Cinema Paraíso** (⊠ 14 Av. 1–04, Zona 1) is a small café that screens artsy films.

Outdoor Activities and Sports

BICYCLING

There's great mountain biking through the hills and villages surrounding Quetzaltenango. **Vrisa Bicicletas** (⊠ 15 Av. 3–64, Zona 1, ☎ 761–3237) rents both on-road and off-road bikes by the day or week and has maps so you can take self-guided tours of the countryside.

HIKING

Quetzaltrekkers (⊠ Casa Argentina, 12 Diagonal 8–67, Zona 1, ☎ 761–2470, WEB beef.brownrice.com/streetschool) is a nonprofit company that supports three major social-service programs by coordinating truly unforgettable hiking trips. The three-day trek to Lago Atitlán and the two-day ascent of Volcán Tajamulco both pass through spectacular countryside and several remote villages.

Shopping

The bustling **Mercado Minerva** (⊠ 6 Calle, Zona 3), next to the main bus terminal, is the best of the city's markets. There are plenty of interesting handicrafts to be found here. But watch your pockets— groups of skillful thieves prey on tourists coming to and from the buses. Artisanía from most of the villages in the region can be found in the **Mercado La Democracia** (⊠ 1 Calle and 15 Av., Zona 3). Since there are relatively few shoppers, prices tend to be lower than elsewhere in the city. Near Parque Centroamérica, the **Centro Comercial Municipal** (⊠ 7 Calle and 11 Av., Zona 1) has a more limited selection of souvenirs.

Quetzaltenango is famous for its beautiful glass. **Vitra** (⊠ 13 Av. 5–27, ☎ 763–5091) is one of the most noted stores. You'll find excellent hand-blown glass at affordable prices.

Zunil

★ ㉓ *9 km (5½ mi) south of Quetzaltenango.*

At the base of an extinct volcano, the radiant village of Zunil is one of the prettiest in the highlands. Mud and adobe houses are clustered around the whitewashed church that marks the center of town. On the outskirts of the village you'll find the local cemetery, which is lined with tombstones painted in soft shades of pink and blue.

Zunil is surrounded by the most fertile land in the valley, so it's no surprise most people make their living off the land. The best day to visit Zunil is Monday, when women wearing vivid purple shawls crowd the covered market hawking fruits and vegetables grown in their own gardens.

Zunil is a good place to pay your respects to a cigar-smoking deity called San Simón. You can ask anyone in town where his likeness is, as almost everyone asks a favor of him at some time or another. The idol has become a tourist attraction, and foreigners are charged a few quetzales to see him. Be sure to bring a small gift, preferably a cigar.

High in the hills above Zunil are the wonderful hot springs of **Fuentes Georginas.** There are four pools, two of which remain in their natural basins. The water ranges from tolerable to near scalding. The springs are tucked in a lush ravine in the middle of a cloud forest, so hikers should take advantage of the beautiful trails that begin here. To get here, take the first left off the main road after passing Zunil.

Lodging

$ ⊡ **Fuentes Georginas.** Although they are a bit rundown, these dozen bungalows have fireplaces that keep you cozy at night. The best part of staying here is having round-the-clock access to the hot springs, which close to the public at 5 PM. ⊠ *8 km (5 mi) from main road,* ☎ *no phone. 8 bungalows. Restaurant. No credit cards.*

Huehuetenango

㉔ *94 km (58 mi) north of Quetzaltenango.*

At the foot of a mountain range called Los Cuchumatanes, Huehuetenango was once part of the powerful Mam Empire, which dominated most of the highland area. It wasn't until much later that the Guatemalan Quiché came into the area to stir things up, pushing the Mam up into the mountains.

Today Huehuetenango is a quiet town, serving mostly a gateway to the magnificent Cuchumatanes and the isolated villages scattered across them. The town surrounds **Parque Central,** where you'll find a pretty fountain and shell-shape bandstand. The butter yellow **Catedral de la Immaculada Concepción** stands guard over the main square.

The ancient city of **Zaculeu,** 4 km (2 mi) from Huehuetenango, was built around AD 600 by the Mam tribe. The site was chosen for its strategic location, as it has natural barriers on three sides. The defenses worked all too well against the Spanish. Realizing they could not take the Zaculeu people by force, the Spaniards chose instead to starve them out. Within two months they surrendered. Today the ruins consist of a few pyramids, a ball court, and a two-room museum that gives a few insights into the world of the Mam.

A short drive north of Huehuetenango, the dirt road begins to wind its way up into the mountains where traditional villages are set between massive rocky peaks. There's a **mirador,** or scenic view, about 6 km (4 mi) from Huehuetenango.

Dining and Lodging

$–$$ ✕ **Las Brasas.** Grilled meats are the specialty at Huehuetenango's best restaurant. Simple red-and-white tablecloths are the only nod toward decor, but because it's the sole place in town with any atmosphere, this is a fairly reassuring sight. The menu has a surprisingly broad range of options. There are even Chinese entrées, which you won't find any-where else in town. ⊠ *2 Calle 1–55,* ☎ *764–6200. AE, DC, MC, V.*

$ ✕ **Jardín Café.** This colorful little corner restaurant has a friendly atmosphere that makes it popular among the locals. Come early for the excellent pancakes served at breakfast, or stop by for beef and chicken dishes at lunch or dinner. The menu includes a few Mexican favorites as well. ⊠ *4 Calle and 6 Av.,* ☎ *769–0769. No credit cards.*

$ ✕ **Pizza Hogareña.** Put together your own pizza from a long list of
★ fresh ingredients at this simple little eatery. If you prefer, you can opt for spaghetti, grilled meat, or sandwiches. ⊠ *6 Av. 4–49,* ☎ *764–3072. No credit cards. Closed Mon.*

$$ 🏨 **Hotel Casa Blanca.** Who would've thought that Huehuetenango would have such a top-notch hotel? Spacious rooms, excellent service, and a central location make it the town's best lodging option. Third-floor rooms have great views, especially when the bougainvillea are in full bloom. At the restaurant you can choose between a table in the shady courtyard or in the cozy dining room warmed by a fireplace. ⊠ *7 Av. 3–41,* ☎ 🖷 *769–0777. 15 rooms. Restaurant, cable TV, meeting rooms. MC, V.*

$$ 🏨 **Hotel Zaculeu.** This hotel north of the main square has welcomed guests for more than a century. When you pass through the front doors, you enter a courtyard overflowing with greenery. The older rooms, set around a portico, are brightened by locally made fabrics. They can be a bit noisy, however, especially those facing the street. The newer ones in the back lack character. ⊠ *5 Av. 1–14,* ☎ *764–1086,* 🖷 *764–1575. 38 rooms. Restaurant. V.*

$ 🏨 **Hotel Mary.** This four-story hotel in the heart of town offers clean, if spartan, accommodations. Ask to see a few rooms, as some are much better than others. ⊠ *2 Calle 3–52,* ☎ *764–1618,* 🖷 *764–7412. 27 rooms. Cable TV. No credit cards.*

Shopping

A few blocks to the east is the **Mercado Central,** where you can pur-chase local handicrafts.

Todos Santos Cuchumatán

㉕ *40 km (24 mi) north of Huehuetenango.*

Although it takes about three hours to cover the short distance from Huehuetenango to Todos Santos Cuchumatán, the bumpy ride is prob-ably the best way to experience the tremendous height of Los Cuchu-matanes. The winding dirt road can be anxiety provoking when one side of the road drops off into a deep ravine. Despite the arduous jour-ney, Todos Santos Cuchumatán is the most frequently visited moun-tain village. Many people come between October 21 and November 1, when the villagers celebrate the Festival de Todos Santos. The high-point of the celebration is a horse race in which the competitors ride bareback.

Market day is Thursday. Men wear the traditional candy-cane-stripe pants and shirts with long embroidered collars. The women wear stun-ning red, pink, and purple huipiles with indigo skirts.

The Western Highlands A to Z

To research prices, get advice from other travelers, and book travel arrangements, visit www.fodors.com.

AIR TRAVEL TO AND FROM THE WESTERN HIGHLANDS

Both Quetzaltenango and Huehuetenango have small airports with service to and from Guatemala City. Taca is the only airline that flies these routes.

➤ AIRLINES AND CONTACTS: **Taca** (☎ 261–2144).

BOAT AND FERRY TRAVEL

With the exception of the service between Panajachel and Santiago Atitlán, Lago Atitlán's public ferries have been replaced by private water taxis. Although they don't follow a schedule, the private boats are much faster and cost about the same. Panajachel has two primary docks, one at the end of Calle del Embarcadero and one at the end of Calle Rancho Grande. The first is for private boats on the San Pedro route, stopping at Santa Cruz, Jaibalito, San Marcos, Santa Clara, and San Pedro. It's about 10 quetzales, no matter where you get off.

The other dock is for hour-long journeys to Santiago, with departures at 8:30, 9, 9:30, 10, 4, and 5 and returns at 6, 11:45, 12:30, 1, 2, and 5. The cost is about 10 quetzales. Private boats occasionally take passengers to Santiago in about half the time.

BUS TRAVEL TO AND FROM THE WESTERN HIGHLANDS

Transportes Rebuli travels from Guatemala City to Panajachel hourly from 5 to 4 daily. Buses bound for Guatemala City leave Panajachel hourly from 6 to 3 daily. The 6 AM and 3 PM buses are more expensive, but they're also much more comfortable. Count on a four-hour trip.

To get to Chichicastenango and Santa Cruz del Quiché, take Veloz Quichelense, which departs from the capital on the half hour between 5 AM and 6 PM and returns on a similar schedule. For Quetzaltenango, take Galgos buses, which leave Guatemala City at 5:30, 8:30, 11, 12:45, 2:30, 5, 6:30, and 7. They depart from Quetzaltenango at 4, 5, 8:15, 9:45, 11:45, 2:45, and 4:45. The trip takes four hours.

To travel to Huehuetenango, you can choose from several companies for the five-hour run from Guatemala City. Los Halcones has departures at 7 and 2. Rápidos Zaculeu runs buses at 6 and 3. Transportes Velasquez also has daily departures at the same time.

Transportes Turisticos Atitrans and Turansa have buses that travel from Antigua to towns in the Western Highlands. You can also catch a public bus at the terminal, which is cheaper but much less comfortable. The one or two direct buses to Panajachel and Quetzaltenango each day, as well as five or six bound for Chichicastenango.

➤ BUS INFORMATION: **Galgos** (✉ 7 Av. 19–44, Zona 1, Guatemala City, ☎ 253–4868). **Los Halcones** (✉ 7 Av. 15–27, Zona 1, ☎ 238–1979). **Rápidos Zaculeu** (✉ 9 Calle 11–42, Zona 1, ☎ 232–2858). **Transportes Rebuli** (✉ 21 Calle 1–34, Zona 1, Guatemala City, ☎ 251–3521). **Transportes Velasquez** (✉ 20 Calle 1–37, Zona 1, ☎ 221–1084). **Veloz Quichelense** (✉ Terminal de Buses, Zona 4, Guatemala City, ☎ no phone).

CAR RENTAL

There is only one national car-rental agency in the Western Highlands, Tabarini Rent-A-Car. If you are considering renting a car, a good option is to do so in Guatemala City.

➤ LOCAL AGENCIES: **Tabarini Rent-A-Car** (✉ 9 Calle 9–21, Zona 1, Quetzaltenango, ☎ 763–0418; ✉ Hotel Los Cuchumatanes, Sector Brasil Zona 7, Huehuetenango, ☎ 764–1951).

CAR TRAVEL

The Pan-American Highway—more country road than highway, really—heads northwest out of Guatemala City, where it is called the Calzada Roosevelt. It passes through Chimaltenango before reaching a crossroads called Los Encuentros. Here you can head north to Chichicastenango, Santa Cruz del Quiché, and Nebaj. Continue on the Pan-American Highway, and you'll pass a turnoff to Panajachel and then another for San Marcos La Laguna and other towns on Lago Atitlán. The Pan-American Highway continues over some impressive ridges and then descends to a crossroads called Cuatro Caminos, about 200 km (124 mi) from the capital. Here the road to Quetzaltenango heads off to the south. About 60 km (37 mi) north of Cuatro Caminos, the road to Huehuetenango cuts off to the right. Many roads to the north of Huehuetenango and Santa Cruz del Quiché are unpaved and pretty rough—this is nerve-racking mountain driving relieved intermittently by memorable views.

EMERGENCIES

In Panajachel, Panamedic Centro Clínico Familiar offers 24-hour medical attention. The doctors, Francisco Ordoñez and his wife, Zulma Ordoñez, both speak English.
➤ EMERGENCY SERVICES: **Ambulance** (☎ 762–4121 in Panajachel; 761–2956 in Quetzaltenango). **Police** (☎ 762–1120).
➤ HOSPITALS: **Panamedic Centro Clínico Familiar** (✉ Calle Principal 0–72, Panajachel, ☎ 762–2174).
➤ PHARMACIES: **Farmacia Nueva Unión** (✉ Calle Santander near Calle Principal, Panajacel). **Farmacia Nueva** (✉ 6 Calle and 10 Av., Zona 1, Quetzaltenango, ☎ 762–4531).

INTERNET

MayaNet is the best Internet café in Panajachel. It is open daily until 9 PM and charges about 20 quetzales per hour.
➤ INTERNET CAFÉS: **MayaNet** (✉ Calle Santander, Panajachel).

MAIL AND SHIPPING

All the villages in the Western Highlands have post offices, but you are probably better off posting your letters from the larger towns. If you are sending something valuable, go with DHL or one of the local companies that will ship packages. Alternativas is in Quetzaltenango, while Get Guated Out is in Panajachel.
➤ OVERNIGHT SERVICES: **Alternativas** (✉ 16 Av. 3–35, Zona 3, Quetzaltenango).**Get Guated Out** (✉ Comercial Pueblito, upstairs, Panajachel). **DHL** (✉ Calle Santander, Panajachel, ☎ 762–1474).
➤ POST OFFICES: **Chichicastenango** (✉ 7 Av. 8–47). **Panajachel** (✉ Calle Santander and Calle 5 de Febrero). **Quetzaltenango** (✉ 15 Av. and 4 Calle, Zona 1).

MONEY MATTERS

All the larger towns in the Western Highlands have ATMs where you can use your bank card. Bancared has branches in Panajachel, Chichicastenango, Quetzaltenango, and Huehuetenango.
➤ BANKS: **Bancared** (✉ 5 Av. and 6 Calle, Chichicastenango; 4 Calle 6–81, Zona 1, Huehuetenango; Calle Principal 0–78, Zona 2, Panajachel; 4 Av. 17–40, Zona 3, Quetzaltenango).

SAFETY
Several groups of travelers have been robbed while hiking around the Lago Atitlán area. It is always a good idea to hire a guide, especially when you are not familiar with your destination.

TOUR OPERATORS
In Panajachel, Atitrans and Centroamericana Tourist Service are both reputable companies. Chichicastenango's only tour company, Chichi Turkaj–Tours, is well-regarded. In Quetzaltenango, Quetzaltrekkers support social service programs in the area. Union Travel in Quetzaltenango also offers tours to just about everywhere in the region.
➤ TOUR COMPANIES: **Atitrans** (⊠ 3 Av. 1–30, Zona 2, Panajachel, ☎ 762–2336). **Centroamericana Tourist Service** (⊠ 3 Av. 4–70, Zona 2, Panajachel, ☎ 762–2496). **Chichi Turkaj–Tours** (⊠ 5 Calle 4–42, Zona 1, Chichicastenango, ☎ 756–2111). **Quetzaltrekkers** (⊠ Casa Argentina, Diagonal 12 8–67, Zona 1, Quetzaltenango, ☎ 761–2470). **Union Travel** (⊠ In Los Pinos Av. Santander, Zona 2, Panajachel, ☎ 762–2426).

VISITOR INFORMATION
The Guatemala tourism agency Inguat has offices in Panajachel, Quetzaltenango, and San Miguel Totonicapán. The staff at the office in Panajachel is particularly helpful.
➤ TOURIST INFORMATION: **Inguat** (⊠ Calle Santander, Panajachel, ☎ 762–1392; ⊠ Parque Centro América, Quetzaltenango, ☎ 761–4931; ⊠ Casa de Cultura, 8 Av. 2–17, next to Hospedaje San Miguel, Zona 1, San Miguel Totonicapán, ☎ 766–1575).

LAS VERAPACES

Northeast of Guatemala City you'll find heavily forested mountains drained by wild rivers running through deep caverns. This region of central Guatemala, known collectively as Las Verapaces, is split between Baja Verapaz, to the south, and Alta Verapaz, to the north. The smaller Baja Verapaz is much drier than Alta Verapaz, where mist-covered mountains are the norm. The area's humid climate, which often comes in the form of a drizzly rain called *chipi-chipi,* has made it the cradle of Guatemala's cardamom and coffee production.

Las Verapaces was once the home of the Rabinal Maya, one of the most feared tribes of the Americas. When the Spanish arrived in the early 1500s, the Rabinal fought back so fiercely that the region became known as Tezulutlán, the "Land of War." Although the Spaniards failed to overcome this tribe with brute force, they finally succeeded with ideology. In 1537 Bartolomé de Las Casas, a Jesuit who crusaded against the maltreatment of indigenous peoples, struck an unusual bargain with his compatriots: if the military stayed away for five years, Las Casas would deliver the land without spilling a single drop of blood. Spain agreed, and Las Casas began translating religious hymns into local languages. The Rabinal chief, realizing the Spanish weren't going to go away, agreed to be baptized. His people followed suit, and the "conquest" of the region meant that the area was soon dotted with orderly Spanish-style villages. It became known as Las Verapaces, "The Lands of True Peace."

Las Verapaces retains a mystical air, particularly because of the presence of the resplendent quetzal, a bird found only in the region's cloud forests. The male has a spectacularly long tail and shiny blue-green feathers, the inspiration for weaving designs and paintings all over Guatemala, as the Maya royalty wore the feathers in their crowns. The pride

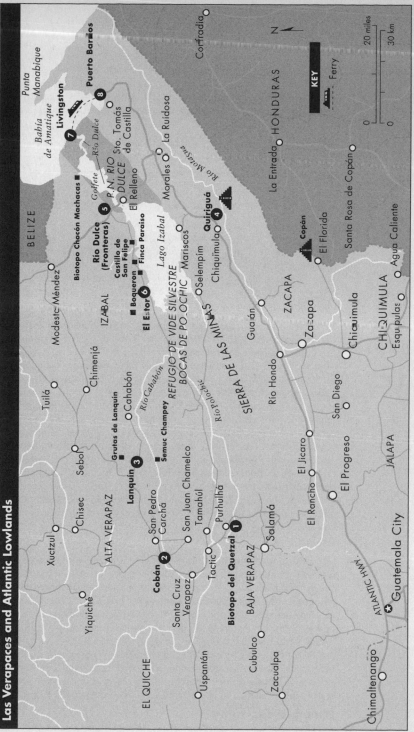

Las Verapaces and Atlantic Lowlands

KEY

⚓ Ferry

N

20 miles

30 km

BELIZE

HONDURAS

Punta Manabique

Bahía de Amatique

Puerto Barrios

Livingston

8

7

Río Dulce

Golfete

P.N. RÍO DULCE

Sto. Tomás de Castilla

El Relleno

5

Biotopo Chocón Machacas ■

Cofradia

La Ruidosa

Río Motagua

Morales

Quiriguá

4

Modesto Méndez

Río Dulce (Fronteras)

Castillo de San Felipe

Finca Paraíso

Baqueron

6

El Estor

Lago Izabal

Mariscos

Selempím

Chiquimula

La Entrada

El Florida

Copán

Santa Rosa de Copán

Agua Caliente

Chimenjá

Cahabón

Río Cahabón

REFUGIO DE VIDE SILVESTRE

BOCAS DE POLOCHIC

Río Polochic

SIERRA DE LAS MINAS

Guastón

ZACAPA

Zacapa

CHIQUIMULA

Chiquimula

Esquipulas

Tuilá

Grutas de Lanquín

Sebol

Semuc Champey

Lanquín

3

Río Hondo

San Diego

Xucutzul

Chisec

ALTA VERAPAZ

San Pedro Carchá

San Juan Chamelco

Tamahú

Purhulhá

El Jicaro

El Progreso

JALAPA

Yiquiché

Cobán

2

Tactic

1

Salamá

El Rancho

Santa Cruz Verapaz

Biotopo del Quetzal

BAJA VERAPAZ

ATLANTIC HWY.

EL QUICHE

Uspantán

Cubulco

✪ Guatemala City

Zacualpa

Chimaltenango

IZABAL

Guatemalans feel for this bird is reflected in the name of the country's currency, the quetzal.

The region's inhabitants are predominantly Pokomchí and Q'eqchí people, who over the years have lost much of their territory to expanding coffee plantations. As a result, they have abandoned some of their traditional ways of sustaining themselves. The region's largest city is Cobán, which has an almost completely indigenous population. Here you'll find a handful of businesses catering to visitors, making it a good base for exploring the region.

Numbers in the text correspond to numbers in the margin and on the Las Verapaces and Atlantic Lowlands map.

Biotopo del Quetzal

★ ❶ *50 km (31 mi) south of Cobán; 164 km (102 mi) northeast of Guatemala City.*

A 2,849-acre tract of cloud forest along the road to Cobán, the Biotopo del Quetzal was created to protect Guatemala's national bird. The resplendent quetzal, known for its brilliant plumage, is endangered because of the indiscriminate destruction of the country's forests. The reserve is also known as the Biotopo de Mario Dary Rivera in honor of the Guatemalan ecologist who fought for its creation.

The elusive quetzal has been revered since the days of the ancient Maya, who called it the winged serpent. Though the Maya often captured quetzals to remove their tail feathers, killing one was a capital offense. The quetzal has long symbolized freedom because it is said the bird cannot live in captivity. Although the female quetzal is attractive, the male is as spectacular a creature as ever took to the air, with a crimson belly, blue-green back, and flowing tail feathers. Its unforgettable appearance notwithstanding, the quetzal remains difficult to spot in the lush foliage of the cloud forest. The reserve offers the chance to see the quetzal in its natural habitat during its mating season, between April and June. The best place to see the birds is not in the park itself, oddly enough, but in the parking lot of the Ranchito del Quetzal, 1½ km (1 mi) north. Since it is easier to spot quetzals around dawn or dusk, it's worth spending a night in the area. Even if you don't catch a glimpse of the legendary bird, there are plenty of other species to spot, and the luxuriant greenery of the cloud forest is gorgeous in its own right.

One of the last remaining cloud forests in Guatemala, the Biotopo del Quetzal is a vital source of water for the region's rivers. Moisture that evaporated from Lago Izabal settles here as fog, which provides sustenance for the towering old-growth trees. Plants like lichens, hepaticas, bromeliads, and orchids abound. If you're lucky, you can see howler monkeys swinging above the two well-maintained trails, the 2-km (1-mi) Los Helechos (The Ferns) and the 4-km (2-mi) Los Musgos (The Mosses). The latter takes a short detour past a series of beautiful waterfalls. Both trails cross a river with concrete bathing pools where you can swim if you don't mind the cold. An interpretive guide is available at the stand at the trailheads. ☎ *No phone.* 🖾 *Free.*

Dining and Lodging

$$ ✕🏨 **Posada Montaña del Quetzal.** This comfortable country inn near
★   the Biotopo del Quetzal is the area's best lodging. Choose between small rooms in the main building and spacious bungalows with two bedrooms and a sitting room warmed by a fireplace. The restaurant overlooks a pool and serves a limited selection of Guatemalan and Continental cui-

sine. Even if you don't spend the night, this is a good spot for a meal or snack. Wander the trails nearby—you might catch a glimpse of a quetzal, ✉ *4 km (2½ mi) south of the Biotopo del Quetzal,* ☎ *335– 1805 in Guatemala City. 8 rooms, 10 bungalows. Restaurant, bar, coffee shop, pool, hiking, fishing. No credit cards.*

Cobán

2 *214 km (133 mi) northeast of Guatemala City.*

Cobán exists because people around the world couldn't get up without their morning cup of coffee. German immigrants flooded into Cobán in the 1880s to establish the vast coffee fincas that still cover the surrounding hillsides. They transformed the city of Cobán from a sleepy village into a wealthy enclave. This period of European high society was short-lived, however. With the onset of World War II, the U.S. government pressured Guatemala to expel the Germans. Traces of their influence remain, however.

The longtime residents of Cobán are the Q'eqchí Maya. Though they are seldom featured in the colorful Guatemalan brochures, many still wear traditional clothing in a style quite different from those of the highlands. *Cortes* (woven skirts), each made of 9 yards of fabric, are gathered and usually worn to just below the knees. They are paired with embroidered huipiles fashioned from a rectangular piece of fabric, with a hole cut out for the neck and the sides sewn up.

Following in the traditions of the ancient Maya, the Q'eqchí are religious people mixing modern theologies with older rituals and beliefs. Many caves around the region are used for religious ceremonies involving candle and incense burning.

A short walk from the prosperous modern markets of central Cobán, **Templo El Calvario** is at the top of a cobblestone path bordered by a series of small shrines, each sheltering a cross darkened with ash. The offerings inside include feathers, hair, and coins stuck to the crosses with gobs of wax. If you sit a while, you might see families muttering prayers in Q'eqchí. The view from the top of the hill is one of the best in the city. ✉ *3 Calle and 7 Av.,* ☎ *no phone.* 🎫 *Free.* ☉ *Daily 7–7.*

The **Catedral de Santo Domingo,** bordering the main square, is worth peeking into. It's one of the more understated churches you'll see. Near the altar is an Englishman's account of his travels to Cobán at the beginning of the century. To the right of the cathedral is the convent. Built first in the late 1500s, it is one of Cobán's oldest surviving buildings. ✉ *1 Av. and 1 Calle.*

Parque National Las Victorias, near Templo El Calvario, sits on what used to be a privately owned plantation. Today the park is filled with winding paths with great views of the town. ✉ *9 Av. and 3 Calle.*

The **Museo El Principe Maya,** a 10-minute walk from the plaza, has a collection of ancient Maya artifacts, mostly recovered from El Petén. Though the exhibit is relatively small, the variety of pieces is impressive. See fearsome masks, giant sacrificial pots, a reconstructed tomb, jade jewelry, and weapons. ✉ *6 Av. 4–26, Zona 3,* ☎ *952–1541.*

OFF THE
BEATEN PATH

SAN PEDRO CARCHÁ – An interesting daily market is the highlight of this traditional little town 6 km (4 mi) east of Cobán. Nearby Las Islas, with a waterfall and pool, is a popular spot for picnics.

At the **Finca Santa Margarita,** three blocks west of Parque Central, you can take a 45-minute tour of an operating coffee farm and witness the process of planting, growing, harvesting, and processing coffee beans. Owned by the Dieseldorff family, which has lived in Cobán for more than a century, the slatted wooden buildings have a distinct old-world feel. ⊠ *3 Calle 4–12, Zona 2,* ☎ *952–1286.* ☉ *Weekdays 8–12:30 and 1:30–5, Sat. 8–noon.*

Run by the friendly Concha de Mittelstaedt, the magnificent orchid farm called **Viveros Verapaz** is a good place for an afternoon jaunt. Mittelstaedt clearly enjoys sharing her passion with visitors, pointing out breathtaking blossoms and describing the painstaking process of coaxing the temperamental ornamentals to bloom. Typically, orchids bloom in late November and early December, the height of the season, culminating in Cobán's International Orchid Festival held annually in early December. Orchid cultivators from as far as Japan come to show off their flowers. ⊠ *Carretera Antigua,* ☎ *952–1133.*

Dining and Lodging

$–$$ ✕ **Kikoe's Tasca.** Kikoe, this establishment's one-eyed owner, makes newcomers feel welcome with his eagerness to chat about anything from his career as a mineralogist to his expertise in all types of beer. With a wraparound bar warmed by a fireplace, Kikoe's is the only real watering hole in Cobán, serving 150 kinds of liquor. The place doesn't get hopping until late and stays open until 1 in the morning. It also has a small but savory menu that will please meat lovers, featuring smoked leg of pork, goulash, and cheese fondue. ⊠ *2 Av. 4–33, Zona 2,* ☎ *952–1248. V. Closed Sun., Mon.*

$ ✕ **Café El Tirol.** The owner of this popular café grew up on a coffee plantation near Cobán. Duly qualified, she serves the largest selection of caffeinated beverages in this coffee-growing region. Hot coffee, cold coffee, coffee with liquor, coffee with chocolate, and a wide assortment of teas make up most of the six-page menu. She also whips up the best breakfasts in town. The café is opposite the church. ⊠ *1 Calle 3–13, Zona 1,* ☎ *951–4042. No credit cards. Closed Sun.*

$$$ ✕🏠 **Hotel La Posada.** True charm pervades La Posada, an attractive
★   colonial inn overlooking Cobán's central plaza. Rooms have wood floors and exposed beams and are furnished with lovely antiques. Some have special touches like wardrobes and writing desks. Blue chairs and cloth hammocks fill the porch overlooking the small garden. A cozy restaurant with a fireplace serves international as well as Guatemalan favorites. ⊠ *1 Calle 4–12, Zona 2,* ☎ *952–1495,* ℻ *951–0646. 14 rooms. Restaurant, café, Ping-Pong, Internet. AE, DC, MC, V.*

$ ✕🏠 **Casa D'Acuña.** The Restaurante Casa D'Acuña is a necessary stop when you're in Cobán, regardless of whether you're a guest at the hotel. Take a seat in the dining room or in out the garden and enjoy a variety of Italian dishes like the cheesy lasagna. Homemade carrot cake and a cup of locally grown coffee make a great dessert or midday snack. A small and clean hostel is adjacent to the restaurant. One room has a double bed; the rest have bunk beds. The proprietors—a lovely Guatemalan–American family—are an invaluable resource. They run excellent two- to five-day ecoadventures to the Biotopo del Quetzal and other sights. ⊠ *4 Calle 3–11, Zona 2,* ☎ *951–0482,* ℻ *952–1547. 7 rooms without bath. Restaurant, café, travel services. AE, MC, V.*

$$ 🏠 **Hostal Doña Victoria.** Built as a convent more than 400 years ago, the colonial-style Doña Victoria is filled with gorgeous antiques. Rocking chairs and overstuffed couches line the stone porch encircling the gardens. Rooms are spacious and have beds piled high with blankets for the cold Cobán nights. ⊠ *3 Calle 2–38, Zona 3,* ☎ *951–4214,* ℻ *951–4213,* WEB *www.lasverapaces.com. 9 rooms. Restaurant, travel services. AE, DC, MC, V.*

Outdoor Activities and Sports

CAVING

The Cuevas de Rey Marco, near the village of San Juan Chamelco, are relatively untouched caves. Tours take you into the caves only a few hundred yards, but the potential for further exploring is limitless, as the caverns stretch for many miles beneath the mountains of the Sierra Yalijux. Getting inside is difficult; expect crawling through the entrance and crossing a waist-high river. Tours can be arranged through **Access Computación** (⊠ 1 Calle 3–13, Zona 1, ☎ 951–4040).

SOCCER

Cobán's more-than-respectable national soccer team, Cobán Imperial, plays regularly in the hilltop **Estadio Verapaz,** five blocks northwest of the bus station. Sit in the bleachers or on the grassy hillside. Look for the sandwich board in the main square for information. Tickets are about 20 quetzales.

Lanquín

❸ *63 km (39 mi) east of Cobán.*

This pretty village is on the doorstep of some impressive natural wonders. The **Grutas de Lanquín,** a system of caves cut through by underground rivers, are easy to explore. A trail with iron railings will help you keep your footing among the huge stalactites and stalagmites. Visit toward sunset and you'll see thousands and thousands of bats leave their dark dwellings and head for the starry night sky. To be let inside, stop in the municipal building in Lanquín.

★ Often praised as the most beautiful spot in Guatemala, **Semuc Champey** appears to be a series of emerald pools surrounded by dense forest. On further investigation you'll notice that the pools are actually the top of a natural arch through which the raging Río Cahabón flows. Local legend has it that various explorers have tried to enter the underground passage by lowering themselves over the lip of the arch; many turned back right away, while some were swallowed up, their bodies never recovered. Semuc Champey is only 10 km (6 mi) south of Lanquín on a dirt road, but you'll need a four-wheel-drive vehicle to reach it.

Dining and Lodging

$$ ✕⌂ **Hotel El Recreo Lanquín Champey.** At the mouth of the Grutas de Lanquín, this concrete-block hotel is a good choice for budget travelers. Lodging is in clean rooms in the main building and in several bungalows out back. The restaurant was built with the expectation of more diners than it typically garners; it serves decent Guatemalan fare. ⊠ *Near Grutas de Lanquín,* ☎ *801–2856,* FAX *951–1492. 30 rooms, 4 bungalows. Restaurant. AE, DC, MC, V.*

Outdoor Activities and Sports

WHITE-WATER RAFTING

Rafting expeditions on the Río Cahabón, a challenging river near Lanquín, usually last from one to three days. Trips can be arranged through the Antigua-based **Area Verde Expeditions** (⊠ 4 Av. Sur 8, Antigua, ☎ 832–3863). The Guatemala City-based **Maya Expeditions** (⊠ 15 Calle 1–91, Zona 10, Guatemala City, ☎ 237–4666) also has trips down the raging river.

Las Verapaces A to Z

To research prices, get advice from other travelers, and book travel arrangements, visit www.fodors.com.

AIR TRAVEL TO AND FROM LAS VERAPACES

There are no airports in Las Verapaces. Most people headed for this region fly into Guatemala City's Aeropuerto Internacional La Aurora.

BUS TRAVEL TO AND FROM LAS VERAPACES

Transportes Escobar runs comfortable buses between Guatemala City and Cobán, passing the Biotopo del Quetzal. The driver will let you off if you ask. Buses depart every hour or so from 4 to 4 at both ends of the route, and the trip takes four hours.

➤ BUS INFORMATION: **Transportes Escobar** (⊠ 8 Av. 15–16, Zona 1, Guatemala City, ☎ 238–1409; ⊠ 2 Calle 3–77, Zona 4, Cobán, ☎ 952–1536).

CAR RENTAL

Several agencies in Cobán rent cars for about 400 quetzales a day, which is a great deal if you want to spend some time exploring the area on your own. Companies with good reputations include Geo, Inque, Sears, and Tabarini. Reserve ahead of time, especially on the weekends.

➤ LOCAL AGENCIES: **Geo Rental** (⊠ 1 Calle 3–13, Zona 1, Cobán, ☎ 952–2059). **Inque** ⊠ 3 Av. 1–18, Zona 4, Cobán, ☎ 952–1994). **Sears** (⊠ 8 Av. 2–36, Zona 4, Cobán, ☎ 952–1530). **Tabarini** (⊠ Av. 227, Cobán, ☎ 952–1504).

CAR TRAVEL

To get to Las Verapaces from Guatemala City, take the Carretera Atlántica to El Rancho, where you'll take Route 17 north to reach Cobán and Lanquín. There are not many gas stations before you reach Cobán, so make sure you fill up before you leave the capital.

EMERGENCIES

➤ EMERGENCY SERVICES: **Police** (☎ 951–1306).
➤ HOSPITALS: **Hospital Regional de Cobán** (⊠ 8 Calle 1–24, Zona 4, Cobán ☎ 952–1315).
➤ PHARMACIES: **Farmacia Central** (⊠ 1 Calle, Zona 1, Cobán, ☎ 951–0581).

MAIL AND SHIPPING

Letters and packages can be shipped from the post office in Cobán, but you're better off bringing them back to Guatemala City and mailing them from there.

➤ POST OFFICES: **Cobán** (⊠ 3 Calle 2–02, Zona 3).

MONEY MATTERS

Currency can be exchanged in Cobán's hotels and banks, but there are very few ATMs, so make sure to bring enough cash. Some banks will give you cash advances on credit cards.

➤ BANKS: **Bancared** (⊠ 1 Av. 2–66, Zona 1, Cobán).

TOUR OPERATORS

Proyecto Ecológico Quetzal specializes in tours of the Biotopo del Quetzal. This nonprofit organization benefits the indigenous Q'eqchí people. Ultimate Flying Tours offers custom-designed private tours of the region, including flights to hard-to-access places.

➤ TOUR COMPANIES: **Proyecto Ecológico Quetzal** (⊠ 2 Calle 14–36, Zona 1, Cobán, ☎ 952–1047). **Ultimate Flying Tours** (⊠ 1 Calle 3–13, Zona 1, Cobán, ☎ 814–0452).

VISITOR INFORMATION

There are no tourist offices in Las Verapaces, but a good place for information is a cybercafé called Access Computación. It provides not only Internet access, but also information on tours to Semuc Champey and other points of interest.

➤ TOURIST INFORMATION: **Access Computación** (✉ 1 Calle 3–13, Zona 1, ☎ 931–4040).

THE ATLANTIC LOWLANDS

Hot and humid, Guatemala's eastern coast was immortalized by Nobel Prize–winning writer Miguel Ángel Asturias in *Viento Fuerte* (1950), *El Papa Verde* (1954), and *Los Ojos de los Enterrados* (1960). Known as the Banana Trilogy, these books chronicle the pain inflicted on the country by the United Fruit Company. Bananas are still big business here, and Dole and Chiquita remain owners of huge plantations in the region's lowlands. From the docks in Puerto Barrios gigantic freight liners leave daily with enormous crates of bananas stacked like children's blocks. Groups of farmworkers can be spotted along the roadside, each carrying nothing more than a small knit bag. Men from one village often seek work as a group to increase their chances of being hired. Although the minimum wage is about $3.50 a day, some will work for half that amount. They usually return home on Sunday, the one day of the week they don't live and work on the farms.

Although the indigenous culture here is not as striking as that in the highlands, you'll run across many people who speak only their native Q'eqchí. Living in remote mountain villages, they sometimes must walk a full day or more to get to the market towns. The coastal towns of Livingston and Puerto Barrios are home to the Garífuna, Afro-Caribbean peoples who speak a language all their own.

Traces of the Maya empire, such as the impressive city of Quiriguá, mark the movement of this ancient people through the lowlands. But even with sights like Quiriguá you won't run into many fellow travelers. The region is practically untouched by tourism, even though it contains treasures such as stunning Lago Izabal. The largest lake in Guatemala, Lago Izabal sits in a tropical valley bordered by two mountain ranges, the Sierra de las Minas, to the south, and the Sierra Santa Cruz, to the north.

You will enjoy your trip to the Atlantic Lowlands much more if you adapt to the local rhythm of life. Wake at sunrise and do most of your activities in the morning. With a good book in hand, find a hammock in which to relax during the steamy midday hours. Hit the street again in the late afternoon and evening, when the temperatures are a bit cooler. The best part of the year to visit is in November and December—the end of the rainy season, when temperatures are tolerable. It is best to avoid the area during March, when the heat is dizzying and farmers are burning their fields, leaving the skies thick with smoke that obliterates the views.

Numbers in the text correspond to numbers in the margin and on the Verapaces and Atlantic Lowlands map.

Quiriguá

★ ❹ *186 km (115 mi) northeast of Guatemala City, 96 km (60 mi) southwest of Puerto Barrios.*

Unlike the hazy remnants of chiseled images you see at most other archaeological sites in Central America, Quiriguá has some that are seemingly untouched by winds and rain. They emerge from the rock faces in breathtaking detail. Quiriguá is famous for the amazingly well-preserved stelae, or carved pillars, that are the largest yet discovered. They depict Quiriguá's ruling dynasty, especially the powerful Cauac Sky. Several monuments, covered with interesting zoomorphic figures, still stand, and the remains of an acropolis and other structures have been partially restored.

In ancient times Quiriguá was an important Maya trading center that stood on the banks of the Río Motagua (the river has since changed its course). The ruins are surrounded by a lush stand of rain forest— an untouched wilderness in the heart of banana country. ⊠ *Near Chiquimula,* ☎ *no phone.* ⌨ *Q25.* ⊙ *Daily 7:30–5.*

Río Dulce

⑤ *30 km (19 mi) northwest of La Ruidosa, where the road to El Petén leaves the Carretera Atlántica.*

Although it sits on the shore of a beautiful waterway, the town of Río Dulce falls sadly short of its potential. A major transportation hub, it's where you'll find the country's longest bridge, which crosses the river that gave this town its name. Drive south, and you'll hit the road leading to the Central Highlands; head north, and you'll eventually reach El Petén. Río Dulce has little to keep you here, although unexpectedly good restaurants and hotels in nearby communities are easily reached by boat. The *launcheros* (captains) who congregate on the river will take you anywhere in the area for under 40 quetzales.

Once an important stop along the Maya trade route, the Río Dulce later became the route over which the conquistadors sent the gold and silver they plundered back to Spain. All this wealth attracted pirates, who attacked both the ships and the warehouses on shore. In hopes of curtailing these buccaneers, colonists built a series of fortresses on the river's northern banks. In the 1950s the Guatemalan government reconstructed the ruined fortress of **Castillo de San Felipe** (⊠ Southwest of Río Dulce, ☎ no phone, ⌨ Q10), named after King Philip II of Spain. From 1655 to 1660 it was used as a prison. You can reach it by the road leading west from Río Dulce or by a short boat ride.

The northern banks of the Golfete, an expansive body of water between Lago Izabal and Río Dulce, are covered by the 17,790-acre **Biotopo Chocón Machacas.** Among the stretches of virgin rain forest and the extensive mangrove swamp here are gentle manatees—shy marine mammals also known as sea cows because of their enormous size. Manatees are as elusive as quetzals, so as you boat through the reserve you're more likely to to see other animals such as sea otters. Some of the creeks go through thick forests where giant mahogany, ceiba, and mangrove trees hang over the water to form tunnels so thick they block out the sun. A tiny island surrounded by the park's dozens of creeks and lagoons has a well-maintained nature trail of a half mile or so that is easily walked by those with stiff boating legs. The trail has such interesting examples of old-growth trees as the San Juan, a tall, straight tree with yellow blossoms, and such exotic plants as orchids and bromeliads.

The only way to get to the reserve is a 45-minute boat trip from Río Dulce or Livingston. Most launches up and down the river will stop at the park entrance if requested, but they rarely enter the park. Most major hotels on the Río Dulce rent boats with guides for individual or group tours. ⊠ *Northeast of Río Dulce,* ☎ *no phone.*

Dining and Lodging

$$$ ✕⚏ **Catamaran Island Hotel.** On the north bank of the Río Dulce, this
★ lovely resort takes advantage of its location with a restaurant built right
over the water. The specialties are grilled steaks and fresh fish, including
the delicious robálo plucked from the river. A string of spacious bun-
galows is cooled by river breezes. The nicest features are the porches,
which are perfect for watching boats. The staff can arrange boat trips
along the river and to Livingston. ✉ *5 km (3 mi) east of Río Dulce,*
☎ *930–5109,* FAX *367–1633. 28 bungalows. Restaurant, fans, pool, bar,
travel services. MC, V.*

$$ ✕⚏ **La Ensenada Hotel & Yacht Club.** Although La Ensenada has less
character than the competition, it is quite close to town. Rooms sur-
round a large pool, and a three-story complex holding a restaurant and
bar overlooks the water. Each of the well-maintained buildings a good
distance from the river has several modern rooms, but the slightly tired
bungalows have much better views. Try windsurfing and other water
sports. ✉ *1½ km (1 mi) east of El Relleno, Km 275 Carretera á Peten,*
☎ *930–5230,* FAX *930–5299,* WEB *www.riodulcegt.com/laensenada.htm.
38 rooms. Restaurant, pool, windsurfing, bar, travel services. AE, DC,
MC, V.*

$$ ✕⚏ **Bruno's.** At this popular hangout for the yachting crowd, many
of the regular patrons arrive by boat. There's plenty of space to dock
at the marina. Bruno's is best known for its lively restaurant featuring
a great international menu. Expats enjoy sandwiches and other light
fare as they watch football on the big-screen TV. The rooms, next to
a pool, are spacious and clean. ✉ *Under bridge, on north side,* ☎ *930–
5174,* FAX *930–5178,* WEB *www.mayaparadise.com. 10 rooms, 7 with
bath. Restaurant, cable TV, pool, boating, marina, bar, laundry ser-
vice. AE, MC, V.*

$ ✕⚏ **Hacienda Tijax.** Built out over the water, this jungle lodge offers
a number of types of accommodations, from cozy birdhouse-shape
cabañas to large two-story bungalows with kitchens and dining rooms.
You can enjoy the breeze while relaxing in one of the hammocks. A
series of swinging bridges over a mangrove swamp lets you stroll to
the adjacent nature reserve. Also nearby is a plantation where you can
learn how rubber is extracted from trees. The lodge is also well known
for its restaurant, which serves a variety of Italian dishes including home-
made pesto. There are also plenty of vegetarian dishes. ✉ *Near Río
Dulce,* ☎ *930–5196,* FAX *902–7523,* WEB *www.tijax.com. 9 rooms.
Restaurant, pool. No credit cards.*

$ ⚏ **Finca Tatin.** A rustic bed-and-breakfast run by a friendly Argentine
family, Finca Tatin is far off the beaten path. The inn, which doubles
as a Spanish school, rents canoes, which are a great way to see the river
without the roar of a motor. Just upstream, Ak'tenamit has a small gift
shop with homemade crafts made by children. ✉ *8 km (5 mi) south
of Livingston,* ☎ *902–0831, fincatatin@hotmail.com. 8 rooms. Restau-
rant. No credit cards.*

Nightlife and the Arts

Head to **Hotel Backpackers** (✉ under bridge on southern end, ☎ 208–
1779) for a beer at the waterfront bar. All the proceeds go to benefit
Casa Guatemala Orphanage, so drink up.

Outdoor Activities and Sports

One of the most beautiful boat trips in the country is the two- to three-
hour ride on the river between the town of Río Dulce and Livingston.
The *collectivos* (public boats) leave from Río Bravo Restaurant when
they have at least eight passengers (the laticheros will keep you wait-
ing all afternoon if the boat is not full). The rate is usually about 70

quetzales per person. Private boats can also be hired, but they cost upwards of 800 quetzales. All public launches stop at Bird Island, a
roosting place for several hundred cormorants, and Flower Lagoon, a
small inlet covered in bobbing water lilies. There's also a stop at a hot
springs that tumbles into a shallow river. Definitely bring your bathing
suit.

El Estor

⑥ *40 km (24 mi) west of Río Dulce.*

Although the vast majority of this little town's population is Q'eqchí,
there's also a decidedly Caribbean influence. Locals describe El Estor
as *tranquilo,* which means easygoing or laid-back, and this becomes
evident as you stroll around the brick streets. The town, which grew
up around the nickel mine to the west, seems to have drifted to sleep
after the facility was shut down. There's a waterfront walk where you
can look for birds along the banks of Lago Izabel. El Estor is on a migratory path, so hundreds of species can be spotted here.

The hour-long drive here from Río Dulce takes you past expansive banana plantations as well as cattle ranches. Look for the massive ceiba
trees along the road. They are sacred to the Maya—the only reason
they were left standing when the rest of the forest was cleared. Also
try to spot strangler figs, which wrap themselves around the trunks of
palms. Eventually they overcome the palms, which die from lack of
sunlight.

★ Perhaps the most beautiful of Guatemala's natural wonders, **El Boqueron**
is a narrow limestone canyon whose 180-meter (590-ft) walls are covered in lush foliage heavy with hanging moss. Hummingbirds dance
around lavish blooms, blue morpho butterflies flutter between branches,
and kingfishers dive at minnows. Sometimes howler monkeys visit the
trees nearby—listen for their thunderous cries in the late afternoon.
All along the canyon you can climb rocks and explore caves filled with
clinging bats. Close to the entrance is a turnoff past a giant ceiba tree
that leads to several thatch huts along the river; the proprietors, Antonio and Miguel, provide roughly fashioned *kayukos* (canoes) that
you can rent for a ride through the canyon. The water is clean and cool
and great for swimming except after a heavy rain, when all the local
rivers turn a muddy brown. ⊠ *3 mi (2 mi) east of El Estor.*

Known for its steaming waterfall, think of **Finca Paraíso** as a natural
spa for the tired traveler. Don't be dissuaded from a trip here even if
the weather is hot and humid, as the falls descend into an icy cold river.
A trail from the front gate leads to a short yet somewhat bumpy climb
to the falls—be careful, as the rocks can be slippery. Around the falls
are small indentations in the rock that serve as natural saunas. You
can also hike upstream to the narrow cave at the source of the river.
The rock formations here are otherworldly. About 2 km (1 mi) down-
stream from the hot springs is a simple restaurant that serves hearty
meals. From here you can also rent horses and ride to the springs. ⊠
10 mi east of El Estor, ☎ *949–7122.* 🎫 *Q5.*

Declared a protected area in 1996, **Refugio de Vida Silvestre Bocas del
Polochic** is home to more than 250 species of birds, including blue herons,
kingfishers, and snowy egrets. If you're lucky, you'll spot the blue-
throated motmot. On the western end of Lago Izabal, the country's
largest wetland encompasses more than 51,000 acres. An organization
called Defensores de la Naturaleza manages the reserve. From the office in El Estor you can arrange a guided boat trip to the reserve and
a visit to the Q'eqchí village of Selempím, with meals prepared by local

women. The organization also runs a remote ecolodge at the base of the Sierra de las Minas. The thatch-roof lodge has rooms with bunk beds and a full kitchen. A midnight thunderstorm is magical, but regardless of the weather you'll hear the roar of howler monkeys long into the night. Rates are $25. ⊠ *Defensores de la Naturaleza, El Estor,* ☎ *369–7777. ecoturismo@defensores.org.net.*

Dining and Lodging

$–$$ ✕ **Restaurante Chaabil.** The name means "beautiful" in the language of the Q'eqchí, and that's an apt description for the best eatery in El Estor. Built over the water, the palm-thatched building is the perfect place for a breakfast with a view of the majestic Sierra de las Minas or for a dinner accompanied by a spectacular sunset over Lago Izabal. You may even get a chance to snap a photo of a fisherman delivering the catch of the day. Call ahead of time to enjoy a bowl of seafood tapado, or stop by anytime for lake perch or river robálo. For dessert try a pineapple or papaya smoothie. ⊠ *West of main square,* ☎ *949–7272. No credit cards.*

$$ ✕🏠 **Hotel Marisabela.** This lakefront hotel has clean, simply furnished rooms overlooking the lake. A third-floor balcony with wooden lounge chairs is the best place in town for an afternoon siesta. Although the restaurant always looks closed, it's open for business. Just call out "¡Buenas tardes!" until one of the workers appears. The Italian dishes are authentic and filling. ⊠ *2 blocks east of the main square,* ☎ *949–7206. 12 rooms. Restaurant. No credit cards.*

$ 🏠 **Hotel Vista al Lago.** This hotel was once the general store that gave El Estor its name. Run by the loquacious Oscar Paz, it has clean, cozy rooms. The wide wooden balcony is a great place to observe the town's waterfront. Before checking in, make sure the town hall next door has no plans for a dance; otherwise the thumping music will keep you awake until 4 AM. ⊠ *Next to town hall,* ☎ *949–7205. 21 rooms. MC, V.*

Shopping

You can watch how the beautiful weavings of Guatemala are made at the **Q'eqchí Women's Weaving Workshop** (⊠ north of main square, ☎ no phone, ☉ Mon.–Sat. 8–noon and 3–5). Every year small numbers of women come from their villages to live at the workshop, where they spend 12 months learning the age-old crafts of loom and belt weaving. Every woman who successfully completes the course is given a loom to take back to her village and is encouraged to teach other women how to weave.

Livingston

★ ❼ *37 km (23 mi) northeast of Río Dulce.*

At the mouth of the Río Dulce, Livingston is known as La Buga, or "the Mouth," by the Garífuna people. Although it's on the mainland, Livingston might as well be a Caribbean island—the only way to get to or from the town is by boat, and the culture is closer to that of Jamaica than to the rest of Guatemala. Once you arrive here, shed your worries and settle under a coconut palm.

Livingston is home to the Garífuna people, who came here from the Lesser Antilles. After two decades of resisting British encroachment, the Garífuna were forcibly removed from their homeland and deposited on Roatán, an island off the coast of Honduras. Most of the Garífuna migrated to the mainland, settling all along the coast from Belize to Nicaragua. Each year from November 24 to 26, Livingston hosts a festival to celebrate the arrival of the Garífuna. The town rejoices with traditional music and dancing. The Feast of St. Isidore, held

May 13–15, is a huge celebration dedicated to the patron saint of corn. The best time to visit Livingston is during these energetic holidays.

Livingston's single paved road is the only evidence left of its heyday as a major port for coffee and other crops during the late 19th century. Livingston's population now makes its living mostly from fishing. By day the soft lick of waves on the shore measures out the slow pace that makes this laid-back community so attractive. At night roving bands of musicians take to the streets. The Garífuna are famous for their *punta* dancing—they may grab you from the crowd and teach you some moves you didn't know your body could make.

Anyone expecting white sandy beaches and azure waters is bound to be disappointed. The narrow beach that stretches north from the river mouth is not especially attractive. It is, however, a great place to explore, as it is home to several bars and a little shop where Pablo Marino sells handmade drums, shakers, and wood carvings. Afternoon breezes off the ocean make resting on the beach a good place to pass the torrid afternoons.

Dining and Lodging

Be aware that young men wait on the town dock to "escort" you to your hotel. You can accept their offer or refuse; either way, they will follow you and ask for money. "Tipping" them to leave you alone is your prerogative.

$–$$ ✕ **Pizzeria Rigoletto.** Wacky stories are the reasons to head to this small restaurant run by a friendly British expat and her Guatemalan husband. They'll talk to you about Garífuna legends and just about anything else you can think of. The limited menu leaves something to be desired, but the pizza really is quite good. ✉ *Near public dock,* ☎ *no phone. No credit cards.*

$–$$ ✕ **Restaurante Bahía Azul.** The walls are literally covered with travel information at Bahía Azul, the most popular tourist restaurant in town. If you're thinking about a trip, you can probably arrange it here. At the curve on the main street, its porch is a great place to watch people stroll past. The large menu includes everything from sandwiches to lobster. Most nights include live drumming by a local band. ✉ *On the main street,* ☎ *947–0049,* 🖷 *947–0136. MC, V.*

$ ✕ **Restaurante Margoth.** Presided over by the well-respected Doña Margoth, this longtime favorite serves the usual fish dishes. It's famous, however, for its delicious seafood tapado with plantains. The stew is a challenge to eat, so tuck your napkin into your collar. The doña keeps a sharp eye on her workers, so the service in this bright and bustling café is speedy. ✉ *North of the main street,* ☎ *947–0019. AE, MC, V. Closed 3 PM–7 PM.*

$$$$ ✕🏠 **Hotel Tucán Dugú.** Livingston's finest hotel, the Tucán Dugú has ★ some great views of the Caribbean from its hilltop perch. The extensive grounds overflow with lush foliage. Spacious rooms, housed in a thatch-roof building, all have ocean views. Palm trees surround the large pool, where you can relax in one of the lounge chairs or order a drink at the bar. The restaurant serves seafood dishes such as coconut shrimp and robálo but is almost always empty. The staff can arrange trips up the Río Dulce and to spots around the Bahía de Amatique. ✉ *On the main street,* ☎ *947–0072; 334–5064 in Guatemala City,* 🖷 *334–5242 in Guatemala City. 46 rooms, 4 suites, 4 bungalows. Restaurant, bar, pool, beach, travel services. AE, DC, MC, V.*

$ ✕🏠 **Casa Rosada.** This string of waterfront bungalows can best be de-★ scribed as Guatemala's most luxurious way of roughing it. Each is furnished with bright highland furniture and a pair of beds draped with mosquito nets. Don't be scared off by the shared baths; they're clean and comfortable, and the showers have hot water The main building houses a restaurant serving excellent meals on a pretty patio overlooking the water. The dinner menu changes daily but always includes lobster and other favorites. Dinner, at 7 sharp, is by candlelight. Owner Cathey Lopez, an American expat, arranges river cruises from Casa Rosado's private dock. ⊠ *Near public dock,* ☎ *947–0303,* FAX *947–0304. 10 bungalows without bath. Restaurant, boating, laundry service, travel services. AE, DC, MC, V.*

$ ⊞ **Hotel Garífuna.** Run by the cordial Livingston family, Hotel Garífuna puts you in the heart of a lively neighborhood. The rooms in this two-story building open onto a porch overlooking the street or a tree-filled backyard. ⊠ *Off the main street,* ☎ *947–0183,* FAX *947–0184. 6 rooms. Laundry service. AE, DC, MC, V.*

Nightlife

Residents of Livingston are famous for their weekend bashes, mostly centering around several beachfront discos. **Barique's Place** is a lively spot at the end of main street, but it's also a good idea to ask around town. Punta music pulls everyone out onto the dance floor. The **Ubafu,** a Rasta-inspired shack (note the Bob Marley posters) is sometimes open for a late-night jam if there are enough beer-drinking customers.

Outdoor Activities and Sports

A short boat ride to the north takes you to a gorgeous little jungle river called Siete Altares, a series of deep pools that are ideal for swimming. Arrange for a guided tour with the cheery and enthusiastic **Rogelio Franzua** (☎ 947–0406). A bag lunch is provided. Tours are about 60 quetzales.

Puerto Barrios

❽   *295 km (183 mi) from Guatemala City, 2 hrs by ferry from Livingston.*

Once a thriving port for the United Fruit Company, the commercial boom has long since subsided for Puerto Barrios, leaving behind paint-chipped wooden buildings. Some old stilt houses built in the traditional Caribbean style line many of the streets. The people are as warm as the tropical air, and a simple "buenas noches" will make even the most hard-hearted dock worker smile.

Dining and Lodging

$$ ✕ **Restaurante Safary.** A longtime favorite in Puerto Barrios, this grass-roof restaurant is one of the few right on the water. On a hot afternoon or steamy night the ocean breezes are a tremendous relief. You sit on wooden benches with lots of locals. ⊠ *End of 5 Av. at water,* ☎ *948–0563. AE, DC, MC, V.*

$$$$ ⊞ **Amatique Bay Resort & Marina.** Sprawling resorts like this waterfront complex are the newest trend in Guatemala. The beautiful natural surroundings are somewhat diminished by all the effort to make things luxurious. The impressive pool, complete with a replica of a Spanish galleon that shoots water from its cannons, has slides for children and an island bar for adults. Few of the sunny suites have views of the ocean, but they are equipped with everything you would find in a well-furnished apartment, including washers and dryers. ⊠ *North of Puerto Barrios,* ☎ *948–1800,* FAX *948–1823.* WEB *www.amatiqueresortandmarina.com 88 rooms. Restaurant, cable TV, boating, jet skiing, marina, bicycles, dance club. AE, DC, MC, V.*

$$$$ ⊞ **Cayos del Diablo.** Set amid a tropical garden, this string of thatch bungalows faces the expansive waters of the Bahía de Amatique. The grounds are adjacent to a forest-draped hill with a small waterfall. You can relax by the pool or the private beach, or arrange a cruise on the

bay and up the Río Dulce. Boats pick up guests at the dock in Puerto
Barrios each hour. ⊠ *13 km (8 mi) west of Puerto Barrios,* ☎ *948–
2361; 800/528–1234 in the U.S.,* ℻ *948–2361. 50 rooms. Restaurant,
bar, pool, beach, waterskiing, meeting room, travel services. AE, DC,
MC, V.*

The Atlantic Lowlands A to Z

*To research prices, get advice from other travelers, and book travel ar-
rangements, visit www.fodors.com.*

AIR TRAVEL TO AND FROM THE ATLANTIC LOWLANDS
Inter Airlines flies from Guatemala City to Puerto Barrios and Río Dulce
on twin-engine planes. Hops between Puerto Barrios and Río Dulce
depart once a day except on Friday and Saturday, when there are two
flights.
➤ AIRLINES AND CONTACTS: **Inter Airlines** (⊠ 7 Av. 14–44, La Galeria,
2nd floor, Zona 9, Guatemala City, ☎ 361–2144).

BOAT TRAVEL
Daily ferry service leaves Puerto Barrios at 10:30 AM and 5 PM and Livingston at 5 AM and 2 PM. The trip takes about two hours. Launches
that connect the two cities take about 34 minutes, but they don't depart until they are full. This can really dent your plans, especially if
you are leaving late in the day.

BUS TRAVEL TO AND FROM THE ATLANTIC LOWLANDS
Bound for Puerto Barrios, comfortable buses leave Guatemala City hourly
from 6 to 5. Be sure to ask for the *especial* service operated by Litegua.
Trips to the capital from Puerto Barrios also leave hourly.

Litegua also has direct service to Río Dulce from the capital. Linea Do-
rada runs between Guatemala City and Flores, but it passes through
Río Dulce. Buses leave the capital every day at 10. The trip takes
about six hours.
➤ BUS INFORMATION: **Linea Dorada** (⊠ 16 Calle 10–03, Zona 1,
Guatemala City, ☎ 232–9658). **Litegua** (⊠ 15 Calle 10–40, Zona 1,
Guatemala City, ☎ 232–7578; ⊠ 6 Av. 9–10, Puerto Barrios, ☎ 948–
1002).

CAR TRAVEL
From Guatemala City most people drive to the Atlantic Lowlands via
the Carretera Atlántica. The journey to Río Dulce or Puerto Barrios is
about five hours on a good day. Descending the curving roads through
the mountains you can feel the temperature and humidity rising.

EMERGENCIES
➤ EMERGENCY SERVICES: **Police** (⊠ Puerto Barrios, ☎ 948–0120).
➤ HOSPITALS: **Hospital Nacional** (⊠ Puerto Barrios, ☎ 948–3077).

HEALTH
The heat and sun in the Atlantic Lowlands can be intense. Be prepared
with a good sun hat and lightweight clothing that covers your arms
and legs. Shorts don't protect legs from the sun, tall grass, insects, and
dust. Also pack plenty of sunscreen and insect repellent.

MAIL AND SHIPPING
Most towns in the Atlantic Lowlands have post offices, but you should
wait to post letters in Puerto Barrios. The main post office here is about
four blocks from the bay.
➤ POST OFFICES: **Puerto Barrios** (⊠ 6 Calle and 6 Av.).

MONEY MATTERS

If you need to exchange cash in the Atlantic Lowlands, the place to do it is Puerto Barrios. There are several banks that will be happy to help you, including Banco Industril.

➤ BANKS: **Banco Industril** (✉ 7 Av. Norte 73, Puerto Barrios).

SAFETY

Robberies have been known to occur in Puerto Barrios, so be on your guard. Use the same precautions you would anywhere—don't wear flashy jewelry and watches, keep your camera in a secure bag, and don't handle money in public. Remain alert for pickpockets, especially in crowded markets.

TIKAL AND THE MAYA RUINS

The jungles of El Petén were once the heartland of the Maya civilization. The sprawling empire—including parts of present-day Mexico, Belize, Honduras, and El Salvador—was once made up of a network of cities that held hundreds of thousands of people, but a millennium ago this fascinating civilization suddenly vanished without a trace. The temples that dominated the horizon were swallowed up by the jungle.

The first major Maya society dates to 2000 BC, based largely on the traditions of the Olmecs, a people living in what is now Mexico. Over the next 2,000 years the Maya proved to be an intellectually curious people. They developed a type of writing (one of the earliest) and a sophisticated system of mathematics (the first to use a zero). The Maya were particularly adept astronomers, mapping the orbits of the sun, moon, and planets with incredible accuracy—the Maya lunar cycle differs from today's calculations by only seven minutes.

From about 250 BC to AD 900 the Maya developed complex social systems, agricultural practices, and religious beliefs, reaching their zenith with the construction of temples like Tikal in El Petén. Around AD 1000, the Maya suffered repeated attacks from rival civilizations, followed by a sudden and mysterious period of decline. The arrival of conquistadors like Hernán Cortés and Pedro de Alvarado in the early 1500s marked the beginning of the subjugation of what was left of the Maya people.

Today El Petén is a sparsely populated backwater where ancient ruins just seem to crop up from the landscape. Nature reigns supreme, with vines and other plants quickly covering everything that stands still a little too long. Whatever your primary interest—archeology, history, birding, biking—you'll find plenty to do and see in this remote region.

It wasn't until 1970 that a dirt road linking the region to the rest of the country finally appeared. It wasn't paved, however, until 1999. Four-wheel-drive vehicles are still required to get to many of the sites, while others are reachable only by boat or on foot. The difficulty doesn't just enhance the adventure, it gives you time to take in the exotic scenery and rare tropical flora and fauna that's with you all the way.

Numbers in the text correspond to numbers in the margin and on the Tikal and the Maya Ruins map.

Flores

★ ❶ *206 km (133 mi) north of Río Dulce, 61 km (38 mi) northeast of Sayaxché.*

The red-roof town of Flores, on an island surrounded by the waters of Lago Petén Itzá, is on the site of the ancient city of Tatyasal. Thi

Tikal and the Maya Ruins

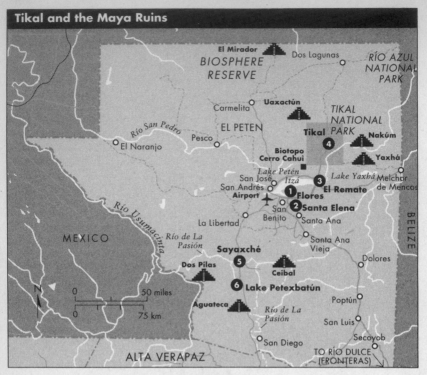

was the region's last unconquered outpost of Maya civilization, until finally falling to the Spanish in 1697. The conquerors destroyed the city's huge pyramids.

Today the provincial capital is a pleasant place to explore, with its narrow streets lined with thick-walled buildings painted pink, blue, and purple. Flowering plants droop over balconies, giving the town a tropical flavor. There's a central square presided over by a colonial church. Connected to the mainland by a bridge, it serves as a base for travelers to El Petén. It is also the center of many nongovernmental organizations working for the preservation of the Mayan Biosphere, an endangered area covering nearly all of northern Petén. Flores is also one of the last remaining vestiges of the Itzá, the people who built Mexico's monumental Chichén Itzá.

In the 1800s, before it was a departure point for travelers headed for the ruins, Flores was called Devil's Island because of the prison on top of the hill where a church now stands. Since 1994 the building has been home to the **Centro de Información sobre la Naturaleza, Cultura, y Artesanía de Petén** (⊠ north side of Parque Central, ☎ 926–0718). The Center for Information on the Nature, Culture, and Crafts of Petén has a small museum with photographs of the region and information about local resources, such as allspice, chicle (a chewing-gum base made from tree sap), and *xate* (a shade palm used in floral decorations). A gift shop sells wood carvings, woven baskets, cornhusk dolls, and even locally made peanut butter.

Dining and Lodging

$–$$ ✕ **Floating Restaurant Don Quijote.** Set on a small boat that is permanently docked on the town's southern shore, Don Quijote is a great place to watch the sunset. The curiously charming owner, Eduardo Fru-

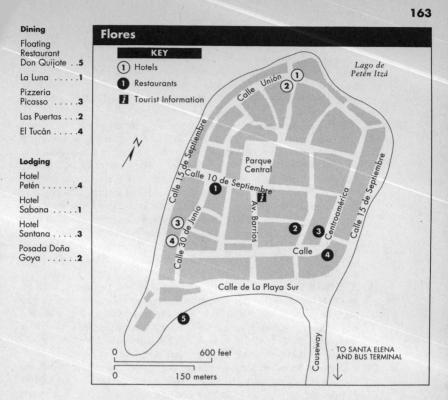

tos, serves up a tasty paella made from a recipe from Valencia. He's proud to announce that travelers have come all the way from Japan bearing pictures of his most famous dish, which appears in a guidebook. His less renowned yet equally regarded dishes include shrimp and fish. ⊠ *2 blocks west of bridge,* ☎ *712–6514. MC, V.*

$–$$ ✕ **La Luna.** With its homemade paper lamp shades illuminating the lovely blue walls, La Luna inspires romance on any moonlit night. You can just as easily fall in love with the place when you stop in for a delicious lunch. Choose from inventive dishes, including wonderful vegetarian options like the stuffed squash in white sauce. Many people drop by for a drink at the bar. ⊠ *Calle 30 de Junio,* ☎ *926–3346. AE, DC, MC, V. Closed Mon.*

$ ✕ **Pizzeria Picasso.** If you find yourself returning to Pizzeria Picasso, it's because the pizza that is baked in a huge brick oven comes out incomparably hot and delicious. The decor, featuring a print of Picasso's *Guernica,* is another draw. If you're not in the mood for pizza, there are a variety of pastas as well. Save room for cheesecake or tiramisu and a cup of steaming cappuccino. ⊠ *Calle Centroamérica,* ☎ *926– 0673. AE, DC, MC, V.*

$–$$ ✕ **Las Puertas.** On a quiet side street, Las Puertas was named for its ★ six screened doors. It's a favorite hangout for locals and travelers alike. The friendly couple who run the place take great pride in serving only the freshest foods. They are famous for their delicious sandwiches made with homemade bread and mozzarella cheese and their giant goblets of incredible iced coffee. In the afternoon you can relax with a fruit drink as you play one of the many board games. Don' forget to stop back at night for a hearty dinner and live music. If mus is not your thing, then slip across the alley to the cinema that sho offbeat films. ⊠ *Calle Central at Av. Santa Ana,* ☎ *926–1061. DC, MC, V. Closed Sun.*

$–$$　✕ **El Tucán.** Toucans and parrots, part of the menagerie belonging to the owner, share the breezy terrace with diners at this pleasant eatery. The small dining room, decorated with highland weavings, also has good views of one of Flores's cobblestone streets. The menu includes a variety of traditional meals, though Mexican cuisine is the specialty here. The bread is baked on the premises. ✉ *Av. 15 de Septiembre and Calle Centroamérica,* ☎ *926–0536. AE, DC, MC V.*

$$$–$$$$　✕🖭 **Ni'tun Ecolodge.** After hiking through the jungle, you'll love return-
★ ing to this charming cluster of cabins. The point is to disturb the environment as little as possible, so the buildings are constructed of stone and wood left behind by farmers clearing land for fields. The common areas, including a massive kitchen downstairs and an airy bar and reading room upstairs, make it difficult not to sit inside and watch the hummingbirds dance around the gardens. But owners Lore Castillo and Bernie Mittelstaedt also run Monkey Eco Tours, so you can choose from itineraries ranging from one-day trips to nearby villages to a seven-day journey to El Mirador, the Maya site with the highest temples. ✉ *2 km (1 mi) west of San Andres,* ☎ *201–0759,* FAX *926–0807; 978/945–6486 in the U.S.,* WEB *www.nitun.com. 4 cabins. Restaurant, travel services. MC, V.*

$$　✕🖭 **Hotel Sabana.** On the northern tip of Flores, this small hotel offers simple rooms that open onto a terrace overlooking the pool. A sun-
deck has nice views of the lake. This is a good choice if you want a few creature comforts like air-conditioning and television. ✉ *Calle Union and Av. Libertad,* ☎ FAX *926–3323,* WEB *www.sabanahotel.com. 28 rooms. Restaurant, cable TV, pool, bar. AE, DC, MC, V.*

$$　✕🖭 **Hotel Santana.** Sitting right on the water, this bright pink hotel is the best lodging on the island. All the rooms open up onto wide bal-
conies with wicker chairs where you can enjoy the view. The sunny central courtyard surrounds a pleasant pool. ✉ *Calle 30 de Junio,* ☎ FAX *926–0662,* WEB *www.santanapeten.com. 32 rooms. Restaurant, air-
conditioning, in-room safes, pool. AE, DC, MC, V.*

$　✕🖭 **Posada Doña Goya.** A rooftop terrace with hammocks swinging in the breeze is the best part of staying at this budget lodging. If you prefer, grab a good book and sink into one of the comfortable lounge chairs. The hotel is clean and well run, which explains why it is so pop-
ular. Come early in the day to secure a room. Stop by for the famous breakfast from 6 to 10. ✉ *Calle Union,* ☎ *926–3538. 6 rooms, 3 with bath. Restaurant, fans. No credit cards.*

$$　🖭 **Hotel Petén.** An arabesque plunge pool graces the central courtyard of this lovely lodging. Taking a dip to escape the midday heat is a treat not to be missed. The rooms are simply furnished. Ask for one facing the lake, as the views are incredible. ✉ *Off Calle 30 de Junio,* ☎ *926–0593. 21 rooms. Restaurant, air-conditioning, pool, travel agency, Internet. AE, DC, MC, V.*

Nightlife

Discoteca Raices (Av. Periferico) is the island's only true disco. The bar at the **Mayan Princess** (✉ Av. La Reforma and Av. 14 de Noviembre) shows nightly movies on a big-screen TV.

Las Puertas (✉ Calle Central at Av. Santa Ana, ☎ 926–1061) has live music every night. The artsy **La Luna** (✉ Calle 30 de Junio, ☎ 926–3346) has a pleasant atmosphere.

Outdoor Activities and Sports

BOATING

Boat trips on Lake Petén Itzá can be arranged through most hotels in Flores or by haggling with boat owners who congregate behind the Hotel Santana. Tours often include a stop at Paraíso Escondido, a small mainland park northwest of Flores.

Santa Elena

➋ *½ km (¼ mi) south of Flores.*

Although it lacks the charms of neighboring Flores, gritty Santa Elena is pretty much unavoidable. Most services that you'll need for your trip to El Petén, from currency exchange to travel planning, are usually offered here. There are also nicer hotels here than in Flores.

Dining and Lodging

$$$$ ✕🏨 **Petén Espléndido.** You're not on Flores, but the views of that pretty island from your private balcony are the next best thing. Every possibly amenity is available at this lakeside hotel, from cable TV to Internet access. The pool, surrounded by palm trees, is a great place to spend an afternoon sunbathing. Sit at one of the shaded tables on the terrace or in the pretty dining room and enjoy the *especial del día* (daily special). The hotel is popular among business travelers, who appreciate the fully equipped convention center that seats 250 people. Families enjoy the paddleboats on the lake. ⊠ *At foot of bridge leading to Flores,* ☎ *926–0880,* FAX *926–0866,* WEB *www.petenesplendido.com. 62 rooms. Restaurant, cable TV, pool, convention center, airport shuttle. AE, DC, MC, V.*

$$$$ ✕🏨 **Villa Maya.** You could lie in bed and count the birds flying by your **★** window at these modern villas on beautiful Lago Petén Itzá. Some 50 species have been spotted in the region. If you're more interested in wildlife, ask an attendant where to find the troop of spider monkeys that roams the grounds and the adjacent rain forest. Explore the jungle by following one of the nature trails or see more of the lake by renting a rowboat. All the rooms, tastefully decorated with colorful weavings and mahogany accents, have terrific views. Vans shuttle you to and from Tikal. ⊠ *12 km (7 mi) east of Santa Elena,* ☎ *926–0086; 334–8136 in Guatemala City,* FAX *334–8134 in Guatemala City,* WEB *www. villasdeguatemala.com. 36 rooms. Restaurant, pool, horseback riding, boating, travel services. AE, DC, MC, V.*

$$$ ✕🏨 **Maya International.** This string of thatch bungalows built over Lago Petén Itzá has lost a bit of its former grandeur. The simple accommodations are surrounded by water lilies, which were sacred to the Maya. From the private balconies you can watch the waterfowl who forage here for their dinner. For your own meals there's the moderately priced restaurant, housed in a round building set out over the water. The set menu changes daily. ⊠ *3 blocks east of bridge to Flores,* ☎ *334–8136,* FAX *334–8134. stpvillas@pronet.net.gt 20 bungalows. Restaurant. AE, DC, MC, V.*

$$ ✕🏨 **Casa Elena Hotel.** An attractive lobby paneled with lots of dark wood welcomes you to this centrally located hotel. Just beyond the entrance is a pretty restaurant that lets the breeze in through lace curtains. There's a wide range of dinner options, from fresh fish to grilled steak. The rooms lack the charm of others in the area, but they are clean and comfortable. There are no balconies—for a view, head to the meeting room on the top floor. The pool has a small waterslide that kids seem to love. ⊠ *6 Av.,* ☎ *926–2239,* FAX *926–0097. 28 rooms. Restaurant, pool, meeting room. AE, DC, MC, V.*

$$$ 🏨 **Hotel del Patio-Tikal.** Built in traditional Spanish style, this modern hotel is know by its barrel-tile roof. Rooms face a small patio with a trickling fountain. All have nice touches like writing desks and ceiling fans. Ask for a room on the first floor, as these have much larger windows. The patio restaurant sits under big arches leading to a grass courtyard, making it a much more pleasant place to relax than the mus bar. ⊠ *2 Calle and 8 Av., Santa Elena,* ☎ *926–0104,* FAX *926–30 21 rooms. Restaurant, pool, gym. AE, DC, MC, V.*

Outdoor Activities and Sports

There are several caves in the hills behind Santa Elena with interesting stalactite and stalagmite formations and subterranean rivers. The easiest to visit is Aktun Kan, just south of town. The bilingual guides of the **Tourist Guide Association of Santa Elena** (✉ Hotel Tayasal, St. Elena and San Benito, ☎ 926–3133) can take you to Aktun Kan and other sites.

El Remate

3 *30 km (18½ mi) northeast of Flores.*

A mellow little town on the eastern shore of Lago Petén Itzá, El Remate is known mostly for its wood carvings by families that have dedicated themselves to this craft for generations. Because it's less than one hour from both Tikal and Yaxhá, El Remate makes a good base for exploring the area.

With more than 1,500 acres of rain forest, **Biotopo Cerro Cahuí** (✉ west of El Remate, 🚶 Q20) is one of the most accessible wildlife reserves in El Petén. It protects a portion of a mountain that extends to the eastern edge of Lago Petén Itzá, so there are plenty of opportunities for hiking. Two well-maintained trails put you in proximity of birds like oscillated turkeys, toucans, and parrots. As for mammals, look up to spot the long-armed spider monkeys or down to see squat rodents called *tepezcuintles.* Tzu'unte, a 6-km (4-mi) trail, leads to two lookouts with views of nearby lakes. The upper lookout, Mirador Moreletii, is known by locals as Crocodile Hill because it looks like the eye of a half-submerged crocodile from the other side of the lake. Los Ujuxtes, a 5-km (3-mi) trail, offers a panoramic view of three lakes. Both hikes begin at a ranger station, where English-speaking guides are sporadically available.

Dining and Lodging

$$ ✕ **La Estancia Cafeteria.** Locals keep this one a secret because the low-key La Estancia Cafetería serves up incredibly flavorful fare. Owner Victor Morales's specialty is an exquisite whitefish served with vegetables sautéed in butter on a wooden platter. Every once in a while he cooks up some fresh venison. Even though the driveway is usually filled with cars, this eatery is easy to miss—look for the Orange Crush sign. ✉ *2 km (1¼ mi) south of El Remate,* ☎ *no phone. No credit cards.*

$$$$ ✕▦ **Camino Real Tikal.** To experience the natural beauty of the jun-
★ gles surrounding Lago Petén Itzá without sacrificing creature comforts, many people head to Camino Real Tikal. It's possible to spend several days at the hotel without exhausting the possibilities—kayaking on the lake, hiking in a private reserve, swimming in the beautiful pool, lounging in the lakeside hammocks, and experiencing a traditional Maya sauna. A dozen thatch-roof villas set high on the hillside hold the rooms, all of which have porches with views of the sparkling lake. A fine terrace restaurant serves international dishes as well as local specialties. Particularly tasty is the sea bass, cooked in a plantain leaf and covered with *salsa pimiento,* a delicate tomato-based sauce. ✉ *5 km (3 mi) west of El Remate,* ☎ *926–0204; 800/228–3000 in the U.S.,* FAX *926–0222. 72 rooms. Restaurant, bar, coffee shop, pool, boating, shop, gym, travel services, airport shuttle, car rental. AE, DC, MC, V.*

$$ ✕▦ **La Mansión del Pajaro Serpiente.** Perched high on the hillside, La Mansión del Pajaro Serpiente has what are perhaps the prettiest accommodations in El Petén. Canopy beds add a festive touch to the bedrooms, each of which adjoins a sitting room. Finished in dark tropical woods, all have big windows that let in lots of light. You can throw open the windows to catch the lake breezes, so sleeping is comfortable.

Up a nearby hill is a swimming pool, and farther up you'll find a covered terrace with several hammocks. The open-air restaurant serves local and international dishes. ⊠ *On main highway south of El Remate,* ☎ FAX *926–4246. 10 rooms. Restaurant, pool, travel services. No credit cards.*

$ ✕⛶ **La Casa de Don David.** As you chat with David Kuhn, the owner of this cluster of bungalows, keep an eye out for his pet parrot. The little fellow sometimes gets jealous. But talking with Kuhn is worth it, as he and his wife, Rosa, have lived in the area for more than 25 years and are a great source of travel tips. Rooms are simple and clean, with private baths. Hammocks are everywhere, including the covered terrace that overlooks the tropical fruit orchard. Perhaps La Casa is most famous for its second-story restaurant, which has good home cooking. Have dinner for two in a booth, or eat at the "friendship table" and make some new acquaintances. Sack lunches are available for day trips, which Kuhn is happy to lead. If you want to set out on your own, you can also use any of the bicycles. ⊠ *On road to Biotopo Cerro Cahuí,* ☎ *306–2190.* WEB *www.lacasadedondavid.com. 15 rooms. Restaurant. No credit cards.*

Outdoor Activities and Sports

The fun folks at **Tikal Canopy Tour** (⊠ Near entrance to Tikal, ☎ 708–0674, tikalcanopy@hotmail.com) have expeditions that take you to the true heart of the rainforest—not on ground level, but more than 100 feet up in the air. In the canopy you'll see monkeys and maybe even a sloth. The tour ends with an exhilarating 300-foot-long ride down a zip line.

Shopping

Although most souvenirs here are similar to those found elsewhere in Guatemala, the beautiful wood carvings are unique to El Petén. More than 70 families in this small town dedicate themselves to this craft. Their wares are on display on the side of the highway right before the turnoff for the Camino Real hotel on the road to Tikal.

Tikal

★ ❹ *35 km (22 mi) north of El Remate, 68 km (42 mi) northeast of Flores.*

You rise shortly before dawn, instinctively aware that creatures out there in the darkness are doing the same. It isn't long before you hear the muffled roars of howler monkeys in the distance. After a quick cup of coffee you and your fellow adventurers follow your guide through the deserted plazas toward the pyramid that towers over everything else. The climb up the side is difficult in the dark, but after scrambling up rickety ladders and over roots and vines you find yourself at the top. You glance to the east, past the endless expanse of jungle, just as the sun starts to rise.

The high point of any trip to Guatemala is a visit to Central America's most impressive ruins. Tikal is one of the most popular tourist attractions in Central America—and with good reason. Smack in the middle of the 575-square-km (222-square-mi) Parque Nacional Tikal, the towering temples are ringed on all sides by miles of virgin forest. The area around the ruins is great for checking out creatures that spend their entire lives hundreds of feet above the forest floor in the dense canopy of trees. Colorful birds like yellow toucans and scarlet macaw are common sights.

Although the region was home to Maya communities as early as 6 BC, Tikal itself wasn't established until sometime around 200 BC. of the first structures to be built here was a version of the N

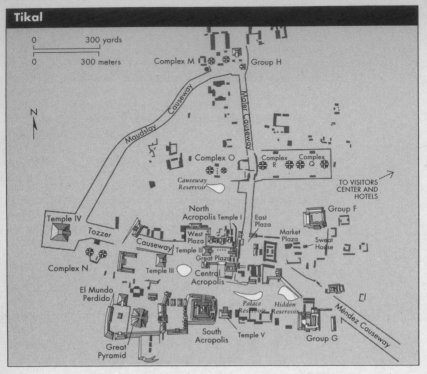

Acropolis. Others were added at a dizzying pace for the next three centuries. By AD 100 impressive structures like the Great Plaza had already been built. But even though it was a powerful city in its own right, Tikal was still ruled by the northern city of El Mirador. It wasn't until the arrival of a powerful dynasty around AD 300 that Tikal arrogated itself to full power. King Great Jaguar Paw sired a lineage that would build Tikal into a city rivaling any of its time. By AD 500 it's estimated that the city covered more than 47 square km (18 square mi) and had a population of close to 100,000.

The great temples that still tower above the jungle were at that time covered with stucco and painted with bright reds and greens, and the priests used them for elaborate ceremonies meant to please the gods and assure prosperity for the city. What makes these structures even more impressive is that the Maya possessed no metal tools to aid in construction, had no beasts of burden to carry heavy loads, and never used wheels for anything except children's toys. Of course, as a hierarchical culture they had a slave class, and the land was rich in obsidian, a volcanic glass that could be fashioned into razor-sharp tools.

By the 6th century Tikal governed a large part of the Maya world, thanks to a leader called Caan Chac (Stormy Sky), who took the throne around AD 426. Under Caan Chac, Tikal became an aggressive military and commercial center that dominated the surrounding communities with a power never before seen in Mesoamerica. The swamps protected the city from attack and allowed troops to spot any approaching enemy. Intensive agriculture in the *bajos* (lowlands) provided food for the huge population. A valuable obsidian trade sprang up, aided by the city's strategic position near two rivers.

Tikal thrived for more than a millennium, forming strong ties with two powerful centers: Kaminal Juyu, in the Guatemalan highlands, and Teotihuacán, in Mexico City. The city entered a golden age when Ah-Cacao (Lord Chocolate) acscended the throne in AD 682. It was Ah-Cacao and his successors who commissioned the construction of most of the city's most important temples. Continuing the tradition of great structures, Ah-Cacao's son commissioned Temple I, which he dedicated to his father, who is buried beneath it. He also ordered the construction of Temple IV, the tallest temple at Tikal. By the time of his death in 768, Tikal was at the peak of its power. It would remain so until its mysterious abandonment around 900.

For almost 1,000 years Tikal remained engulfed by the jungle. The conquistadors who came here searching for gold and silver must have passed right by the overgrown ruins, mistaking them for rocky hills. The native Peténeros certainly knew of the ancient city's existence, but no one else ventured near until 1848, when the Guatemalan government dispatched archaeologists to the region. Tikal started to receive international attention in 1877, when Dr. Gustav Bernoulli commissioned locals to remove the carved wooden lintels from across the doorways of Temples I and IV. These items headed to a museum in Basel, Switzerland.

In 1881 and 1882 English archaeologist Alfred Percival Maudslay made the first map showing the architectural features of this vast city. As he began to unearth the major temples, he recorded his work in dramatic photographs—you can see copies in the museum at Tikal. His work was continued by Teobert Maler, who came in 1895 and 1904. Both Maler and Maudsley have causeways named in their honor. In 1951 the Guatemalan air force cleared an airstrip near the ruins to improve access for large-scale archaeological work. Today, after more than 150 years of digging, researchers say that Tikal includes some 3,000 buildings. Countless more are still covered by the jungle. ⊠ *Parque Nacional Tikal,* ☏ *no phone.* ⊟ *Q50.* ⊙ *Daily 6–6.*

The Tikal Ruins

As you enter the Tikal, keep to the middle trail. You'll soon arrive at the ancient city's center, filled with awe-inspiring temples and intricate acropolises. The pyramid that you approach from behind is **Temple I,** known as the Temple of the Great Jaguar because of the feline represented on one of its carved lintels. It's in what is referred to as the **Great Plaza,** one of the most beautiful and dramatic in Tikal. The Great Plaza was built around AD 700 by Ah-Cacao, one of the wealthiest rulers of his time. His tomb, comparable in magnitude to that of Pa Cal at the ruins of Palenque in southern Mexico, was discovered beneath the Temple of the Great Jaguar in the 1960s. The theory is that his queen is buried beneath **Temple II,** called the Temple of the Masks for the decorations on its facade. It's a twin of the Temple of the Great Jaguar. In fact, construction of matching pyramids distinguishes Tikal from other Maya sites.

The **North Acropolis,** to the west of Ah-Cacao's temple, is a mind-boggling conglomeration of temples built over layers and layers of previous construction. Excavations have revealed that the base of this structure is more than 2,000 years old. Be sure to see the stone mask of the rain god at Temple 33. The **Central Acropolis,** south of the Great Plaza, is an immense series of structures assumed to have served as administrative centers.

If you climb to the top of one of the pyramids, you'll see the gray r combs of others rising above the rain forests canopy but still trap within it. **Temple V,** to the south, is waiting to be restored to some blance of its former grandeur. In 2001 about $3 million was all for its reconstruction. **Temple IV,** to the west, is the tallest-know

HISTORY OF THE MAYA

THE IMMENSE STONE STRUCTURES at Tikal and other archaeological sites in Guatemala are certainly impressive, but they barely suggest the culture that once existed here. The first thing you must remember is that these streets and plazas were once full of people. Archaeologists estimate that nearly 100,000 people lived in the region surrounding Tikal. Many lived in the city itself, while some lived beyond its borders on farms. When you consider that Tikal is but one of the dozens of cities that once dotted the region, it becomes clear that this was a major metropolitan area.

The pyramids were not always the faded gray you see today. In ancient times this was a vibrant city, with the facades of the buildings covered with stucco painted vivid shades of red and green. If you wonder what a temple might have looked like, head to the ruins of Copán in Honduras. You can go underground to see the remains of the Rosalila Temple, then head to the nearby museum to see a re-creation of that beautiful structure.

The buildings might have been colorful, but the people also adorned themselves in bright clothing. Especially fine were the rulers, who decorated themselves with the long feathers of resplendent quetzals and jewelry made of jade and other precious stones. Depictions of these rulers in the stellae that still stand in many of the sites show just how elaborate these costumes could be.

Besides the ruins of the great cities, other traces of the Maya survive. Their works in pottery and jade are unmatched in the ancient world. The Museo Popol Vuh, in Guatemala City, has fascinating examples of the artistic sensibilities of the Maya, from religious figurines of mythological creatures to burial urns covered with fearsome skulls.

Traditionally, Western anthropologists have divided Mayan history into three main periods: the Preclassic, Classic, and Postclassic. Although academics question the validity of such a uniform chronology, traditional labels are still in use.

The **Preclassic** (2,000 BC–AD 250) period is characterized by the influence of the Olmec, a civilization in what is present-day Mexico. The Maya adopted many of the customs of that culture. During this period cities began to sprout up here and there, especially in the southern highlands of Guatemala and El Salvador. The Maya language also began to take shape.

By the **Late Preclassic** (300 BC–AD 250) period, the Maya experienced a burst of creativity. They developed an advanced mathematical system, a impressively precise calendar, and one of the world's first writing systems. It was during this time that some of the great Maya cities of the north, including Tikal, were founded.

During the **Classic** (250 BC–AD 900) period, Maya artistic, intellectual, and architectural achievements literally reached for the stars. Vast city-states were crisscrossed by numerous paved roadways, some of which still exist today. The great cities of Palenque, in Mexico, and Uaxactún and Quiriguá, in Guatemala, were just a few of the powerful centers that controlled the Classic Maya world. But none matched the majesty and power of Tikal.

The single largest unsolved mystery about the Maya is their rapid decline during the **Terminal Classic** (800–900) period. The current theory is that siege warfare caused rural people to seek shelter in the cities. The growing urban populations drained the agricultural potential of the land around the cities. As crops failed, famine ensued, causing a mass exodus out of the cities and into smaller, sustainable populations.

The Maya of the **Postclassic Period** (900–1511) were heavily affected by growing powers in central Mexico. Architecture, ceramics, and carvings from this period show considerable outside influence. Although still dramatic, Postclassic cities such as Mayapán, Chichén Itzá, and Uxmal pale in comparison to their Classic predecessors. By the time the Spanish conquest reached the Yucatán, the Maya were scattered, feuding, and easy to conquer.

— *by Mark Sullivan and Melisse Gelula*

ture built by the Maya. Although the climb to the top is difficult, the view is unforgettable.

To the southwest of the plaza lies the **South Acropolis**, which hasn't been reconstructed, and a 105-ft-high pyramid, similar in construction to those at Teotihuacán. A few jungle trails, including the marked Interpretative Benil-ha Trail, offer a chance to see spider monkeys and other wildlife. Outside the park, a somewhat overgrown trail halfway down the old airplane runway on the left leads to the remnants of old rubber-tappers' camps and is a good spot for bird-watching.

At park headquarters you'll find two archaeological museums that display Mayan artifacts. They are a good resource for information on the enigmatic rise and fall of the Maya people.

Other Nearby Ruins

Although Tikal is the most famous, El Petén has hundreds of archaeological sites, ranging from modest burial chambers to sprawling cities. The vast majority have not been explored, let alone restored. Within a few miles of Tikal are several sites that are relatively easy to reach. Because they are in isolated areas, it's a good idea to go with a guide.

Nakúm lies deep within the forest, connected to Tikal via jungle trails that are sometimes used for horseback expeditions. You cannot visit during the rainy season, as you'll sink into mud up to your ankles. Two building complexes and some stelae are visible. ⊠ *26 km (16 mi) east of Tikal.*

The 4,000-year-old city of **Uaxactún** was once a rival to Tikal's supremacy in the region. It was conquered by Tikal in the 4th century and lived in the shadow of that great city for centuries. Inscriptions show that Uaxactun existed longer than any other Mayan city, which may account for the wide variety of structures. Here you'll find, if you can imagine, a Maya observatory.

Uaxactún is surrounded by thick rain forest, so the trip can be arduous. The rock-and-dirt road is passable during the drier seasons and nearly impossible at other times without a four-wheel-drive vehicle. You'll need to secure a permit to visit Uaxactún. The administration building in Tikal is on the road between the Jaguar Inn and the Jungle Lodge. Sometimes police will ask to accompany you on the trip, which is helpful for two reasons: it prevents potential robberies and, most important, will give you an extra person to push if your vehicle gets stuck. The permits to visit the ruins are free. ⊠ *24 km (16 mi) north of Tikal.*

Overlooking a beautiful lake of the same name, the ruins of **Yaxhá** are divided into two sections of rectangular structures that form plazas and streets. The city was probably inhabited between the Preclassic and Postclassic periods. The ruins are currently being restored by a German organzation. Lake Yaxhá, surrounded by virgin rain forest, is a good bird-watching spot. During the rainy season only a four-wheel-drive vehicle—or setting out on horseback or on foot—will get you to Yaxhá; the rest of the year the road is passable. ⊠ *10 km (6 mi) east of Tikal.*

A popular ecotourism destination, **El Zotz** is where you'll find the remnants of a Maya city. On a clear day you can see the tallest of the ruins at Tikal from these unexcavated ruins. The odd name, which means "the bat" in Q'eqchí, refers to a cave from which thousands of bat make a nightly exodus. Troops of hyperactive spider monkeys seem to have claimed this place for themselves, swinging through the treetop and scrambling after each other like children playing a game of Unlike those in Tikal, however, these long-limbed creatures are not to people and will shake branches and throw twigs and fruit to scare you away. During the rainy season the mosquitoes can be fierce, so bring your strongest repellent. ⊠ *24 km (15 mi) west of Tikal.*

Dining and Lodging

$$ ✕⊞ **Tikal Inn.** This cluster of comfortable bungalows wraps around
★ a well-manicured garden and a pool. It's set apart from the other lodgings, affording a bit of privacy. The rooms have a modern feel, yet they have thatch roofs and stucco walls decorated with traditional fabrics. A small restaurant has a menu that changes daily. Rates include breakfast and dinner. ⊠ *Parque Nacional Tikal,* ☎ *926–1917,* ☎ 〒 *926–0065. 22 rooms. Restaurant, pool. No credit cards.*

$$$ ⊞ **Jungle Lodge.** Built to house archaeologists working at Tikal, this hotel has cute duplexes. There's a lack of privacy, as the dividing wall between the rooms does not meet the ceiling. The rooms are clean, but the furnishings are dated. ⊠ *Parque Nacional Tikal,* ☎ *477–0570,* 〒 *476–0294. 46 rooms, 34 with bath. Restaurant, pool. V.*

$$$ ⊞ **El Campamento del Sombrero.** This cluster of wooden cabins is a restful place to spend the night. There's no electricity in the rooms, but they each have two double beds and a private bath. The restaurant serves three meals a day. ⊠ *Yaxká,* ☎ *926–5229,* 〒 *926–5198. 9 rooms. Restaurant. No credit cards.*

Sayaxché

❺ *61 km (38 mi) southwest of Flores.*

Down a bumpy dirt road from Flores, this muddy frontier town on the southern bank of the Río de La Pasión is a good base for exploring the southern reaches of El Petén. This is river country, and the La Pasión and Petexbatún lead to a number of important yet largely unvisited ruins in various stages of excavation.

★ Upriver from Sayaxché are the impressive ruins of a city called **Ceibal,** which served as a tollgate, if you will, for barges plying the river. Its archaeological attractions include several restored temples, including the only circular one known to exist. Here you will also find intricately carved stelae. Interestingly, a number of anomalies were found in these monuments, which hint at a foreign influence, most likely from the Toltecs of central Mexico. Though it can be reached via a dirt road that floods during the rainy season, Ceibal is best accessed by boat on the Río de la Pasión, followed by a half-hour ascent through the forest. ⊠ *On the Río de la Pasión.*

Dining and Lodging

$$ ✕⊞ **La Montaña.** On the Río Petexbatún, this jungle lodge was built in a clearing hacked out of the rain forest. Rustic bungalows have cement floors and bamboo walls, but they do have private baths. Family-style meals are served in an open-air dining hall. The staff can book tours of local archaeological sites. For reservations contact Viajes Turísticos La Montaña. ⊠ *Sayaxché,* ☎ *928–6114,* 〒 *928–6169. 8 rooms. Dining room, travel services. MC, V.*

$ ⊞ **Hotel Guayacan.** By the south bank of the Río de La Pasión, this place looks run-down but has clean, comfortable rooms on the second floor. It even has air-conditioning. The owner can arrange boat trips to nearby Maya ruins. ⊠ *Sayaxché,* ☎ *928–6111. 25 rooms, 19 with bath. Travel services. No credit cards.*

Outdoor Activities and Sports

The lowland Río de la Pasión flows into the Usumacinta, which winds for countless miles through the rain forest. Both rivers were important Maya trade routes and thus pass numerous archaeological sites. Local agencies book expeditions to the sites that can last from a day to more than a week. Along the way you can catch a glimpse of the area's many animal inhabitants, including turtles, crocodiles, and a vast array of birds.

A day trip to one of the ruins costs $30–$60, depending on the number of passengers. The rate is not set in stone, so feel free to bargain. A reputable company in Sayaxché is **Viajes Don Pedro** (☎ 928–6109). **Viajes Turísticos La Montaña** (☎ 928–6114) also offers trips on the river.

Lake Petexbatún

6 *2 hrs by boat from Ceibal.*

This impressive rain-forest lagoon was the site of a 6th-century kingdom that was likely ruled by a power-hungry prince who fled Tikal and engaged in battles for territory from two twin capitals, Dos Pilas and Aguateca. A three-hour hike from Sayaxché brings you to **Dos Pilas**. Recent archaeological finds here indicate that continual warfare may have caused an ecological imbalance that led to the collapse of the Maya civilization. Most spectacular of the ancient structures found here is a limestone staircase covered with carvings that recount the battles the upstart ruler waged against his brother at Tikal. Unlike most other Maya cities, this one was surrounded by a defensive wall.

On the southern shore of the lake lies **Aguateca,** a small site by a 200-ft escarpment. It was likely the final capital after Dos Pilas was subsumed by Tikal. Few of the ruins have been excavated, but the trip here is a wonderful adventure.

The fortress of **Punta de Chimino,** 2½ mi north of Aguateca, was the last residence of the area's besieged royal family. The defenders dug several moats into the peninsula where the fort stood, turning it into an island.

Dining and Lodging

$$$ ✕▣ **Chiminos Island Lodge.** Archaeologists speculate that Punta de Chimino was once the retreat of Maya nobility, and now it can be your retreat, too. Beautiful cabins are scattered along the peninsula's edges, with private views of the lake and the jungle beyond. Rooms have hardwood floors and screened walls that keep the jungle near and the insects at bay. Delicious meals using local ingredients like *anacates* (mushrooms) and *loroco* (an herb) are served in an open-air restaurant. Tours of nearby archaeological sites for both the hearty or the delicate are included. Transportation (a 1½-hour boat ride) is arranged from Sayaxché. ⌧ *Punta de Chimino,* ☎ 337–0009. *ecoadventure@guate.net. 6 bungalows. Restaurant, travel services. No credit cards.*

Tikal and the Maya Ruins A to Z

To research prices, get advice from other travelers, and book travel arrangements, visit www.fodors.com.

AIR TRAVEL TO AND FROM EL PETÉN

Grupo Taca, Racsa, and Tikal Jets operate flights from Guatemala City to Santa Elena that take less than an hour and cost about $60 each way. Several daily flights leave the capital around 7 AM and return around 4 PM. Air service between Santa Elena and the Mexican resort of Cancún is offered by Aviateca and Aerocaribe. Aerocaribe also offers flights to the ruins of Pelenque.

Aeropuerto Internacional Santa Elena is less than 1 km (½ mi) outside town. Taxis and shuttles meet every plane and charge about 20 quetzales to take you into town. Plans to build a new runway are on t drawing boards. This would allow direct international flights from the United States to land in Santa Elena.

➤ AIRLINES AND CONTACTS: **Aerocaribe** (☎ 926–0923). **Grupo Taca** (☎ 926–1238). **Racsa** (☎ 926–1477). **Tikal Jets** (☎ 926–0386 or 332–5070).

BUS TRAVEL TO AND FROM EL PETÉN

Linea Dorada offers direct bus service between Guatemala City and Santa Elena and Flores. The 10-hour trip on air-conditioned buses with comfortable reclining seats, TVs, and bathrooms costs $30–$50 round-trip. Call at least one day ahead for reservations. Inexpensive local service is available, but these buses stop in every village along the way, which adds hours to the trip.

➤ BUS INFORMATION: **Linea Dorada** (✉ Calle Principal, Santa Elena; ✉ Calle de la Playa, Flores, ☎ 926–0528 in Santa Elena, 232–9658 in Guatemala City).

BUS TRAVEL WITHIN EL PETÉN

In Santa Elena the San Juan Hotel serves as the local bus terminal. Here you can catch a bus operated by San Juan Travel that makes the two-hour trip to Tikal at 6, 8, 10 AM and return trips at 2, 4 and 5 PM. Local buses serving other destinations like Sayaxché depart from the market in Santa Elena. They are inexpensive but very slow.

➤ BUS INFORMATION: **San Juan Travel** (✉ San Juan Hotel, Santa Elena, ☎ 926–0041).

CAR RENTAL

If you're not booked on a tour, the best way to get around El Petén is by renting a four-wheel-drive vehicle. The major rental agencies, including Budget and Hertz, have offices at Aeropuerto Internacional Santa Elena. Koka, a local company, rents four-wheel-drive vehicles from an office in the Camino Real Tikal near El Remate. San Juan Travel, at the San Juan Hotel in Santa Elena, rents four-wheel-drive vehicles and passenger vans.

➤ LOCAL AGENCIES: **Budget** (✉ Aeropuerto Internacional Santa Elena, ☎ 950–0741). **Koka** (✉ Camino Real Tikal, El Remate, ☎ 926–1233). **Hertz** (✉ Aeropuerto Internacional Santa Elena, ☎ 950–0204). **San Juan Travel** (✉ San Juan Hotel, Santa Elena, ☎ 926–2013).

CAR TRAVEL

Roads in El Petén are often in poor repair and not very well marked. Some roads are impassable during the rainy season, so check with the tourist office before heading out on seldom travelled roads, such as those to the more-remote ruins surrounding Tikal. A four-wheel-drive vehicle is highly recommended.

To be on the safe side, never travel at night. If you come upon a fallen tree across the road, do not get out of your car to remove the debris. Robbers have been known to fell trees to get tourists to stop. Turn around as quickly as possible.

EMERGENCIES

Medical facilities in El Petén are not as modern as in the rest of the country. If you're really sick, consider getting on the next plane back to Guatemala City.

➤ EMERGENCY SERVICES: **Police** (☎ 926–1365).

➤ HOSPITALS: **Hospital del Instituto Guatemalteco de Seguridad Social** (✉ Santa Elena, ☎ 926–0619).

➤ PHARMACIES: **Farmacia Nueva** (✉ Av. Santa Ana, Flores, ☎ 926–1387). **Farmacia San Carlos** (✉ 4 Calle 1–92, Zona 1, Santa Elena, ☎ 926–0753).

MAIL AND SHIPPING

The main post office in Flores is a a half block east of the main square. In Santa Elena the post office is a block east of the bridge leading to Flores. Mail service is slow, so expect to get back home before your letter does.

➤ POST OFFICES: **Flores** (✉ Calle 10 de Noviembre, Flores).**Santa Elena** (✉ 2 Calle and 7 Av., Flores).

MONEY MATTERS

There are several banks in Santa Elena, but nowhere else in the region. Make sure to exchange your money before heading off on your jungle adventure. Some high-end hotels will exchange dollars for a small commission.

➤ BANKS: **Banco Industrial** (✉ Calle Principal, Santa Elena, ☎ 926–0281).

TOUR OPERATORS

Flores-based Martsam Travel, run by Lileana and Benedicto Grijalva, offers many different types of tours in the area. The El Petén environmental group ProPetén offers adventure trips led by rubber-tappers who once worked at plantations in the forest.

Guatemala City-based Adventuras Naturales and Flores-based Expedition Panamundo specialize in tours of the Maya world and bird-watching expeditions. Guatemala City–based Maya Expeditions has trips down Sayaxché area rivers and the nearby archaeological sites. From Antigua, Inter Quetzal, Sin Fronteras, and Vision Travel all offer tours of El Petén.

➤ TOUR COMPANIES: **Adventuras Naturales** (✉ 9 Calle 18–17, Zona 14, Guatemala City, ☎ FAX 333–6051). **Expedition Panamundo** (✉ Av. Reforma, Flores, ☎ 926–0501). **Inter Quetzal** (✉ 7 Av. 1–20, Zona 4, Guatemala City, ☎ 331–9282). **Martsam Travel** (✉ Calle Centroamérica and Av. 30 de Junio, Flores, ☎ 926–0346, ☎ FAX 926–3225). **Maya Expeditions** (✉ 15 Calle 1–91, Zona 10, Guatemala City, ☎ 363–4955). **Sin Fronteras** (✉ 3 Calle Poniente, Antigua, ☎ 832–1226). **Vision Travel** (✉ 3 Av. Norte 3, Antigua, ☎ 832–3293, WEB www.guatemalainfo.com).

VISITOR INFORMATION

Arcas, which returns illegally captured animals to the wild, is a great resource on the flora and fauna of El Petén. Inguat has two offices in El Petén, one in Flores and one at Aeropuerto Internacional Santa Elena.

➤ TOURIST INFORMATION: **Arcas** (✉ 10 km [6 mi] east of Santa Elena, FAX 591–4731). **Inguat** (✉ On Parque Central, Flores, ☎ 926–0669; ✉ Aeropuerto Internacional Santa Elena, ☎ 926–0533 at the airport).

GUATEMALA A TO Z

To research prices, get advice from other travelers, and book travel arrangements, visit www.fodors.com.

AIR TRAVEL TO AND FROM GUATEMALA

Guatemala has two international airports: Aeropuerto Internacional La Aurora, at the edge of Guatemala City, and the smaller Aeropuerto Internacional Santa Elena, in El Petén.

Domestic carriers fly between Guatemala City and Santa Elena, Puerto Barrios and Río Dulce on the Atlantic coast, and Quetzaltenango and Huehuetenango in the highlands.

BUS TRAVEL TO AND FROM GUATEMALA

There is bus service from Guatemala City to cities on the Mexican and Honduran borders, as well as to destinations in Belize and El Salvador. To La Mesilla, on the Mexican border, El Condor departs at 4, 8, 10, 1, and 5 for the seven-hour trip. To Tecún Umán, on the Mexican border, Fortaleza has hourly departures from 1 AM to 6 PM; the journey takes five hours. For service to El Carmen/Talismán, also on the Mexican border, contact Galgos. Departures for the five-hour ride are at 5:30, 10, 1:30, and 5. Maya Mundo runs buses to Quintana Roo, Mexico.

Melva International has service to San Salvador. Eight buses a day depart between 4 AM and 6 PM for the five-hour journey. For service to Esquipulas, on the border of Honduras, try Rutas Orientales. Buses run almost hourly from 5 AM to 6 PM and take four hours. For El Florido take the bus to Chiquimula at 7 AM, 10 AM, or 12:30 PM and change there. Linea Dorada operates from Santa Elena to destinations in Belize. ➤ BUS INFORMATION: **El Condor** (✉ 19 Calle 2–01, Zona 1, Guatemala City, ☎ 232–8504). **Fortaleza** (✉ 19 Calle 8–70, Zona 1, Guatemala City, ☎ 220–6730). **Galgos** (✉ 7 Av. 19–44, Zona 1, Guatemala City, ☎ 253–4868). **Melva International** (✉ 3 Av. 1–38, Zona 9, Guatemala City, ☎ 331–0874). **Rutas Orientales** (✉ 19 Calle 8–18, Zona 1, Guatemala City, ☎ 238–3894). **Mundo Maya** (✉ Calle de la Playa. Edificio Hotel Itza 1, Flores, ☎ 926–0070).

BUS TRAVEL WITHIN GUATEMALA

Buses are the most widely used form of public transportation, with myriad companies running buses to almost every community that can be reached by road. Buses range from comfortable coaches with reclining seats and rest rooms to run-down school buses carrying twice as many people as they were built to hold, as well as a few animals.

If you decide to travel point to point without a plan, be sure the bus driver knows where you're going, and ask several times during the trip where you should get off. If you're friendly and give reminders you're there, the driver will almost always be helpful.

CAR TRAVEL TO AND FROM GUATEMALA

It's possible to enter Guatemala by land from Mexico, Belize, El Salvador, and Honduras. The Pan-American Highway, which passes through most major cities, connects the country with Mexico at La Mesilla and with El Salvador at San Cristobal Frontera. It's also possible to travel to El Salvador via the coastal highway, crossing at Ciudad Pedro de Alvarado, or Valle Nuevo. Pacific routes to Mexico pass through Tecún Umán and El Carmen/Talismán.

To reach Belize, take the highway east from Flores, passing El Cruce before reaching the border town of Melchor de Mencos. There are also two routes into Honduras, through El Florido or Esquipulas.

Travelers often get harassed or swindled at border towns. There is no entry fee, although you may be asked for a bribe. Crossing the border in a rental car can be troublesome; if you need to do so, ask your rental agency for advice. When in a border town, always watch your belongings carefully.

CAR TRAVEL WITHIN GUATEMALA

You need a valid driver's license from your own country to drive in Guatemala. Most roads leading to larger towns and cities are paved; those leading to small towns and villages are generally dirt roads. *Doble-tracción,* or four-wheel drive, is a necessity in many remote areas, especially at the height of the rainy season. Gas stations can be also scarce, so be sure to fill up before heading into rural areas. Consider bringing some extra fuel along with you. Don't count on finding repair shops outside the major towns.

Many locals ignore traffic laws, so you should be on your guard. *Alto* means "stop" and *Frene con motor* (brake with motor) means that a steep descent lies ahead. Travel only by day, especially if you are driving alone. Keep your eyes peeled for children or animals on the road.

DISABILITIES AND ACCESSIBILITY

People with disabilities will find Guatemala's cobbled streets and lack of wheel-chair access nearly impossible to negotiate. This said, most high-end hotels and tour providers are able to accomodate people with disabilities.

EMBASSIES

➤ EMBASSIES: **Canada** (✉ Edificio Edyma Plaza, 8th floor, 13 Calle 8–44, Zona 10, Guatemala City, ☎ 333–6102). **United Kingdom** (✉ Centro Financiero Torre II, 7th floor, 7 Av. 5–10, Zona 4, Guatemala City, ☎ 332–1601). **United States** (✉ Av. La Reforma 7–01, Zona 10, Guatemala City, ☎ 331–1541).

HEALTH

The most common health hazard for visitors to Guatemala is traveler's diarrhea. To avoid this problem, drink only bottled water. Remember to avoid raw vegetables unless you know they've been thoroughly washed and disinfected. Be wary of strawberries and other unpeeled fruits for the same reason. Heat stroke is another risk, but one that can easily be avoided. The best way to steer clear of heat stroke is to do as the locals do (wake early and retire at midday for a siesta) and drink lots of water.

MAIL AND SHIPPING

There are post offices in most communities, but the best way to mail letters and packages is often through your hotel. If at all possible, bring the items home with you, as Guatemala brings new meaning to the concept of "snail mail."

MONEY MATTERS

You can exchange U.S. dollars at any bank and in most hotels. It's far more difficult to exchange other currencies. If you are traveling with currency other than U.S. dollars, it would be wise to change the money into dollars or quetzales before you arrive. Traveler's checks are accepted only in larger hotels.

ATMS

There are ATMs that work on the Cirrus and Plus systems in most major cities. In smaller cities you will be hard pressed to find an ATM, but you should be able to go to the bank to withdraw money from your account using your ATM card. Make sure you only have a four-digit pin number, as many ATMs only take four digits.

CREDIT CARDS

In smaller cities and towns you will be hard pressed to find an ATM, but you should be able to go to the bank to withdraw money from your account using your bank card. Make sure you have a four digit pin number, as many ATMs will not accept those with five or more digits.

CURRENCY

Guatemalan currency is called the quetzal, after the resplendent national bird. There are 1-, 5-, 10-, and 25-centavo coins. Bills come in denominations of one-half, 1, 5, 10, 20, 50, and 100 quetzales. At pres time $1 was worth roughly Q8.

SAFETY

Most crimes directed at tourists have been pickpocketings and muggings, as well as thefts from cars. In the cities you should do the same as you would in any metropolitan area—leave flashy jewelry and watches at home, keep your camera in a secure bag, and don't handle money in public. Hire taxis only from official stands at the airport, outside hotels, and at major intersections. When traveling outside the cities, it's a good idea to hire a guide. Some of the volcanoes near Antigua and Lago Atitlán have been frequented by muggers.

If you can avoid it, don't drive after sunset. Watch out on the roads, as one common ploy used by highway robbers is to construct a roadblock, such as logs strewn across the road, and then hide nearby. When unsuspecting motorists get out of their cars to remove the obstruction, they are waylaid. If you come upon a deserted roadblock, don't stop; turn around.

Avoid participating in local rallies, as protesters are not always treated well. Several Guatemalans were killed protesting a bus fare increase in spring 2000. The increase in adoption of Guatemalan children has provoked the fear by many here, particularly rural villagers, that children will be abducted by foreigners. In April 2000 two Japanese tourists suspected of this were killed in a market area of Todos Santos Cuchumatán. Limit your interaction with children you do not know, and be discreet when taking photographs.

TELEPHONES

Public phones are few and far between in Guatemala, but most towns have offices where you can place both national and international calls. The easiest way to place a call is from your hotel.

Guatemala's country code is 502; there are no local area codes.

TIPPING

A tip of about 10 percent is standard at most Guatemalan restaurants. Bellhops and maids expect tips only in the more expensive hotels. Tip tour guides about 10 percent of the tour price.

VISITOR INFORMATION

The staff at Inguat is courteous, professional, and knowledgeable. There are offices in Guatemala City, Antigua, Quetzaltenango, Panajachel, Flores, and Santa Elena.

➤ TOURIST INFORMATION: **Inguat** (✉ 7 Av. 1–17, Zona 4, Guatemala City, ☎ 331–1333; ✉ Palacio de los Capitanes, Antigua, ☎ 832–0763; ✉ 7 Calle 11–35, Zona 1, Quetzaltenango, ☎ 761–4931; ✉ Calle Santander 1–30, Zona 2, Panajachel, ☎ 762–1392; Parque Central, Flores, ☎ 926–0669; ✉ Santa Elena Airport, Santa Elena, ☎ 926–0533).

4 BACKGROUND AND ESSENTIALS

"Busing It in Guatemala"

Books

Wildlife Glossary

Spanish Vocabulary

BUSING IT IN GUATEMALA

THE SUN IS RISING in the highlands of Guatemala. Along bumpy back roads, a school bus bounces over rocks and ruts to the whine of *ranchero* drinking music akin to country, declaring the woes of lost loves and long days of working the fields. Outside, villages show the first signs of waking—men carrying machetes walk to their *milpa* or cornfields; girls carrying plastic bowls full of corn dough return from the neighborhood grinder ready to make the day's tortillas; women stoke the cooking fires. Inside the restyled Virginia Public School Bus #121, young students aren't aboard, but a wide range of travelers, from newborns swaddled in hand-woven cloth, toothless grandmas with unflinching stares, cowboy-hat-wearing men in bright patchwork pants and wool skirts, to a European couple reading travel guides.

The driver uses the windshield as a tableau of personal expression: stickers of the Virgin Mary, the Tasmanian Devil, a winking Jesus, the Playboy bunny, and a baby wearing a leather jacket and sunglasses are juxtaposed here, a cast of characters assembled nowhere else, it would seem. Highlighting the driver's more sensitive side is a small menagerie of stuffed animals dangling from the rear-view mirror. As he passes a jalopy on a blind, cliff-side curve, the early morning passengers appear unconcerned. Maybe that's because the sticker above the NO SMOKING sign declares in red glistening letters, *Yo manejo, pero Jesus me guia* (I drive, but Jesus guides me.) The driver's helper, his *ayudante*, is busy carrying 100-pound bags of beans up the ladder to the bus's rooftop. It's difficult to keep an eye fixed on him: one minute he's squeezing down the aisle selling tickets, the next, he's swinging out the emergency exit used as the back door and climbing along the outside of the speeding bus. He leans out the front door, pointing at the people on the roadside and flipping his hand upward. *"¿Donde?"* Where do you want to go? He jumps off the bus and helps a woman toting a little baby to climb aboard. *"¡Dále!"* he then yells. Then in English, "Put the pedal to the metal!" Young boys look on with ad-

miration as the ayudante runs alongside and jumps aboard just when it seems the bus has picked up too much speed. With his spare moments he pulls up a turned-over bucket and from his perch keeps the driver company by leaning close and telling him any number of fables or rumors or jokes; so animated his face and so attentive is the driver, you wish you could listen in for a while over the din.

The bus roars off leaving a group of colorfully dressed women and their children on the roadside. It is almost noon in a small Guatemalan town on market day. With the children grabbing at their skirts, the women wander off, silently entering a mass of crowded stalls packed with everything from *típica*, traditional clothes, to superglue. They pass by a little girl concentrating on balancing a bowl of hot beef soup in her hands, carrying it to her parents who are busy peddling a dozen different varieties of hot peppers. A little old woman clutches two chickens by the feet and haggles with a man over their price, yanking them up and down in air as she bargains. Behind her, a peddler is enticing some tourists into a sale by showing them an impressive selection of thick wool blankets, even though it's 95°. There are no price tags or cash registers or express aisles; shopping on market day is not an expedient experience—it's a social transaction, in which every purchase requires a discussion or at least a certain amount of feigned indecision.

Being Sunday, the market is filled with churchgoers as well as shoppers. A procession leaves the church and descends into the market led by elderly men wearing black robes, swinging golden globes of incense. One man beats a small drum while another blows into a wooden reed instrument with a ducklike honk. Boys stride ahead and, unconcerned, with long poles, raise the electrical wires to make room for an 18-ft statue of the Virgin Mary to pass. When the procession is gone, the market swings back to its regular affairs and is once again quiet and *tranquilo*. Only a few noises rise above the pitch of hushed talking. Ice-cream vendors ring small bells. A young girl drags a snorting pig along on a leash. Several young boys playing marbles on a dirt patch behind the market argue about the ownership of a shooter. And off in the distance is the ubiquitous cry of ranchero music rising from the radios of the townspeople who peek out of their houses inspired by the passing of strangers and buses.

The sun is setting on the Central American isthmus. The ayudante hoses down the bus while the driver counts the day's take. The peddlers in the market load their wares into woven baskets and boxes and haul them away. The young children drag their feet home for dinner. The bus driver heads off and greets a circle of friends gathered around a domino game at a local drinking house. He orders a round of beers and raises the bottle for a toast, "For a day well done."

–Joanna Kosowsky

BOOKS

Belize

Two histories stand out: *The Making of Modern Belize,* by C. H. Grant, and *A Profile of the New Nation of Belize,* by W. D. Setzekorn. *Jaguar,* by Alan Rabinowitz, an interesting book about the creation of the Cockscomb Basin Wildlife Sanctuary, unfortunately tells you too much about the man and too little about the cat. Aldous Huxley, who wrote *Beyond the Mexique Bay,* is always hard to beat. If you're interested in the Maya, Ronald Wright's *Time Among the Maya* ties past and present together in one perceptive whole. Classic works on the Maya include *The Maya* by Michael Coe, a compendious introduction to the world of the Maya, and *The Rise and Fall of the Maya Civilization,* by one of the grand old men of Maya archaeology, J. Eric S. Thompson. For natural history enthusiasts, three books belong in your suitcase: *A Field Guide to the Birds of Mexico* by E. P. Edwards; *Guide to Corals and Fishes of Florida, the Bahamas and the Caribbean* by I. Greenberg; and *An Introduction to Tropical Rainforests* by T. C. Whitmore.

Guatemala

For travel literature, try Ronald Wright's *Time Among the Maya* or Aldous Huxley's *Beyond the Mexique Bay,* which describes his travels in 1934. Nobel laureate Miguel Angel Asturias is the country's most famous author, and his *Men of Maize* is full of history and cultural insight. Francisco Goldman's *The Long Night of White Chickens* is a lyrical novel that touches on some contemporary social issues. Michael Coe's *The Maya* is an authoritative book on the lost societies of the region's prehistory, as is J. Eric S. Thompson's *The Rise and Fall of the Maya Civilization.* Tour Tikal with a copy of Coe's *Tikal: A Handbook of the Ancient Maya Ruins.* It can often be purchased in the airport, at the area's larger hotels, and sometimes at the park entrance. For a guide to Guatemala's flora and fauna, try John C. Kricher's *A Neotropical Companion.* For historical and political background, try James Painter's *Guatemala: False Hope, False Freedom,* or Jean-Marie Simon's *Guatemala: Eternal Spring, Eternal Tyranny,* which has excellent photographs. Victor Perera's *Unfinished Conquest* is a thorough and fascinating account of Guatemala's guerilla war, while Rigoberta Menchú's memoir, *I, Rigoberta Menchú; An Indian Woman in Guatemala,* opened the world's eyes to the human-rights abuses perpetrated during the country's 36-year "dirty war," and earned the author a Nobel Prize.

WILDLIFE GLOSSARY

An AMAZING ARRAY OF CREATURES make their homes in Belize and Guatemala. Many are not terribly difficult to see, thanks to their brilliant coloring. Others are likely to elude you completely. A rundown of some of the region's most attention-grabbing mammals, birds, reptiles, amphibians—even a few insects—are listed below. Common names are given, so you can understand the local wildlife lingo.

Agouti (*guanta, paca, tepezcuintle*): A 20-inch tailless rodent with small ears and a large muzzle, the agouti is known locally as the gibnut. It's reddish brown on Guatemala's Pacific coast, more tawny orange on Belize's Caribbean slope. You might spot one sitting on its haunches and eating large seeds and fruit. Largely nocturnal, the agouti is more likely to be seen on a menu than in the wild. Known as the royal rat, it was served to Queen Elizabeth on her last visit to Belize.

Anteater (*oso hormiguero*): Three species—giant, silky, and collared—are found in this region. Only the collared, or vested, anteater is commonly seen (and too often as a roadkill). This medium-size anteater (30 inches long with an 18-inch tail) has long sharp claws for ripping into insect nests. You may spot one lapping up ants and termites with its long sticky tongue.

Aracari (*cusingo*): These slender toucans, known for their strikingly colored bills, eat ripe fruit. They often travel in groups of six or more. Collared aracaris on the Caribbean coast have a chalky upper mandible.

Armadillo (*cusuco*): These are the same animals that are found in southern U.S. Mostly nocturnal and solitary, this edentate roots in the soil with its long muzzle for a varied diet of roots, insects, and small animals. They are sometimes found on the menu in local restaurants.

Basilisk (*gallego*): Flaps of skin on their long toes enable the "Jesus Christ lizard" to run across water. The emerald basilisk in the Caribbean lowlands is marked with turquoise and black on its green body. Adult males grow to 3 feet and have crests on its heads, backs, and tails.

Booby: This red-footed bird received its unflattering name because it was unafraid of humans. Because of this it became the easy prey of hungry sailors landing at Belize's Half Moon Caye, where 4,000 now live in a protected nature reserve. Look for nests with fuzzy white chicks.

Caiman (*cocodrilo*): The spectacled caiman is a small crocodile that subsists mainly on fish. It's most active at night (its eyes glow red when illuminated by a flashlight), basking in the sun by day. It's distinguished from its American cousin by its sloping brow and smooth back scales.

Capuchin monkey (*mono carablanca*): With black fur and pink faces surrounded by wisps of white, capuchin monkeys are found singly or in groups of up to 20. They are extremely active foragers, sometimes even coming to the ground to search for food.

Coati (*pizote*): A long-nose relative of the raccoon, the coati has a slender, ringed tail it often holds straight up. Lone males or groups of females with young are active during the day, either on the ground or in the trees. Omnivorous, they feed on fruit and seeds as well as mice and rats.

Cougar (*puma*): Growing to 5 ft in length, mountain lions are the largest unspotted cats in Central America. Rarely seen, they live in most habitats in the region and feed on vertebrates ranging from snakes to deer.

Crocodile (*lagarto*): Although often referred to as alligators, crocodiles reign supreme in this region. They are distinguished from the smaller caiman by their flat heads, narrow snouts, and spiky scales. The American crocodile can reach 16 ft in length, while the smaller Morelet's crocodile only grows to 8 ft. The territories of both species overlap in estuaries and brackish coastal waters, but only the American crocodile is able to filter excess salt from its system, allowing it to venture to the more distant cayes. Crocodiles seldom attack humans, preferring fish, birds, and the occasional small mammal. Both species are endangered and protected by international law.

Ctenosaur (*garrobo*): Known in Creole as the wish willy, this 36-inch-long lizard is mostly tan with four dark bands on its body and a tail ringed with rows of sharp, curved spines. This cousin of the iguana sleeps in burrows or tree hollows and is most commonly seen along the coast of Belize. Though largely vegetarian, it won't turn its nose up to a meal of a small creature.

Dolphin (*delfin*): Several species are frequently spotted off the Pacific shores. They often travel in groups of 20 or more and play around vessels. Look for spotted dolphins, which are 6 ft long and have pale markings on their posterior.

Eagle Ray: One of the Caribbean's most graceful swimmers, these flat-bodied rays range in size from 6 to 8 ft. They have a white underside and numerous white spots and circular markings over their darker backs. Their pronounced heads have flattened, tapered snouts, and their long, thin tails have one to five venomous spines at the base. They prefer cruising sandy areas, occasionally stopping to dig for mollusks.

Fer-de-lance (*barba amarilla*): One of the most dangerous of all pit vipers, the fer-de-lance has a host of names, such as tommygoff in Belize and tomagasse in Guatemala. This aggressive snake grows up to 8 ft in length and is distinguished by the bright yellow patches on its head.

Frigate Bird (*tijereta del mar*): These black birds with slender wings and forked tails are some of the most effortless and agile fliers of the avian world. Coastal dwellers, they are more common on the Pacific than on the Atlantic. When mating season approaches, males inflate a scarlet pouch beneath their beaks in an effort to attract females.

Frog (*rana*): Some 120 species of frogs can be found in Belize and Guatemala. Most are nocturnal in an effort to avoid being eaten, but the brightly colored poison dart frogs—whose brilliant red, blue and green coloration warns predators that they don't make a good meal—can be spotted during the day. Red-eyed leaf frogs are among

the showiest of nocturnal species. They firmly attach themselves to plants with neon-orange legs, scarlet eyes bulging out from a metallic green body splashed with white dots and blue patches. Large brown marine toads are also common at night.

Howler monkey (*mono congo*): These chunky-bodied monkeys travel in troops of up to 20. A bit on the lethargic side, they eat leaves, fruits, and flowers. The deep, resounding howls of the males serve as communication among and between troops. Erroneously termed "baboons" by Belizeans, these dark-faced monkeys travel only from tree to tree, limiting their presence to dense jungle canopy. They are increasingly difficult to spot in the wild.

Iguana (*iguana*): The largest lizards in Central America, these scaly creatures can can grow to 10 ft. They are good swimmers, and will often plop into a body of water when threatened by a predator. Only young green iguanas are brightly colored; adult females are grayish, while adult males are olive (with orangish heads during mating season). They are considered a delicacy among Belizeans, who call them "bamboo chicken."

Jacana (*gallito de agua*): These birds are sometimes referred to as "lily trotters" because their long toes allow them to walk on floating vegetation. They eat aquatic plants and animals and are found at almost any body of water. They expose their yellow wing feathers when in flight. The liberated females lay eggs in several floating nests tended by males.

Jaguar (*tigre*): The largest feline in the western hemisphere grows up to 6 ft long can weigh up to 250 pounds. Exceedingly rare, this nocturnal predator is most often spotted near the Cockscomb Basin Wildlife Sanctuary in Belize.

Kinkajou (*martilla*): A nocturnal relative of the raccoon, kinkajous are known for their 20-inch-long prehensile tails. They actively and often noisily forage for fruit, insects, and the occasional sip of nectar. (If you aren't sure what you have spotted is a kinkajou, simply look at the picture on Belize's $20 note.)

Leaf-cutter ant (*zompopa*): Called wee wee ants in Creole, leaf-cutter ants are the region's the most commonly noticed ants. They are found in all lowland habitats. Columns of these industrious little guys, all carrying clippings of leaves, sometimes extend for several hundred yards from plants to the underground nest. The leaves are used to cultivate the fungus that they eat.

Macaw (*lapas*): The beautiful scarlet macaw is the only species of this bird found in Belize and Guatemala. Huge, raucous birds with long tails, they use their immense bills to rip apart fruits to get to the seeds. Their nests are in hollow trees. They are endangered because of poachers and deforestation.

Magpie jay (*urraca*): A southern relative of the blue jay, magpie jays have long tails and distinctive crests of forwardly curved feathers. They are residents of Guatemala's Pacific slope. Omnivorous, bold, and inquisitive, with amazingly varied vocalizations, these birds travel in noisy groups of four or more.

Manatee: An immense and gentle mammal, the manatee is often called the sea cow. Living exclusively in the water, particularly in shallow and sheltered areas, manatees are said to be the basis of myths about mermaids. Scarce today, these vegetarians have been hunted for thousands of years for their tasty flesh; their image frequently appears in ancient Maya art.

Margay (*caucel*): This nocturnal, spotted cat is similar to the somewhat larger ocelot, but has a longer tail. Mobile ankle joints allow it to climb down trunks head first. The margay eats small vertebrates.

Morpho (*morfo*): This spectacular butterfly doesn't fail to astound first-time viewers. Easy to overlook when resting, their color is only apparent when they take flight. One species has brilliant-blue wings, while another is distinguished by its intense violet color. Adults feed on fallen fruit, never flowers.

Motmot (*pajaro bobo*): Handsome birds of the forest, motmots sit patiently while scanning for large insects and small vertebrates. The four species found in Belize and Guatemala make their nests in burrows.

Ocelot (*manigordo*): These medium-size spotted cats have shorter tails than their cousins the margays. They are active night and day, feeding on rodents and other small animals. Their forepaws are rather large in relation to their bodies, hence the Creole name that translates as "fat hand."

Oropéndola (*oropéndola*): These crow-size birds, members of the oriole family, have bright yellow tails. They nest in colonies with the female building pendulous nests in isolated trees. Males make unmistakable gurgling calls. They are fairly omnivorous, but subsist mostly on fruit.

Parrot (*loro*): A prerequisite of any tropical setting, there are five species of parrot in Central America. All are clad in green, which means they virtually disappear upon landing in the trees. Most have a splash of color or two on their head or wings.

Pelican (*pelícano*): Their large size, big bills, and flapping throat pouches make brown pelicans unmistakable inhabitants of both coasts (although they are far more abundant on the Pacific side). A white American variety prefers freshwater locations. They often fly in V formations and dive for fish.

Quetzal (*quetzal*): One of the world's most exquisite and elusive birds, resplendent quetzals were revered as sacred by the Mayas. The glittering green plumage and long tail feathers of the males were used in Maya ceremonial costumes. No longer found in Belize, they can be seen in and around Guatemala's Biotopo del Quetzal from February to April.

Roseate spoonbill (*garza rosada*): Pink plumage and distinctive bills set this wader apart from all other wetland birds. They feed by swishing their bills back and forth in the water while using their feet to stir up bottom-dwelling creatures.

Sea turtle: Sea turtles on the coasts of Belize and Guatemala come in three varieties: green, hawksbill, and loggerhead. All have paddlelike flippers and have to surface to breathe.

Spider monkey (*mono colorado, mono araña*): These lanky, long-tailed monkeys hang out in groups of two to four. Their diet consists of ripe fruit, leaves, and flowers. These incredible aerialists can swing effortlessly through the trees using their long arms and legs and prehensile tails. Caribbean and southern Pacific populations are dark reddish brown, while their cousins in the north-west are blond.

Tapir (*danta*): The national animal of Belize is also known as the mountain cow. Something like a small rhinoceros without the armor, it has a stout body, short legs, and small eyes. Completely vegetarian, it uses its prehensile snout for harvesting vegetation. The shy creature lives in forested areas near streams and lakes, where it can sometimes be spotted bathing.

Toucan (*tucán, tucancillo*): Recognizable to all who have ever seen a box of Fruit Loops, the toucan is common in Belize and Guatemala. The largest are the keel-billed and chestnut-mandibled toucans, growing to 22 inches long. The much smaller and stouter emerald toucanet and yellow-ear toucanet are among the most colorful. All eat fruit with their curved, multihued beaks.

— Elbert Greer

SPANISH VOCABULARY

English	Spanish	Pronunciation
Basics		
Yes/no	Sí/no	see/no
Please	Por favor	por fah-*vore*
May I?	¿Me permite?	may pair-*mee*-tay
Thank you (very much)	(Muchas) gracias	(*moo*-chas) *grah*-see-as
You're welcome	De nada	day *nah*-dah
Excuse me	Con permiso	con pair-*mee*-so
Pardon me/what did you say?	¿Como?/Mánde?	pair-*doan*/*mahn*-dey
Could you tell me?	¿Podría decirme?	po-*dree*-ah deh-*seer*-meh
I'm sorry	Lo siento	lo see-*en*-toe
Good morning!	¡Buenos días!	*bway*-nohs *dee*-ahs
Good afternoon!	¡Buenas tardes!	*bway*-nahs *tar*-dess
Good evening!	¡Buenas noches!	*bway*-nahs *no*-chess
Goodbye!	¡Adiós!	ah-dee-*ohss*
	¡Hasta luego!	ah-stah-*lwe*-go
Mr./Mrs.	Señor/Señora	sen-*yor*/sen-*yore*-ah
Miss	Señorita	sen-yo-*ree*-tah
Pleased to meet you	Mucho gusto	*moo*-cho *goose*-to
How are you?	¿Cómo está usted?	*ko*-mo es-*tah* oo-*sted*
Very well, thank you.	Muy bien, gracias.	*moo*-ee bee-*en*, grah-see-as
And you?	¿Y usted?	ee oos-*ted*
Hello (on the telephone)	Bueno	*bwen*-oh

English	Spanish	Pronunciation
Numbers		
1	un, uno	oon, *oo*-no
2	dos	dos
3	tres	trace
4	cuatro	*kwah*-tro
5	cinco	*sink*-oh
6	seis	sace
7	siete	see-*et*-ey
8	ocho	*o*-cho
9	nueve	new-*ev*-ey
10	diez	dee-*es*
11	once	*own*-sey
12	doce	*doe*-sey
13	trece	*tray*-sey
14	catorce	kah-*tor*-sey

15	quince	*keen*-sey
16	dieciséis	dee-es-ee-*sace*
17	diecisiete	dee-*es*-ee-see-*et*-ay
18	dieciocho	dee-*es*-ee-o-cho
19	diecinueve	*dee-es*-ee-new-*ev*-ay
20	veinte	*vain*-tay
21	veinte y uno/veintiuno	*vain*-te-oo-no
30	treinta	*train*-tah
32	treinta y dos	train-tay-*dose*
40	cuarenta	kwah-*ren*-tah
43	cuarenta y tres	kwah-*ren*-tay-*trace*
50	cincuenta	seen-*kwen*-tah
54	cincuenta y cuatro	seen-*kwen*-tay *kwah*-tro
60	sesenta	sess-*en*-tah
65	sesenta y cinco	sess-*en*-tay *seen*-ko
70	setenta	set-*en*-tah
76	setenta y seis	set-*en*-tay *sace*
80	ochenta	oh-*chen*-tah
87	ochenta y siete	oh-*chen*-tay see-*yet*-ay
90	noventa	no-*ven*-tah
98	noventa y ocho	no-*ven*-tah o-cho
100	cien	see-*en*
101	ciento uno	see-en-toe oo-no
200	doscientos	doe-see-*en*-tohss
500	quinientos	keen-*yen*-tohss
700	setecientos	set-eh-see-*en*-tohss
900	novecientos	no-veh-see-*en*-tohss
1,000	mil	meel
2,000	dos mil	dose meel
1,000,000	un millón	oon meel-*yohn*

Colors

black	negro	*neh*-grow
blue	azul	ah-*sool*
brown	café	kah-*feh*
green	verde	*vair*-day
pink	rosa	*ro*-sah
purple	morado	mo-*rah*-doe
orange	naranja	na-*rahn*-hah
red	rojo	*roe*-hoe
white	blanco	*blahn*-koh
yellow	amarillo	ah-mah-*ree*-yoh

Days of the Week

Sunday	domingo	doe-*meen*-goh
Monday	lunes	*loo*-ness
Tuesday	martes	*mahr*-tess
Wednesday	miércoles	me-*air*-koh-less
Thursday	jueves	who-*ev*-ess
Friday	viernes	vee-*air*-ness
Saturday	sábado	*sah*-bah-doe

Months

January	enero	eh-*neh*-ro
February	febrero	feh-*brair*-oh
March	marzo	*mahr*-so
April	abril	ah-*breel*
May	mayo	*my*-oh
June	junio	*hoo*-nee-oh
July	julio	*who*-lee-yoh
August	agosto	ah-*ghost*-toe
September	septiembre	sep-tee-*em*-breh
October	octubre	oak-*too*-breh
November	noviembre	no-vee-*em*-breh
December	diciembre	dee-see-*em*-breh

Useful Phrases

Do you speak English?	¿Habla usted inglés?	*ah*-blah oos-*ted* in-*glehs*
I don't speak Spanish	No hablo español	no *ah*-blow es-pahn-*yol*
I don't understand (you)	No entiendo	no en-tee-*en*-doe
I understand (you)	Entiendo	en-tee-*en*-doe
I don't know	No sé	no *say*
I am American/ British	Soy americano(a)/ inglés(a)	soy ah-meh-ree-*kah*-no(ah)/ in-*glace*(ah)
What's your name?	¿Cómo se llama usted?	*koh*-mo say *yah*-mah oos-*ted*
My name is . . .	Me llamo . . .	may *yah*-moh
What time is it?	¿Qué hora es?	keh o-rah es
It is one, two, three . . . o'clock.	Es la una; son las dos, tres	es la oo-nah/sone lahs dose, trace
Yes, please/ No, thank you	Sí, por favor/ No, gracias	*see* pore fah-*vor*/no *grah*-see-us
How?	¿Cómo?	*koh*-mo
When?	¿Cuándo?	*kwahn*-doe
This/next week	Esta semana/ la semana que entra	*es*-tah seh-*mah*-nah/lah say-*mah*-nah keh *en*-trah
This/next month	Este mes/el próximo mes	*es*-tay mehs/el *proke*-see-mo mehs
This/next year	Este año/el año que viene	*es*-tay *ahn*-yo/el *ahn*-yo keh vee-*yen-ay*
Yesterday/today/ tomorrow	Ayer/hoy/mañana	ah-*yair*/oy/mahn-*yah*-nah
This morning/ afternoon	Esta mañana/tarde	*es*-tah mahn-*yah*-nah/*tar*-day
Tonight	Esta noche	*es*-tah *no*-cheh
What?	¿Qué?	keh
What is it?	¿Qué es esto?	keh es *es*-toe

Why?	¿Por qué?	pore *keh*
Who?	¿Quién?	kee-*yen*
Where is . . . ?	¿Dónde está . . . ?	*dohn*-day es-*tah*
the train station?	la estación del tren?	la es-tah-see-*on* del *train*
the subway station?	la estación del Metro?	la es-ta-see-*on* del *meh*-tro
the bus stop?	la parada del autobús?	la pah-*rah*-dah del oh-toe-*boos*
the post office?	la oficina de correos?	la oh-fee-*see*-nah day koh-*reh*-os
the bank?	el banco?	el *bahn*-koh
the . . . hotel?	el hotel . . . ?	el oh-*tel*
the store?	la tienda?	la tee-*en*-dah
the cashier?	la caja?	la *kah*-hah
the . . . museum?	el museo . . . ?	el moo-*seh*-oh
the hospital?	el hospital?	el ohss-pea-*tal*
the elevator?	el ascensor?	el ah-*sen*-sore
the bathroom?	el baño?	el *bahn*-yoh
Here/there	Aquí/allá	ah-*key*/ah-*yah*
Open/closed	Abierto/cerrado	ah-be-*er*-toe/ ser-*ah*-doe
Left/right	Izquierda/derecha	iss-key-*er*-dah/ dare-*eh*-chah
Straight ahead	Derecho	der-*eh*-choh
Is it near/far?	¿Está cerca/lejos?	es-*tah* sair-kah/ *leh*-hoss
I'd like . . .	Quisiera . . .	kee-see-air-ah
a room	un cuarto/una habitación	oon *kwahr*-toe/ oo-nah ah-bee-tah-see-*on*
the key	la llave	lah *yah*-vay
a newspaper	un periódico	oon pear-ee-*oh*-dee-koh
a stamp	un timbre de correo	oon *team*-bray day koh-*reh*-oh
I'd like to buy . . .	Quisiera comprar . . .	kee-see-*air*-ah kohm-*prahr*
cigarettes	cigarrillo	ce-gar-*reel*-oh
matches	cerillos	ser-*ee*-ohs
a dictionary	un diccionario	oon deek-see-oh-*nah*-ree-oh
soap	jabón	hah-*bone*
a map	un mapa	oon *mah*-pah
a magazine	una revista	oon-ah reh-*veess*-tah
paper	papel	pah-*pel*
envelopes	sobres	*so*-brace
a postcard	una tarjeta postal	oon-ah tar-*het*-ah post-*ahl*
How much is it?	¿Cuánto cuesta?	*kwahn*-toe *kwes*-tah
It's expensive/ cheap	Está caro/barato	es-*tah* kah-roh/ bah-*rah*-toe

A little/a lot	Un poquito/mucho . . .	oon poh-*kee*-toe/*moo*-choh
More/less	Más/menos	mahss/*men*-ohss
Enough/too much/too little	Suficiente/demasiado/muy poco	soo-fee-see-*en*-tay/day-mah-see *ah*, doe/*moo*-ee poh-koh
Telephone	Teléfono	tel-*ef*-oh-no
Telegram	Telegrama	teh-leh-*grah*-mah
I am ill/sick	Estoy enfermo(a)	es-*toy* en-*fair*-moh(ah)
Please call a doctor	Por favor llame un médico	pore fa-*vor* ya-may oon *med*-ee-koh
Help!	¡Auxilio! ¡Ayuda!	owk-*see*-lee-oh ah-*yoo*-dah
Fire!	¡Encendio!	en-*sen*-dee-oo
Caution!/Look out!	¡Cuidado!	kwee-*dah*-doh

On the Road

Highway	Carretera	car-ray-*ter*-ah
Causeway, paved highway	Calzada	cal-*za*-dah
Route	Ruta	*roo*-tah
Road	Camino	cah-*mee*-no
Street	Calle	*cah*-yeh
Avenue	Avenida	ah-ven-*ee*-dah
Broad, tree-lined boulevard	Paseo	pah-*seh*-oh
Waterfront promenade	Malecón	mal-lay-*cone*
Wharf	Embarcadero	em-bar-cah-*day*-ro

In Town

Church	Templo/Iglesia	*tem*-plo/e-*gles*-se-ah
Cathedral	Catedral	cah-tay-*dral*
Neighborhood	Barrio	*bar*-re-o
Foreign Exchange Shop	Casa de Cambio	*cas*-sah day *cam*-be-o
City Hall	Ayuntamiento	ah-yoon-tah-mee *en*-toe
Main Square	Zócalo	*zo*-cal-o
Traffic Circle	Glorieta	glor-e-*ay*-tah
Market	Mercado (Spanish)/Tianguis (Indian)	mer-*cah*-doe/tee-*an*-geese
Inn	Posada	pos-*sah*-dah
Group taxi	Colectivo	co-lec-*tee*-vo
Group taxi along fixed route	Pesero	pi-*seh*-ro

Items of Clothing

Embroidered white smock	Huipil	whee-*peel*
Pleated man's shirt worn outside the pants	Guayabera	gwah-ya-*beh*-ra
Leather sandals	Huarache	wah-*ra*-chays
Shawl	Rebozo	ray-*bozh*-o
Pancho or blanket	Serape	seh-*ra*-peh

Dining Out

A bottle of . . .	Una botella de . . .	*oo*-nah bo-*tay*-yah deh
A cup of . . .	Una taza de . . .	*oo*-nah *tah*-sah deh
A glass of . . .	Un vaso de . . .	oon *vah*-so deh
Ashtray	Un cenicero	oon sen-ee-*seh*-roh
Bill/check	La cuenta	lah *kwen*-tah
Bread	El pan	el pahn
Breakfast	El desayuno	el day-sigh-*oon*-oh
Butter	La mantequilla	lah mahn-tay-*key*-yah
Cheers!	¡Salud!	sah-*lood*
Cocktail	Un aperitivo	oon ah-pair-ee-*tee*-voh
Dinner	La cena	lah *seh*-nah
Dish	Un plato	oon *plah*-toe
Dish of the day	El platillo de hoy	el plah-*tee*-yo day oy
Enjoy!	¡Buen provecho!	bwen pro-*veh*-cho
Fixed-price menu	La comida corrida	lah koh-*me*-dah co-*ree*-dah
Fork	El tenedor	el ten-eh-*door*
Is the tip included?	¿Está incluida la propina?	es-*tah* in-clue-*ee*-dah lah pro-*pea*-nah
Knife	El cuchillo	el koo-*chee*-yo
Lunch	La comida	lah koh-*me*-dah
Menu	La carta	lah *cart*-ah
Napkin	La servilleta	lah sair-vee-*yet*-uh
Pepper	La pimienta	lah pea-me-*en*-tah
Please give me	Por favor déme	pore fah-*vor* *day*-may
Salt	La sal	lah sahl
Spoon	Una cuchara	*oo*-nah koo-*chah*-rah
Sugar	El azúcar	el ah-*sue*-car
Waiter!/Waitress!	¡Por favor Señor/Señorita!	pore fah-*vor* sen-*yor*/sen-yor-*ee*-tah

INDEX

Icons and Symbols

★ Our special recommen-
dations
✕ Restaurant
🏠 Lodging establishment
✕🏠 Lodging establishment
whose restaurant war-
rants a special trip
🔔 Good for kids (rubber
duck)
☞ Sends you to another
section of the guide for
more information
✉ Address
☎ Telephone number
🕐 Opening and closing
times
💲 Admission prices
🔗 Sends you to
www.fodors.com/urls
for up-to-date links to
the property's Web site

Numbers in white and black
circles ③ ❸ that appear on
the maps, in the margins, and
within the tours correspond
to one another.